Mayflower Increasings

Mayflower Increasings

2nd Edition

by
Susan E. Roser

Genealogical Publishing Co., Inc.

1st Edition 1989
2nd Edition 1995, 1996
Copyright © 1989, 1995
Genealogical Publishing Co., Inc.
1001 N. Calvert Street, Baltimore, MD 21202
All Rights Reserved
Library of Congress Card Catalogue Number 95-76482
International Standard Book Number 0-8063-1479-6
Made in the United States of America

"... And seeing it hath pleased him to give me to see 30 years compleated since these beginings. And that the great works of his providence are to be observed I have thought it not unworthy my paines, to take a view of the decreasings & increasings of these persons, and such changes as hath passed over them & theirs in this thirty years. It may be of some use to such as come after ..."

William Bradford, 1651

Contents

Preface

This revision of *Mayflower Increasings* contains a great deal more data than is found in the original which was published in 1989. As was my intention in 1989, I have attempted to lay a solid foundation for the first three generations of Mayflower passengers. We may never know absolutely everything about our ancestors, but as each year passes, new information is uncovered, however small, which sheds light on a missing date or an unknown parent. The genealogies found herein are by no means complete: there are missing names, dates, and sources. However, I have added many more names, dates, and sources that were missing from the original. Since the original was published in 1989 I have had three books published: *Mayflower Marriages* (1990), *Mayflower Births & Deaths* (2 vols., 1992), and *Mayflower Deeds & Probates* (1994). These books have been a tremendous help in completing this revision. The time spent on these books and my position as Historian of the Canadian Society of Mayflower Descendants (branch of The General Society) have gained me much needed experience in the field of genealogy and Mayflower research.

Twenty-seven Mayflower families are treated in this book, which gives genealogical data on Mayflower passengers and their children and grandchildren. As with all my books, heavy emphasis is placed on providing sources for each date or piece of data. Having Mayflower lines means we all have non-Mayflower lines which are just as important to our family tree. I have included data on these non-Mayflower spouses as well, including parentage and additional marriages. Each third generation listing includes references as to which records or sources will help the researcher find fourth generation children. Included with each Mayflower family is a "Probate Appendix" in which wills and probate records are transcribed in order to assist the reader in identifying fourth and fifth generation children.

Along with the birth, death, and marriage dates will be found epitaphs and obituaries, which are interesting to read whether or not the person was your ancestor. Mention will be found of pre-marital relations (too numerous to count!) and illegitimate children; adulterous relationships including one with an Indian and another with a negro servant; one case of murder and another of manslaughter; men killed by Indians or going off to war or sea, never to return; a case of a conscientious objector who was imprisoned for refusing to go to war; siblings fighting over their parents' estates; a firsthand account of a person imprisoned for witchcraft. All of these examples serve to remind us that our ancestors were real people, with real emotions. Stephen Vincent Benet, in "Western Star," explains it best in two simple lines:

> *"In fact, there were human beings aboard the Mayflower,*
> *Not merely ancestors."*

I have also included as Appendices Gov. Bradford's "List of the Mayflower Passengers" and the "1627 Cattle Division," as both are of monumental importance to the research of the early Mayflower generations. Following this is a Reference List of sources mentioned throughout the text. The text is fully indexed (according to my word processor) and contains references to over 6,000 names or persons.

Introduction

esearch on Mayflower families is never-ending, with new bits of information appearing in print all the time. Although we are fortunate in knowing a great deal about our ancestors, there remains much that has yet to be uncovered. Many birth, death, and marriage dates have yet to be found and therefore have to be estimated. Perhaps the most frustrating of all is the unknown maiden names of the women who married "our men." Who was Susanna, wife of William White? Rose and Barbara, wives of Capt. Standish? Elizabeth, wife of Richard Warren? The unknown wife of James Chilton? Eleanor, wife of John Billington? Mary, wife of William Brewster? Martha and Mary, wives of Peter Brown? Sarah, wife of Francis Eaton? The unknown wife of Edward Fuller? The unknown first wife of Stephen Hopkins? Elizabeth, wife of Thomas Rogers? Who knows what interesting lines would be opened up if we only knew who they were! The same applies to children who have disappeared from the records. What became of John Alden's daughters Mary and Priscilla? Peter Brown's unnamed child? Francis Eaton's "idiot" child? Dr. Samuel Fuller's daughter Mercy? Stephen Hopkins' daughter Elizabeth? Thomas Rogers' daughters Elizabeth and Margaret (did they come to New England with brother John as Bradford suggests?)? Myles Standish's son Charles? John Tilley's son John (did he come to New England?)? The second and third generations have even more unidentified wives and children who, if found or identified, could open up new Mayflower lines.

Fortunately, there are many dedicated individuals who are using their time and expertise in researching the families of the Mayflower. Books on Mayflower ancestry are being published every year and scholarly articles appear constantly in the various genealogical publications. What would we do without such publications as *The New England Historical and Genealogical Register, The Mayflower Descendant, The Mayflower Quarterly, The American Genealogist,* and *The Genealogist* (to name a few), all of which provide the means for researchers to update, correct and expand the Mayflower genealogies! We also owe a debt of gratitude to The Five Generations Project of The General Society of Mayflower Descendants for their commitment to Mayflower research which, in the past twenty years, has resulted in the publication of eight 5-generation (silver) books and eight 4-generation booklets, representing twenty-one Mayflower families. And gratitude is also due to Elizabeth P. White for her research and publications (two, with more to come) on the twenty-second Mayflower family. It is due to the efforts and accomplishments of all of the above that I have been able to compile and revise *Mayflower Increasings*.

•   •   •

Births, Marriages, Deaths

As I have already stated, despite what we know about our ancestors, many dates of birth, death, or marriage are unknown. The possibilities are clear: either they were never recorded, the records were lost, or they have not been found. Where a birth record is lacking, an approximate birth date is derived from the age at death (which may or may not be accurate). Where an age at death is unknown, the birth date may be estimated from the marriage date or births of children. In some cases an estimated birth date is based solely on family positioning, e.g., it might be the only year which would fit in relation to the other siblings. In families where the birth dates of some or all of the children are unknown, the order of births is estimated and may or may not be accurate. The same reasoning applies to an unknown marriage date. An approximate date is calculated from the date of the birth of the first child, from the ages of the marriage partners or from a deed or probate record in which the first mention of a woman using her married name is found.

Quite often a discrepancy will be found in the records as to a person's age at death. I have cited depositions in which a person gives his age, only to find his gravestone gives an age at death that disagrees. George Bowman (*The Mayflower Descendant*—hereafter *MD*—2:45) addressed this problem: "Occasionally a deposition proves that the age at death contained in a town record or gravestone inscription is incorrect, for a man's own statement of his age must be considered better authority than a record made after his death."

Probate Appendix

At the end of each Mayflower family will be found a Probate Appendix in which will be found data on wills and probate records. I have included these records for the sole purpose of aiding in the identification of children, thereby widening the scope of this book beyond the third generation grandchildren to

xii

include fourth and sometimes fifth generations. With this in mind, I make no reference to anything in the probate records other than family members. I have made exceptions in cases where the records cite unusual happenings, such as siblings accusing each other of trying to steal the family fortune. In the case of wills, I give the date the will was written and the first date in the probate records that would indicate the death of the testator, be it the date the inventory was taken, witnesses sworn, or date the will was probated. The purpose of this is to help pinpoint an unknown death date.

Old and New Style Dating

We have all come across the dreaded double dating—Old Style and New Style. What does it all mean? An excellent explanation can be found in *MD* 1:17–22, but for the benefit of those who have not read this article, I will give a summary.

The Old Style (O.S.) was the Julian calendar in which each new year began on March 25th; thus March was considered the first month, April the second and so on. In March 1582, Pope Gregory XIII abolished the Julian calendar and in an attempt to bring uniformity between the calendar and actual time (which differed by ten days), the vernal equinox was restored by deleting ten days; thus 5 October 1582 became 15 October 1582. This new Gregorian calendar, with New Style (N.S.) dating, began each new year on January 1st instead of March 25th.

All would be simple for present day researchers if only England had adopted the Gregorian calendar in 1582—but it delayed until 1752. Holland made the switch in 1582, therefore all events which occurred in Leyden while the Pilgrims resided there are dated in the New Style and do not require changing. When our ancestors arrived in 1620, they reverted back to the Julian calendar, or Old Style dating, that England was still using; thus dates before 1752 are ten days behind, and between January 1st and March 25th they are off by one year. Double dating the year for the months of January, February and March was often (but not always) practiced by our ancestors and continues today as a way of clarifying a date. For example, if a couple recorded the birth of two children thus: Mary, b. 5 Dec. 1651 and Sarah, b. 2 Mar. 1652, these impossible births make sense only if we use double dating—5 Dec. 1651 and 2 Mar. 1652/53. We now have fifteen months between the births instead of only three months.

Gov. Bradford's List and the 1627 Cattle Division

I have included as Appendices Gov. Bradford's passenger list and his "increasings & decreasings" (from *MD* 1:9–16) as well as the 1627 Cattle Division (from *MD* 1:148–54), as I refer to them often in the text.

Bowman (*MD* 1:161–3) has estimated the time period in which Bradford wrote his list. Bradford refers twice to "this year 1650 . . . this present year 1650," therefore it was written before 24 march 1650 (O.S.) which was considered the last day of the year. He mentions John Alden's eldest daughter had five children—Elizabeth (Alden) Pabodie's fifth child, Martha, was born 24 February 1650 (O.S.). Therefore, the list was written between 24 February 1650 (O.S.) and 24 March 1650 (O.S.), or 6 March 1651 (N.S.) and 3 April 1651 (N.S.). Bradford's list is not without error or omission; he was recalling events that occurred over a thirty-year period to over 100 fellow passengers and their children and grandchildren. One such omission I have come across is in the Hopkins family where Bradford states that Gyles Hopkins has four children. According to the records, Gyles' son Caleb was born January 1650/1, which would give Gyles five children living. Bradford does not account for Caleb, yet he does account for the above Martha Pabodie who was born a month after Caleb.

The Cattle Division, dated 22 May 1627, serves as the first census of Plymouth Colony, as it is thought to include all those who resided in Plymouth, numbering 156 persons. Not only does it tell us who had arrived in Plymouth by 1627, it also indicates, from their omission, who had moved on or died, or those who had not yet arrived. It tells us who had married and who were still single. The listing of children is particularly helpful as in many cases the births of these children were not recorded. The children also appear to be listed either in order of birth, or sons first (in order) followed by daughters (in order).

Index

The Index will be easier to use if I explain the reasoning behind some of the entries. All names found in the text will (hopefully) be found in the index—except for names without surnames (example 1: John SMITH (son of Robert & Mary)—John Smith is indexed, Robert & Mary are not; example 2: Sarah SMITH wf of John—Mrs. Sarah Smith is indexed, John is not). The only exception occurs in the Probate Appendix where daughters are named by first name only. Thus, if John SMITH mentions daughters Elizabeth and Mary in his will, they are indexed as Elizabeth SMITH and Mary SMITH.

There are other instances where female names are indexed by identification and not precisely as they appear in the text. For example, if a woman appears as Mary Smith, but she is identified as a wife or daughter, I have attempted to include this identification in the index, thus Mrs. Mary Smith, Mary (Brown) Smith, Mary Smith. This is to make a search for a particular person easier for the reader. The only occasion in which this type of identification was not always possible was in indexing daughters who were named in their mothers' wills. Unless these daughters were specifically identified, they could be single, married, or widowed. Therefore, there will be cases where a woman is found in the index without her true identification or marital status. (This is a very important point to remember, because if you are looking for Elizabeth (Brown) Smith she may appear in the index as Elizabeth Smith, a single woman.) As with any index, bear in mind the possibility of multiple listings for a name on any given page. If the name you have found on a page isn't the person you are looking for, there may be another on the page who is. There are also instances where the same person is mentioned more than once on the same page.

Variations in the spelling of surnames must not be overlooked. Since I have tried to retain the original spelling as found in the records, there are quite a few unusual variations to watch for (including the double "F", as in Ffuller).

Susan E. Roser

Abbreviations

ack.—acknowledged
adm.—administration, administered
admr.—administrator
admx.—administratrix
ae.—age
aft.—after
app'td.—appointed
b.—born
bpt.—baptized
bth.—birth
betw.—between
bur.—buried
c.—circa
cem.—cemetery
ch.—child
chil.—children
ChR—Church Records
Co.—County
Col.—Colony
d.—died
dau(s)—daughter(s)
dec., dec'd—deceased
dep.—deposition
div.—division
dth.—death
d.y.—died young
est.—estate
exr.—executor

exx.—executrix
fam.—family
fath.—father
g.s.—gravestone
gdn.—guardian
hus.—husband
incl.—including
int.—marriage intentions
inv.—inventory
m., marr.—married
ment.—mentions
mth(s).—month(s)
N.S.—New Style dating
O.S.—Old Style dating
poss.—possibly
PR—Probate Records
pre—before
prob.—probably
rec., rcd(s)—record(s)
rep.—representatives
sett.—settlement
TR—Town Records
unm.—unmarried
VR—Vital Records
wf—wife
wit.—witness(es)
y.m.d.—years, months, days
yr(s)—year, years

JOHN ALDEN

John Alden was born in England c1598/9 <MD 2:114, 3:120 (ae 83 or "therabouts" in 1682 deposition, PCR 2:32), 7:64 (lived 88 yrs), 39:111 (narrows it down to betw. 6 July - 12 Sept. 1598 "or thereabouts")> and died 12 Sept. 1687 (O.S.), Duxbury <MD 2:64,3:10,9:129>. He married by 1623 at Plymouth, Priscilla MULLINS <MD 2:114, 39:111; Stratton:233,416 (Priscilla is not listed in the 1623 land division, therefore she must have been married and accounted for with John who is listed.) Priscilla was born c1602 (dau of William & Alice) and died betw. 1 Dec. 1680 (funeral of Josiah WINSLOW) <MQ 48:143> - 12 Sept. 1687, probably at Duxbury. (See ALDEN Probate Appendix for estate of John Alden. See also the MULLINS Family.)

(See also: TAG 53:235, John Alden - Beer Brewer of Windsor?; MD 39:111-22,40:133-36, John Alden: Theories on English Ancestry, Part 1 & 2 (Alicia C. Williams makes use of English records to put together several possibilities including the very interesting fact that the step-father of Capt. Christopher Jones (Master of the Mayflower) was the brother-in law of Elizabeth Russell, 2nd wife of a John Alden.); MD 9:129-31,193-96, 31:49-52,144, 34:49-53 for rare broadsides on the death of John Alden.)

John & Priscilla had 10 children:

I.   Elizabeth, b. c1624, Plymouth (94th yr at dth.)
II.   John, b. c1626, Plymouth (listed in 1627 Cattle Division <MD 1:150>; ae 75 at dth)
III.   Joseph, b. aft. 22 May 1627, Plymouth (not listed in Cattle Division, MD 1:150)
IV.   Sarah, b. c1629, d. pre 13 June 1688
V.   Jonathan, b. c1632 (65th yr at dth.)
VI.   Ruth, b. c1634-5
VII.   Rebecca, b. pre 1649
VIII.   Mary, b. (   ), living 13 June 1688, unm.
IX.   Priscilla, b. (   ), living 13 June 1688, unm.
X.   David, b. c1646 (ae 73 at dth.)

* * * * * * * * * * * * *

I.   **ELIZABETH ALDEN**[2], b. c1624, Plymouth, d. 31 May 1717, 94th yr, Little Compton RI <MD 34:98; NEHGR 115:263>; m. 26 Dec. 1644, Duxbury, **William PABODIE** <PCR 8:288;MD 1:163,6:129,8:231,34: 97; Duxbury VR 1:1; Plymouth Court Orders 2:107>, b. c1619/20, d. 13 Dec. 1707, 88th yr, Little Compton RI <MD 6:129,132,34:97>. (See ALDEN Probate Appendix for will of William PABODIE and obituary of Elizabeth (ALDEN) PABODIE.)

   13 PABODIE Children: <MBD 1:6; MD 1:163; Duxbury VR 1:21; MD 9:171 (1-10), 172 (11-13), 34: 100 (bth John), 101 (remaining 12)>

1.   **John PABODIE**[3], b. 4 Oct. 1645, Duxbury; d. 17 Nov. 1669, Duxbury, unm. <Duxbury VR 1:164; MD 12:30,31 (duplicate), 34:101>

2.   **Elizabeth PABODIE**[3], b. 24 Apr. 1647, Duxbury; d. betw. 4 May 1677 (bth last ch.) <MD 9:172> - 21 Oct. 1679 (hus. 2nd marr.) <MD 19:192>; m. Nov. 1666, Duxbury, **John ROGERS**[3] <Duxbury VR 1:2; MD 8:232, 34:100>, (son of John ROGERS[2] & Anna CHURCHMAN). (See ROGERS Family.)

3.   **Mary PABODIE**[3], b. 7 Aug. 1648, Duxbury; d. aft. 11 Dec. 1727 (adm.hus.est.) <MD 18:244>; m. 16 Nov. 1671, Duxbury, **Edward SOUTHWORTH** <Duxbury VR 1:2; MD 8:232, 18:244, 34:100>, (son of Constant SOUTHWORTH[2] (Edw.[1]) & Elizabeth COLLIER), b. (   ), d. betw. 11 June 1719 (will) - 7 Nov. 1727 (wit.sworn) <MD 18:244>. <See MBD 1:12 for bth. of chil.> (See ALDEN Probate Appendix for will of Edward SOUTHWORTH.)

4.   **Mercy PABODIE**[3], b. 2 Jan. 1649/50, Duxbury; d. betw. 26 Sept. (will) - 8 Nov. 1728 (inv.), Duxbury <MD 19:51,53; MDP:11>; m. 16 Nov. 1669, Duxbury, **John SIMMONS** <Duxbury VR 1:2; MD 8: 232, 19:51, 34:100>, b. (   ), d. pre 9 Feb. 1715/16 (adm.), Duxbury <MD 19:51,52; MDP:11>. <See MBD 1:15 & MD 9:172-3 for bth. of chil.> (See ALDEN Probate Appendix for will of Mercy (PABODIE) Simmons & estate of John SIMMONS.)

5.   **Martha PABODIE**[3], b. 24 Feb. 1650/1, Duxbury; d. 25 Jan. 1711/2, Little Compton RI <RI VR 4:6: 116>; m.1st 4 Apr. 1677, Duxbury, **Samuel SEABURY** <Duxbury VR 1:2; MD 8:232, 34:100>, (son of John & Grace), b. 10 Dec. 1640, Boston <Boston Rcd.Com.9:10>, d. 5 Aug. 1681, Duxbury <MD 8: 232> (Samuel m.1st 16 Nov. 1660, Duxbury, Patience KEMP <MD 8:232; see also MDP:6 for proof of marr., in 1709 action among heirs>), who d. 29 Oct. 1676, Duxbury <MD 12:31>; they had 8 chil. <MBD 1:8; MD 9:172 (5),12:30 (2),31 (1)>.) Martha m. 2nd c1682, **William FOBES** <MD 6: 131>, b. c1650, Little Compton RI; d. 6 Nov. 1712, Little Compton RI <RI VR 4:6:116>. <See MBD 1:7-8 for 3 Seabury & 4 Fobes chil., MD 9:173 for 2 Seabury chil.> (See ALDEN Probate Appendix for will of William FOBES.)

6. **Priscilla PABODIE**[3], b. 16 Nov. 1652, Duxbury; d. 2 Mar. 1652/3, Duxbury <Duxbury VR 1:164; MD 12:31, 34:101>.

7. **Priscilla PABODIE**[3], b. 15 Jan. 1653/4, Duxbury; d. 3 June 1724, ae 71, Kingston g.s. <MD 7: 224, 19:1, 22:1; MSR:237>; m. 2 Dec. 16(79), Duxbury, **Rev. Ichabod WISWALL** <Duxbury VR 1:2 (last two numbers worn in rcds., the entry falls betw. those dated 1677-81 and since their 1st child was born Oct. 1680, a marr. date of 1679 is likely), MD 8:232, 34:100>, b. 3 June 1637 <   >, d. 23 July 1700, 63rd yr, S. Duxbury g.s. <MD 10:172, 19:1> (Ichabod m.1st, (   ) and had dau Elizabeth.) <See MBD 1:19; MD 9:229, 19:1 for data on chil.> (See ALDEN Probate Appendix for will of Rev. Ichabod WISWALL.)

8. **Sarah PABODIE**[3], b. 7 Aug. 1656, Duxbury; d. 27 Aug. 1740, Little Compton RI <   >; m. 10 Nov 1681, Duxbury, **John COE** <Duxbury VR 1:2; MD 8:232, 34:100>, b. 30 June 1649, Gloucester <   > d. betw. 4 Dec. 1728 (will) - 1 Jan. 1729 (pr.) <MDP:15>. <See MBD 1:22; MD 9:173; Little Compton VR for bth. of chil.> (See ALDEN Probate Appendix for will of John COE.)

9. **Ruth PABODIE**[3], b. 27 June 1658, Duxbury; d. betw. 25 Apr. 1724 (swore to hus.inv.) - 27 Mar. 1725 (div.hus. real estate) <MD 18:177>; m. Dec. 167(6) or 167(8), Duxbury (rcds.worn), **Benjamin BARTLETT**[4] <Duxbury VR 1:2; MD 8:232, 18:242, 34:100>, (son of Benjamin BARTLETT[3] (Mary Warren[2]) & Sarah BREWSTER[3] (Love[2])), b. prob. 27 June 1658, Duxbury <MFIP, Warren #49>, d. betw. 10 Dec. 1717 (will) - 10 Apr. 1724 (wit.sworn) <MD 18:177>. <See MD 18:177-83,242-44 & MBD 2:395-6 for data on children.> (See ALDEN Probate Appendix for will of Benjamin BART-LETT. See WARREN Family for ancestry of Benjamin BARTLETT.)

10. **Rebecca PABODIE**[3], b. 16 Oct. 1660, Duxbury; d. 3 Dec. 1702, Little Compton <RI VR 4:6:168>; m. c1680, **William SOUTHWORTH**[3] <   >, (son of Constant SOUTHWORTH[2] (Edw.[1]) & Elizabeth COL-LIER), b. c1659 <   >, d. 25 June 1719, Little Compton RI <RI VR 4:6:168>. (William m.2nd, Martha (   ), who d. betw. 13 June 1729 (will) - 8 Apr. 1738 (pr.) <MDP:15>.) <See MBD 1:21 for chil.> (See ALDEN Probate Appendix for will of William SOUTHWORTH & 2nd wife Martha.)

11. **Hannah PABODIE**[3], b. 15 Oct. 1662, Duxbury; d. 29 Apr. 1723, 61st yr, Plymouth g.s. <Kingman: 12; MBD 1:6>; m. 1st 2 Aug. 1683, Duxbury, **Samuel BARTLETT**[4] <Duxbury VR 1:2; MD 8:232, 34: 100>, (son of Benjamin BARTLETT[3] (Mary Warren[2]) & Sarah BREWSTER[3] (Love[2])), b. (   ), prob. Duxbury <MFIP, Warren #51>, d. pre 9 Dec. 1713 (adm.) <MDP:493, Plymouth Co.PR 3:255>. Hannah m.2nd, 4 Mar. 1715, Plymouth, **Serjant John CHURCHILL** <MD 14:37>, b. c1658, d. 13 June 1723 <   >. (Did John m.1st, 28 Dec. 1686, Plymouth, Rebecca Delano <MD 13:204> who d. 7 Apr. 1709 <MD 16:64>?) <See MBD 1:6 & MD 9:174 for bth. of chil.> (See WARREN Family for ancestry of Samuel BARTLETT.)

12. **William PABODIE**[3], b. 24 Nov. 1664, Duxbury; d. 17 Sept. 1744, 80th yr, Little Compton RI g.s. <MD 34:99; NEHGR 115:263>; m.1st 27 June 1693, **Judith TILDEN** <TAG 53:246-8>, (dau of Steven) b. 1 June 1670, Scituate <MSR:624; (MSR:319 - bpt. 14 Aug. 1670)>, d. 20 July 1714, 45th yr, Little Compton RI g.s. <MD 34:99; NEHGR 115:263>. **William m.2nd, 20 Mar. 1715/6, Elizabeth (THROOPE) Peck** <TAG 53:246-8>, b. 1672, Barnstable <MBD 1:23,65>, d. 14 Dec. 1717, "ae about 45", Little Compton RI g.s. <MD 34:99; MBD 1:23>. **William m.3rd, aft. 1717, Mary (MORGAN) Starr** <TAG 53:246-8>, b. 20 Mar. 1670, New London CT <   >, d. 14 Sept. 1765, Stonington CT <   >. <See MBD 1:23 for chil.> (See ALDEN Probate Appendix for will of Deacon William PABODIE.)

13. **Lydia PABODIE**[3], b. 3 Apr. 1667, Duxbury; d. 13 July 1748, Saybrook CT <Barbour/Saybrook CT VR:54>; m. c1683, **Daniel GRINNELL** <MD 6:130>, b. c1668, Portsmouth RI <   >, d. 7 Jan. 1740/1, Saybrook CT <Barbour/Saybrook CT VR:54>. <See MBD 1:6 for chil.>

II **JOHN ALDEN**[2], b. c1626, Plymouth, d. 14 Mar. 1701/2, ae 75, Boston (5:00 p.m.) <MD 6:193>; m.1st, c1658, **Elizabeth (   )** <Boston Rec.Com.9:69>, b. (   ), d. prob. Dec. 1659 (bth. of only ch.). John m.2nd, 1 Apr. 1660, Boston, **Elizabeth (PHILLIPS) Everill** <MD 34:176>, b. pre 1640 (dau of William PHILLIPS), bur. 7 Feb. 1695/6, Boston <Sewall's Diary>. (She m.1st 6 July 1655, Boston, Abiel EVERILL <Boston Rcd.Com.9:52> and had two chil.: James, b. 4 Apr. 1656 and Abiel bpt. 28 Apr. 1667 <Boston Rcd.Com.9:54,106>.) <See also MDP:16,17 for court & probate records relating to heirs, dated 23 Apr. 1734 and 15 Apr. 1736.> (See ALDEN Probate Appendix for will of Capt. John ALDEN and the account of his imprisonment during the 1692 witchcraft hysteria in Salem.)

   13 ALDEN Children: (one by 1st wf, rest by 2nd wf), b. Boston <See MD 10:76-83; MBD 1:24>

1. **Mary ALDEN**[3], b. 17 Dec. 1659, Boston <Boston Rec.Com.9:69>, d. betw. 1665/6 - 28 Apr. 1667, prob. Boston <   >.

2. **John ALDEN**[3], b. 20 Nov. 1660, Boston <Boston Rcd.Com.9:73>, d. pre 12 Mar. 1662/3 (bth. of another son John).

3. **Elizabeth ALDEN**[3], b. 9 May 1662, Boston, d. 14 July 1662, Boston <Boston Rcd.Com.9:83,85>.

4. **John ALDEN**[3], b. 12 Mar. 1662/3, Boston <Boston Rcd.Com.9:106>, d. 1 Feb. 1729/30, ae 67, Boston <Historical Sketches of King's Chapel:42>; m.1st c1686/7, **Elizabeth PHELPS** <MM:9; NEHGR 6:205 says 1684>, b. c1669, d. 26 Nov. 1719, ae 50, Boston <King's Chapel:42>. **John** m.2nd, 22 Nov. 1722, Boston, **Susanna WINSLOW**[4] <Boston Rcd.Com.29:104; MD 12:129>, dau of Edward Winslow[3] (Mary Chilton[2]) & Elizabeth Hutchinson), b. 31 July 1675, Boston <MD 12:129>, d. aft. 17 Sept. 1734 (swore to hus.inv.) <MD 10:81>. <See MBD 1:26 & Boston Rcd.Com. for bth. of chil.> (See ALDEN Probate Appendix for will of Capt. John ALDEN.)

5. **William ALDEN**[3], b. 16 Mar. 1663/4, Boston, d. 7 June 1664, Boston <Boston Rcd.Com.9:91,94>.

6. **Elizabeth ALDEN**[3], b. 9 Apr. 1665, Boston <Boston Rcd.Com.9:95>, d. aft. 15 Apr. 1736 <MDP:17; an unknown source says she d. aft. 1 Sept. 1739>; m.1st, c1683, **John WALLEY**, mariner <MM:8>, b. 27 Aug. 1662, Boston < >, d. pre 30 Apr. 1702, overseas (adm.) <MDP:17, Suffolk Co.PR #2750, 15:14,56; MD 10:76-77; MBD 1:25>. **Elizabeth** m.2nd, betw. 30 Apr. 1702 - 31 July 1702, Boston, **Simon WILLARD**, shop keeper <Bowman gives the date 30 Apr. 1702 with the source Boston Rcd.Com.28:6, however this is the date she administered her 1st husband's estate as "Elizabeth WALLEY; she made oath to the inventory on 31 July 1702 as "Elizabeth WILLARD">, b. 6 Dec. 1676, Boston < >, d. betw. 13 Nov. 1709 (will) - 11 Jan. 1713 (pr.) of Boston <MD 10:77; MBD 1:25; MDP:17>. <See MBD 1:25 & Boston Rcd.Com. for bth. of chil.> (See ALDEN Probate Appendix for will of Simon WILLARD.)

7. **William ALDEN**[3], b. 5 Mar. 1665/6, Boston <Boston Rcd.Com.9:99>, d. pre 10 Sept. 1669 (bth of another son William).

8. **Zachariah ALDEN**[3], b. 8 Mar. 1667, Boston <Boston Rcd.Com.9:99>, d. pre 18 Feb. 1672/3 (bth of another son Zachariah).

9. **Nathaniel ALDEN**[3], b. 9 July 1668, Boston < >, d. pre 24 July 1702, mariner,Antequa (adm.) <MD 10:77; Suffolk Co.PR 15:48,49,62,150,175,223-4> (he was dec. by 17 Feb. 1701, his father's will; unknown source says d. 1 July 1700); m. 1 Oct 1691, Boston, **Hepzibah MOUNTJOY** <Boston Rcd.Com.9:198>, (dau of George), bpt. 9 8mth 1673, Boston <Boston Rcd.Com.9:131>, d. aft. 15 Apr. 1736 (agreement of heirs of John Alden[1]) <MDP:17, Middlesex Co.PR #122/#247>. (Hepzibah m.2nd 8 June 1703, Boston, John MORTEMORE <MD 10:78 (she is called Hepzibah MORTIMORE on 8 July 1703)>. <See MBD 1:29 & Boston Rcd.Com. for bth. of chil.> (See ALDEN Probate Appendix for estate of Capt. Nathaniel ALDEN.)

10. **William ALDEN**[3], b. 10 Sept. 1669, Boston <Boston Rcd.Com.9:110>, d. 9 or 10 Feb. 1728/9, ae 60, mariner, Boston < >; m. 21 May 1691, Boston, **Mary DRURY** <Boston Rcd.Com.9:198>, b. 10 July 1672 < >, d. 11 Feb. 1727, Boston, ae 56 <King's Chapel g.s.; MBD 1:29>. <See MBD 1:29 & Boston Rcd.Com. for bth. of chil.> (See ALDEN Probate Appendix for will of Capt. William ALDEN.)

11. **Zachariah ALDEN**[3], b. 18 Feb. 1672/3, Boston <Boston Rcd.Com.9:122>, d. pre 18 Aug. 1709 (adm.) <MD 10:79, Suffolk Co.PR 16:602,17:38>; m. 13 Jan. 1700, Boston, **Mary VIALL** <Boston Rcd.Com.28:1>, b. 10 Oct. 1676, Boston < >, d. aft. 15 Apr. 1736 (agreement of heirs of John Alden[1]) <MDP:17, Middlesex Co.PR #122/#247; (an unknown source says she d. aft. 13 Oct. 1737)>. <See MBD 1:29 for bth. of chil.>

12. **Nathan ALDEN**[3], b. 17 Oct. 1677, Boston <Boston Rcd.Com.9:140>, d. pre 17 Feb. 1701/2 (fath. will) <MD 6:193-200>.

13. **Sarah ALDEN**[3], b. 27 Sept. 1681, Boston <Boston Rcd.Com.9:154>, d. pre 17 Feb. 1701/2 (fath. will) <MD 6:193-200>.

III **JOSEPH ALDEN**[2], b. aft. 22 May 1627, Plymouth; d. 8 Feb. 1696/7, Bridgewater <MD 6:71,73>; m. c1665 (based on bth. of 1st ch.), **Mary SIMMONS** <MD 6:71, 31:60 (her fath. will); MM:11>, (dau of Moses), b. ( ), d. aft. 10 Mar. 1696/7 (hus.adm.) <MD 6:73>. (See ALDEN Probate Appendix for will of Joseph ALDEN.)

6 ALDEN Children:: <MD 6:110-111; MBD 1:33>

1. **Isaac ALDEN**[3], b. c1667, d. 24 June 1727, Bridgewater <MD 20:49,51>; m. 2 Dec. 1685, Bridgewater, **Mehitable ALLEN** <MD 3:9, 20:49; MSR:6>, (dau of Samuel), b. 20 Jan. 1664, Bridgewater <MD 2:91,20:49>, d. aft. 30 Oct. 1727 (hus.pr.) <MD 20:51>. <See MD 3:9 & MBD 1:33 for bth. of chil.> (See ALDEN Probate Appendix for will of Isaac ALDEN.)

2. **Joseph ALDEN**[3], b. c1668, d. 22 Dec. 1747, ae 80, Bridgewater <MD 3:143>; m. c1690, **Hannah DUNHAM** <MD 3:142 (bth. of 1st ch.> (& bth. of chil.)>, (dau of Daniel), b. c1670, d. 14 Jan. 1747/8, ae 78, Bridgewater <MD 3:143>. <See MBD 1:42 & MD 3:142-3 for bth. of chil.>

3. **Mercy ALDEN**[3], b. c1670, d. aft. 28 July 1727 (hus.will); m. 26 June 1688, Taunton, **John BURRILL** <MSR:628; NEHGR 13:251>, b. ( ), d. 16 Nov. 1731, Weymouth <Weymouth VR 2:252>. <See

MBD 1:45 & Weymouth VR for bth. of chil.> (See ALDEN Probate Appendix for will of John BURRILL.)

4.   **Elizabeth ALDEN[3]**, b. c1673, d. 8 May 1705, Bridgewater <MD 14:203 (& bth. of chil.); m. 12 Dec. 1693, Bridgewater, **Benjamin SNOW[3]** <MD 26:38>, (son of William SNOW & Rebecca BROWN[2]). (See BROWN Family and BROWN Probate Appendix for will.)

5.   **John ALDEN[3]**, b. c1674/5, Middleboro, d. 29 Sept. 1730, 56th yr, Middleboro <MD 6:111,23:111; Middleboro Dths.:1>; m. c1690-1700, Middleboro, **Hannah WHITE** <MD 6:111,23:111>, (dau of Ebenezer[2] (Tho.[1])), b. 5 May 1681, Weymouth <Weymouth VR 1:339; NEHGR 4:57 says 12 May 1681>, d. 5 Oct. 1732, 52nd yr, Middleboro <MD 6:111,23:111; Middleboro Dths.:1>. <See MBD 1:37 for bth. of chil. & MD 2:201 for bth. of 4 daus.> (See ALDEN Probate Appendix for wills of John & Hannah ALDEN.)

6.   **Hopestill ALDEN[3]**, b. (   ), d. aft. 18 Dec. 1753 (hus.dth.); m. c1689, **Joseph SNOW[3]** <MD 6: 110, 14:208 (& bth. of chil.)>, (son of William Snow & Rebecca Brown[2]). (See BROWN Family.)

IV   **SARAH ALDEN[2]**, b. c1629, d. pre 13 June 1688 (sett.fath.est.) <MD 3:10-11>; m. (   ) **Alexander STANDISH[2]** <MQ 52:146>. (See STANDISH Family.)

V   **JONATHAN ALDEN[2]**, b. c1632, d. 14 Feb. 1696/7, 65th yr, Duxbury g.s. <MD 9:159>; m. 10 Dec. 1672, Duxbury, **Abigail HALLETT** <MD 8:232,14:67>, (dau of Andrew), b. c1645, d. 17 Aug. 1725, 81st yr, Duxbury g.s. <MD 9:159>. <See MD 14:140-42 for data & deeds pertaining to chil.> (See ALDEN Probate Appendix for estate of Jonathan ALDEN.)

    6 ALDEN Children: <See MD 14:140-42 for children's deeds>

1.   **Elizabeth ALDEN[3]**, b. c1673/74 <MD 14:67>, d. betw. 21 Feb. 1738 (ack.deed) <Plymouth Co. Deeds 34:199,200> - 2 May 1757 (pr.2nd hus.will) <MDP:21>; m.1st pre 2 July 1711, **Edmund CHANDLER[3]** (Joseph[2], Edmund[1]), blacksmith <MD 14:141 (deed)>, b. (   ), d. betw. 4 Apr. 1715 - 28 Sept. 1717 <MD 14:66,140,141>; (his estate was adm. 5 Feb. 1721 <MDP:22>). <See MD 14: 65-70 for Chandler Notes.> **Elizabeth** m.2nd, 12 July 1722, Duxbury, **Pelatiah WEST** <Duxbury VR; MD 11:240,14:66>, (son of Samuel WEST & Tryphosa PARTRIDGE) b. 8 Mar. 1674, Duxbury <MD 9: 173>, d. 7 Dec. 1756, Duxbury <Duxbury ChR 1:248>. (See ALDEN Probate Appendix for will of Pelatiah WEST.)

2.   **Anna ALDEN[3]**, b. (   ); d. 8 June 1705, Bridgewater <MD 6:7>; m. 21 Dec. 1699, Duxbury, **Josiah SNELL** <MD 9:109>, (son of Thomas), b. 5 May 1674, Bridgewater <MD 2:242>, d. 4 Apr. 1753, Bridgewater <MD 6:7>. <See MBD 1:30 & MD 6:7 for bth. of chil.>

3.   **Sarah ALDEN[3]**, b. c1679, d. 26 June 1738, 59th yr, S. Duxbury g.s. <MD 10:170,19:25>; m. c1701, **Thomas SOUTHWORTH[4]** <MD 14:140,18:244,19:25>, (son of Edward SOUTHWORTH[3] (Constant[2], Edw.[1]) & Mary PABODIE[3] (Elizabeth Alden[2]), b. c1675/6, d. 2 Sept. 1743, 68th yr, S. Duxbury g.s. <MD 10:170,19:25>. <See MD 9:231,19:25 MBD 1:14 for bth. of chil.> (See ALDEN Probate Appendix for will of Thomas SOUTHWORTH.)

4.   **John ALDEN[3]**, b. c1681/2, d. 24 July 1739, 58th yr, S. Duxbury g.s. <MD 8:233,9:159,20:12>; m. 12 Jan. 1709/10, Scituate, **Hannah BRIGGS** <Scituate VR 1:2:18>, b. 8 May 1684, Scituate <   >, d. 8 Feb. 1739/40, 56th yr, S. Duxbury g.s. <MD 8:233,9:159,20:12>. <See MBD 1:31 & MD 11:22 for bth. of chil.> (See ALDEN Probate Appendix for estate of Col. John ALDEN & will of Hannah (BRIGGS) Alden.)

5.   **Andrew ALDEN[3]**, b. (?aft. 1681), d. aft. Mar. 1754, Duxbury or Connecticut <   >; m. 4 Feb. 1713/4, Duxbury, **Lydia STANFORD** <MD 11:24>, b. (   ), d. (   ). <See MD 10:185 & MBD 1:30 for bth. of chil.>

6.   **Jonathan ALDEN[3]**, b. cMar. 1686, d. 10 July 1770, ae 84y4m, Gorham ME <History of Gorham:387>; m.1st 17 Jan. 1717/8, Marshfield, **Elizabeth (ARNOLD[5]) Waterman** <Marshfield VR:36; MD 8:43; MSR:245>, (dau of Seth ARNOLD & Elizabeth GRAY[4] (Mary Winslow[3], Mary Chilton[2])), b. (   ), d. betw. 26 Oct. 1729 (bpt. last ch.)) - 5 May 1731 (div. of 1st hus. est. ordered) <MFIP, Warren #174>. (Elizabeth m. 1st c1709, Marshfield, Anthony WATERMAN[4] <MFIP, Warren #174>, son of Joseph WATERMAN & Sarah SNOW[3] (Abigail Warren[2]), b. 4 June 1684, Marshfield <Marshfield VR:11>, d. 3 Apr. 1715, 31st yr, Marshfield <Marshfield VR:33,389>; they had 4 chil. <Marshfield VR 32 (2), 42 (1), 45 (1)>.) Jonathan m.2nd 25 Nov. 1731, Bridgewater, **Mehetable ALLEN** <MD 16:98>, (dau of Samuel Jr. & Rebecca), b. 18 Dec. 1694, Bridgewater <MD 2:244>, d. (   ). <See MBD 1:30 & MD 31:124,162,163,164,168 for 5 chil., Marshfield VR:87 (4); (note: the son b. Mar. (worn) <MD 9:186; Marshfield VR:48> is poss. the 5th ch. <MD 31:168>.>

VI   **RUTH ALDEN**, b. 1634/5, d. 12 Oct. 1674, Braintree <Braintree VR:640>; m. 3 Feb. 1657, Braintree, **John BASS** <Braintree VR:716; MQ 42:90; (?12 May 1657)>, bpt. 18 Sept. 1630, Saffron,

Waldon, Essex, Eng. <MQ 42:90>, d. 12 Sept. 1716, ae 84, Braintree <Braintree VR:724; MD 4:
202>, (John m.2nd 21 Sept. 1675, Hannah/Ann STURTEVANT <MM:16> who d. aft. 25 June 1716
(hus.will).) <See PN&Q 2:49-52 & MBD 1:50-51 for chil.> (See ALDEN Probate Appendix for will
of John BASS.)

7 BASS Children:

1. **John BASS**[3], b. 26 Nov. 1658, Braintree <Braintree VR:691>, d. 30 Sept. 1724, Braintree
   <Braintree VR:726>; m.1st c1687, **Abigail ADAMS**[3] <PN&Q 2:49>, (dau of Joseph[2] (Henry[1])),
   b. 27 Feb. 1658, Braintree <Braintree VR:818>, d. 26 Oct. 1696, Braintree <Braintree VR:693>.
   John m.2nd 17 Mar. 1698/9, Braintree, **Rebecca SAVIL** <   >, b. 3 July 1672 <   >, d. aft.
   30 Nov. 1724 (adm.hus.est.) <MD 18:107>. <See MBD 1:52 & Braintree VR for bth. of chil.>
   (See ALDEN Probate Appendix for will of John BASS.)

2. **Samuel BASS**[3], b. 25 Mar. 1660, Braintree <Braintree VR:642>, d. 20 Feb. 1751, E. Bridgewater
   <MBD 1:50>; m.1st prob. Lynn, **Ann KIRTLAND** <   >, b. 16 Apr. 1658, Lynn <   >, d. (   );
   Samuel m.2nd 29 Nov. 1689, Braintree, **Mercy MARSH** <   >, b. 2 Apr. 1669, Braintree <   >;
   Samuel m.3rd pre 18 July 1694, **Mary ADAMS**[3] (her fath.will) <PN&Q 2:49-51>, (dau of Joseph[2]
   (Henry[1]), b. 25 Feb. 1667, Braintree <Braintree VR:646>, d. 9 Mar. 1706, Braintree <Braintree
   VR:695>; Samuel poss. m.4th, c1707-10, **Bethia NIGHTINGALE** <Thayer Mem.1:59,60>. <See MBD 1:
   60-61 for chil.> (Note: The Bowman Files give only wives Mary Adams & Bethia Nightingale.)

3. **Ruth BASS**[3], b. 28 Jan. 1662, Braintree <Braintree VR>, d. 5 June 1699, Braintree <Braintree
   VR:694>; m. c1683, **Peter WEBB**[3] <PN&Q 2:49>, (son of Christopher[2-1]), b. 1 Dec. 1657, Brain-
   tree <Giles Mem.:501; MBD 1:60>, d. 12 Feb. 1717, Salem g.s. <Giles Mem.:501; MBD 1:60>.
   <See MBD 1:60 & Braintree VR:662-4 for bth. of chil.> (Peter m.2nd betw. 1700-1703, Amy HAY-
   DEN[3] <MBD 1:60>, (dau of Jonathan[2] (John[1])), b. 16 Sept. 1672, Braintree <MBD 1:60; Giles
   Mem.:501-2>, d. 8 Nov. 1732, Boston <MBD 1:60; Giles Mem.:501-2>. <See MBD 1:60 & Braintree
   VR:684-92 for bth. of chil.>)

4. **Joseph BASS**[3], b. 5 Dec. 1665, Braintree <Braintree VR:645>, d. 22 Nov. 1733, prob. Boston
   <MD 18:107>; m.1st 5 June 1688, Braintree, **Mary BELCHER** <Braintree VR:720>, (dau of Moses &
   Mary), b. 8 Sept. 1668, Braintree <Braintree VR:647>, d. 2 Nov. 1707, Braintree <Braintree
   VR:694>. Joseph m.2nd 23 Feb. 1707/8, Lynn, **Lois (IVORY)(Blye) Rogers** <MM:17>, b. 7 Feb.
   1660, Lynn <   >, d. aft. 26 June 1734 (hus.est.) <MD 18:110>. <See MBD 1:53,54 & Brain-
   tree VR:666-85 for bth. of chil.> (See ALDEN Probate Appendix for will of Joseph BASS.)

5. **Hannah BASS**[3], b. 22 June 1667, Braintree <Braintree VR:646>, d. 24 Oct. 1705, Braintree
   <Braintree VR:695; MQ 42:90>; m. 8 Feb. 1687/8, prob. Braintree, **Joseph ADAMS**[3] <Braintree VR;
   MQ 42:90; PN&Q 2:49 (no date)>, (son of Joseph[2] (Henry[1])), b. 24 Dec. 1654, Braintree
   <Braintree VR:630>, d. 12 Feb. 1736/7, Braintree <Braintree VR:732; NEHGR 9:153>. (Joseph
   m.1st 20 Feb. 1682, Mary CHAPIN <Braintree VR:719>, b. 27 Aug. 1662, Braintree <Braintree
   VR:819>, d. 14 June 1687, Braintree <Braintree VR:660>; he m.3rd Elizabeth (   ), b. c1669,
   d. 14 Feb. 1739/40 ae 71 <NEHGR 9:153; MBD 1:51>.) <See MBD 1:51 & Braintree VR:665-685 for
   bth. of chil.> (See ALDEN Probate Appendix for will of Joseph ADAMS.)

6. **Mary BASS**[3], b. 11 Feb. 1669, Braintree <Braintree VR:647>, d. ?10 Apr. 1725, bur. Randolph
   <   >; m.1st 24 3mth 1686, Braintree, **Christopher WEBB**[3] <Braintree VR:664; PN&Q 2:49 (no
   date)>, (son of Christopher[2-1]), b. 25 Mar. 1663, Billerica <Billerica VR>, d. Mar. 1689/90,
   at sea off Nantasket (smallpox) <Braintree VR:658>. Mary m.2nd 13 Apr. 1694, Braintree,
   William COPELAND <Braintree VR:721; PN&Q 2:49 (no date)>, (son of Laurence & Lydia), b. 15
   Nov. 1656, Braintree <Braintree VR:636>, d. 30 Oct. 1716, Braintree <Braintree VR:724>.
   (Mary was app'td admx. of his estate 31 Dec. 1716 <Suffolk Co.PR #3802, 19:239; MDP:36).
   Mary m.3rd c1718, **Ebenezer SPEAR** <   >, b. 3 Aug. 1654, Braintree <   >, d. 21 Mar. 1719,
   Braintree <   >.

7. **Sarah BASS**[3], b. 29 Mar. 1672, Braintree <Braintree VR:649>, d. 19 Aug. 1751, bur. Braintree
   <MBD 1:51; Thayer Gen.:590>; m. 7 Jan. 1691/2, Braintree, **Ephraim THAYER** <Braintree VR:647>,
   b. 17 Jan. 1669, Braintree <Braintree VR:647>, d. 15 June 1757, Braintree <   > <MD 18:113
   states he died in 88th yr betw. 10 Apr. 1755 (will) - 15 July 1757 (prob.)>. <See MBD 1:62
   for bth. of chil.> (Ephraim m.2nd aft. 1751, Mary (   )(Burill) KINGMAN <MD 18:105; Thayer
   Mem.2:3> who d. aft. 10 Apr. 1755 (hus.will).) (See ALDEN Probate Appendix for will of
   Ephraim THAYER.)

VII **REBECCA ALDEN**[2], b. pre 1649, d. pre 13 June 1688 (sett. fath. est.) <MD 3:10; Stratton:281
tells of an unrecorded deed dated 2 July 1685, ack. by John ALDEN and witnessed by Thomas &
Rebecca De Lano which would place Rebecca's dth. betw. 1685-1688>; m. pre 30 Oct. 1667, **Dr.
Thomas DELANO** <PCR 4:168 (fined 10 pounds for copulation with unnamed wife before marriage)>,
(son of Phillip DELANO & Hester DEWSBURY), b. 21 Mar. 1642 <   >, d. 13 Apr. 1723, Duxbury
<   > <MD 6:22 states he died betw. 5 Oct. 1722 (will) - 22 Apr. 1723 (oath of wit.)> (See
ALDEN Probate Appendix for will of Dr. Thomas DELANO.)

9 DELANO Children: <See MBD 1:46-7; MD 6:23, 8 chil. listed in fath. will>

1. **Benoni DELANO**[3], b. 30 Oct. 1667, Duxbury < >, d. 5 Apr. 1738, 71st yr, Duxbury g.s. <MD 9:160>; m. ( ), **Elizabeth DREW** <MD 20:31-2>, (dau of John & Hannah), b. 5 Feb. 1673, Plymouth <PCR 8:67; MD 1:146,20:31>, d. pre 21 Aug. 1733 (deed) <MD 20:31; Plymouth Co.Deeds 28:67>. <See MBD 1:47 for 4 chil> (See ALDEN Probate Appendix for estate of Dr. Benoni DELANO.)

2. **Thomas DELANO**[3], b. 12 Nov. 1668/9, Duxbury < >, d. aft. 15 Aug. 1725 (joined Plym.Church) <Plymouth ChR 1:228-9>; m. 24 Oct. 1699, Duxbury, **Hannah ( ) Bartlett** <MD 9:109; The Plymouth Quarter Sessions, 1687-1721, p.164 contain this entry: "17 Sept. 1700 Hannah ye Wife of Thomas DELANO junr. presented for Committing ffornication while single person: Appeared & pleaded not Guilty & put her self on Tryall by a Jury who found her not Guilty".>; (poss. the dau of John & Abigail (Bryant) BRYANT, b. 2 Dec. 1688, prob. Duxbury <MFIP, Warren #52>), d. aft. 15 Aug. 1725 (joined Plym.Church) <Plymouth ChR 1:228-9>. (Hannah m.1st, (c1693?), prob. Duxbury, Ebenezer BARTLETT[4], son of Benjamin BARTLETT[3] (Mary Warren[2]) & Sarah BREWSTER[3] (Love[2]), b. pre Aug. 1670 <MFIP, Warren #52>, d. pre 1 Mar. 1697/8 (inv.) <MDP:491; Plymouth Co.PR #1259, 1:288>.)

3. **Deborah DELANO**[3], b. c1672 <MQ 46:58>, d. pre 1 Oct. 1717 (hus.2nd marr.) <NEHGR 70:162; MQ 46:58>; m. c1695, **John WESTON** <MQ 46:58; MFIP, Soule #40 says c1697>, (son of Edmund), b. c1662 <MQ 46:58>, d. pre 18 Nov. 1736 (pr.) <Plymouth Co.PR 7:238,255-6>. <See , for 6 or 7 chil.> (John m.2nd 1 Oct. 1717, Duxbury, Rebecca PETERSON[3] <Duxbury VR; MQ 46:57>, (dau of John PETERSON & Mary SOULE[2], see SOULE Family.) <See MQ 46:57-59, Who Was Deborah WESTON?>

4. **Jonathan DELANO**[3], b. Dec. 1675, d. 6 Jan. 1765, ae 89y2wks, Duxbury <Duxbury ChR 1:250>; m. 12 Jan. 1698, Duxbury, **Hannah DOTY**[3] <Duxbury VR:67 or 244; MD 12:33>, (dau of Thomas DOTY[2] & Mary CHURCHILL) - see DOTY family. <See MBD 1:48 & MD 12:33 for bth. 11 chil.>

5. **David DELANO**[3], b. (c1677?), d. betw. 30 July 1750 ( ) - 2 July 1755 ( ), Middleboro < >; m. 9 Jan. 1705/6, Middleboro, **Elizabeth EDDY** <MD 2:157>, b. c1684, Middleboro < >, d. aft. 30 July 1750 < >.

6. **Mary DELANO**[3], b. c1680, d. 7 Nov. 1756 < >.

7. **Sarah DELANO**[3], b. ( ), d. aft. 15 May 1746 (oath to hus.inv.) <MD 7:114,117>; m. ( ), **John DREW** <MD 6:23,7:114>, (son of John & Hannah), b. 29 Aug. 1676, Plymouth <MD 1:146,7:114> d. betw. 17 Apr. 1742 (will) - 10 July 1745 (pr.), Halifax <MD 7:114>. <See MBD 1:49 for chil.> (See ALDEN Probate Appendix for will of John DREW Sr.)

8. **Ruth DELANO**[3], b. ( ), d. aft. 5 Oct. 1722 (fath.will) <MD 6:23>; m. ( ), **Samuel DREW**, (son of John & Hannah), b. 21 Feb. 1678, Plymouth <MD 1:146>, d. ( ).

9. **Joseph DELANO**[3], b. 1 Sept. 1685, Duxbury < >, d. 22 May 1770, Duxbury < >; m. 16 Oct. 1719, Marshfield, **Hannah (BARTLETT**[5]**) Arnold** <Marshfield VR:38 (gives the date as 1714 but this is corrected in TAG 37:143-4>, (dau of Samuel BARTLETT[4] (Benjamin[3], Mary Warren[2]) (Sarah Brewster[3], Love[2]) & Hannah PABODIE[3] (Elizabeth Alden[2])), b. c1690, d. 16 Jan. 1763, ae 73, Duxbury <Duxbury VR>. (Hannah m.1st, 8 Mar. 1713/4, Duxbury, Benjamin ARNOLD[5] <MD 11:24,25:35>, (son of Seth ARNOLD & Elizabeth GRAY[4], Mary Winslow[3], Mary Chilton[2]), b. ( ), d. betw. 19 Jan. 1715/6 - 16 July 1718 <MF5G 2:90 (no reason given for dates; he was ment. as living in his fath. will of 11 Dec. 1715 <MDP:148; MD 25:36-7>; see MBD 1:299-300 & MD 8:233 for bth. 1 son.) <See MD 12:165 for bth. 6 chil.>

VIII **MARY ALDEN**, b. ( ), living 13 June 1688, unm. (sett. fath. est.) <MD 3:10-11>.

IX **PRISCILLA ALDEN**, b. ( ), living 13 June 1688, unm. (sett. fath. est.) <MD 3:10-11>.

X **DAVID ALDEN**[2], b. c1646 <MD 7:64 (arrived to the age of 73 at dth.)>, d. betw. 5 June 1718 (deed) <MD 9:147> - 1 Apr. 1719 (adm.) <MD 6:239>; m. by 1667, **Mary SOUTHWORTH**[3] (Constant SOUTHWORTH[2] (Edward[1]) & Elizabeth COLLIER), b. ( ) < >, d. betw. 28 Mar. 1718 (deed) <MD 9:147; Plymouth Co.Deeds 14:55> - 1 Apr. 1719 (not ment. in hus.pr.) <MD 6:239>. <See MD 6:239-43 for estate of David ALDEN>

6 ALDEN Children:

1. **Ruth ALDEN**[3], b. c1674, d. 2 July 1758, ae 84, Rochester <Rochester VR 2:101>; m. 29 Nov. 1694 Duxbury, **Samuel SPRAGUE** <MD 9:25>, b. c1669, d. 25 July 1740, ae 71, Rochester <MD 20:192>. <See MDP:5 for estate of Samuel SPRAGUE & deed of heirs. See MD 9:25 & MBD 1:4 for 8 chil.>

2. **Elizabeth ALDEN**[3], b.? 9 Apr. 1675, Duxbury <NEHGR 54:181>, d. 4 Jan. 1771, Stonington CT, bur Groton CT < >; m. 9 Dec. 1697, Duxbury, **John SEABURY** <Duxbury VR:211; MD 9:108>, b. c1673 prob. Duxbury, d. 17 Dec. 1759, ae 86, Hempstead, Long Island NY < >. <See MBD 1:3 & Groton CT VR for bth. of chil.>

3. **Priscilla ALDEN**[3], b. ( ), d. aft. 19 Jan. 1735/6 (hus.will) <MDP:5; New London CT PR D:248> m. 4 Jan. 1699/1700, Duxbury, **Samuel CHESEBROUGH Jr.** <MD 9:109>, b. 14 Feb. 1673/4, Stoning-

ton CT <   >, d. 2 Mar. 1735/6, Stonington CT <New London CT PR D:319 (inv. gives death
date)>. <See MBD 1:4 & Stonington CT VR 1:101 for bth. of chil.> (See ALDEN Probate Appendix for will of Samuel CHESEBROUGH   )

4. **Alice ALDEN**[3], b. c1685/6, d. 12 July 1774, 89th yr, bur. Dennis <PN&Q 5:126>; m. 5 Dec. 1706,
    Duxbury, **Judah PADDOCK** <MD 9:108; PN&Q 5:126>, (son of Zachary), b. 15 Sept. 1681, Yarmouth
    <MD 3:247>, d. 31 Mar. 1770, 89th yr, bur. Dennis <PN&Q 5:126> <See MBD 1:1,2 & MD 13:233 for
    bth. of chil.>

5. **Benjamin ALDEN**[3], b. (   ), d. 14 Apr. 1741, drowned, Duxbury <MD 8:233,24:74>; m. betw. 3 Oct
    1707 (deed) <MD 20:115> - 1 Jan. 1709/10 (bth.1st ch.) <MD 10:185>, **Hannah BREWSTER**[4], (dau of
    Wrestling BREWSTER[3] (Love[2]) & Mary (   )), b. cSept. 1688, d. 8 Jan. 1763, ae 7464m12d, Dux-
    bury <Duxbury ChR 1:249; MD 8:233,24:74>. <See MD 10:185,24:74; MBD 1:2 for bth. of chil.>
    (See ALDEN Probate Appendix for estate of Deacon Benjamin ALDEN.)

6. **Samuel ALDEN**[3], b. cDec. 1688 <MD 7:64 (age 85 in 1773)>, d. 24 Feb. 1781, ae 92y2m3d, bur. S.
    Duxbury <MD 9:159,20:76>; m. 26 Feb. 1727/8, Duxbury, **Sarah SPRAGUE** <MD 11:80,20:76>, b. cMay
    1701, d. 28 Mar. 1773, 72nd yr, bur. S. Duxbury <MD 9:159,20:76>. <See MBD:6 & MD 11:236,12:
    163 for bth. of chil.> (See ALDEN Probate Appendix for will of Capt. Samuel ALDEN.)

ALDEN PROBATE APPENDIX

===

Will of **Joseph ADAMS**: <MD 18:112-13; Suffolk Co.PR 33:82,83>
...1 Mar. 1733/4, mentions wf Elezebeth, sons Joseph ADAMS, John ADAMS, Samuel ADAMS & Josiah
ADAMS; daus Hannah OWEN, Ruth WEBB, Bethiah ADAMS; heirs of dau Abagail CHAPING; son Ebenezer
ADAMS & his "Sisters Children". Pr. 22 Mar. 1736/7
===

Estate of **Deacon Benjamin ALDEN**[3] (David[2]): <MD 24:74-81; MDP:4; Plymouth Co.PR #63, 8:371, 375,
410,431,19:77>...Division of estate, 5 Oct. 1741, among following children, viz: David ALDEN
(eldest son), Bezaleel ALDEN, Wrestling ALDEN, Abiathar ALDEN, Elizabeth ALDEN, Mary WADSWORTH.
===

Will of **Hannah (BRIGGS) Alden**: <MD 20:14-15; Plymouth Co.PR 8:153,154>
...1 Feb. 1739/40, mentions sons Samuel ALDEN, Judah ALDEN, Briggs ALDEN; daus Anna & Abigail.
Pr. 5 Mar. 1739/40. (<8:166,176> - Guardianship rcds. show Briggs & Abigail were minors.)
===

Will of **Isaac ALDEN**[3] (Joseph[2]): <MD 20:49-51; Plymouth Co.PR 5:344,345>
...24 Apr. 1727, mentions wf Mehittabell, sons Isaac ALDEN, Ebenezer ALDEN, John ALDEN; grandchildren (chil. of dec'd dau Mehittabell RICHARDS), viz: Joseph RICHARDS, Daniel RICHARDS, James
RICHARDS, Mehittabel RICHARDS & Sarah RICHARDS; daus Sarah CARY, Mary WEBB, Mercy PACKARD &
Jemima ALLDEN. Pr. 30 Oct. 1727.
===

Estate of **John ALDEN**[1]: <MD 3:10-11; Plymouth Co.PR 1:10,16>
...Settlement of estate, 13 June 1688, the following heirs ack. that they have received their
shares from brother Jonathan ALDEN, viz: Elexender STANDISH (in right of dec'd wf Sarah), John
BASS (in right of dec'd wf Ruth), Mary ALDEN, Thomas DILLANO, John ALDEN, Joseph ALDEN, David
ALDEN, Priscilla ALDEN, William PAYBODY.
===

Will of **Capt. John ALDEN**[2] (mariner): <MD 6:193-200; Suffolk Co.PR 15:5>
...17 Feb. 1701, mentions eldest son John ALDEN, sons William ALDEN, Zechariah ALDEN; dau Elizabeth WALLEY; chil. of dec'd son Nathaniel ALDEN. Inv. 2 June 1702.

(Capt. John ALDEN was a distinguished and respected citizen, having lived in Boston for over 30
years. He was an experienced mariner and had served as a naval commander. As a military offi-
cer he had served in the French and Indian wars and as late as 1690 served as commissioner in
conducting negotiations with the natives. Imagine his amazement to find himself before the Salem
magistrates, 31 May 1692, "upon the accusation of a company of poor distracted or possessed crea-
tures or witches" on a charge of witchcraft! He was interrogated for many hours, during which
time his sword was taken from him (he was accused of using it to afflict his accusers) and he was
further degraded by one accuser who stated, "he sells powder and shot to the Indians and French,
and lies with the Indian squaws, and has Indian papooses". The evidence against him? During the
interrogation he was said to pinch his accusers, strike them down with his look and heal them
with his touch. Capt. Alden was taken to Boston jail where he was held in custody for fifteen
weeks and, in his own words, "...and then, observing the manner of trials, and evidence then
taken, was at length prevailed with to make his escape". He made his escape about the middle of
September and it was probably just in time as soon after this nine of the accused were executed.
Alden probably made his way to Duxbury where relatives & friends hid him, but his experience was
not yet over. In Apr. 1693 when it appeared the witchcraft hysteria was over and people were
coming to their senses, Alden turned himself in and was bound over to the Superior Court at Bos-

ton the last Tuesday of Apr. 1693. When no one came forward to prosecute, he and 150 others were released. The judicial proceedings were finally over, at the expense of 20 innocent lives. <Salem Witchcraft: With an Account of Salem Village and A History of Opinions on Witchcraft and Kindred Subjects, vol.2, Upham, Charles W., pp.243-5 (John ALDEN's own account.)>>

Will of **John ALDEN**[3] (John[2]): <MD 10:79; Suffolk Co.PR 27:82,83,31:27>
...5 May 1727, mentions wf Susanna; chil. of dec'd son John ALDEN; sons Nathaniel ALDEN, Thomas ALDEN; daus Elizabeth ALDEN, Hannah JONES, Anne ALDEN. Pr. 9 Feb. 1729.

Will of **John ALDEN**[3] (Jos.[2]): <MD 23:112-15; Plymouth Co.PR>
...23 Sept. 1730, mentions wf Hannah; sons John ALDEN (under 21), David ALDEN, Joseph ALDEN (under 21), Noah ALDEN; daus Thankfull EATON, Hannah WOOD, Lydia ALDEN, Mary ALDEN, Abigail ALDEN; 20 acres where grave stone of son Lemuel ALDEN lies to be reserved as a burying place. Witnesses sworn 17 Dec. 1730.

Will of **Hannah (WHITE) Alden**: (widow) <MD 23:112-15; Plymouth Co.PR 6:279,280>
...8 Sept. 1732, mentions daus Thankful, Hannah, Lydia, Mary, Abigail; brother Benjamin WHITE; requests "a pair of Grave Stones for their Fathers Grave and also for a Pair for my own Grave". Pr. 1 Jan. 1732 (O.S.).

Estate of **Capt. Jonathan ALDEN**[2]: <MD 6:174-8; Plymouth Co.PR 1:255,2:28>
...Inventory taken 3 Mar. 1697. Settlement, 7 Jan. 1703, mentions eldest son John ALDEN; widow Abigail; 3 unnamed sons (including John) and 3 unnamed daus.

Will of **Joseph ALDEN**[2]: <MD 6:71-4; Plymouth Co.PR 1:256-7>
...14 Dec. 1696, mentions sons Isaac ALDEN, Joseph ALDEN, John ALDEN; wf Mary. Inv. 3 Mar. 1696/7 Pr. 10 Mar. 1696/7. (Note: He does not mention his 3 daus who were then living.)

Estate of **Capt. Nathaniel ALDEN**[3] (John[2]): <MD 10:77-9; Suffolk Co.PR 15:48,49,62,150,175,223-4>
...Adm. 24 July 1702 to widow Hephzibah ALDEN. Petition 8 July 1703 of widow Hephzibah MORTIMORE. Guardian app'td 9 July 1703 for the children (all minors), viz: Mary, Nathaniel, Hepsheba and "Phillips".

Will of **Capt. Samuel ALDEN**[3] (David[2]): <MD 20:76-78; Plymouth Co.PR 28:38,41>
...10 Nov. 1779, mentions daus Rebeckah FRAZIER wf of Thomas, Sarah BRADFORD wf of Gamaliel, Alethea LORING wf of William; chil. of dec'd dau Alice SEABURY; dau Abagail WINTER wf of Rev. Francis; grandchildren John ALDEN & Rebeckah Partridge ALDEN; son Samuel ALDEN. Pr. 5 Mar. 1781.

Will of **Capt. William ALDEN**[3] (John[2]): <MD 10:79; Suffolk Co.PR 27:82,83,31:27>
...14 Jan. 1728, mentions youngest dau Mary ALDEN; daus Elisabeth BETTERLY, Lydia BRITON. Pr. 3 Mar. 1728.

Will of **John BASS**: <MD 4:202-6; Suffolk Co.PR #378, 19:202,203,270>
...25 June 1716, mentions son John BASS & his wife & his sons John & Samuel; sons Samuel BASS, Joseph BASS; daus Mary COPELAND & Sarah THAYER "as they come of age"; unnamed granddaughters (some of age), the daus of dec'd daus Ruth & Hannah. Petition of heirs, 22 Oct. 1716, signed by son Joseph BASS states (in part) that his father "was under great insanity of mind...(and) was perswaded by his Son John BASS & wife to cutt off his son Joseph by making this new will and being Stricken in years was much awed by his grandson John BASS...(and he) has given Legacys to the Daughters of his Children Ruth WEBB and Hannah ADAMS both dec'd and has totally Excluded their Sons." (The matter was evidently dropped as their is no further mention of it in the records.)

Will of **John BASS**[3]: <MD 18:105-7; Suffolk Co.PR 23:425>
...10 Jan. (or July) 1723, mentions wf Rebecca; sons Ebenezer BASS, Samuel BASS, John BASS. Pr. 30 Nov. 1724.

Will of **Joseph BASS**[3]: <MD 18:107-12; Suffolk Co.PR 32:59>
...latter end Oct. 1733 (or Sept. 1733), mentions sons Alden BASS, Joseph BASS, Moses BASS, Benjamin BASS; dau "Miller"; seven unnamed children. On 25 Feb. 1733/4, son Alden BASS petitioned the General Court at Boston and stated that two days after his father's decease the family read the will (dated latter end Oct. 1733), after which the eldest son Joseph BASS took the will home with him and it disappeared. The will was never found; in his petition, Alden related the contents of the will as he remembered. Alden seemed very suspicious of his brother Joseph and what became of the will, particularly in view of the fact that Joseph attempted to have administration of the estate granted to him with the estate rendered intestate. Alden states in his petition, "...all the Family wellknows and he (Joseph) himself in particular That the Same is a Testate Estate and that Such Attempts are a notorious Violation of the Will of the Deceased & detestable in the Sight of God & man and loudly crys for the Interposition of your Excellency & Honours, otherwise no Person can dye with Assurance that his Will tho' made with the utmost Deliberation can take Effect". Alden goes on to use such phrases as "embezelment or concealing the said will...evil practices...ill minded persons...evil intents". The Committee app'td to look into the matter questioned the witnesses to the will (who stated they signed on or about the 22 Sept. 1733) and the widow & children who confirmed Alden's account of the will. The Committee's findings were thus, "that Some Clandestine Methods have been made use of to secrete & destroy the (will) thereby to frustrate the Intent of the Dec'd as to the Disposition of his Estate after his Death" and that Alden's account would serve as the will. Pr. 11 Feb. 1734/5.

Will of **John BURRILL** (husbandman): <MDP:28; Suffolk Co.PR #6180, 29:230,321>
...28 July 1727, mentions wf Mercy; dau Mary RIPLEY; son John BURREL. Pr. 13 Dec. 1731.

Will of **Samuel CHESEBROUGH**: <MDP:5; New London CT PR #D:248,319>
...19 Jan. 1735/6, mentions wf Priscilla; son Amos CHESEBROUGH; daus Mary HEWIT, Priscilla PALMER
Hannah SHAW, Sarah & Prudence (both under 18); grandchildren Nathaniel HEWIT and Mary & Priscilla
CHESEBROUGH. Inv. taken 6 May 1736 (gives his dth. date).

Will of **John COE** (husbandman): <MDP:15; Bristol Co.PR 6:195,198,199>
...4 Dec. 1728, mentions wf Sarah; Samuel COE (eldest son); John COE (2nd son); Joseph COE (3rd
son); eldest dau Lydia BAILEY wf of John Jr.; 2nd dau Sarah TOMKINS wf of Samuel; 3rd dau Elizabeth BURGESS wf of Edward; youngest dau Hannah COE. Inv. taken 6 Jan. 1728.

Estate of **Dr. Benoni DELANO**: <MD 20:33-4; Plymouth Co.PR 7:386>
...Pr. 27 Apr. 1738. Division of estate, 12 Sept. 1738 to following chil., viz: Beriah DELANO
(eldest son); Lemuel DELANO (2nd son); chil. or rep. of Hannah HARLOW dec'd, viz: Eliphaz HARLOW,
Lemuel HARLOW and Eleazer HARLOW; Rebekah TURNER wf of Amasa.

Will of **Dr. Thomas DELANO**: <MD 6:22-24; Plymouth Co.PR 4:358,359>
...5 Oct. 1722, mentions sons Benoni DELENO, Jonathan DELENO, David DELENO; daus Mary DELENO,
Sarah DREW, Ruth DREW; granddaughter Deborah WESTON; son Joseph DELENO. Witnesses sworn 22 Apr.
1723. Inv. taken 29 Apr. 1723.

Will of **John DREW Sr.**: <MD 7:114-17; Plymouth Co.PR 9:506-8,10:163>
...17 Apr. 1742, mentions wf Sarah; eldest son John DREW; son Thomas DREW; daus Elizabeth DREW,
Jemima READ, Mary BENNET; grandsons Peter DREW (under 21), Silvanus DREW, Isaac BENNET (under
21); son Thomas DREW's eldest son (under 21); grandson Charles READ (under 21). Widow's oath to
inventory, 15 May 1746. Pr. 10 July 1745.

Will of **William FOBES**: <MDP:7; Bristol Co.PR 3:111-2,114-5,187,535-8;8:133>
...4 Nov. 1712, mentions son-in-law Joseph SEABERY; son-in-law Josiah SAWYER & his wife Martha
SAWYER; dau Elizabeth BRIGGS wf of William & their eldest son Louet BRIGGS; dau Constant LITTLE
& husband John LITTLE; grandchildren Fobes SOUTHWORTH (under 21) & his sister Rebecca SOUTHWORTH
(under 21), Samuel SEABERY & John SAWYER. Inv. taken 12 Nov. 1712 (gives dth. date).
(Note: On 14 Nov. 1712 the will was contested by Edward SOUTHWORTH.)

Obit of **Elizabeth (ALDEN[2]) Pabodie**: <MD 34:98>
Death Notice in The Boston News-Letter, issue of 17 June 1717: "Little Compton, May 31. This
Morning died here Mrs. Elizabeth PAYBODY late wife of Mr. William PAYBODY in the 93rd Year of her
Age. She was the Daughter of John ALDEN, Esq: and Priscilla his Wife Daughter of Mr. William
MULLINS. This John ALDEN and Priscilla MULLINS were Married at Plymouth in New-England where
their Daughter Elizabeth was born. She was Exemplarily Vertuous and Pious and her Memory is
blessed: Has left a very numerous Posterity: Her Granddaughter BRADFORD is a Grand-mother."

Will of **William PABODIE**: <MD 6:129-35; Bristol Co.PR 2:193-5,268>
...13 May 1707, mentions unnamed wife; son William PABODIE; dau Lidea GREENILL; grandson Stephen
SOUTHWORTH (son of dec'd dau Rebecca); grandsons John & William PABODIE (sons of son William);
daus Mary, Mercey, Martha, Priscilla, Ruth, Sarah, Hannah & Lidia; heirs of dau Elizabeth; heirs
of dau Rebecah; mentions deeds in reference to sons-in-law William FOBES & Ichabod WISWALL. Inv.
taken 13 Dec. 1707. (Note: MD 34:98 says will was dated 17 May.)

Will of **Deacon William PABODIE[3]**: <MD 23:105-7; Bristol Co.PR 8:446-7>
...7 Aug. 1743, mentions wf Mary; sons Joseph PABODIE, Benjamin PABODIE; daus Elisabeth GRAY wf
of Edward, Rebeckah FISH wf of Joseph, Priscilla WILCOX wf of William, Judith CHURCH wf of Benjamin and Mary FISH wf of Nathaniel. Inv. taken 12 Oct. 1744. Pr. 12 Nov. 1744.

Will of **Samuel SEABURY**: <MDP:6; Plymouth Co.PR 4:1;93,94>
...21 Sept. 1680, mentions wf Martha; eldest dau Elizabeth; 2nd dau Sarah; eldest son Samuel SEA-
BURY; 3rd dau Hannah; dau Martha; 2nd son John SEABURY; son Joseph SEABURY; mentions land had of
father William PAYBODY. Codicil 8 Oct. 1680 mentions "former wives death"; dau Elizabeth; present wf Martha "to be with child". Inv. taken 27 Oct. 1681.

Estate of **John SIMMONS**: <MDP:11; Plymouth Co.PR #18343, 3:388,400>
...Division 11 Feb. 1715/6, mentions widow Mercy and following chil., viz: John SIMMONS (eldest
son), William SIMMONS, Isaac SIMMONS, Benjamin SIMMONS, Joseph SIMMONS, Joshua SIMMONS, Moses
SIMMONS (youngest son), Martha WEST wf of Samuel, Rebeckah SOUTHWORTH wf of Constant.

Will of **Mercy (PABODIE[3]) Simmons** (widow): <MDP:11; Plymouth Co.PR #18371, 5:487-89>
...26 Sept. 1728, mentions following chil., viz: John SIMMONS, William SIMMONS, Isaac SIMMONS,
Benjamin SIMMONS, Joseph SIMMONS, Joshua SIMMONS, Martha and Rebecca. Inv. taken 8 Nov. 1728.

Will of **Edward SOUTHWORTH**: <MD 18:244-47; Plymouth Co.PR 5:360>
...11 June 1719, mentions sons Thomas SOUTHWORTH (eldest son), Constant SOUTHWORTH, Benjamin
SOUTHWORTH, John SOUTHWORTH; daus Mercy SOULE wf of Moses, Elizabeth WESTON wf of Samuel and
Priscilla SOUTHWORTH; grandson Cornelius SOUL; wf Mary. Witnesses sworn 7 Nov. 1727. Pr. 11 Dec.

Will of **Thomas SOUTHWORTH**: <MD 19:28-30; Plymouth Co.PR 9:4>
...21 Aug. 1742, mentions dau Hannah SOUTHWORTH widow of dec'd son Jedediah SOUTHWORTH; grandson John SOUTHWORTH (under 21); unnamed chil. of late son Jedediah; to granddaughter Deborah LORING wearing cloaths of late wife at the house of Joshua LORING; grandson James SOUTHWORTH; sd five chil. of dec'd son Jedediah. Pr. 22 Sept. (1742? - Thomas d. 2 Sept. 1743.)

Will of **William SOUTHWORTH**: <MDP:14; Bristol Co.PR 3:575-6,4:96>
...8 May 1719, mentions wf Martha; sons Benjamin SOUTHWORTH, Joseph SOUTHWORTH, Edward SOUTH-WORTH, Samuel SOUTHWORTH, Nathaniel SOUTHWORTH, Thomas SOUTHWORTH, Stephen SOUTHWORTH, Gideon SOUTHWORTH, Andrew SOUTHWORTH; daus Elizabeth LITTLE, Alice COOKE; grandsons William & Constant SOUTHWORTH. Inv. taken 31 July 1719.

Will of **Martha SOUTHWORTH** (widow): <MDP:15; Bristol Co.PR 9:22>
...13 June 1729, mentions sons Joseph BLAGUE, Andrew SOUTHWORTH, Gideon SOUTHWORTH; dau Mary SOUTHWORTH; grandson William SOUTHWORTH; granddaughter Mary BLAGUE; son-in-law Joseph SOUTH-WORTH. Pr. 8 Apr. 1738 states she was of Saybrook CT.

Will of **Ephraim THAYER**: <MD 18:113-15; Suffolk Co.PR 52:507,508>
...10 Apr. 1755, mentions wf Mary & her "sons Kingmans"; sons Ephraim THAYER, Philip THAYER, Joseph THAYER, Shadrack THAYER, Naphtali THAYER, Peter THAYER; granddaughter Ruth VINTON dau of dau Sarah DORMAN; daus Hannah BLANCHER, Ruth CAPEN, Esther FRENCH, Priscilla FORD, Abigail RICH-ARDS; sons Christopher THAYER, James THAYER. Pr. 15 July 1757.

Will of **Pelatiah WEST** (husbandman): <MDP:21; Plymouth Co.PR 14:330,332,15:254>
...31 Jan. 1731/2, mentions wf Elizabeth; brother Samuel WEST of Lebanon CT; kindsman Benjamin SOUTHWORTH Jr. of Duxbury, the son of sister Abigail COLE wf of Nathaniel COLE. Pr. 2 May 1757.

Will of **Simon WILLARD** (shopkeeper): <MDP:17; Suffolk Co.PR 18:220>
...13 Nov. 1709, "shortly designing a voyage by Sea and not knowing how it may please God to dis-pose of me therein"; mentions wf Elizabeth and following chil., viz: Samuel WILLARD, Abigail WIL-LARD, Katherine WILLARD. Pr. 11 Jan. 1713.

Will of **Rev. Ichabod WISWALL**: <MD 19:1-5; Plymouth Co.PR 1:325,326>
...25 May 1700, mentions eldest dau Elizabeth WADSWORTH wf of Elisha; wf Presilla; son Peleg WIS-WALL; daus Mercy, Hannah, Prissilla & Deborah. Pr. 19 Aug. 1700.

NOTES:

ISAAC ALLERTON

Isaac ALLERTON was born prob. Suffolk Co., England, c1585/6 <MQ 47:14; MD 4:109-10 (ae about 53 in 1639 deposition), 40:7; Banks 1:29> and died between 1 Feb. (court appearance) - 15 Feb. 1658/9, New Haven CT. <MD 2:155> He married 1st, 4 Nov. 1611, Leyden, Holland, Mary NORRIS of Newbury, England <MD 7:129-30,22:15>, who died 25 Feb. 1620/1, Plymouth (two months after the birth of her stillborn child) <MD 1:88,30:3,97; MQ 47:15>. Isaac married 2nd, bet-ween 1623 (in the 1623 allotment of land Fear is single) - 1626 (she is included in the 22 May 1627 Cattle Division as Isaac's wife with mention of a Sarah ALLERTON who is now thought to be their first child. If they had a child by May 1627, they had to have married by 1626 at the latest), Fear BREWSTER[2] (dau of Elder William & Mary - See BREWSTER Fam.). Fear died not long before 12 Dec. 1634, Plymouth <MD 30:98 (date of letter of Gov. Winthrop of the Bay Colony to his son in which he relates the death of some at Plymouth)>. Isaac married 3rd, between 1635 - 1644 (1st mention of a wife Joanna), poss. Marblehead, Joanna SWINNERTON <MQ 47:15-16; MD 2:114; NEHGR 124:133>, who died between 14 May 1680 - 10 Mar. 1682/3 (mentioned in deeds) <MD 2:254; MQ 44:41; NEHGR 44:291,124:133>. (See ALLERTON Probate Appendix for will of Isaac ALLERTON.)

(See also: MQ 47:14-18, The Children of Isaac Allerton; MQ 48:170-171, Isaac Allerton, The First Yankee Trader; MQ 45:23, The Unproved Allerton Family Lineage; MQ 44:39-44, The Taylor Family of Virginia; MD 40:7-10, Bartholomew Allerton and the Fairfax Family of Bramfield, Suffolk; Isaac Allerton of the Mayflower and His Descendants for Four Generations (MFIP - Mayflower Families In Progress), by Robert S. Wakefield, FASG, 2nd Ed., 1992.)

Isaac had 5 children by 1st wife Mary and 2 children by 2nd wife Fear: <MQ 47:17>

I.   Bartholomew, b. c1612/3, Leyden, Holland
II.   Remember, b. c1614/5, Leyden, Holland
III.   Mary, b. c1617, Leyden, Holland
IV.   Child, bur. 5 Feb. 1620, Leyden, Holland <MQ 47:15>
V.   Son, stillborn, 22 Dec. 1620, Provincetown Harbour <Mourt's Relation (Dexter):66>
VI.   Sarah, b. betw. 1625-May 1627, Plymouth, d. pre 1651
VII.   Isaac, b. betw. May 1627-1630, Plymouth

* * * * * * * * * * * * * *

I. **BARTHOLOMEW ALLERTON**[2], b. c1612/3, Leyden, Holland <MD 40:7>, d. betw. 15 Oct. 1658 (will) - 19 Feb. 1658/9 (pr.) <MD 40:8>; m.1st (   ), England, **Margaret (   )** <MD 40:7>, d. pre 1658 (hus.will). **Bartholomew** m.2nd (   ), England, **Sarah FAIRFAX** <MD 40:7,8>, (dau of Ben-jamin FAIRFAX & Sarah GALLIARD), b. (   ), poss. Rumburgh Parish, Eng. <MD 40:8>, d. betw. 13 Sept. 1678 (will) - 6 Nov. 1679 (pr.), of Halesworth, Suffolk co., England. <MD 40:8-9>. (See ALLERTON Probate Appendix for wills of Bartholomew & Sarah ALLERTON.)

4 ALLERTON Children: <MD 40:7-10; MFIP #2; Bradford: "Bartle is married in England">

1. **Isaac ALLERTON**[3],   b. (   ), d. aft. 13 Sept. 1678 (mother's will).
2. **Mary ALLERTON**[3],   b. (   ), d. aft. 13 Sept. 1678 (mother's will); m. (   ) AUGER.
3. **Dorothy ALLERTON**[3], b. (   ), d. aft. 13 Sept. 1678 (mother's will); m. (   ) RAUSHAM.
4. **John ALLERTON**[3],   b. (   ), d. aft. 13 Sept. 1678 (mother's will).

II. **REMEMBER ALLERTON**[2], b. c1614, Leyden, Holland, d. betw. 12 Sept. 1652 (bpt.last ch.) - 22 Oct. 1656 (hus.2nd marr.), Marblehead <MD 2:114-5>; m.pre 6 May 1635, Marblehead, **Moses MAVERICK** <MD 2:115,5:129>, (son of John MAVERICK & Mary GUY), bpt. 3 Nov. 1611, Huish, Devon co., Eng. <NEHGR 96:232,358-60>, d. 28 Jan. 1685/6, ae 76, Marblehead <Marblehead 1st ChR:1; MD 2:115,5:130>. (Moses m.2nd, 22 Oct. 1656, Boston, Eunice (COLE) Roberts (widow of Thomas ROBERTS) <Torrey:628; see MBD 1:90 for bth. of chil. Mary, Moses, Sarah & Aaron>, d. aft. 5 Dec. 1698 <MD 5:141 (ack. agreement of heirs of hus.est.)>) (See ALLERTON Probate Appendix for will of Moses MAVERICK.)

7 MAVERICK Children: <Salem, Essex Inst.Hist.Coll.6:228-43; MBD 1:89; NEHGR 96:358-60>

1. **Rebecca MAVERICK**[3], bpt. 7 Aug. 1639, Marblehead <Salem 6:228; NEHGR 96:359>, d. 4 Nov. 1659, Lynn <Lynn VR 2:497; MD 17:223,224>; m. 3 June 1658, Lynn, **John HAWKS** <Essex Co.Court Rec.; MD 17:223,224>, (son of Adam & Ann), b. 13 Aug. 1633, Charlestown <Hawkes Gen.(Smith):29; d. 5 Aug. 1694, Lynn <MD 17:224>. (John m.2nd 11 Nov. 1661, Lynn, Sarah CUSHMAN[3] <see under Mary ALLERTON[2]>). <See MD 17:222-34 for data on chil. & Hawkes notes.>

2. **Mary MAVERICK**[3], bpt. 14 Feb. 1640/1, Salem <Salem 6:237; Salem 1st ChR:18>, d. 24 Feb. 1655 Boston <Boston Rcd.Com.9:52>.

3. **Abigail MAVERICK**[3], bpt. 12 Jan. 1644/5, Salem <Salem 6:240; Salem 1st ChR:20; Salem VR 2:67>, d. pre 1683/4 (hus.2nd marr.) <MD 5:13 (dec'd in fath. will of Jan. 1685/6)>; m. c1660-2, Ip-

swich, **Samuel WARD**, (son of Samuel & Mary), bpt. 18 Nov. 1638, Hingham < >, d. betw. 30 July 1689 (will) - 12 Mar. 1690/1 (pr.) <Essex Co.PR #28928; MDP:49>. (Samuel m.2nd, c1684, Sarah (BRADSTREET) Hubbard. <See MBD 1:90,103 for bth. of 2 chil.>) <See MBD 1:90,103 & Salem 1st ChR:29,30,33 for bth. of chil.> (See ALLERTON Probate Appendix for will of Maj. Samuel WARD.)

4. **Elizabeth MAVERICK**[3], bpt. 3 Dec. 1646, Salem <Salem 6:240; Salem 1st ChR:21; NEHGR 7:270>, d. pre Sept. 1649 (birth of another dau Elizabeth).

5. **Samuel MAVERICK**[3], bpt. 19 Dec. 1647, Salem <Salem 6:241; Salem 1st ChR:21>, d. betw. 1668/9 - Jan. 1685/6 (fath.will).

6. **Elizabeth MAVERICK**[3], bpt. 30 Sept. 1649, Salem <Salem 6:242; Salem 1st ChR:22; NEHGR 7:270, 96:360>, d. betw. Jan. 1685/6 (fath.will) - 3 Nov. 1698 (gdn. app'td for her minor chil.) <Suffolk Co.PR 8:305-6>; m.1st 6 Apr. 1665, Marblehead, **Nathaniel GRAFTON** <Salem VR; NEHGR 7: 270,96:360>, (son of Joseph GRAFTON & Mary MOORE), bpt. 24 Apr. or 1 May 1642, Salem <Salem VR>, d. 11 Feb. 1670/1, Barbadoes <Salem, Essex Inst.Hist.Coll.2:97>. **Elizabeth** m.2nd, c1676 prob. Boston, **Thomas SKINNER** (baker) <Boston VR 28:34>, b. c1644, d. 28 Dec. 1690, ae 46, Boston <Boston Rcd.Com.9:194>. (Thomas m.1st 28 Dec. 1669, Mary GOULD <MFIP #8>.) <See Salem VR & MBD 1:95 for bth. of chil.>

7. **Remember MAVERICK**[3], bpt. 12 Sept. 1652, Salem <Salem 6:243; Salem 1st ChR:23; NEHGR 7:270>, d. betw. Jan. 1685/6 (fath.will) - 22 Sept. 1693 (gdn. app'td for minor chil.) <MD 5:139>; m. c1671, Salem, **Edward WOODMAN**, b. ( ), d. betw. 22 Sept. 1693 (app'td gdn. of his chil.) - 25 Oct. 1698 (gdn. app'td for his chil.) <Suffolk Co.PR 8:302>. <See MBD 1:99,104 for bth. of chil.>

II **MARY ALLERTON**[2], b. c1617, Leyden, Holland, d. 28 Nov. 1699, ae 83, Plymouth (g.s. says aged about 90 years) <MD 2:115,4:37,16:63; Plymouth VR 1:203; Drew:10>; m. c1636, Plymouth, **Thomas CUSHMAN** <MD 2:115>, (son of Robert CUSHMAN & Sarah REDER), bpt. 8 Feb. 1607/8, Canterbury, Kent co., England <NEHGR 68:185; MD 2:115 (b. Feb. 1608)>, d. 10/11 Dec. 1691, ae 84, Plymouth g.s. <MD 4:37,38; Plymouth VR 2:202 (MD 16:62) states he d. 10 Dec., "being entered into the 84 yeare of his age"; Plymouth ChR I:V:22 states "11 Dec., having within two moneths finished the 84th yeare of his life"; Plymouth ChR 1:2:165-6 states, "...chosen & ordained Elder of this chh. April 6: 1649: he was neere 43 yeares in his office, his sicknesse lasted about 11 weekes...he was grave, sober, holy & temperate...He dyed December 11: neere the end of the 84th yeare of his life. December 16 was kept as a day of Humiliation for his death... much of Gods prescence went away from this chh. when this blessed Pillar was removed".> <See MD 10:193 for Cushman's parents> (See ALLERTON Probate Appendix for will of Thomas CUSHMAN.)

(Note: The order of the birth of the following Mary & Sarah is uncertain. Sarah was married and having children at least 15 years earlier than Mary, had children born between 1662-1677 and her husbands were born in 1632 and 1633. Mary's first known child was not born until after Feb. 1677/8 which gives an approx. marriage date of 1676 or later; her husband was born c1630 but as this was his second marriage, Mary could very well have been younger than him. For these reasons I have placed Sarah as the second child. See MQ 52:28-32)

8 CUSHMAN Children: <MD 4:39; MBD 1:68; See MQ 52:28-32>

1. **Thomas CUSHMAN**[3], b. Sept. 1637, Plymouth, d. 23 Aug. 1726, ae 89 wanting a month, Plympton <MD 2:235, 10:112 (89th yr)>; m.1st 17 Nov. 1664, Plymouth, **Ruth HOWLAND**[2] <PCR 8:25> (See HOWLAND Family), d. betw. 29 May 1672 (fath.will) <MD 2:70-3> - 16 Oct. 1679 (hus.2nd marr.). **Thomas** m.2nd, 16 Oct. 1679, Rehoboth, **Abigail (TITUS) Fuller** <PCR 8:87; Rehoboth VR:116; MD 22:115>, (dau of John TITUS & Abigail CARPENTER), b. 18 Feb. 1652/3, Rehoboth <Rehoboth VR:755>, d. 31 May 1734, 82nd yr, Attleboro g.s. <Attleboro VR:656>. (Abigail m.1st, 25 Apr. 1673, Rehoboth, John FULLER <Rehoboth VR:365>). < See MBD 1:84-5 for bth. of chil.>

2. **Sarah CUSHMAN**[3], b. c1640 (1639-45), Plymouth, d. (*); m.1st 11 Apr. 1661, Lynn, **John HAWKS** <MD 17:224>, (son of Adam & Ann), b. 13 Aug. 1633, Charlestown <Hawkes Gen.:29>, d. 5 Aug. 1694, Lynn <MD 17:224>. (John m.1st 1658, Rebecca MAVERICK[3] (Remember Allerton[2]).) **Sarah** m.2nd (int.) 7 Nov. 1695, Lynn, **Daniel HUTCHINGS** <Lynn VR; Torrey:376>, b. c1632 <Hawkes Gen.:41 (ae about 50 in Mar. 1682/3 deposition as Daniel "HITCHINS")>, d. (*). (Daniel m.1st Eleanor ( ).) (*Could Sarah & Daniel HUTCHINGS be the following: Daniel HITCHENS d. c15:2:1731 ae about 100 and Mrs. Daniel HITCHENS, widow, bur. 12:5:1737 - ?? <MBD 1:95; Lynn VR; Zach.Collins Diary>) <See MBD 1:81 & MD 17:224 for bth. of chil.>

3. **Mary CUSHMAN**[3], b. c1643 (1640-45), Plymouth <MQ 52:31>, d. betw. 1685 (last ch. prob. born) <MQ 52:31> - 22 Oct. 1690, Lynn (fath.will) <MD 4:38-41>; m. c1676-80, Lynn, **Francis HUTCHINSON** <MQ 52:31 gives a possible marriage entry (torn & incomplete), found in Marblehead VR:108 and listed after a Cushman entry: "CUS( ), Mary, and ( )ison of Reading, May 17, (1680?)">, b. c1630 <MQ 52:30>, d. 12 Nov. 1702, Reading <Middlesex Co.PR>. (Francis m.1st, 11 Dec. 1661, Lynn, Sarah LEIGHTON who d. 23 Dec. 1661 <Lynn VR:505>; he m.2nd Martha (STEARNS) Parker who d. 15 Aug. 1708, Reading <Reading VR:532>.) <See MQ 52:28-32 for this family> (See ALLERTON Probate Appendix for will of Francis HUTCHINSON.)

4. **Isaac CUSHMAN**[3], b. 8 Feb. 1648/9, Plymouth <MD 15:27; PCR 8:5 says 1647/8 but see MD 15:25 for correction>, d. 21 Oct. 1732, 84th yr, Plympton g.s. <MD 10:111,17:139; Plympton VR:470>; m. c1675, Plymouth, poss. **Rebecca HARLOW**[4] <TAG 26:144-7; MFIP, Allerton #13>, (dau of William HARLOW & Rebecca BARTLETT[3] (Mary Warren[2]) - see WARREN Family), b. 12 Jan. 1655, Plymouth <PCR 8:17>, d. 3 Sept. 1727, 73rd yr, Plympton g.s. <MD 1:178,10:112; Plympton VR:471>. <See MBD 1:74 for bth. 6 chil.; MD 1:210 for bth. 5 chil. & Plymouth ChR 1:274 for bpt. 6th> (See ALLERTON Probate Appendix for will of Rev. Isaac CUSHMAN.)

5. **Elkanah CUSHMAN**[3], b. 1 June 1651, Plymouth <MD 5:20,16:237; PCR 8:12>, d. 4 Sept. 1727, 77th yr, Plympton <MD 1:178,5:20,10:111>; m.1st 10 Feb. 1677/8, Plymouth, **Elizabeth COLE** <MD 13:203>, (dau of James COLE & Abigail DAVENPORT), b. c1660, Plymouth, d. 4 Jan. 1681/2, Plymouth <MD 13:203,15:213>. **Elkanah** m.2nd, 2 Mar. 1683/4, Plymouth, **Martha COOKE**[3] <MD 13:203>, (dau of Jacob COOKE[2] & Damaris HOPKINS[2] - See COOKE & HOPKINS families). <See MBD 1:72 & MD 1:142 for bth. 9 chil.; MD 1:142 for bth. 8 chil. & Plymouth ChR 1:271 for bpt. 9th> (See ALLERTON Probate Appendix for will of Elkanah CUSHMAN.)

6. **Feare CUSHMAN**[3], b. 20 June 1653, Plymouth <MD 17:70; PCR 8:15>, d. pre 22 Oct. 1690 (fath. will) <MD 4:38-40>.

7. **Eleazer CUSHMAN**[3], b. 20 Feb. 1656, Plymouth <MD 17:71; PCR 8:16>, d. aft. 14 Oct. 1723, Plympton (deed) <MDP:39; Plymouth Co.Deeds 18:140; MFIP #15 states he d. aft. a Nov. 1733 petition in which his land is mentioned but does not say if he himself is mentioned as living nor is a source given>; m. 12 Jan. 1687/8, Plymouth, **Elizabeth COOMBS** <MD 13:205>, (dau of John & Elizabeth), b. 30 Nov. 1662, Boston <Boston Rcd.Com.9:83>, d. aft. 14 Oct. 1723, Plympton (deed) <MDP:39; Plymouth Co.Deeds 18:140>. <See MBD 1:68 for 6 chil.; MD 1:212 for bth. 2.>

8. **Lydia CUSHMAN**[3], b. c1660 (1658-62), Plymouth, d. 11 Feb. 1718/9, Plymouth <NEHGR 14:229>; m. cJan. 1682/3, Plymouth, **William HARLOW**[4] <Plymouth ChR 1:251 (Under 15 Apr. 1683, "William Harlow & Lydia his wife were called before the church & charged with uncleanesse, their child being borne within six weekes after marriage, & for disobedience to parents, engaging one to another without knowledge & against consent of parents, sinfully also hiding & denying their guilt, they manifested soe much Repentance for all charged, as that the Church would not reject them, only voted Admonition, which was applyed by the Pastour,")>, (son of William HARLOW & Rebecca BARTLETT[3] (Mary Warren[2]) - see WARREN family), b. 2 June 1657, Plymouth <PCR 8:17; MD 12:195; TAG 23:189>, d. 28 Jan. 1711/12, Plymouth <MD 16:64>. <See MBD 2:437 for bth. 9 chil.; MD 1:207 (3), Plymouth ChR 1:271 (bpt. 1).> (See ALLERTON Probate Appendix for estates of William & Lydia HARLOW.**)**

VII **ISAAC ALLERTON**[2], b. betw. 22 May 1627 (Cattle Division) <MD 1:153> - 1630 <MD 7:173; MQ 47:18 (of legal age (i.e. 21) 21 Sept. 1652)>, Plymouth. (After his mother's death in 1634, Isaac seems to have been raised by his grandfather, William BREWSTER, then his uncle Love BREWSTER. The agreement of heirs of William BREWSTER, 20 Aug. 1645, provides "for the dyett of Isaack Allerton, a grandchild of the sd William, which hee had placed with his sonn Love to table". <Plymouth Co.Deeds 1:198; MD 3:27-30>). Isaac d. betw. 25 Oct. (will) - 30 Dec. 1702 (pr.), Westmoreland Co.VA <MD 7:173-6; MQ 44:41>; m.1st c1652, poss. New Haven CT, Elizabeth ( ) <MD 7:173> who d. c1655 (bth. of ch.; dec'd by 1658 settlement of est. of Isaac ALLERTON[1]). **Isaac** m.2nd c1663, Westmoreland Co.VA, **Elizabeth (WILLOUGHBY)(Oversee) Colclough** <MD 7:173; MQ 44:41; betw. 8 Sept. 1662 when she adm. est. of 2nd hus. <Northumberland Co.VA Order Bk 2:160> - 30 May 1664, an order to audit the account of Isaac ALLERTON[2] "who married the relict and administrator of Major George COLCLOUGH dec'd" <Northumberland Co.VR Rec.Bk 15:130a, b,131a,b.>>, (dau of Thomas & Alice WILLOUGHBY), b. c1635, d. aft. 1672, prob. Westmoreland Co.VA <MD 42:118>. (Elizabeth m.1st c1659, Northumberland Co.VA, Simon OVERZEE who marr. as his first wife Sarah THOROUGHGOOD <Adventurers of Purse & Person:360>. Elizabeth m.2nd c1661 VA, George COLCLOUGH who d. pre 8 Sept. 1662 (adm.- above) and who m. as his 1st wife Ursala BISSHE <Virginia Mag.3:323>.) (See ALLERTON Probate Appendix for will of Isaac ALLERTON.)

    5 ALLERTON Children: (2 by 1st, 3 by 2nd) <See MFIP; MD 42:117; VG 32:92, 33:171>

1. **Elizabeth ALLERTON**[3], b. 27 Sept. 1653, New Haven CT <New Haven CT VR 1:9; MD 7:174>, d. 17 Nov. 1740, New Haven CT <New Haven CT VR 1:625>; m.1st 23 Dec. 1675, New Haven CT, **Benjamin STARR** <MD 7:174>, (son of Thomas & Rachel), b. 6 Feb. 1647/8, Yarmouth <PCR 8:3>, d. 1678, ae 31, New Haven CT <NEHGR 91:288; MD 7:174>. **Elizabeth** m.2nd 22 July 1679, New Haven CT, **Simon EYRES/AYRES** <New Haven CT VR 1:72; Torrey:256; MD 7:174>, (son of Simon AYRES & Lydia STARR), b. 6 Aug. 1652, Boston <Boston Rcd.Com.9:36; NEHGR 91:288>, d. c1695 <Underhill 2:844; MFIP, #17>. <See Boston Rcd.Com.9:196 & New Haven CT VR 1:67,78,81,87,136 for bth. 7 chil.>

2. **Isaac ALLERTON**[3], b. 11 June 1655, New Haven CT <VR 1:12>, d.y. poss. 1655 <See MQ 45:23-4.>

3. **Willoughby ALLERTON**[3], b. c1664, Westmoreland Co.VA <VG 32:171>, d. 1724, Westmoreland Co.VA <MD 7:174; VG 32:171 says betw. 16 Jan. 1723/4 (will) - 8 Apr. 1724 (will rec.); MFIP #18 says betw. 17 Jan. 1723/4 (codicil) - 25 Mar. 1724 (pr.)>; m.1st by 1698, Westmoreland Co.VA, **Rosamond FITZHUGH** <VG 32:171>, (dau of Col. William FITZHUGH & Sarah TUCKER), b. c1680 <VG 32:171>, d. c1700, Westmoreland Co.VA <VG 32:171>. **Willoughby** m.2nd c1702, Westmoreland Co. VA, **Sarah (TAVERNER) Travers** <VG 32:171>, (dau of John & Elizabeth), b. 7 Jan. 1679/80, N.

Farnham Parish, Richmond Co.VA <VG 32:171>, d. c1720, Westmoreland Co.VA <VG 32:172>. (Sarah m.1st, c1697, Westmoreland Co.VA, Rawleigh TRAVERS (brother of Samuel below) who d. betw. 20 Feb. 1701 (will) - 4 Mar. 1701/2 (pr.) <VG 32:172, Richmond Co.VA Wills & Inventories:42>.) **Willoughby** m.3rd, c1722, Westmoreland Co.VA, **Hannah (KEENE) Bushrod** <VG 32:172>, (dau of William KEENE & Elizabeth ROGERS), b. 14 Feb. 1676/7, Northumberland Co.VA <VG 32:172, St. Stephen's Parish Register>, d. betw. 26 Dec. 1738 (will) - 29 May 1739 (pr.) <Westmoreland Co. Deeds & Wills 9:25,26>. (Hannah had 7 chil. by 1st hus. John BUSHROD (m.c1694), (son of Richard & Apphia), b. 30 Jan. 1663/4, Gloucester Co.VA, d. 6 Feb. 1719/20 <VG 27:280,32:172>; she m.3rd c1725, Westmoreland Co., Dr. John COOPER who d. c1735 <VG 32:173>.) <See MFIP #18 & VG 32:173 for 2 chil. by 2nd wife.> (See ALLERTON Probate Appendix for wills of Willoughby ALLERTON & Hannah COOPER.)

4. **Frances ALLERTON**[3], b. c1668, Westmoreland Co.VA <VG 32:175>, d. pre 25 Oct. 1702 (fath.will) <MD 7:173-6; and soon after her husband's death in 1698 <Richmond Co.VA Orders 4:112>; m. 1 July 1685, Rappahannock Co.VA, **Capt. Samuel TRAVERS** <VG 32:175>, (son of William TRAVERS & Rebecca HUSSEY), b. c1660, Rappahanock Co.VA <VG 32:175>, d. pre 7 Sept. 1698 (order to appraise est.) <Richmond Co.VA Orders 2:232>. <See VG 32:176 & MFIP, #20 for bth. 4 chil.>

5. **Sarah ALLERTON**[3], b. c1670, Westmoreland Co.VA <VG 32:176; MD 7:174>, d. 17 May 1731, ae 60, Wicomico, Northumberland Co.VA <MD 7:174; VG 32:176 says Westmoreland Co.>; m.1st c1693, ( ) **NEWTON** <MD 42:117-23>. **Sarah** m.2nd c1700, Westmoreland Co.VA, **Hancock LEE** <MD 42:122>, (son of Col. Richard LEE & Ann CONSTABLE) b. c1653, Dividing Creek, Northumberland Co.VA <VG 32:176; MQ 44:41>, d. 25 May 1709, ae 56, Wicomico or Dividing Creek, Northumberland Co.VA <MQ 44:41>. (He m.1st c1675, Mary KENDALL who d. 24 Dec. 1694 ae 33 <MQ 44:41;MD 42:122>.) <See MD 43:1 for correction to MFIP, #21 & MD 42:123, (Hancock & Sarah LEE did have a daughter Ann who m. William Eustace.); MD 42:123 for bth. 1 Newton ch. and 4 Lee chil.>

ALLERTON PROBATE APPENDIX

Will of **Bartholomew ALLERTON**[2]: <MD 40:7-8; Prerogative Court of Canterbury 92 Pell>
...15 Oct. 1658, of Bramfield, Co. Suffolk, Eng., ment. dec'd wf Margaret, wf Sarah, unnamed chil Pr. 19 Feb. 1658/9.

Will of **Sarah ALLERTON** (widow): <MD 40:8-9; Court of the Archdeacon of Suffolk, Probate Rec.
                                    1644-1700, W109/92, R73/208>
...13 Sept. 1678, of Halesworth, Co. Suffolk, Eng., ment. son Isaac ALLERTON; daus Mary AUGER, Dorothy RAUSHAM; son John ALLERTON; "brother Johnson & his wife"; brothers Benjamin FAIRFAX, John FAIRFAX, Nathaniel FAIRFAX; "brother Harlock & his wife"; sisters Priscilla FAIRFAX, Anne FAIRFAX; Sarah, Mary & Elizabeth, the daus of brother Benjamin FAIRFAX; Elizabeth, dau of brother John FAIRFAX; Sarah, dau of brother Nathaniel FAIRFAX; all the children of the three brothers (not before mentioned). Pr. 6 Nov. 1679.

Will of **Isaac ALLERTON**[1]: <MD 2:155-7; New Haven CT PR 1:1:82,83>
...(no date), ment. son Isaac ALLERTON; unnamed wf; "brother Bruster". Inv. taken 12 Feb. 1658. Will presented 19 Oct. 1659. (This is more an account of debts due & owed than it is a will.)

Will of **Isaac ALLERTON**[2]: <MD 7:173-6; Westmoreland Co.VA PR 3:115>
...25 Oct. 1702, ment. dau Sarah LEE; grandson Allerton NEWTON (under 21); dau Elizabeth STARR (alias AYERS); dec'd dau TRAVERSE & her daus Elizabeth TRAVERSE, Rebecca TRAVERSE, Winifred TRAVERS; son Willoughby ALLERTON. Pr. 30 Dec. 1702.

Will of **Willoughby ALLERTON**[3]: <VG 32:171; Westmoreland Co.VA Wills & Deeds 8:9-10>
...17 Jan. 1723/4, ment. wf Hannah and her daus Hannah & Sarah; son Isaac ALLERTON; dau Elizabeth ALLERTON. Rec. 8 Apr. 1724.

Will of **Hannah COOPER** (widow): <VG 32:172; Westmoreland Co.VA Wills & Deeds 9:25-26>
...26 Dec. 1738, ment. son Thomas BUSHROD (under 21); William SANFORD, son of sister Elizabeth SANFORD; dau Elizabeth MERIWETHER; dau Sarah BERRYMAN; son John BUSHROD; dau Hannah NEALE; late husband Col. Willoughby ALLERTON; son in law William FAUNTLEROY; dau Apphia FAUNTLEROY; son Richard BUSHROD & his dec'd father Richard BUSHROD. Pr. 29 May 1739.

Will of **Deacon Elkanah CUSHMAN**[3]: <MD 5:20-1; MDP:41; Plymouth Co.PR #5813, 5:330,331>
...14 Oct. 1725, ment. son Allerton CUSHMAN; dau Martha HOLMES; granddaughters Elizabeth DELANOE & Hannah CUSHMAN; son Josiah CUSHMAN. Pr. 26 Sept. 1727.

Will of **Rev. Isaac CUSHMAN**[3]: <MD 17:139-40; Plymouth Co.PR 6:248,267,365>
...25 Oct. 1727, ment. dec'd son Isaac CUSHMAN; dau Rebeckah MITCHELL; chil. of dec'd daus Mary WATERMAN & Sarah BRIANT; dau Fear STURTEVANT; son in law Robert WATERMAN. Sworn to 30 Oct. 1732.

Will of **Elder Thomas CUSHMAN**: <MD 4:37; Plymouth Co.PR 1:129-32>
...22 Oct. 1690, ment. wf Mary; sons Thomas CUSHMAN, Isaac CUSHMAN, Elkanah CUSHMAN, Eleazer CUSHMAN; daus Sarah HOAKS/HAWKS, Lidiah HARLOW; 3 chil. of dec'd dau Mary HUTCHINSON. Sworn to 16 Mar. 1691/2.

Epitaph of **Elder Thomas CUSHMAN**: <Burial Hill (Drew):9,10; MSR:505>
"Here lyeth buried ye body of that precious servant of God Mr. Thomas Cushman, who after he had served his generation according to the will of God, and particularly the church of Plymouth for many years in the office of a ruleing elder fell asleep in Jesus Decemr. ye 10, 1691 & in ye 84. year of his age.
This stone placed at the grave of Elder Cushman by the First Church in Plymouth, was removed to this situation in 1858, to make room for a more endureing memorial which now exactly occupies its original position." (The new 25 foot monument is inscribed on four sides in memory of Thomas, his wife Mary and his father Robert Cushman.)
==
Estate of **Lydia (CUSHMAN[3]) Harlow**: (widow): <MDP:510; MD 12:196-7; Plymouth Co. PR 4:231,249,250>
...Division, 24 Dec. 1720, ment. heirs: Thomas HARLOW, William HARLOW, Robert HARLOW, Isaac HARLOW; Thomas DOTY Jr., son of Elizabeth DOTY late wf of Thomas DOTY dec'd; Lydia CHURCHILL wf of Barnabas; Rebecca HARLOW.

Estate of **William HARLOW**: <MDP:509; MD 12:195-6; Plymouth Co.PR 3:107,135>
...Settlement, 21 June 1712, ment. widow Lidia; dec'd dau Elizabeth DOTEN & her son Thomas DOTEN; eldest son Thomas HARLOW; 2nd son William HARLOW; 3rd son Robert HARLOW; 4th son Isaac HARLOW; 2nd dau Mary; 3rd dau Lidia; youngest dau Rebecca.
==
Estate of **John HAWKES**: <MD 17:228-32>
...Settlement, 4 Sept. 1694, ment. widow Sarah; sons John HAWKES, Thomas HAWKES, Ebenezer HAWKES; to son Moses HAWKES, land grandfather Adam HAWKES willed him; dau Mercy HAWKES.
==
Will of **Francis HUTCHINSON**: <Middlesex Co.PR #12336>
...18 Feb. 1698, ment. sons Francis HUTCHINSON, Thomas HUTCHINSON, John HUTCHINSON. Inv. states he d. 12 Nov. 1702.
==
Will of **Hancock LEE**: <Northumberland Co.VA Rec.Bk:29-32>
...31 Dec. 1706, ment. unnamed wf; dau Mrs. Anna ARMSTEAD; son Richard LEE; brother Richard LEE; sons Isaac LEE, John LEE; "child that my wife is now with". Pr. 20 July 1709.
==
Will of **Moses MAVERICK**: <MD 5:129-41; MDP:49; Essex Co.PR #1472, 9:293,295>
...Jan. 1685/6, ment. wf Eunice; Moses HAWKS only surviving child of dec'd dau Rebecca; four children of dec'd dau Abigail, viz: Samuel WARD, Abigail HINDS, Mary DOLLABER & Martha WARD; daus Elizabeth SKINNER, Remember WOODMAN, Mary FERGUSON & Sarah NORMAN; son in law Archibald FERGUSON. (Will was unsigned.) Presented for probate 30 Mar. 1686 but some of the children objected. On 15 July 1686, widow Eunice was app'td admx. Agreement of heirs, 29 Nov. 1698, signed by: Eunice MAVERICK, Archibald FERGUSON, Moses HAWKS, John NORMAN, Sarah NORMAN, Samuel WARD, Elizebeth HEWES, Thomas JACKSON, Thomas PERKINS. Ack. by John NORMAN, 15 Sept. 1699. Ack. by rest, 5 Dec. 1698.
==
Will of **Maj. Samuel WARD**: <MDP:49; Essex Co.PR #28928>
...29 July 1689, "Whearas the Governor and Counsill have orderid me upon an expeditian to Cannade by gods asistans agaienst the Comon enemie", ment. wf Sarah, "god having given me a living child by her"; dau Mercy (unm.); to son in law John TUTTELL "the leggasie which my dau Martha had given her from herr grandfather"; dau Marie DOLIVER; father BRADSTREET; son Samuel WARD; surviving children of dau Abigail HINDS; children of dau Remember WILSON; he asks his wife "to be as kiend to my Children as I have ben to herr Children". Inv. 12 Mar. 1690/1. Pr. 22 Apr. 1691.
(Note: The witnesses testified the will was left with them "on his goeing to Canada on ye 30th of July 1690...at that time he was a disposeing mind and...was well composed, being seriously melancholy in haste to looke after his souldiers". The wording of the will (e.g. being ordered upon an expedition) and the fact that he left the will with witnesses 30 July 1690, seems to imply the will was written just before he left, i.e. 29 July 1690, not 1689.)

NOTES:

JOHN BILLINGTON

John BILLINGTON was born c1580, possibly from Spaulding, Lincolnshire, Eng. <NEHGR 124:116-8>. He was executed for murder in Sept. 1630 (See BILLINGTON Probate Appendix for Bradford's account) John was married in England by 1604 to Eleanor (   ) (identity unknown) <MD 2:115>, who was born c1580, poss. the same area of England as her husband and died aft. 2 Mar. 1642/3 when she is mentioned in a deed <PCR 12:93-4>. Eleanor remarried between 14-21 Sept. 1638, Plymouth, Gregory Armstrong <PCR 12:33,37> who died 5 Nov. 1650, Plymouth <PCR 8:11; MD 2:115>.

(See: Mayflower Families Through Five Generations (MF5G), John Billington of the Mayflower, by Harriet Woodbury Hodge, vol.5, 1991; NEHGR 124:116-118, Francis Billington of Lincolnshire; MQ 52:137-143, Desire Billington And Her Grandfather Francis Billington's Estate; TG 3:228-48, Some Descendants of Francis Billington of the Mayflower.)

John & Eleanor had two children: <MD 2:115; MBD 1:106>

I. John, b. c1604, England
II. Francis, b. c1606, England

* * * * * * * * * * * * * * * *

I. **JOHN BILLINGTON**[2], b. c1604, England, d. betw. 22 May 1627 (Cattle Division) <MD 1:152 - Sept. 1630, Plymouth <Bradford:234,446>, no known issue.

II. **FRANCIS BILLINGTON**[2], b. c1606, England (ae 68 in 1674 dep.) <MD 2:46,115; MF5G 5:31,36 gives a possible birth date of c1609 based on English records of a Francis Billington, son of John, who in 1613 was named heir to a lease of crown land in Lincolnshire. The 1650 survey of crown lands states this Francis Billington "was living a year since in New England aged forty years or thereabouts". MF5G interprets this statement to mean he was aged forty "in the previous year, thus b. ca1609". However, with only this phrase to work with and not seeing the original record, my interpretation would read that this Francis had been living in New England one year, age forty (b. c1610) or thereabouts (b. c1609-11). Does this sound like Francis Billington[2], b. c1606 (by his own statement) who had, by 1650, been living in New England for 30 years?? Two other statements give a clue to his year of birth. He is called age 80 at death and a Mar. 1703/4 petition of his son Isaac states he died "near 80 years" - both of these statements bring his year of birth further away from c1609. See also NEHGR 124:116-18.> Francis d. 3 Dec. 1684, Middleboro <Middleboro Dths.:20 (says ae 80 which would place his birth at c1604; however, credibility should be given to his deposition in which he himself states his age, rather than the age given by family or friends after his death). Francis married July 1634, Plymouth, **Christian (PENN) Eaton** <PCR 1:31; MD 2:115>, b. c1607, England, d. c1686 <Plymouth Co.PR #2001 (The petition of son Isaac, dated 1 Mar. 1703/4 states his parents "were near 80 years old when they dyed; & it is now 18 years since". Since we know Francis died in 1684, the "18 years since" must refer to his last surviving parent, his mother, which places her year of death at 1686 - and being "near 80" coincides with her approximate year of birth of c1607.> (Christian m.1st c1624-5, Plymouth, Francis EATON - See EATON Family.) (See also BILLINGTON Probate Appendix for Isaac's petition.)

9 BILLINGTON Children: <MQ 52:142-3; MBD 1:110>

1. **Elizabeth BILLINGTON**[3], b. 10 July 1635, Plymouth <PCR 2:38 (18 Apr. 1642 she was apprenticed or "bound out">, d. aft. 22 Mar. 1709/10, Providence RI (deed) <MQ 52:142-3>; m.1st 21 Sept. 1660, Rehoboth, **Richard BULLOCK** <Rehoboth VR:67>, b. c1622, England (ae 25 in 1647) <MSR: 514>, d. betw. 13 Feb. 1663/4 (deed) <Plymouth Co.Deeds 3:122> - 22 Nov. 1667 (inv.) <MSR: 538; MD 17:28; MF5G 5:37 cites TAG 39:65-73 & Plymouth Co.PR 2:2:47 and states he died pre 22 Oct. 1667>. (Richard m.1st 4 Aug. 1647, Rehoboth, Elizabeth INGRAHAM <Rehoboth VR> who d. 7 Jan. 1659/60 <Rehoboth VR>. See Rehoboth VR for bth. of 6 chil. betw. 1648-1659.) **Elizabeth** m.2nd 25 June 1673, Rehoboth, **Robert BEERS/BEERE** <VR; MQ 52:142>, poss. of Newport RI <TAG 39:65>, d. 29 Mar. 1676, Rehoboth (killed by Indians) <PCR 8:63; TAG 39:65>. **Elizabeth** m.3rd c1679, **Thomas PATTE/PATEY** <MQ 52:142> who drowned on the Seekonk River near Providence, 19 Aug. 1695 <MQ 52:143>. <See Rehoboth VR:563 & MBD 1:110 for bth. of chil.>

2. **Joseph BILLINGTON**[3], b. c1636/7, Plymouth (ae 6 or 7 in Jan. 1642/3 when he and two sisters, aged 5 yrs & younger, were "bound out") <Plymouth TR 1:12; PCR 2:58,59 relates how young Joseph often ran off from his master to return to his family. Since the boy was too young to be punished, the Court tried a preventative measure with his parents, Francis & Christian. The records state that "if either the said Francis or Christian, his wyfe, do receive him, if he shall againe dept <depart> from his said master wthout his lycence...the said Francis and Christian, his wyfe, shalbe sett in the stocks...as often as he or shee shall so receive

him".>, d. aft. 7 Jan. 1684/5 (land grant), prob. Block Island RI <MQ 52:143; New Shoreham RI TR 1:57>; TG 3:228-48>; m. 16 Sept. 1672, New Shoreham RI, **Grace (   )** <New Shoreham VR 1: 45> who d. aft. 13 Oct. 1680, Block Island (charged with theft) <TG 3:228-48; New Shoreham TR 1:55>. <See MF 5:40 & NEHGR 106:103-5 for chil.>

3. **Martha BILLINGTON**[3], b. c1638, Plymouth (ae 5, 14 Jan. 1642/3 when she was "bound out") <Ply-mouth TR 1:12>, d. betw. 9 June 1704 (deed) <Plainfield CT Deeds 1:17> - 2 Mar. 1722 (son's deed) <Plymouth Co.Deeds 20:10>; m.1st 10 Jan. 1660/1, Plymouth, **Samuel EATON**[2] <PCR 8:22; MSR:544> (See Eaton Family.). **Martha** m.2nd aft. 7 Dec. 1687 (ante-nuptial contract), **Robert CROSSMAN** <MSR:43; NEHGR 62:233>, (prob. son of John), b. c1621 <NYGBR 22:77-8>, d. pre 27 Oct 1692 (inv. which states he d. ae 71) <NEHGR 63:139>. (Robert m.1st 25 May 1652, Dedham, Sarah KINGSBURY <NYGBR 22:77-8>, by whom he had 12 children <Taunton VR 1:109-12>.) (See EATON Family for chil.)

4. **Mary BILLINGTON**[3], b. c1640, prob. Plymouth (under ae 5, 14 Jan. 1642/3 when she was "bound out") <Plymouth TR 1:12>, d. aft. 28 June 1717, Rehoboth (ack.deed) <Bristol Co.Deeds 12:300-301>; m. 20 Jan. 1663/4, Rehoboth, **Samuel SABIN** <Rehoboth VR:331>, (son of William), b. c1640 d. 23 Sept. 1699, Rehoboth <Rehoboth VR:874>. <See Rehoboth VR:736,737 & MBD 1:108-9 for bth. of chil.> (See BILLINGTON Probate Appendix for will of Samuel SABIN.)

5. **Isaac BILLINGTON**[3], b. c1644, prob. Plymouth, d. 11 Dec. 1709, 66th yr, Middleboro <MD 1:223; Middleboro Dths.:20 says 9 Dec.>; m. pre 1675, **Hannah GLASS** <MQ 52:142>, (dau of James GLASS & Mary PONTUS), b. 24 Dec. 1651, Plymouth <PCR 8:13; MD 16:237>, d. bew. 30 Aug. 1704 (deed) <Plymouth Co.Deeds 6:5> - 9 Dec. 1709 (not ment. in deed) <Plymouth Co.Deeds 7:314>. <See MF5G 5:44 for 6 chil.> (See BILLINGTON Probate Appendix for 1703/4 petition of Isaac.)

6. Child, b. pre 1651 <MD 1:14, Bradford - 8 children living in 1651>.

7. **Rebecca BILLINGTON**[3], b. 8 June 1647 <MD 15:27; PCR 8:4 says 1648 but see MD 15:25 for correc-tion>, poss. d.y.

8. **Dorcas BILLINGTON**[3], b. c1650, Plymouth, d. aft 1 Aug. 1707 (deed) of Plymouth <Plymouth Co. Deeds 7:326; Hist. of Plympton:84 (poss. d. aft. 1711 if she is the Dorkaj Macy on membership list of Plympton Ch.)> (On 7 June 1672, Dorcas was fined five pounds for committing forn-ication; the records show she was whipped, which indicates that she was unable to pay the fine <PCR 8:137>. The Middleboro records show that Dorcas had an illegitimate son, at the 20 July 1683 town meeting it was decided that her father, Francis BILLINGTON, "being in pre-sent want and for his relief they have left it to ye wisdom and discretion of ye selectmen... to ye disposing of his daughter Dorcas her lad" <Middleboro Proprietors' Rec.:43>. It is clear that neither Dorcas nor her father were in a position to financially care for the boy which is a strong indication that Dorcas was single at this time. It is also apparent that Dorcas never revealed the name of the boy's father, for if she had, the courts would have or-dered the father to support the child.) **Dorcas** m. pre 20 May 1686 (when his 1st wife was known to be dec'd), **Edward MAY** <MQ 52:142; MF 5:45>, b. (   ), d. 10 Aug. 1691, Plymouth <MD 16:62>. (The Settlement of Edward's estate (no date) mentions widow Dorcas, two sons and two daughters (unnamed) <MD 31:104>.) (Edward m.1st pre 1670, Hannah KING, dau of Samuel KING Sr. & Anna FINNEY, b. c1653 <NEHGR 148:326-7>.) <See MF5G 5:45 for chil.>

9. **Mercy BILLINGTON**[3], b. 25 Feb. 1651/2, Plymouth <PCR 8:13, MD 16:237 (no first name)>, d. 28 Sept. 1718, Rehoboth <Rehoboth VR:848; MQ 49:177>; m. 27 June 1681, Rehoboth, **John MARTIN** <Rehoboth VR:239; PCR 8:76; MSR:547>, (son of Richard MARTIN & Elizabeth SALTER), bpt. 20 Jan. 1652/3, Ottery St. Mary, Devonshire, Eng. <MQ 49:177>, d. 28 Aug. 1720, Rehoboth <Reho-both VR:848; MQ 49:177>. (John m.2nd, 28 May 1719, Rehoboth, Abigail READ <Rehoboth VR:239>, who d. 17 Apr. 1721, Rehoboth <Rehoboth VR:857; MQ 49:177>.) < See MBD 1:109 & Rehoboth VR for bth. of chil. and MQ 49:170-179, The Martins Of Swansea And The Martins Of Rehoboth.>

BILLINGTON PROBATE APPENDIX

The Death of **John BILLINGTON**[1]: <Of Plimouth Plantation, 1620-1647, by William Bradford (Morison edition, 1952), p.234>
"This year <1630> John BILLINGTON the elder, one that came over with the first, was arraigned and both by grand and petty jury found guilty of wilful murder, by plain and notorious evidence. And was for the same accordingly executed. This, as it was the first execution amongst them, so was it a matter of great sadness unto them. They used all due means about his trial and took the ad-vice of Mr. Winthrop and other the ablest gentlemen in the Bay of the Massachusetts, that were then newly come over, who concurred with them that he ought to die, and the land to be purged from blood. He and some of his had been often punished for miscarriages before, being one of the profanest families amongst them; they came from London, and I know not by what friends shuffled

into their company. His fact was that he waylaid a young man, one John Newcomen, about a former quarrel and shot him with a gun, whereof he died."

==

Petition of **Isaac BILLINGTON**[2]: <MDP:57; Plymouth Co.PR #2001>
(I include portions of this petition because of its interesting nature and the information it gives on Francis & Christian BILLINGTON. The full petition can be found in MDP.)
...1 Mar. 1703/4...A true Narrative or Relation or A Bill of Changes drawn up by Isaac BILLING-TON and his wife Hannah...concerning the great expence & charge they were at, in keeping their aged parents, Francis & Christian BILLINGTON, late of Middleborough...deceased; for the space of 7 years, even to their Death & Burial. They were neare 80 years old when they dyed; & it is now 18 years since. Soon after ye former, never to be forgotten, impoverishing indian Warrs, my aged Father, Francis BILLINGTON, came to me and told me he must return again to Middleborough for he could no longer subsist at Plymouth, & urged me with ye greatest importunity to goe with him, alledging that he should perish if I did not, for there his lands & living were; whereupon (tho then I lived comfortably at Marshfield) I removed with my family to Middleborough to take care off & provide for my aged Parents...And Lieut. TOMPSON then Selectman of ye Town promised me that if I would take care of them & not suffer them to want, I should have all ye estate that my fath-er left at his decease...Now my humble request to ye honoured Court is, that (seeing I have no other recompence but ye lands) it may be settled upon me & mine...

==

Will of **Samuel SABIN**: <Bristol Co.PR 2:7,8; MF 5:42>
...14 July 1690, "called forth to war against the French", ment. wife, sons Samuel SABIN, Israel SABIN; daus Mercy & Sarah; unnamed youngest dau (unm.). Presented for probate 16 Oct. 1699.

NOTES:

WILLIAM BRADFORD

William BRADFORD was baptized 19 Mar. 1589/90 at Austerfield, co. York, England, the son of William BRADFORD & Alice HANSON <MD 7:65>. He died 9 May 1657, ae 67 years and almost two months, at Plymouth <MD 7:65; Burial Hill (Drew):211 ("William Bradford of Austerfield Yorkshire England. Was the son of William and Alice Bradford He was Governor of Plymouth Colony from 1621 to 1633 1635 1637 1639 to 1643 1645 to 1657. Under this stone rest the ashes of Will(ia)m Bradford a zealous Puritan & sincere Christian Gov. of Ply. Col. from 1621 to 1657 (the year he died) aged 69, except 5 yrs. which he declined".)>. He married 1st (ae 23), 10 Dec. 1613, Amsterdam, Holland, to Dorothy MAY <MD 9:115-117,22:63-4>. Dorothy was born c1597 (ae 16, from Wisbeach, England in marriage intention record). Her parentage is uncertain, her father is believed to have been either John MAY or Henry MAY, see Stratton:325 for discussion. (I find the wording in the marriage intention record interesting, "William Bradford...declaring that he has no parents, on the one part and Dorothy May...assisted by Henry May on the other part". One might interpret the wording to mean that William was not attended by a parent but Dorothy was; however, proof is still needed to make a positive identification.) Dorothy died 7 Dec. 1620 of accidental drowning at Cape Cod Harbour <MD 29:97-102,31:105>. William married 2nd, 14 Aug. 1623, Plymouth, Alice (CARPENTER) Southworth <MD 30:4>. (Alice m.1st, 28 May 1613, Leiden, Holland, Edward Southworth <MD 10:1,38:90> and had two children, Constant & Thomas who both settled in Plymouth.) Alice was the daughter of Alexander CARPENTER and was baptized 3 Aug. 1590, Wrington, Sommerset co., England <MD 38:90>. (It is interesting to note that Alice had three sisters, viz: Juliana, Mary & Priscilla who settled in Plymouth and a sister Agnes who was the first wife of Dr. Samuel Fuller) Alice died 26 Mar. 1670/1, Plymouth <MD 15:213; MSR:548 ("a most excellent woman, ae about 80"); MD 18:68 ("Mistris Allic Bradford sen[r] Changed this life for a better haveing attained to fourscore yeares of age or therabouts shee was a godly Maton and much loved while shee lived and lamented tho aged when shee Died and was honorably enterred on the 29th" - in her will she had asked to be buried near her husband). (See BRADFORD Probate Appendix for wills of Gov. William Bradford & his wife Alice.)

(See also: Mayflower Families in Progress (MFIP): William Bradford of the Mayflower and His Descendants for Four Generations, by Robert S. Wakefield, FASG, 3rd Ed., 1991 and NEHGR 83:439,84:5, Ancestry of the Bradfords of Austerfield, County York - Records Extending the Ancestral Line of Gov. William Bradford.)

William had one child by 1st wf Dorothy and three children by 2nd wf Alice:

I.   John, b. c1618, Leyden, Holland
II.   William, b. 17 June 1624, Plymouth
III. Mercy, b. pre May 1627 (Cattle Division), Plymouth
IV.   Joseph, b. c1630, Plymouth

* * * * * * * * * * * * * * *

I.   JOHN BRADFORD[2], b. c1618, Leyden, Holland <MFIP #2>, d. pre 21 Sept. 1676, Norwich CT. (will exhibited) <New London Co.CT Court Rec.3:83>; m. pre 1650 (Marshfield town record in which he is married <MFIP #2>, **Martha BOURNE** <MD 16:24; MSR:534 (her father's will of 1664 calls her "Daughter Bradford")>, (dau of Thomas & Elizabeth), b. c1614, prob. England, d. betw. 20 Feb. 1679/80 (sold land) - 1683 <MFIP #2>. (Martha m.2nd c1679, Thomas TRACY who remarried in 1683 <MFIP #2>.) John & Martha had no known issue. (See BRADFORD Probate Appendix for data regarding their wills.)

II. WILLIAM BRADFORD[2], b. 17 June 1624, Plymouth <MD 30:4; MD 1:151 (listed in 1627 Cattle Division), d. 20 Feb. 1703/4, neare 80 yrs, Plymouth <MD 4:143,15:212; Plymouth ChR 1:195 ("dyed Maj. William Bradford in the 80th year of his age. He was the son of ye Honourable Governour Bradford, and did for many years sustaine the place of Leivtenant Governour of ye Colony of New Plimouth and did almost from his Youth serve God and his Generation in both civill & military posts. He dyed in a good old age and went to his grave in peace"); (Drew):207 ("Here lies the body of/ye honourable Major/William Bradford/who expired Feb. 20/1703-4 aged 79 years/He lived long but still was doing good/& in his countres service lost much blood/After a life well spent he's now at rest/His very name and memory is blest.")> **William** m.1st betw. 23 Apr. 1650 <MD 9:65; Plymouth Co.Deeds 3:204 (marriage settlement from father)> - 28 Jan. 1650/51 <MD 9:90 (petition of heirs of Thomas RICHARDS)>, **Alice RICHARDS**, (dau of Thomas RICHARDS & Welthean LORING), b. c1627, England <MFIP #3>, d. 12 Dec. 1671, ae about 44, Plymouth <MSR:548; PCR 8:33; MD 18:68 ("Mistris Allice Bradford Jun[r] Changed this life for a better about the age of 44 yeeres Shee was a gracious Woman liveed much Desired Died much lamented and was buried on the 14th.")>.
William m.2nd, c1674, **Mrs. (   )(FITCH) Wiswall** who d. pre 1676/7 <MFIP #3>. **William** m.3rd, c1676, Plymouth, **Mary (WOOD) Holmes** <NEHGR 144:23-28>, (dau of John WOOD/ATWOOD & Mary MASTERSON), b. c1643, Plymouth, d. 6 Jan. 1714/5, Plymouth <MD 15:212>. (Mary m.1st, 11 Dec. 1661 Plymouth, John HOLMES <PCR 8:23>, b. (   ), d. 24 Dec. 1675 <Stratton:306> & had

chil., Joseph, Mary & Isaac.) (See BRADFORD Probate Appendix for will of Maj. Wm. Bradford.)

15 BRADFORD Children: (10 by 1st wf, 1 by 2nd, 4 by 3rd) <MD 9:91; MBD 1:117, MFIP #3>

1. **John BRADFORD[3]**, b. 20 Feb. 1652/3, Plymouth <MD 16:238,20:133; PCR 8:14>, d. 8 Dec. 1736, 84th yr, Kingston g.s. <MD 7:23,20:133>; m. 6 Jan. 1674/5, Plymouth, **Mercy WARREN[3]** <MD 13: 205,17:192,20:133>, (dau of Joseph WARREN[2] & Priscilla FAUNCE - see WARREN Family), b. 23 Sept. 1653, Plymouth <PCR 8:33; MD 18:69,20:133>, d. Mar. 1747, ae 93y6m, Kingston g.s. <MD 7:23,20:133>. <See MD 1:147 & MBD 1:139 for bth. 7 chil.> (See BRADFORD Probate Appendix for will of Major John Bradford.)

2. **William BRADFORD[3]**, b. 11 Mar. 1654/5, Plymouth <MD 17:71; PCR 8:16>, d. 5 July 1687, Plymouth <MD 15:213; MBD 1:117 (According to the Quarter Sessions, 1687-1721,p.26, an inquest was held into his death, "a cart overturned on him".)>; m.c1679, Plymouth, **Rebecca BARTLETT[4]** <MD 6:45 (Rebecca Bradford in father's will of 1691)>, (dau of Benjamin BARTLETT[3] (Mary Warren[2]) & Sarah BREWSTER[3] (Love[2])), b. pre 1664, d. 14 Dec. 1741, Duxbury <Duxbury VR>. (Rebecca m.2nd 1691/92, Robert Stanford who d. 1721/22 <MFIP, Warren #50 (they had one child, Robert)> and who marr. as his 1st wife, 22 Jan. 1679, Mary (Howland) Williamson <Marshfield VR:1>. Rebecca m.3rd, 30 Jan. 1728/9, Caleb Samson[2], son of Henry Samson[1] and Ann Plummer; see SAMSON Fam.) <See MBD 1:163 for bth. 3 chil.>

3. **Thomas BRADFORD[3]**, b. c1657/8, Plymouth, d. 1 Oct. 1731, ae 73, Windham CT g.s. <TAG 11:12-14> m.1st c1681, **Anne RAYMOND** <TAG 11:12-14; MM:54>, (dau of Joshua RAYMOND & Elizabeth SMITH), b. 12 May 1664, New London CT <New London CT VR 1:14>, d. pre 8 May 1705 (will of Aunt Mary Raymond) <New London CT PR 1:299>. **Thomas** m.2nd, ( ), **Katherine ( )** who d. 6 Nov. 1733, Lyme CT <Lyme CT VR:219>. <See MBD 1:162,172 for bth. 6 chil.>

4. **Alice BRADFORD[3]**, b. c1659, Plymouth, d. 15 Mar. 1745/6, (84th yr), Canterbury CT g.s. <Canterbury CT VR 1:148>; m.1st 29 Mar. 1680, Dedham, **Rev. William ADAMS** <Dedham VR 1:17; Torrey: 6>, (son of William), b. 27 May 1650, Ipswich <MBD 1:117>, d. 17 Aug. 1685, Dedham <Dedham VR 1:20>. (William m.1st, 15 Oct. 1674, Dedham, Mary MANNING & had 3 chil <MFIP #9>). **Alice** m.2nd, 8 May 1687, Norwich CT, **Maj. James FITCH** <Norwich CT VR 1:6; MM:39>, (son of James FITCH & Abigail WHITFIELD), b. 2 Aug. 1649, Saybrook CT <NEHGR 70:344>, d. 10 Nov. 1727, Canterbury CT <NEHGR 70:344>. (James m.1st, Jan. 1676/7, Norwich, Elizabeth MASON & had 4 chil. <Norwich CT VR 1:6>.) <See Dedham VR 1:17,18,21 & MBD 1:117 for bth. of 4 Adams chil. and MBD 1:117 for bth. of 11 Fitch chil.>

5. **Mercy BRADFORD[3]**, bpt. 2 Sept. 1660, Boston <Boston Rcd.Com.9:77>, d. pre 5 Apr. 1720, Hartford CT (adm.) <MDP:74; Hartford CT PR #5196>; m. 16 Sept. 1680, Hartford CT, **Samuel STEELE** <MM:48>, (son of John STEELE & Mary WARNER), b. 15 Mar. 1652, Farmington CT <MFIP #10>, d. pre 2 Jan. 1709/10, Farmington CT (adm.) <MDP:74; Hartford CT PR #5198>. <See MBD 1:150 for bth. 8 chil.> (See BRADFORD Probate Appendix for probates.)

6. **Hannah BRADFORD[3]**, b. 9 May 1662, Plymouth <Bradford Desc.:4; Waterman Gen.1:626; MFIP #11>, d. 28 May 1738, 76th yr, Windham CT g.s. <Windham CT VR 1:188; MD 28:101,102 (ae about 75)>; m. 28 Nov. 1682, Plymouth **Joshua RIPLEY** <Windham CT VR A:16; MD 28:97,101; NEHGR 121:211>, (son of John RIPLEY & Elizabeth HOBART), b. 9 Nov. 1658, Hingham <MD 28:97>, d. 18 May 1739, 81st yr, Windham CT g.s. <Windham CT VR 1:188; MD 28:98, 101 (ae about 80), 102 (81st yr)>. <See MBD 1:132, MD 28:99-100 & Windham CT VR A:16,17 for bth. 12 chil. (incl. 2 sets twins).> (See BRADFORD Probate Appendix for will of Joshua Ripley & epitaphs.)

7. **Melatiah BRADFORD[3]**, b. 1 Nov. 1664, Plymouth <Bradford Desc.:4; MFIP #12>, d. aft. 24 Apr. 1739 (deed) <Killingworth CT Deeds 6:270>; m.1st, c1689, **John STEELE** <MM:48; MFIP #12>, (son of James STEELE & Bethia BISHOP), b. c1660, Hartford CT <MFIP #12>, d. 6 Mar. 1697/8, Hartford CT <MDP:74,82; Hartford CT PR #5188 (inv. gives dth. date). **Melatiah** m.2nd, aft. 23 June 1702, prob. Killingworth CT <MFIP #12 (when her father in law James STEELE was app'td gdn. of the children)>, **Samuel STEVENS**, (son of William STEVENS & Mary MEIGGS), b. 1 Mar. 1656, Guilford CT <Guilford CT VR 1:60>, d. pre 7 July 1712, Killingworth CT (inv.) <New London CT PR 1:653>. (Samuel m.1st Elizabeth ( ) & had 5 chil. <MFIP #12>.) <See MBD 1: 150 for bth. 3 Steele & 2 Stevens chil.>

8. **Samuel BRADFORD[3]**, b. c1667/8, Plymouth, d. 11 Apr. 1714, ae 46, Duxbury g.s. <MD 9:160; Duxbury VR>; m. 31 July 1689, Plymouth, **Hannah ROGERS[4]** <MD 13:205>, (dau of John ROGERS[3] (John[2]) & Elizabeth PABODIE[3] (Elizabeth Alden[2]) - see ALDEN & ROGERS Families), b. 16 Nov. 1668, Duxbury <Duxbury VR; MD 9:172>, d. Sept. 1754, Hingham <Hingham VR 2:15>. <See MBD 1:151 & MD 2: 18 for bth. 7 chil.> (See BRADFORD Probate Appendix for wills of Samuel & Hannah Bradford.)

9. **Mary BRADFORD[3]**, b. 1668, prob. Plymouth, d. 7 May 1720, Chilmark <MBD 1:149,171; MSR:108 ("May 8. 1720, Mrs. Hunt sen[r] departed this life yesterday about five of the clock afternoon and was buryed this evening.">; m. c1686/7, **William HUNT** <MM:49; NEHGR 4:59>, (son of Ephraim HUNT & Ebbet BRIMSMEAD), b. 1655, Weymouth <Weymouth VR>, d. (2) Jan. 1726/7, Chilmark <Chilmark VR; MSR:111 ("Jan. 8. 1726/7 - Last night before sundown <e.g. 7 Jan.> Old William Hunt departed this life, he was a man of good age, had been long fraile. He died suddenly, none of his family knowing when he died. (Aged about 73 gravestone).")>. (William m.2nd Hannah (Skiffe) Mayhew.) <See MBD 1:149 for chil.> (See BRADFORD Probate Appendix for will of Wm.)

10. **Sarah BRADFORD**[3], b. 1671, prob. Plymouth, d. betw. 18 Oct. 1705 (bth. of twins) <MD 6:21> - 29 Sept. 1712, Marshfield (hus. will) <MD 24:27>; m. c1687, poss. Marshfield, **Kenelm BAKER** (based on bth. 1st ch.) <MD 5:234,24:27>, (son of Samuel BAKER & Eleanor WINSLOW), b. 23 Mar. 1657/8, Marshfield <Marshfield VR:4; MD 2:7>, d. betw. 29 Sept. 1712 (will) - 30 Mar. 1713 (inv.), Marshfield <Plymouth Co.PR 3:236; MD 24:27-30>. <See Marshfield VR:20,21,26, MD 5: 234-5, 6:20,21, 24:27 & MBD 1:161 for bth. of 10 chil. & MD 11:122 for bpt. 1702 of 7 chil.> (See BRADFORD Probate Appendix for will of Kenelm Baker.)

11. **Joseph BRADFORD**[3], b. 18 Apr. 1675, Plymouth <Bradford Desc.:4>, d. 16 Jan. 1747, 73rd yr, New London CT <Montville Cem.Rec.:11>; m.1st 5 Oct. 1698, Lebanon CT, **Anna FITCH** <Lebanon VR 1:20>, (dau of James FITCH & Priscilla MASON), b. 6 Apr. 1675, Norwich CT <Norwich CT VR 1: 39>, d. 7 Oct. 1715, Lebanon CT <Lebanon CT VR>; **Joseph** m.2nd, int. 25 Feb. 1715/6, New London CT, **Mary (SHERWOOD) Fitch** <MFIP #16>, (dau of Mathew SHERWOOD & Mary FITCH), b. 1674 <MFIP #16>, d. 16 Sept. 1752, Montville CT <Hist. Montville:344>. (Mary m.1st, 4 Mar. 1698, Preston CT, Daniel Fitch <Torrey:269> and had five children.) <See Lebanon CT VR 1:20 for bth of 10 chil and MBD 1:146-7 for bth of 11 chil. (incl. 3 sets of twins).> (See BRADFORD Probate Appendix for will of Joseph Bradford.)

12. **Israel BRADFORD**[3], b. c1677/8, Plymouth, d. 26 Mar. 1760, 83rd yr, Kingston g.s. <MD 7:23,18: 243; MSR:236>; m. 27 Nov. 1701, Plymouth, **Sarah BARTLETT**[5] <MD 13:207,18:243>, (dau of Benjamin BARTLETT[4] (Benjamin[3], Mary Warren[2] - see WARREN Family) & Ruth PABODIE[3] (Elizabeth ALDEN[2] - see ALDEN Family), b. c1681, prob. Duxbury <MD 18:243>, d. 3 Apr. 1761, 80th yr, Kingston g.s. <MD 7:23,18:243; MSR:236>. <See MD 13:167-8 & MBD 1:137 for bth. 7 chil.>

13. **Ephraim BRADFORD**[3], b. 1685, Plymouth, d. betw. 20 Feb. 1743/4 (deed) <Plymouth Co.Deeds 36: 204> - 6 Oct. 1746, Kingston (pr.) <MD 21:189-90>; m. 13 Feb. 1709/10, Plymouth, **Elizabeth BREWSTER**[4] <MD 14:36 (VR errs in giving her name as Elizabeth Bartlett), 21:189>, (dau of Wrestling BREWSTER[3] (Love[2] - see BREWSTER Family) & Mary (   )), b. c1690, d. 5 Dec. 1741, 51st yr, Kingston g.s. <MD 7:23; MSR:237>. <See MD 13:32 for bth. 10 chil. & MBD 1:130 for bth. 14 chil.> (See BRADFORD Probate Appendix for will of Lieut. Ephraim Bradford.)

14. **David BRADFORD**[3], b. pre 1687, prob. Plymouth <MFIP #19>, d. 16 Mar. 1729/30, Kingston <Kingston VR:319; see MD 23:181-85 for probate & family data>; m. 23 Feb. 1713/4, Plymouth, **Elizabeth FINNEY** <MD 14:37,23:181>, (dau of Jonathan FINNEY[2] (John[1]) & Joanna KINNICUT), bpt. 27 Oct. 1695, Bristol <NEHGR 60:68>, d. aft. 9 Oct. 1746, Braintree (deed) <MD 23:183; Plymouth Co.Deeds 38:122>. (Elizabeth m.2nd, int. 10 Aug. 1733, Benjamin Ludden <MD 23:182-3>.) <See MD 12:85 for bth. 4 of 5 chil., Kingston VR for bth of 5th and MD 23:182 & MBD 1:121 for bth. 5 chil.>

15. **Hezekiah BRADFORD**[3], b. pre 1687, prob. Plymouth, d. aft. 10 Apr. 1761 (deed) <Plymouth Co. Deeds 52:74>; m. 21 May 1714, Plymouth, **Mary CHANDLER** <MD 14:37>, (dau of Joseph & Mercy), b. (   ), Duxbury, d. aft. 23 Apr. 1761 (deed) <Plymouth Co.Deeds 52:74>. <See MFIP #20 for bth. one child.>

II. **MERCY BRADFORD**[2], b. pre May 1627, Plymouth (Cattle Division) <MD 1:153>, d. prob. pre 9 May 1657 (not ment. fath. will) <MD 2:228-34>; m. 21 Dec. 1648, Plymouth, **Benjamin VERMAYES** <MD 15:28; PCR 8:5; MSR:544>, b. c1624 (ae 30 or thereabouts in deposition of 1 June 1754) <Suffolk Co.Deeds 2:27>, d. pre 28 9mth 1665, "Ginne" (adm.) <Essex Co.PR 2:21>.

No known issue.

III. **JOSEPH BRADFORD**[2], b. c1630, Plymouth, d. 10 July 1715, Plymouth <MD 5:217 (85th yr), 15:212 (neare 84 yrs), 16:85 (ae 84), Plymouth ChR 1:214 (85th yr); Burial Hill (Drew):206 ("Here lyes interred ye body of Mr. Joseph Bradford son of the late Honourable William Bradford Esq[r] Governour of Plymouth Colony who departed this life July the 10th 1715 in the 85th year of his age.")>; m. 25 May 1664, Hingham, **Jael HOBART** <Hist.Hingham 2:90>, (dau of Rev. Peter HOBART & Elizabeth ILBROOK), bpt. 30 Dec. 1643, Hingham <Hist. Hingham 2:90>, d. 14 Apr. 1730 87th yr, Kingston g.s. <MD 7:23>. (See BRADFORD Probate Appendix for wills of Joseph & Jael Bradford.)

3 BRADFORD Children: <MBD 1:116>

1. **Joseph BRADFORD**[3], b. 18 Apr. 1665, Plymouth <PCR 8:25>, d. pre 8 Oct. 1712 (fath. will) <MD 5:217-224>.

2. **Elisha BRADFORD**[3], b. c1669, prob. Plymouth <PN&Q 2:136 (ae 29 yrs or thereabout in June 1698 deposition)>, d. 16 June 1747, ae 78 <MBD 1:116; NEHGR 111:242 (bible)>; m.1st pre 28 Jan. 1702/3, **Hannah COLE** (deed) <MD 8:256; Plymouth Co.Deeds 5:229; MD 27:42>, (dau of James COLE & Abigail DAVENPORT), b. (   ), d. Aug. 1718, Plymouth <MD 27:41; Plymouth ChR 1:219 (She did not die 15 Aug. as stated in MFIP #21. The first entry in the church records is that of Martha Howland who died Aug. 15, then follows: "Hannah, wf of Elisha Bradford ye same month & in ye same house".)>; **Elisha** m.2nd, 7 Sept. 1719, Plymouth, **Bathsheba LeBROCKE/BROCK** <MD

14:38,27:42, 18:142 (int.)>, (dau of Francis BROCK & Sarah HOBART), b. 21 May 1703, Scituate
<Scituate VR 1:50; MD 18:127>, d. aft. 17 Nov. 1758 (deed) <Plymouth Co.Deeds 41:85>. (Bath-
sheba m.2nd, int. 21 Mar. 1752, Kingston, Joshua OLDHAM <NEHGR 4:47>.) <See MD 13:112 for
bth. 5 chil. and NEHGR 1:275-6 & MBD 1:116 for bth. 15 chil. (all by 2nd wf).>

3. Peter BRADFORD[3], b. 1 Mar. 1676/7, Hingham <Hingham VR 1:39>, d. pre 8 Oct. 1712 (fath. will)
    <MD 5:217-24>

BRADFORD PROBATE APPENDIX

Will of **Kenelm BAKER**: <MD 24:27-30; Plymouth Co.PR 3:236>
...29 Sept. 1712, ment. sons Kenelm BAKER (eldest son), Samuel BAKER, William BAKER (under 21),
Edward BAKER (under 21); dau Sarah SHERMAN wf of John; daus Alice, Elanor, Abigale, Bethiah (under 18), Keziah (under 18); uncle Capt. Nathaniel WINSLOW; brother Maj. John BRADFORD; kinsman
Isaac WINSLOW. Inv. 30 Mar. 1713. Pr. 6 Apr. 1713.

Will of **Lieut. Ephraim BRADFORD[3] (Wm.[2])**: (yeoman) <MD 21:189-91; Plymouth Co.PR 10:343-4,13:75.
...16 Dec. 1741, ment. 3 sons & 3 daughters (no names). Pr. 6 Oct. 1746.

Estate of **John BRADFORD[2] & wf Martha**: <MDP:91>
The wills of John BRADFORD and his wife Martha have been lost. MDP:91 gives three deeds, found
in Norwich CT Deeds which mention the will of Martha (BOURNE) (Bradford) Tracy. In the first,
dated 12 Apr. 1690, William BRADFORD deeds to son Thomas BRADFORD the "one nineth received from
my sister Martha BRADFORD widow of my brother John BRADFORD by her **will**". The second is dated 10
June 1690, "...wheras my respected aunt Martha formerly the widow of my uncle John BRADFORD late
of Norwich deceased by her **will** left me all her real & personal estate in New London CT..." -
John BRADFORD sells his one ninth share to brother Thomas BRADFORD. The third deed dated 1 Apr.
1691 mentions Thomas BRADFORD paying his father William BRADFORD, uncle Joseph BRADFORD and brother John BRADFORD "who were legatees unto Mrs. Martha TRACY deceased (formerly Bradford)".

Will of **John BRADFORD[3] (Wm.[2])**: (gentleman) <MD 20:133-7; Plymouth Co.PR>
...2 Oct. 1732, ment. wf Marcy; grandson Robert BRADFORD the son of dec'd son John BRADFORD; son
Samuel BRADFORD; dau Allice HEARSY wf of Joshua; dau Marcy CUSHMAN widow of Isaac Jr.; dau Pricilla CHIPMAN wf of Seth, & her children; grandsons James BRADFORD, Zadock BRADFORD, Samuel BRAD-
FORD, Eliphalet BRADFORD & William BRADFORD, the sons of dec'd son William BRADFORD; granddaughter Hannah BRADFORD dau of dec'd son William BRADFORD. Pr. 21 Dec. 1736.

Will of **Joseph BRADFORD[2]**: (planter) <MD 5:217-24; Plymouth Co.PR>
...8 Oct. 1712, ment. wf Jael & son Elisha BRADFORD. Inv. 27 July 1715. (The lengthy records
state that the Judge of Probate refused to approve the will. Testimony from witnesses showed
that the will Joseph signed was not the will he had intended. Joseph had stated that he fully
intended to leave all his lands to his only son Elisha, however his signature appears on a will
in which he leaves half to his son and half to his wife & her heirs. From the testimony given it
appears that Joseph's wife Jael, along with her brother David HOBART, deceived Joseph into signing their own version of the will so that the Hobarts would inherit half of Joseph's lands.)

Will of **Jael (HOBART) Bradford**: (widow) <MD 16:114; Plymouth Co.PR 5:753>>
...25 Mar. 1729, ment. (grand)daughter Hannah BRADFORD dau of son Elisha BRADFORD; grandsons Joseph BRADFORD, Nehemiah BRADFORD; granddaughter Uranie BRADFORD; Kinsmen, Seth CHIPMAN, Henry WET-
HERTON. Sworn 22 May 1730.

Will of **Joseph BRADFORD[3] (Wm.[2])**: <MDP:81; New London CT PR #667, 5:53,7:93>
...14 Sept. 1731, ment. wf Mary; eldest son Joseph BRADFORD; son John BRADFORD; eldest dau Anne
DIMMOCK/DEMICK; daus Priscilla HIDE, Sarah TUTHILL, Hannah BUELL, Elizabeth BRADFORD, Alithea
BRADFORD, Irene BRADFORD. Pr. 10 Mar. 1746/7.

Will of **Samuel BRADFORD[3] (Wm.[2])**: <MD 16:116-9; Plymouth Co.PR 3:301>
...26 Jan. 1713/4, ment. eldest son Gershom BRADFORD; son Perez BRADFORD; dec'd father William
BRADFORD; youngest son Gamaliel BRADFORD (under 21); dau Hannah GILBERT wf of Nathaniel; daus
Elisabeth BRADFORD, Jerusha BRADFORD & Welthea BRADFORD (all under 21); wf Hannah. Pr. 16 June
1714.

Will of **Hannah (ROGERS) Bradford**: (widow) <Suffolk Co.PR #12505>
...16 Apr. 1734, ment. sons Gershom BRADFORD, Peres BRADFORD, Gamaliel BRADFORD; daus Hannah GIL-
BURD/GILBERT, Elizabeth WHITON, Jerusha GAY, Welthean LANE; son in law Peter LANE. Codicil 1 June
1747. Sworn 5 Nov. 1754.

Will of **William BRADFORD[1]**: <MD 2:228-234; MSR:526-7; Plymouth Co.PR 2:1:53-59>
...9 May 1657, ment. sons John BRADFORD, William BRADFORD, Joseph BRADFORD; wf Alice. Inv. 22 May
1657.

Will of **Alice (CARPENTER) (Southworth) Bradford:** (widow) <MD 3:144-9; Plymouth Co.PR 3:1:2-5>
...29 Dec. 1669, ment. sister Mary CARPENTER; sons Constant SOUTHWORTH, Joseph BRADFORD, Capt.
William BRADFORD; grandchild Elizabeth HOWLAND dau of dec'd son Thomas SOUTHWORTH (for the benefit of her son James HOWLAND). Pr. 7 June 1670.
==

Will of **Maj. William BRADFORD**[2]: <MD 4:143-7; Plymouth Co.PR 2:40-43>
...29 June 1703, ment. wf Mary; sons David BRADFORD, Ephraim BRADFORD, Hezekiah BRADFORD; eldest
son John BRADFORD to have "my father's manuscript, viz: a Narrative of the beginning of New Pli-
mouth"; grandson William BRADFORD (under 21) son of dec'd son William BRADFORD; to son Thomas
BRADFORD lands in Norwich CT which were the lands of my brother John BRADFORD; sons Samuel BRAD-
FORD, Joseph BRADFORD, Israel BRADFORD; grandsons John BRADFORD & William BRADFORD, sons of son
John BRADFORD; daus Mercy STEEL, Hannah RIPLEY, Melatiah STEEL, Mary HUNT, Alce FITCH, Sarah BAK-
ER; Hannah, wf of son Samuel BRADFORD. Pr. 10 Mar. 1703/4.
==

Will of **William HUNT:** (yeoman) <Dukes Co.PR 2:19-20>
...13 Mar. 1721/2, ment. son William HUNT; granddaughters Mary KNOWLES, Rebecca KNOWLES, Malatiah
KNOWLES. Pr. 5 Apr. 1727.
==

Will of **Joshua RIPLEY:** <MDP:77; MD 28:102-3; Windham CT PR 2:204-5,212-3>
...6 Jan. 1738/9, ment. sons Joshua RIPLEY, Hezekiah RIPLEY, David RIPLEY; dau Jerusha RIPLEY;
grandchildren An(n) BINGHAM, Abigall MANING, Samuell MANING; daus Alce EGERTON, Hannah WEBB, Leah
COOK, Rachel TRACEY, Faith BINGHAM dec'd (& her dau), Margret SEBURY, Irene MANNING dec'd (& her
daus), Ann WHEAT. Pr. 27 June 1739.

(<MD 28:102> Windham CT gravestones: "Here Lies Interred ye/Body of Joshua Ripley/Esq[r] One of His
Maies/ties Justices for the/County of Windham/Husband of Mrs Hann[h]/Ripley Departed This/Life May
the 18. 1739/in ye 81 Year of his age." "Here Lies Interred the/Body of That Worthy/Vertuous and
Most Ingenious/Gentlewoman Mr[s] Hannah/Ripley the well Beloveed Con/sort of Joshua Ripley Esq[r]/Who
After She Had Lieved/A Holy and Frieutful Life/Fell Aslepe in Jesus May Ye/28:1738 in ye 70 y[r] of
her age".)
==

Estate of **Samuel STEEL/STEELE:** <MDP:74; Hartford CT PR #5198>
...28 Feb. 1711/2, distribution to wf Mercy and children, viz: Thomas STEEL (eldest son), William
STEEL, Daniel STEEL, Eliphalet STEEL, Abiel STEEL.

Estate of **Mercy (BRADFORD**[3]**) Steel (Wm.**[2]**):** (widow) <MDP:74; Hartford CT PR #5196>
...Apr. 1724, agreement among heirs to divide estate of mother Mercy and brother William STEEL,
viz: Thomas STEEL, Daniel STEEL, Eliphalet STEEL and John WEBSTER in right of wf Abiell.

NOTES:

WILLIAM BREWSTER

William BREWSTER was born c1566/7 <MQ 51:161 (ae around 42 in 1609)>; Bradford:324 ("near four-score years of age (if not all out) when he died")>, poss. Doncaster, Yorkshire, England, (son of William BREWSTER & Mary (SMYTHE) Simkinson) <NEHGR 124:250; TAG 41:1-5; Stratton:251>. His date of death at Plymouth is questionable <NEHGR 18:18-20>. Bradford states in his history <:324> that Elder BREWSTER died "about the 18th of April" (1643/4). Nathaniel Morton, in copying from Bradford's manuscript history upon the Plymouth Church Records 1:38 gives the date as "about" the 16th of Apr. 1644. The Brewster Book <MD 1:7> gives the date as 10 Apr. 1644. In reviewing the above, NEHGR 18:18-20 comes to the conclusion that the true date of death is probably 16 Apr. 1644. Bradford gives a good account of Elder Brewster's life and death in his history <:324-28>. William married c1590, poss. at Scrooby, Nottinghamshire, England, Mary (   ). Although many have attempted to identify her (e.g. Mary Wentworth, Mary Wyrall) conclusive evidence is still lacking. Mary was born c1569, England <MQ 51:161 (ae around 40 in 1609)> and died 17 Apr. 1627, Plymouth <MD 1:7,2:115,32:2>. Bradford, in his writings of the increasings & decreasings, states she died "aged". In a letter dated 20 Dec. 1623 to Elder Brewster, Rev. John ROBINSON writes, "And I hope Mrs. Brewster's weak and decayed state of body will have some repairing by the coming of her daughters", so obviously Mary BREWSTER did not fare well in the New World <Bradford:376>. Elder Brewster did not leave a will; on 5 June 1644 his "onely" two sonnes surviveing", Jonathan & Love, were appointed administrators of his estate. As one would expect from such a learned man, his inventory included 63 Latin books and 300-400 English books <Plymouth Co.Wills 1:53; MD 3:15; MSR:511>.

(See also: Mayflower Families In Progress, William Brewster of the Mayflower and His Descendants for Four Generations, 1994, by Barbara L. Merrick; NEHGR 53:109,283-8, Early Generations of the Brewster Family; NEHGR 18:18-20, The True Date of the Birth and Death of Elder Brewster; TAG 41: 1-5, New Light On The Brewsters of Scrooby & New England; NEHGR 124:250, The Mother of Elder William Brewster of the Mayflower; MD 4:109, William Brewster (His True Position In Our Colonial History); MD 1:1-5, for a description of The Brewster Book; A Notebook on the Descendants of Elder William Brewster of Plymouth Colony, 1985, by Milton E. Terry & Anne Borden Harding; The Brewster Genealogy, 1566-1907. A Record of the Descendants of William Brewster of the Mayflower, Ruling Elder of the Pilgrim Church which Founded Plymouth Colony in 1620, 2 vols., 1908, by Emma Jones; Pilgrim, A Biography of William Brewster, 1982, by Mary B. Sherwood.)

William & Mary had 6 known children:

I.   Jonathan, b. 12 Aug. 1593, Scrooby
II.   Patience, b. c1600, prob. Scrooby
III. Fear, b. c1606, prob. England
IV.   child, b. Leyden, d. 20 June 1609, Leyden, Holland
V.   Love, b. c1611, Leyden, Holland
VI.   Wrestling, b. c1614, Leyden, Holland

* * * * * * * * * * *

I. **JONATHAN BREWSTER[2]**, b. 12 Aug. 1593, Scrooby, England <MD 1:7,32:2; MQ 51:161>, d. 7 Aug. 1659, New London CT, bur. Preston CT <MQ 52:72; MD 1:72,5:194>; m. 10 Apr. 1624, Plymouth, **Lucretia OLDHAM** <MD 1:8,32:2; MQ 51:161,52:72>, (dau of William OLDHAM & Phillipa SOWTER), bpt. 14 Jan. 1600, Parish of All Saints, Derby/Darby, England <NEHGR 111:242; MQ 52:72>, d. 4 Mar. 1678/9, Norwich CT, bur. Preston CT <MD 1:168; NEHGR 53:112-3; MQ 52:74>. (See BREWSTER Appendix for letter written by Jonathan in 1656 in which he implies he has decided to return to England ("resolved for Old England").

8 BREWSTER Children: <MD 1:7,8, 32:2; MQ 52:72-83 ; MBD 1:178>

1. **William BREWSTER[3]**, b. 9 Mar. 1625, Plymouth <MD 1:7,32:2>, d. prob. pre 1658 when he was not ment. in father's deed <MQ 52:74; PN&Q 2:158>; m. 15 Oct. 1651, (   ), **Mary PEAME** "of London" <MD 1:8,32:3>. Nothing further is known about William & Mary or any possible children.

2. **Mary BREWSTER[3]**, b. 16 Apr. 1627, Plymouth <MD 1:7,11:7,31:1,32:2>, d. aft. 23 Mar. 1697/8, prob. Scituate (receipt) <MD 5:41,31:1,2; PN&Q 2:158>; m. 10/12 Nov. 1645, Plymouth, **John TURNER** <Plymouth VR:655; MD 1:8,5:41,13:86,31:1,32:3>, b. prob. Essex, England <MQ 52:75>, d. betw. 4 Mar. 1695 (will) - 20 May 1697 (inv.), Scituate <MD 5:41,31:1,32:28>. <See MBD 1:184 & MD 32:30-1 for bth. 13 chil., Scituate VR & MD 17:75 for bth. 5 chil.> (See BREWSTER Probate Appendix for will of John TURNER.)

3. **Jonathan BREWSTER[3]**, b. 17 July 1629, Plymouth <MD 1:7,32:2>, d. aft. 2 Jan. 1659/60 (debtor) <NEHGR 53:112-3; MQ 52:74>.

4. **Ruth BREWSTER[3]**, b. 3 Oct. 1631, Plymouth (now Duxbury) <MD 1:7,32:2>, d. 30 Apr. or 1 May 1677, New London CT <MD 1:73; New London CT VR 4:315; MQ 52:76 ("a woman of great worth, died

comfortably and christianly")>; m.1st, 14 Mar. 1651, New London CT, **John PICKETT** <MD 1:8, 32: 3>, (?son of John PICKETT & Elizabeth IVES), b. (   ), d. 16 Aug. 1667, at sea returning from Barbadoes <NEHGR 8:326,9:44>. <See MQ 52:77 for bth. 6 Pickett chil.; MBD 1:183 & New London CT VR 4:327,328 for bth. 3 chil.; MD 1:170 for bth. 1 ch.> **Ruth** m.2nd, 2 or 16 July 1668, New London CT, **Charles HILL** <MD 1:173 (2nd); New London CT VR 4:324 (16th)>, (son of George of Barley/Barlow, Derbyshire/Darbyshire, England) <MD 1:73; MQ 52:76>, b. (   ), prob. Eng., d. Oct. 1684, New London CT <TAG 10:34; MQ 52:76>. <See MBD 1:183, MQ 52:77-8 & New London CT VR 4:315,318,319,321,323 for bth. 5 Hill chil.; MD 1:73 for bth 2 chil.> (Charles m.2nd, 12 June 1678, New London CT, Rachel MASON <MBD 1:183,262; MQ 52:76>, (dau of John MASON & Anne PECK) <Torrey:494>, b. Oct. 1648, prob. Saybrook CT <MQ 52:76>, d. 4 Apr. 1679, New London CT ("Rachell, ye beloved wife of Charles Hill was snatched away by death in child bearing one dau being borne dead another child at ye birth".) <MBD 1:183; New London CT VR 4:314>.)

5. **Benjamin BREWSTER**[3], b. 17 Nov. 1633, Plymouth (now Duxbury) <MD 1:7,32:2>, d. 14 Sept. 1710, Norwich CT, bur. Preston CT <Norwich CT VR 1:21; MD 1:8>; m. last day (28) Feb. 1659/60, Norwich CT, **Ann (ADDIS) Darte** <Norwich CT VR 1:21; MD 1:72,5:194; NEHGR 53:283>, (dau of William ADDIS & Millicent WOOD) <TAG 58:215>, bpt. 17 Mar. 1628, Frampton on Severne, Gloucestershire Eng. <TAG 57:183; NYGBR 58:19,22>, d. 9 May 1708 or 1709, Norwich CT, bur. Preston CT <MD 1:73,195>. <See MBD 1:178, MQ 52:79, MD 1:72,74 & Norwich CT VR 1:21 for bth. 8 chil.> (Ann m.1st, 24 4mth (June) 1653, Boston, Ambrose DARTE <NEHGR 53:283> and had son William b. 1 Jan 1654/5, Boston <Boston Rcd.Com.9:43>.) (See BREWSTER Probate Appendix for will of Benjamin BREWSTER.)

6. **Elizabeth BREWSTER**[3], b. 1 May 1637, Plymouth (now Duxbury) <MD 1:7,32:2>, d. Feb. 1708, New London CT g.s. <Hist.New London:317; Calkins:277>; m.1st, 7 Sept. 1653, New London CT, **Peter BRADLEY** <MD 1:71>, b. (   ), d. 3 Apr. 1662/3, mariner, New London CT g.s. <MD 1:72,5:194; TAG 18:104>. **Elizabeth** m.2nd, betw. 13 July 1676 (1st wife's dth.) <Hist.New London:317; TAG 18:104> - 26 Mar. 1680 (deed) <New London CT Deeds 5:101; MFIP #10 says pre 5 June 1677; considering their history together, they were prob. married soon after his wife's dth.>, prob. New London CT, **Christopher CHRISTOPHERS** <MQ 52:80>, b. c1631, prob. England <MQ 52:80; MFIP #10 says prob. b. Cherston-Ferrers, Devonshire, Eng.>, d. 23 July 1687, 56th yr, New London CT g.s. <MD 1:77; TAG 18:104>. <See MBD 1:181, MD 1:71,72, MQ 52:80-1 & New London CT VR 4: 328 for bth of 4 Bradley chil. & 2 Christophers chil.> (Christopher m.1st, 16 Aug. 1654, New London CT, Mary BERRY <Torrey:152>, b. c1621, d. 13 July 1676, ae 55, New London CT <MBD 1: 261 #6; MQ 52:79> and had two children who married two of Elizabeth's "Bradley" children.) (Although Christopher's first wife, Mary, did not die until 1676, he and Elizabeth had children born in 1668 & 1673. Elizabeth was brought before the courts on 16 Sept. 1673 and found guilty of committing fornication with Christopher, "which sin of hers is highly aggravated as being the second of yt nature with the same party who is a married man" <New London CT Court Rec.3:63>.)

7. **Grace BREWSTER**[3], b. 1 Nov. 1639, Duxbury <MD 1:7,32:2>, d. 22 Apr. 1684, New London CT <MD 1: 75>; m. 4 Aug. 1659, New London CT, **Daniel WETHERELL** <MD 1:71,74; New London CT TR 1:3>, (son of Rev. William WETHERELL & Mary FISHER), b. 29 Nov. 1630, Maidstone, Kent, Eng. <MD 1:74; New London CT TR 1:51>, d. 14 Apr. 1719, 89th yr, New London CT <New London CT VR:363; New London CT TR 1:51>. <See MBD 1:183, New London CT VR 4:322,323,327 & MQ 52:81 for bth. 9 chil.; MD 1:74,75 for bth. 8 chil.> (See BREWSTER Probate Appendix for will of Daniel WETHERELL.)

8. **Hannah BREWSTER**[3], b. 3 Nov. 1641, Duxbury <MD 1:8,32:2>, d. aft. 25 Nov. 1691 (church member) <New London CT 1st ChR:7; MD 1:227>, m. 23 Dec. 1664, New London CT, **Samuel STARR** <New London VR 4:326; New London TR 1:39; MD 1:226>, (son of Dr. Thomas & Rachel), b. c1641 (ae 20 in 1661 <MFIP #12>), Duxbury or Yarmouth <NEHGR 90:152,269; MQ 52:82>, d. pre 2 Feb. 1687/8 (deed), prob. New London CT <New London CT Deeds 5:111; MQ 52:82; MD 1:226>. <See MQ 52:82 for bth. 4 chil.; MBD 1:184 for bth. 3 chil.; New London CT VR 4:324,325 for bth. 2 chil.>

II **PATIENCE BREWSTER**[2], b. c1600, prob. Scrooby, England. (Although she is usually given a birthdate of c1605, this is surely too late. When the marriage banns of Anna Crackstone were published in Leiden in 1618, she was accompanied by Patience BREWSTER, her acquitance <MQ 40: 117>. It would therefore seem more plausible that Patience was born c1600, rather than the frequently given c1605 which would make her a 13 year old witness & acquaintance of a woman of marriageable age which seems unlikely.) Patience is called deceased in a letter dated 12 Dec. 1634 from Gov. Winthrop of the Bay Colony to his son in which he relates the death of some at Plymouth <MD 30:97-8>. Patience married 5 Aug. 1624, Plymouth, **Thomas PRENCE** <MD 6: 230,30:4>, (son of Thomas PRENCE & Elizabeth TODLERBY, of Lechlade, Gloucestershire and All Hallows Barking, London, Eng.) <MFIP #3; Stratton:340>, b. c1600, d. 29 Mar. 1673, ae 73, Plymouth <MD 3:203,6:230,33:97; MSR:548; MD 15:212 & Plymouth TR 1:198 ("Mr Thomas Prince Esquir deceased on the 29 of Mar 1673: Who for sixteen years past was governer of Plimouth Coloney and god made him a great blesing to his people therein". Note: MBD 1:214 has a typo error, his death should read 1673 not 1783.)> (See BREWSTER Probate Appendix for will & obituaries of Thomas PRENCE.) (Thomas m.2nd, 1 Apr. 1635, Plymouth, Mary COLLIER <MD 13:83>, (dau of William COLLIER & Jane (   ) Clark), bpt. 18 Feb. 1611/2, St. Olave Parish, Southwark, Eng. <Savage 3:477; TAG 49:215,51:92> who d. pre 8 Dec. 1662 (c1658?) and they had 5 children. He m.3rd, pre 8 Dec. 1662, Apphia (QUICKE) Freeman <MD 6:230; Plymouth Co.Deeds 3: 201> who d. pre 1 Aug. 1668 <MD 6:233; Plymouth Co.Deeds 3:146>. Apphia m.1st, 14 July 1624, St. Anne, Blackfriar, London, Eng., Samuel FREEMAN <Torrey:283> and had son Samuel. Thomas m.4th, betw. 26 Feb. 1665/6 (when she swore to 1st hus. inv.) <MD 6:232> - 1 Aug. 1668 (deed) <MD 6:233; Plymouth Co.Deeds 3:146>, Mary (   ) Howes (widow of Thomas HOWES), who d. 9 Dec. 1695, Yarmouth <Yarmouth VR 3:37; Yarmouth TR 3:338; MD 6:230>.

4 PRENCE Children: <MBD 1:214-5>

1. **Thomas PRENCE**[3], b. c1625 (pre 22 May 1627, Cattle Division), prob. Plymouth <MD 1:150,153, 6: 233>, d. pre 13 Mar. 1672 (fath.will), prob. England <MD 6:233>; m. (   ) and had one known child, Susannah <MD 6:233; MFIP #13>.

2. **Rebecca PRENCE**[3], b. c1627 (pre 22 May 1627, Cattle Division), prob. Plymouth <MD 1:151>, d. pre 18 July 1651 (hus.2nd marr.), prob. Sandwich <MD 14:109; Plymouth VR:655 (poss. bur. 23 Mar. 1648/9)>; m. 22 Apr. 1646, prob. Eastham, **Edmond FREEMAN** <MD 13:86; Plymouth VR:655>, (son of Edmund FREEMAN & Bennet HODSOLL), bpt. 26 Nov. 1620, Billingshurst, Sussex, Eng. <TAG 40:103>, d. pre 5 Jan. 1703/4 (adm.), prob. Sandwich <TAG 4:105; MDP:126>. <See MBD 1:261 for bth. 2 chil.> (See BREWSTER Probate Appendix for estate of Edmond FREEMAN.) (Edmond m. 2nd, 18 July 1651, Sandwich, Margaret PERRY <MD 14:109> and had 6 chil. <MBD 1:261; MD 14: 109-10>. Margaret d. aft. 2 Mar. 1684/5 (deed) <MDP:126; Plymouth Co.Deeds 5:379> and prob. pre 5 Jan. 1703/4 (hus.pr.) <MFIP #14 says pre Mar. 1696/7>.)

3. **Mercy PRENCE**[3], b. c1631, Plymouth, d. 28 Sept. 1711, ae 80, Eastham g.s. <MD 5:143,8:2>; m. 13 or 14 Feb. 1649/50, Eastham, **John FREEMAN** <MD 16:122,17:199; PCR 8:26; MSR:544,545>, (son of Edmund FREEMAN & Bennet HODSOLL), bpt. 28 Jan. 1626/7, Billingshurst, Sussex, Eng. <TAG 17:94; MDP:120 (ae about 77 years in 3 July 1704 testimony)>, d. 28 Oct. 1719, 98th yr, Eastham g.s. <MD 5:143,8:2>. <See MBD 1:225 for bth. 11 chil.; for 5 chil. see PCR 8:26, MD 17: 199-200 & MSR:545 and for 2 chil. see MD 17:110.> (See BREWSTER Probate Appendix for will of John FREEMAN.)

4. **Hannah PRENCE**[3], b. pre 1633, Plymouth, d. pre 23 Nov. 1698 (hus.marr.), Eastham <MD 8:4,14: 87>; m.1st 13 Feb. 1649/50, Eastham, **Nathaniel MAYO** <MD 17:200; MSR:436,545>, (son of Rev. John MAYO & Tamsin LUMPKIN), b. c1627, Eng., d. betw. 19 Dec. 1661 (will) - 24 Feb. 1661/2 (inv.) <MD 17:215; MDP:118>. <See MBD 1:215 for bth. 6 Mayo chil., MD 17:200 for bth. 5.> (See BREWSTER Probate Appendix for will of Nathaniel MAYO.) **Hannah** m.2nd, betw. 5 June 1667 <PCR 4:147> - 11 Sept. 1671 (deed) <Plymouth Col.Deeds 5:257> Eastham, **Jonathan SPARROW** <MD 14:198>, (son of Richard & Pandora), b. c1633/4, Eng. <MBD 1:215>, d. 21 Mar. 1706/7, ae 73, Eastham g.s. <MD 8:4; MSR:436>. <See MBD 1:215, MD 14:193-203 & MD 17:201 for bth. 2 (poss. 3) Sparrow chil.> (Jonathan m.1st, 28 Oct. 1654, Eastham, Rebecca BANGS <MD 5:23; MSR:545 says 26th>, (dau of Edward) & had 6 chil. <MD 14:194-5>. He m.3rd, 23 Nov. 1698, Barnstable, Sarah (LEWIS) Cobb <MD 14:87>, (dau of George LEWIS & Sarah JENKINS), b. 2 Feb. 1643, Barnstable <MD 10:249>, d. 11 Feb. 1735, 92nd yr, Barnstable <Otis 1:172>. Sarah m.1st, 26 Dec. 1663, Barnstable, James COBB <Otis 1:172>, (son of Henry COBB & Patience HURST), b. 14 Jan. 1634, Plymouth <Otis 1:171>, d. 1695, Barnstable; they had 11 chil. <Otis 1:172-3>.)

III **FEAR BREWSTER**[2], b. c1606, prob. England, d. pre 12 Dec. 1634, Plymouth <MD 30:97-8 (Gov. Winthrop's letter); m. betw. 1623-26, Plymouth, **Isaac ALLERTON**.

(See ALLERTON Family for 2 children.)

IV. **Child**, bur. 20 June 1609, Leyden, Holland

V. **LOVE BREWSTER**[2], b. c1611, prob. Holland <MD 2:203-6>, d. betw. 1 Oct. 1650 (will) - 31 Jan. 1650/1 (inv.), Duxbury <MD 2:203-6; MSR:515>; m. 15 May 1634, Plymouth (now Duxbury), **Sarah COLLIER** <MD 13:83; Plymouth VR:652>, (dau of William COLLIER & Jane (   ) Clark), bpt. 30 Apr. 1616, St. Olave, Southwark, Surrey, Eng. <TAG 49:215,51:58>, d. 26 Apr. 1691, 76th yr, Plymouth <Plymouth ChR 1:271; MD 3:192,4:128>. (Sarah m.2nd, aft. 1 Sept. 1656 (letter), Richard PARKE <MD 8:164-5> who d. aft. 12 July 1665, Cambridge (will) <MD 2:115,3:192>. (See BREWSTER Probate Appendix for will of Love BREWSTER & 1656 letter to Sarah.)

4 BREWSTER Children: <MBD 1:209>

1. **Sarah BREWSTER**[3], b. c1635, Plymouth (now Duxbury) <MQ 51:131>, d. betw. 5 Mar. 1667/8 - 21 Jan. 1678/9, prob. Duxbury <PCR 4:80; MQ 51:131>; m. aft. 4 Apr. 1654 (c1656), Duxbury, **Benjamin BARTLETT**[3] <MD 8:171-2; MQ 51:131>, (son of Robert BARTLETT & Mary WARREN[2]). See WARREN Family.

2. **Nathaniel BREWSTER**[3], b. (   ), Plymouth (now Duxbury), d. pre 11 Oct. 1676 (appraisal of estate) <MBD 1:209; MDP:115; Plymouth Col.Court Orders 5:146>; m. (   ) who d. aft. 2 Nov.
   1676. (No known issue.) (See BREWSTER Probate Appendix for nun-cupative will of Nathaniel
   BREWSTER.)

3. **William BREWSTER**[3], b. c1645, Plymouth (now Duxbury), d. 3 Nov. 1723, near 78th yr, S. Duxbury
   g.s. <Duxbury VR:356; MD 9:160,12:31; NEHGR 53:283>; m. 2 Jan. 1672, Duxbury, **Lydia PARTRIDGE**
   <Duxbury VR:226; MD 8:232; NEHGR 53:283>, (dau of George PARTRIDGE & Sarah TRACY), b. pre
   1655, Duxbury, d. 2 Feb. 1742/3, Duxbury <Duxbury VR:355; MD 12:31; NEHGR 53:283>. <See MBD
   1:209 & MD 9:173,229,232 for bth. 8 chil.>

4. **Wrestling BREWSTER**[3], b. (   ), prob. Duxbury, d. 1 Jan. 1696/7, Duxbury <MD 20:113; NEHGR
   53:283>; m. pre 1678, **Mary** (   ) <MD 20:112>, b. Nov. 1661, d. 12 Nov. 1742, ae 80y11m27d,
   Kingston g.s. <MD 7:168,20:113; NEHGR 53:283; MSR:236 (says d. ae 80y11m<u>29</u>d)>. <See MBD 1:
   211 & MD 20:112 for bth. 8 chil. and MDP:116 & MD 20:114 for estate & heirs.> (Mary m.2nd,
   23 May 1700, John PARTRIDGE <MD 20:113 & 2 chil.>, (son of George PARTRIDGE & Sarah TRACY)
   who d. 5 Apr. 1731, 73rd yr <MD 20:113; NEHGR 53:283>. John m.1st, 24 Dec. 1684, Duxbury,
   Hannah SEABURY <Duxbury VR:283>, (dau of Samuel SEABURY & Patience KEMP - see pg. 1), b. 7
   7 July 1668, Duxbury <Duxbury VR:149>.)

VI **WRESTLING BREWSTER**[2], b. c1614, prob. Holland, d. betw. 22 May 1627 (Cattle Division) - 5 June
    1644 (adm.fath.est.) <MD 3:115>.

BREWSTER PROBATE APPENDIX

Will of **Benjamin BREWSTER**[3] (Jonathan[2]): <New London CT PR #685>
...28 June 1709, ment. sons Benjamin BREWSTER, Daniel BREWSTER; son-in-law Thomas ADGATE; grandsons Jonathan BREWSTER & Joseph BREWSTER, the sons of son Jonathan BREWSTER. Rec. 20 Nov. 1710.
===
Letter from **Jonathan BREWSTER**[2]: <MD 8:164-5; Plymouth Co.Deeds 2:1:193>
...(to sister in law Sarah BREWSTER, widow of brother Love)...dated 1 Sept. 1656, "Loveing and
kind sister I thank you for youer loveing letter I Received being glad to heare of youer well
Doeing in youer affliction of widdowhood the lord will make up youer losses and healp you to bee
thankfull for Raising youer good brother to bee Instead of an husband to you; In my Judgement I
would advise you to marry one whom you could love; I would to god I were nearer you I should Doe
somthing for you but I fear I shall the next year goe further from you for I with my whole family
Resolve for old England and there I shalbee able to Doe very little for you and youers whom I
love and Respect being glad to heare of youer Daughters Improvement both in Sperituall and Temp-
orall thinges the Lord bestow his further blessing upon her and the Rest of youers; I Doe heer by
this give unto her all my Interest in the pcells of Land which was left by my father lying near
Plymouth Southward To her and her heires for ever; I pray you Remember my love and Respects to
the Capt. and his wife and Children with the Rest of my frinds with you to whom I cannot write
excuse mee to them all thuse with my best love Remembered to you and youers; I Pray to the Lord
to blesse and keep you in all youer wayes in his fear Amen and Doe Rest
              Moheken this 1 of September 1656
              youer unfeigned Brother Jonathan Brewster

The abovewritten Letter was sent from M[r] Jonathan Brewster unto M[is] Sarah Brewster widdow now
liveing in the towne of Duxburrow In the Gov[r]ment of New Plymouth."
===
Will of **Love BREWSTER**[2]: <MD 2:203-6; MSR:515>
...1 Oct. 1650, ment. wf Sarah, sons Nathaniell BREWSTER (eldest son), William BREWSTER (2nd son)
Wrestling/Wrasteling BREWSTER (youngest son) and dau Sara. Inv. taken 31 Jan. 1650/1.
===
Estate of **Edmund FREEMAN**: <MDP:126; Barnstable Co.PR 2:166,171,190>
...Distribution of estate, 9 June 1705, to following children, viz: Edmond FREEMAN, Alice POPE wf
of Isaac, Margaret FISH wf of John, Rachel LANNDERS wf of John, Patience BURG (widow), Rebekah
PERRY wf of Ezra; payment also made to Richard ALLEN.
===
Will of **Maj. John FREEMAN**: <MD 5:143-51; Barnstable Co.PR 3:527-30>
...dated 1 June 1716, ment. sons John FREEMAN, Edmond FREEMAN, Nathaniel FREEMAN (youngest son);
grandson William FREEMAN; son John MAYO; daus Mercy KNOWLES, Hannah MAYO, Patience PAINE; chil.
of son John FREEMAN; dau Rebeckah FREEMAN widow of Thomas; granddaughter Lydia GODFREE;..."To my
Negro man Tobye one Cow and a small Iron pot and y[e] meanest of my Wearing clothes...I Give To my
Negroes Toby and Bess Their Freedom and I Desire you my Children To put Them into such a way as
they may not Want". Codicil 16 June 1716..."to Toby my Negro The use of four acres of Land...
during his life...I Give him a hoe and an ax and some small Things in The kitchen and hay Ground
To keep a Cow and Room to Live in part of my old house and wood for firing and fensing and con-

venient bedding". <3:597-99>...Whereas There is and hath Been some uneasyness and Dissattisfaction among the Children and Heirs...there may be a peacable & Quiet Settlement". An agreement was made 27 Jan. 1719/20.

Will of **Nathaniel MAYO**: <PCR 4:8; MD 17:215; Barnstable Co.PR; MDP:118 (heirs)>
...19 Dec. 1661, ment. sons Thomas MAYO (eldest son), Nathaniel MAYO, Theophilus MAYO; dau Hannah; wf Hannah; father Thomas PRENCE; brothers John Ffreeman, Nathaniel BACON;..."if it please god to blesse my wife and to give her to enjoy the life of that which shee is now Reddy to bring forth that shee bee mindfull to bestow somethinge upon it as a token of my love and alsoe my will is that my Children bee all brought up to write and Read." Pr. 4 Mar. 1661/2.

Will of **Gov. Thomas PRENCE**: <MD 3:203-6; Plymouth Co.PR 3:1:58-70; MD 33:97-100 (heirs)>
...13 Mar. 1672, ment. wf Mary; daus Jane SNOW wf of Mark, Mary TRACYE, Sarah HOWES, Elizabeth HOWLAND, Judith BARKER; grandchild Theophilus MAYO; grandchild Susanna PRENCE dau of dec'd son Thomas PRENCE; my seven daus, Hannah, Marcye, Jane, Mary, Elizabeth, Sarah, Judith. Codicil 28 Mar. 1673, ment. son John FREEMAN; dau Elizabeth HOWLAND; Lydia STURTIVANT (no relationship stated); dau Jane; grandson Theophilus MAYO; brother Thomas CLARKE. Pr. 5 June 1673.

<PCR 8:34> "Thomas Prence, Esquire, Govr of the jurisdiction of New Plymouth, died the 29th of March, 1673, and was interred the 8th of Aprill following. After hee had served God in the office of Govr sixteen yeares, or neare therunto, hee finished his course in the 73 yeare of his life. Hee was a worthy gentleman, very pious, and very able for his office, and faithfull in the discharge therof, studious of peace, a welwiller to all that feared God, and a terrour to the wicked. His death was much lamented, and his body honorably buried att Plymouth the day and yeare above mensioned."

<Plymouth ChR 1:147> "In 1673: was a very awfull frowne of God upon this chh & colony in the death of Mr Thomas Prince the Governour in the 73d yeare of his Age; when this Colony was in a hazardous condition upon the death of Govr Bradford the lott was cast upon Mr Princ to be his successour, God made him a repairer of breaches & a meanes to setle those shakings that were then threatning, he was excellently qualifyed for the office of a Governour, he had a countenance full of majesty & therein as well as otherwise was a terrour to evill doers, he was very amiable & pleasant in his whole conversation & highly esteemed of the saints & acknowledged by all; In the time of his sicknesse the chh sought God by Fasting & Prayer, but God would not be intreated any longer to spare him, but he dyed on Mar 29: & was honourably interred April 8."

Will of **Jonathan SPARROW**: <Barnstable Co.PR 3:380-8>
...10 Mar. 1706/7, ment. sons John SPARROW, Jonathan SPARROW, Richard SPARROW; daus Rebecka, Lydia, Patience; the chil. Capt. Samuel FREEMAN had by dau Elizabeth; Benoney GRAY; grandchild John SPARROW; grandson Jonathan SPARROW; William FREEMAN & Lydia GODFREE (one half of their mother's part). Pr. 3 Apr. 1707.

Will of **John TURNER**: <MD 5:41-6; MDP:99; Plymouth Co.PR 1:266-70>
...4 Mar. 1695, ment. sons Jonathan TURNER, Joseph TURNER, Ezekiel TURNER; grandchildren Isaac TURNER, John JAMES, Thomas PRINCE, Margret TURNER, Alice PRINCE and eldest child of son Ezekiel; sons John TURNER, Elisha TURNER, Amos TURNER; dau Grace CHRISTOPHERS; four daus Lydia, Mary, Ruth Grace; son Benjamin TURNER; wf Mary. Inv. 20 May 1697.

Will of **Daniel WETHERELL**: <New London CT PR #5625>
...11 Apr. 1719, ment. grandchildren John PICKETT, Mary BUTTLOR, Grace HALLAM, Phebe DENISON (ment. land given to Edward HALLAM), Hannah HOUGH, Borradel DENISON, Daniel DENISON, Wetherell DENISON; youngest granddaughters Anne DENISON & Sarah DENISON, daus of George DENISON. Pr. 4 May 1719.

NOTES:

PETER BROWN

Peter BROWN was born pre 1600 (to be of age in 1620 to sign the Mayflower Compact) <MD 1:79>, poss. at Great Burstead, Essex, England <MQ 53:10; Banks' Planters 2:50>. He died at Plymouth between 25 Mar. 1633 (tax list) <PCR 1:10> - 10 Oct. 1633 (inv.) <MD 1:79-82,2:115; MSR:507;MQ 53:10>. Peter married 1st, c1624, Plymouth, Martha (   ) FORD (she is widow Ford in the 1623 Land Division) <PCR 12:11; MD 1:227-9,2:115-6; MQ 53:10>. Martha was prob. born in England and died between 22 May 1627 (Cattle Division) <MD 1:152> - c1630/1 <MD 2:116; MQ 53:10; TAG 42:39>, at Plymouth. Martha's first husband, (   ) Ford (proof is lacking that his name was William), died between 11 Dec. 1621 and March 1623 <MQ 53:10> at Plymouth, having arrived in Plymouth in Nov. 1621. Mary had three children by her first husband <MQ 53:10>. Peter married 2nd, c1630, Plymouth, Mary (   ) <TAG 42:35-42; MD 2:116; MQ 53:10> who died between 27 Mar. 1634 (taxed) <PCR 1:26-28> and 27 Oct. 1647 (no mention of widow's dower in deed) <MD 5:30-34>. (MQ 53:13 questions the "unlikely" possibility that Peter's widow Mary married James Lendall of Duxbury, based on a May 1653 deed in which James sold two acres in Duxbury "which sometimes was the meddow of Peeter Brownes Children" <MD 2:169> and further states the will of James Lendall, dated 4 Mar. 1652, mentioned wife Mary. However, James' will was dated 10 Aug. 1652 (it was exhibited at court 4 Mar. 1652/53) and the inventory was taken 29 Oct. 1652 - which proves James Lendall died between Aug.-Oct. 1652. If he was deceased by Oct. 1652, he could not have been the James Lendall who sold land in May 1653. (This could be explained by a son named James but his will mentions only one son, Timothy.) James' wife, Mary (whoever she was) was deceased by 8 Feb. 1652/3 when a review of the inventory was taken.)

(See: Mayflower Families Through Five Generations (MF5G), vol.7, Peter Brown of the Mayflower, by Robert S. Wakefield, F.A.S.G., 1992.)

Peter had four children: (2 by 1st wife, 2 by 2nd) <MBD 1:268>

I.   Mary, b. c1626, Plymouth
II.   Priscilla, b. aft. 22 May 1627, Plymouth
III. Rebecca, b. c1631, Plymouth
IV.   child, b. pre 1633, Plymouth

*   *   *   *   *   *   *   *   *   *   *   *   *   *

I.   **MARY BROWN**[2], b. c1626 (In 1633 Mary was placed with John DOANE until "shee should accomplish the age of seaventeene yeares"; this term ended 10 Oct. 1644, therefore she was most probably 18 at this time <PCR 1:18,76; MQ 53:10-12>, d. aft. 8 Oct. 1679 (deed) <MD 5:32; Plymouth Co. Deeds 5:197; MF5G 7:5 states she died aft. Nov. 1689 when she consented to sale of land betw. sons John & Elkiah/Helkiah, however it does not cite this deed further (nor give a source for it) nor is it mentioned in the sections dealing with the two sons. A check of MDP:133 found a partial abstract of this deed dated 6 Nov. 1689 from Bristol Co.Deeds 7:457. The abstract (as given by Bowman) does not mention Mary, but perhaps the original complete copy does.> **Mary** m. c1646, Plymouth, **Ephraim TINKHAM/TINCOM** <MF5G 7:5; Stratton:363>, b. prob. England, <MQ 60:222-24 suggests he was the Ephraim, son of John TINCOMBE & Martha BEARE, bpt. 23 Feb. 1617/8, Barnstaple Parish, co. Devon, Eng.)>, d. betw. 17 Jan. 1683/4 (will) - 20 May 1685 (inv.) <MD 4:122>. (See BROWN Probate Appendix for will of Ephraim TINCOM Sr.)

9 TINKHAM Children: <MBD 1:268 (8); MF5G 7:6>

1.   child, b. c1647, Plymouth, living 1651 <Bradford>.

2.   **Ephraim TINKHAM**[3], b. 5 Aug. 1649, Plymouth <PCR 8:7; MD 16:120>, d. 13 Oct. 1714, 66th yr, Middleboro <MQ 15:101; Middleboro Dths.:201>; m. soon aft. 9 June 1676, Plymouth, **Hester/Esther WRIGHT**[3] <MD 24:83, MDP:161 (when she signed as Esther Wright for portion of brother's estate)>, (dau of Richard WRIGHT & Esther COOKE[2] - See Cooke Family). <See MBD 1:272 for bth. 6 chil.; MD 1:221,222,223 (4); Middleboro VR 1:2,3,4 (4); Plymouth ChR 1:271 (1).> (See BROWN Probate Appendix for will of Ephraim TINCKOM.)

3.   **Ebenezer TINKHAM**[3], b. 30 Sept. 1651, Plymouth <PCR 8:12; MD 16:237,17:186>, d. 8 Apr. 1718, ae 67, Nemasket g.s., Middleboro <Middleboro VR:28; MD 15:100,17:186; Middleboro Dths.:201 ("His wife died Morning, he died evening"); MD 4:73 (70th yr. of his age)>; m. pre 7 July 1676, **Elizabeth BURROWS/BURROUGHS** <MD 17:162, 186 (div. of her brother's est.; although Middleboro Dths.:201 says her maiden name was "Liscom", Bowman states it was not)>, (dau of Jeremiah BURROWES & (   ) HEWES), b. 5 Mar. 1654, Marshfield <Marshfield VR:4; MD 2:6,17:186; MSR:315>, d. 8 Apr. 1718, ae 64, Nemasket g.s., Middleboro <Middleboro VR:28; MD 4:74, 15:101; Middleboro Dths.:201>. <See MBD 1:268 for bth. 7 chil.; MD 1:221 for bth. 3 and Plymouth ChR 1:257,262,268,274 for bpt. of remaining 4.> (See BROWN Probate Appendix for will of Ebenezer TINKHAM.)

4.   **Peter TINKHAM**[3], b. 25 Dec. 1653, Plymouth <PCR 8:15; MD 17:70>, d. 30 Dec. 1709, ae 56, Middleboro <MD 15:102; Middleboro Dths.:201 (says 20 Dec.)>; m. c1690, **Mercy MENDALL** <MF5G 7:8>,

(dau of John), b. 3 Aug. 1666, Marshfield <Marshfield VR:15; MD 3:42>, d. aft. 10 May 1711
(fath.will) <PN&Q 2:55>. <See MBD 1:277-8 for bth. 4 chil.> (See BROWN Probate Appendix for
estate of Peter TINKHAM.)

5. **Helkiah TINKHAM**[3], b. 8 Feb. 1655, Plymouth <PCR 8:16; MD 17:71>, d. betw. 1724 (church member) <Plymouth ChR 1:227> - 25 Sept. 1731 (pr.) <MD 12:147>; m. c1684, **Ruth (   )** <MD 4:110>,
b. (   ), d. aft. 2 Apr. 1737 (deed) <Plymouth Co.Deeds 31:44>. <See MBD 1:275, MD 4:110-
111 & Plymouth VR for bth. 9 chil.> (See BROWN Probate Appendix for will of Helkiah TINKCOME)

6. **John TINKHAM**[3], b. 7 June 1658, Plymouth <PCR 8:17; MD 17:72>, d.y.

7. **Mary TINKHAM**[3], b. 5 Aug. 1661, Plymouth <PCR 8:26; MD 17:186>, d. 1731, ae 67, Middleboro
g.s. <MD 14:219; Middleboro Dths.:194 (no day or month on g.s.)>; m. c1680, **John TOMSON**[3],
(son of John TOMSON & Mary COOKE[2]). (See COOKE Family.)

8. **John TINKHAM**[3], b. 15 Nov. 1663, Plymouth <PCR 8:26; MD 17:186>, d. pre 15 Jan. 1739/40, Dartmouth (adm.) <MDP:128,133; Bristol Co.PR 9:314>; m. pre 1720, **Sarah (   )** <MF5G 7:13>, b.
(   ), d. aft. 10 Apr. 1759, prob. Dartmouth (deed) <Bristol Co.53:383>. <See MBD 1:277 for
bth. 5 chil.; Dartmouth VR:185 for bth. 3 of 5.> (See BROWN Probate Appendix for estate of
John TINKCOM.)

9. **Isaac TINKHAM**[3], b. 11 Apr. 1666, Plymouth <PCR 8:31; MD 18:56>; d. betw. 1 Oct. 1730 (deed)
<Plymouth Co.Deeds 25:221> - 5 Apr. 1732 (pr.), Plympton <MD 17:166>; m. 17 Nov. 1692, Ply-
mouth, **Sarah KING** <MD 13:206,17:162>, b. (   ), d. aft. 9 Dec. 1734 (deed) <Plymouth Co.
Deeds 29:91; Plymouth ChR 2:527 (poss. the Sarah TINKHAM, nurse, in the 1742 list of church
members.> No known issue. (See BROWN Probate Appendix for will of Isaac TINKHAM.)
(Note: Sarah KING's identity is unknown. I have not yet investigated the possibility that
she was the dau. of Thomas KING & Elizabeth CLAPP, bpt. 18 Sept. 1670, Scituate <MSR:319>.)

II. **PRISCILLA BROWN**[2], b. aft. 22 May 1627 (Cattle Division) <MD 1:152; PCR 1:19,2:89 & MQ 53:11
(In 1633 she was placed for 12 years with William GILSON; if, like her sister, she had com-
pleted her 17th year when the term ended 28 Oct. 1645, she would have been born betw. May -
Oct. 1627)>, d. aft. 17 Feb. 1697/8 (hus.will) <MD 32:26; Barnstable Co.PR 2:210>; m. 21 Mar.
1649, Sandwich, **William ALLEN** <PCR 8:9; MD 16:122; MSR:544>, (son of George ALLEN & Catherine
(?STARKES), b. c1627, England <MF5G 7:6>, d. 1 Oct. 1705, Sandwich (stated in inv.) <Barns-
table Co.PR 2:211; MDP:136>. No known issue. (See BROWN Probate Appendix for will of William ALLEN.)

III. **REBECCA BROWN**[2], b. c1631, Plymouth, d. aft. 9 Mar. 1698/9 (hus.will) <MD 8:101>; m. c1654,
William SNOW <MF5G 7:7>, b. c1617, England <Drake:23 & Banks' Planters:132 (if he is the
William Snow, aged 18 who arrived in New England in 1635 in the Susan & Ellen)>, d. 31 Jan.
1708, Bridgewater (stated in inv.) <MD 8:101,103>. (See BROWN Probate Appendix for will of
William SNOW.)

8 SNOW Children: <MBD 1:279>

1. **Mary SNOW**[3], b. (   ), d. aft. 9 Mar. 1698/9 (fath.will) <MD 8:101>.

2. **Lydia SNOW**[3], b. (   ), d. aft. 9 Mar. 1698/9 (fath.will) <MD 8:101>.

3. **William SNOW**[3], b. c1662, prob. Bridgewater, d. pre 7 Nov. 1726, prob. Bridgewater (adm.)
<MD 22:47-8; MDP:139; Plymouth Co.PR #18729>; m. last of (30) Nov. 1686, Bridgewater, **Naomi
WHITMAN** <Bridgewater VR; MD 2:242,22:47; MSR:6>, (dau of Thomas WHITMAN & Abigail BYRAM), b.
c1664 prob. Bridgewater <MF5G 7:14>, d. aft. 12 Jan. 1711 (fath.will) <Plymouth Co.PR
#22802> and poss. pre 22 Nov. 1726 (not ment. in heirs of hus.est.) <MD 22:47-8>. <See MBD
1:284, Bridgewater VR & MD 15:47 for bth. 6 chil.> (See BROWN Probate Appendix for estate
of William SNOW.)

4. **Joseph SNOW**[3], b. pre 1664, prob. Bridgewater, d. 18 Dec. 1753, Bridgewater <MD 14:209>; m.
c1689, prob. Bridgewater, **Hopestill ALDEN**[3], (dau of Joseph ALDEN[2] & Mary SIMMONS - See ALDEN
Family). <See MBD 1:281, MD 14:208 & Bridgewater VR for bth. 7 chil. (incl. twins).>

5. **Hannah SNOW**[3], b. c1664, prob. Bridgewater, d. 29 Mar. 1723, 59th yr, prob. Yarmouth <NEHGR
100:321; MSR:433>; m.1st, 7 Nov. 1683, Plymouth, **Giles RICKARD** <MD 13:204>, (son of Giles
RICKARD[2-1] & Hannah DUNHAM), b. 1659 <MF5G 7:16>, d. 29 Jan. 1709/10, Plymouth <Plymouth ChR
1:209; Drew:266 (states his age is hard to read - either 30 or 50 - 50 fits.)>. **Hannah** m.2nd
9 Mar. 1713/4, Plymouth, **Joseph HOWES** <MD 14:37>, (son of Joseph HOWES & Elizabeth MAYO)
<MF5G 7:16>, b. c1660, d. 24 Dec. 1743, 84th yr, prob. Yarmouth <NEHGR 100:321; MSR:433>. No
known issue. <See BROWN Probate Appendix for will of Giles RICKARD.> (Joseph HOWES m.1st,
28 Nov. 1689, Yarmouth, Mary VINCENT <Yarmouth VR 1:128> who d. 14 Mar. 1712, 49th yr <MSR:
433> and had 7 chil.)

6. **Benjamin SNOW**[3], b. c1669, prob. Bridgewater, d. 28 May 1743, Bridgewater <Bridge.VR 2:558>;
    m.1st, 12 Dec. 1693, Bridgewater, **Elizabeth ALDEN**[3] <Bridgewater VR; Gen.Adv.1:2>, (dau of
    Joseph ALDEN[2] & Mary SIMMONS - See ALDEN Family). **Benjamin** m.2nd, 25 Oct. 1705, Bridgewater,
    Sarah (ALLEN) Cary <MSR:7>, (dau of Samuel ALLEN & Sarah PARTRIDGE), b. 14 Apr. 1667, Bridge-
    water <Bridgewater VR>, d. aft. 12 Sept. 1738 (hus.will) <MD 22:99>. <See Bridgewater VR &
    MD 14:203 for 5 chil. by 1st wf and 1 ch. by 2nd wf.> (Sarah m.1st, c1687, prob. Bridgewater,
    Jonathan CARY <MD 22:99> and had 3 chil.). (See BROWN Probate Apendix for will of Benjamin
    SNOW.)

7. **Rebecca SNOW**[3], b. c1671, prob. Bridgewater, d. 4 Apr. 1740, ae about 69, Plympton g.s. <MD
    11:116, 1:177 (says ae about 63); Plympton VR>; m. 31 Dec. 1689, Plymouth, **Samuel RICKARD** <MD
    13:205>, (son of Giles RICKARD[2-1] & Hannah DUNHAM), b. 14 Jan. 1662, Plymouth <PCR 8:23>, d.
    7 Sept. 1727, ae about 63, Plympton g.s. <MD 1:177,11:116>. <See MBD 1:283-4 for bth. 9 chil
    and MD 1:211 (2), 3:15 (4), 94 (2).>

8. **JAMES SNOW**[3], b. (   ), d. pre 14 May 1691 (inv.) <MD 31:17 ("who Dyed in y[e] Expedition to
    Canada in ye year 1690"); Gen.Adv.2:62>.

IV. **Child**, b. pre 11 Nov. 1633 ("the widow having two children by the sd Peter"), d. pre 1647
     (div.) <MD 5:29-37>.

BROWN PROBATE APPENDIX

Will of **William ALLEN**: <MD 32:26-7; MDP:136; Barnstable Co.PR 2:210-11,229>
...17 Feb. 1697/8, ment. nephew Daniel ALLEN the son of brother George ALLEN dec'd; wf Priscilla;
"my friends called Quakers". Inv. taken 26 Oct. 1705 (gives his dth. date).
==
Will of **Giles RICKARD**: <Plymouth Co.PR #16896>
...13 Dec. 1709, ment. adopted child Desire DOTEN; kinsman Samuel RICKARD the son of brother Henry RICKARD; kinsman John RICKARD the son of brother John RICKARD; Giles RICKARD, eldest son of
brother Josiah RICKARD; Samuel RICKARD the son of brother Samuel RICKARD; Sarah, dau of brother
Eliezor RICKARD; John WHITING the son of sister Abigail; Elezor FAUNCE the son of sister Judith;
Mercy EATON the dau of sister Hannah; wf Hannah. Pr. 10 Mar. 1709/10.
==
Will of **Benjamin SNOW**[3] (**Rebecca Brown**[2]): <MD 22:99-100; MDP:136-7; Plymouth Co.PR 9:83-4,117>
...12 Sept. 1738 (husbandman), ment. sons Benjamin SNOW, Solomon SNOW, Ebenezer SNOW (youngest
son); wf Sarah; daus Rebecca CAMPBELL, Elizabeth CARVER; grandson Seth PRATT (under 21) the son
of dec'd dau Sarah. Pr. 6 June 1743.
==
Will of **William SNOW Jr.**: <MD 8:101-103; Plymouth Co.PR 2:175-77>
...9 Mar. 1698/9, "being very weak & Lame and my wife being aged", ment. unnamed wf; sons Joseph
SNOW, Benjamin SNOW, William SNOW; daus Mary, Lidia, Hannah, Rebeckah. Pr. 4 Mar. 1708.
==
Estate of **William SNOW**[3] (**Rebecca Brown**[2]): <MD 22:47-8; MDP:139; Plymouth Co.PR #18729, 5:160,181>
...Agreement of heirs, 22 Nov. 1726, ment. children: James SNOW, William SNOW, Eleazer SNOW, John
SNOW, Bethiah HOWARD wf of Elisha, Susannah ALGER wf of Israel.
==
Will of **Ephraim TINCKOM**: <MD 17:162-4; MDP:130; Plymouth Co.PR 3:358-60>
...17 Sept. 1714, ment. wf Esther; daus Martha SOUL, Mary TINCKOM; sons John TINCKOM (eldest son)
Isaac TINCKOM, Samuell TINCKOM; chil. of dec'd son Ephraim TINCKOM. Pr. 3 Mar. 1714/5.
==
Will of **Ephraim TINCOM Sr.**: <MD 4:122-24; Plymouth Co.PR 4:2:110-11>
...17 Jan. 1683/4, ment. wf Mary; sons Ephraim TINCOM (eldest son), Ebenezer TINCOM, Peter TINCOM
Elkiah TINCOM, John TINCOM, Isaack TINCOM; dau Mary TOMSON. Inv. 20 May 1685.
==
Estate of **John TINKCOM**[3] (**Mary Brown**[2]): <MDP:133; Bristol Co.PR 9:314,365,386,481>
...Division of real estate, 20 Apr. 1741, ment. children: John TINKHAM (eldest son), Peter TINK-
HAM, Hezekiah TINKHAM, Mary TABOR, Martha TINKHAM.
==
Will of **Helkiah TINKCOME**[3] (**Mary Brown**[2]): <MD 12:145-8; Plymouth Co.PR>
...14 Dec. 1716, ment. wf Ruth; sons Helkiah TINKCOME, John TINKCOME, Jacob TINCOME, Caleb TINCK-
COME; daus Mary COURTIS, Ruth TINKCOME; sons Ebenezer TINKCOME, Peter TINKCOME; son in law Eben-
ezer COURTIS. Codicil, 20 May 1718, ment. dec'd dau Mary COURTIS & her children, Jacob, Caleb,
Mary & Sarah (all under age). Pr. 29 Sept. 1731.
==
Will of **Deacon Ebenezer TINKHAM**[3] (**Mary Brown**[2]): (yeoman) <MD 17:164-5>
...3 Apr. 1718, ment. wf Elizabeth; sons Ebenezer TINKHAM, Shuball TINKHAM; chil. of son Jeremiah
TINKHAM, viz: Jeremiah, Ebenezer & Joanna (all minors) & their mother Joanna TINKHAM; dau Joanna
MACOMBER; granddaughter Elizabeth TINKHAM. Wit. sworn 28 Apr. 1718.
==

Will of **Isaac TINKHAM**[3] **(Mary Brown**[2]**):** (yeoman) <MD 17:166; Plymouth Co.PR 6:160>
...25 Feb. 1708/9, wf Sarah to receive one half of lands (he does not dispose of the other half, perhaps he did so in his lifetime). Pr. 5 Apr. 1732.

==

Estate of **Peter TINKHAM**[3] **(Mary Brown**[2]**):** <MDP:135; Plymouth Co.PR #20895, 2:115,3:56-7>
...Settlement of estate, 22 Sept. 1710, ment. children: Samuel TINKHAM, Seth TINKHAM, Mercy TINK-HAM, Joanna TINKHAM.

NOTES:

JAMES CHILTON

James CHILTON was born pre 1563 (freeman in 1583), Canterbury, Kent co., England, the son of Lyonell CHILTON. He d. 8 Dec. 1620, Provincetown, Cape Cod Harbour <MD 30:3 (O.S.); MD 2:116 (N.S.-18th)>. James married c1585, prob. Canterbury, (   ). Although her name is frequently given as Susanna, Bowman states there is no foundation for this claim which first appeared in Mitchell's History of Bridgewater in 1840. Bowman states that Dr. Nathaniel B. Shurtleff of Boston wrote to Judge Mitchell asking his source for the name and received the following reply, "I cannot now say how I learnt the name of James Chilton's wife, but I am very certain I had good authority for calling it Susanna - perhaps I may stumble upon it again" <MBD 1:312, #1>. MF5G 2:5 suggests he married Susanna FURNER, the daughter of his step-mother, Isabell (   )(Furner) Chilton. James' wife died shortly after 11 Jan. 1620/21 <MF5G 2:5>.

See TAG 38:244, Origins of the Chiltons of the Mayflower; Mayflower Families Through Five Generations (MF5G), James Chilton, vol.2, by Robert M. Sherman, F.A.S.G.

James & wife had 10 children, only two of whom are carried further: (b. England) <MF5G 2:5>

I.   Isabella, bpt. 15 Jan. 1586/7, St. Paul's Parish, Canterbury
II.   Jane, bpt. 8 June 1589, St. Paul's Parish, Canterbury
III. Mary, bur. 23 Nov. 1593, St. Martin's Parish, Canterbury
IV.   Joel, bur. 2 Nov. 1593, St. Martin's Parish, Canterbury
V.   Elizabeth, bpt. 14 July 1594, St. Martin's Parish, Canterbury
VI.   James, bpt. 22 Aug. 1596, St. Martin's Parish, Canterbury
VII. Ingle, bpt. 29 Apr. 1599, St. Paul's Parish, Canterbury
VIII. Christian, bpt. 26 July 1601, St. Peter's Parish, Sandwich
IX.   James, bpt. 11 Sept. 1603, St. Peter's Parish, Sandwich
X.   Mary, bpt. 31 May 1607, St. Peter's Parish, Sandwich

* * * * * * * * * * * *

I. **Isabella CHILTON[2]**, bpt. 15 Jan. 1586/7, Canterbury, Eng. <MF5G 2:5>, d. (   ); m. 21 July 1615, Leyden, Holland, **Roger CHANDLER** <MD 11:129>, b. (   ) <MD 11:129 (from Colchester, Eng.)>, d. betw. 1658 <PCR 8:174 (freeman of Duxbury)> - 11 Oct. 1665, prob. Duxbury <PCR 4:110>. MF5G 2:6 states in Oct. 1665 the Plymouth Court granted 150 acres to the three daus of Roger Chandler. It goes on to state that, of his three daus, Mary is "with virtual certainty the Mary, wife of Edmund Burfe" who died in 1658 - this would leave only two daus alive in 1665.

4 CHANDLER Children: <TAG 27:1-6,37:212-7>

1. **Samuel CHANDLER[3]**, b. pre 15 Oct. 1622, Leyden, Holland, poss. d.y.

2. **Sarah CHANDLER[3]**, b. pre 15 Oct. 1622, Leyden, Holland, d. poss pre 27 Oct. 1675, Bridgewater (hus.adm.) <Plymouth Co.PR #12697>; m. c1640, Duxbury, **Solomon LEONARD/LEONARDSON** MF5G 2:10> b. c1610, prob. Monmouthshire, Eng. <MF5G 2:10>, d. pre 1 May 1671, Bridgewater (son's deed) <Plymouth Co.Deeds 4:217-8>. <See MF5G 2:11 for 6 chil.>

3. **Mary CHANDLER[3]**, b. aft. 1622, prob. Leyden, Holland, d. prob. 15 Aug. 1658, Boston <Boston Rcd.Com.9:67>; m. (   ), **Edmond BRUFF/BROUGH** <MF5G 2:11>, b. (   ), d. aft. 1658 (wf's dth.) <MF5G 2:11>. <See MF5G 2:12 for one chil.>

4. **Martha CHANDLER[3]**, b. aft. 1622, prob. Leyden, Holland, d. 1 May 1674, Taunton <PCR 8:36>; m. pre 1649, **John BUNDY** <MF5G 2:12>, b. c1617, Eng., d. betw. Apr. - 29 Oct. 1681, Taunton <Plymouth Co.PR #3310 (will & pr.)>. <For 6 chil. see MBD 1:287 and Boston Rcd.Com.9:29,41 (2), NEHGR 16:324 (4), PCR 8:35 (1), 36 (2).>

X. **MARY CHILTON[2]**, bpt. 31 May 1607, Sandwich, Eng. <MQ 43:56>, d. shortly before 1 May 1679, Boston <MD 1:65 (executor declined)>; m. betw. July 1623 (land division) - 22 May 1627 (Cattle division) <MD 1:228,151>, **John WINSLOW** <MD 1:151>, (son of Edward WINSLOW & Magdalen OLLYVER), b. 16 Apr. 1597, Droitwich, Worcestershire, Eng. <MD 3:129>, d. betw. 12 Mar. - 21 May 1674, Boston <MD 3:129 (will & pr.)>. (See CHILTON Probate Appendix for wills of Mary & John WINSLOW.)

10 WINSLOW Children: <MBD 1:288>

1. **John WINSLOW[3]**, b. betw. 22 May 1627 (Cattle Division) - 1630, Plymouth, d. betw. 3-12 Oct. 1683, Boston <MD 10:54-5 (will & pr.); m.lst c1662/3, **Elizabeth (   )**, d. aft. 7 Aug. 1670, Boston <MF5G 2:13 (bth.last ch.)>. **John** m.2nd, (   ), **Judith (   )**, bur. 18 Dec. 1714, ae near 90, Boston <MA Hist.Coll.(5th series) 5:7:30 (Sewall's Diary). <For 4 chil. see MBD 1:

294,313 and Boston Rcd.Com.9:94,98,112,116.> (See CHILTON Probate Appendix for will of John WINSLOW.)

2. **Susanna WINSLOW[3]**, b. betw. 22 May 1627 (Cattle Division) - 1630, Plymouth, d. prob. aft. 14 Nov. 1685, E. Bridgewater <Plymouth Co.Deeds 5:28; MDP:150; PN&Q 1:10-11 (The will of her brother John, dated 3 Oct. 1683, calls her dec'd. On 14 Nov. 1685, Robert & Susanna Latham acknowledged a deed. It is hard to imagine that her own brother could be mistaken about whether or not she was alive, but either he was mistaken or Robert remarried to another Susanna and it was he and his second wife who acknowledged the 1685 deed)>; m. c1649, prob. Plymouth, **Robert LATHAM**, b. c1623, prob. England, d. betw. 14 Nov. 1685 <Plymouth Co.Deeds 2:26; MDP:151; MF5G 2:13 (d. ae 76)>. (On 4 Mar. 1654/5 Robert was indicted for felonious cruelty causing the death of his 14 year old servant, John WALKER. A jury found him guilty of manslaughter and he was sentenced to be burned on the hand and, since he owned no land, to have his personal property confiscated. The courts charged wife Susanna with complicity but she was never tried. See Stratton:185-86.) <See MBD 1:303,314 for 8 chil. and MD 16:235 for one.>

3. **Mary WINSLOW[3]**, b. c1631, Plymouth, d. betw. 28 Oct. 1663 - 2 Nov. 1665 <MF5G 2:15>; m. 16 Jan 1650/1, Plymouth, **Edward GRAY** <PCR 8:11; MD 16:235>, b. c1629, d. last of June 1681, ae about 52, Plymouth g.s. <Drew:95 (oldest original stone on Burial Hill)>. (Edward m.2nd, 12 Dec. 1665, Plymouth, Dorothy LETTICE <PCR 8:31; MD 18:56>, (dau of Thomas), who d. aft. 5 Mar. 1684/5 <Plymouth Court Orders 6:2:21>; they had 6 chil. <MBD 1:294,313>.) <See MBD 1:294 for 6 chil. and MD 16:237 (1), 17:70 (1), 183 (3), 18:56 (1), PCR 8:12 (1), 15 (1), 22 (3).> (See CHILTON Probate Appendix for estate of Edward GRAY.)

4. **Edward WINSLOW[3]**, b. c1635, Plymouth, d. 19 Nov. 1682, 48th yr, Boston <MD 12:129>; m.1st, pre 1661, (   ), **Sarah HILTON**, (dau of William HILTON & Sarah GREENLEAF), b. June 1641, Newbury <MF5G 2:16>, d. 4 Apr. 1667, ae 26, Boston g.s. <Boston Rcd.Com.; MF5G 2:16>. **Edward** m.2nd, 8 Feb. 1668, Boston, **Elizabeth HUTCHINSON** <Boston Rcd.Com.; MD 12:129>, (dau of Edward HUTCH-INSON & Catherine HAMBY), b. 4 Nov. 1639, Boston <NEHGR 19:15; MD 12:129>, d. 16 Sept. 1728, 89th yr, Boston <MD 12:129>. <See MBD 1:289 & Boston Rcd.Com.9:80 for bth. 3 chil. by 1st wf and MBD 1:289 & MD 12:129 for bth. 5 chil. by 2nd wf.> (See CHILTON Probate Appendix for will of Edward WINSLOW.)

5. **Sarah WINSLOW[3]**, b. c1638, Plymouth, d. 9 Apr. 1726, ae 88, Boston <MD 21:1,2; NEHGR 15:308>; m.1st 19 July 1660, Boston, **Myles STANDISH[2]** <MD 21:1>, (son of Myles STANDISH[1] - see STANDISH family). **Sarah** m.2nd, Nov. 1666 or 1667, Boston, **Tobias PAYNE** <MD 21:1>, b. poss. Fownhope, Hereford, Eng. <MF5G 2:17>, d. 12 Sept. 1669, Boston <MD 21:1>. **Sarah** m.3rd, c1672, **Richard MIDDLECOTT** <MD 21:1>, (son of Edward & Mary), b. c1640, Wiltshire co., Eng. <MF5G 2:17>, d. 13 June 1704, Boston <MD 21:1>. <See MBD 1:301 & MD 21:1 for bth. 1 ch. by 2nd hus.; see MBD 1:301 & MD 21:1 for 4 chil. by 3rd hus. and Boston Rcd.Com.9:133 (1), 146 (1).> (See CHILTON Probate Appendix for wills of Tobias PAYNE and Richard MIDDLECOT and estate of Sarah.)

6. **Samuel WINSLOW[3]**, b. c1641, Plymouth, d. 14 Oct. 1680, ae 39, Boston g.s. <MF5G 2:18>; m. pre 22 June 1675 (deed), **Hannah BRIGGS** <Suffolk Co.Deeds 9:212>, (dau of Walter & Mary), b. c1650, Scituate, d. aft. 4 Nov. 1714, prob. Boston <Suffolk Co.Deeds 28:180>. (Hannah m.2nd, Capt. Thomas JOLLS <MF5G 2:18>.) <See MBD 1:291 for 2 chil. & Boston Rcd.Com.9:147 (1).> (See CHILTON Probate Appendix for will of Samuel WINSLOW.)

7. **Joseph WINSLOW[3]**, b. c1642, Plymouth, d. pre 7 Aug. 1679 (distribution of mother's est.), Long Island NY <Suffolk Co.PR 12:321,326 (pre 3 Oct. 1679, adm., mariner of Boston)>; m. pre 10 Oct. 1668 (deed) <MF5G 2:19>, **Sarah LAWRENCE**, (dau of Thomas of Newtown, Long Island NY), b. (   ) <MF5G 2:19>, d. prob. pre 1693 (fath.will) <MF5G 2:19>. (Sarah m.2nd, Charles LeBROS) <See MBD 1:294 for 2 chil.>

8. **Isaac WINSLOW[3]**, b. c1644, Plymouth, d. betw. 26-29 Aug. 1670, Port Royal, Jamaica <MDP:140 (will & pr.)>; m. 14 Aug. 1666, Charlestown, **Mary NOWELL** <MF5G 2:20>, (dau of Increase NOWELL & Parnell GRAY), b. 26 May 1643, Charlestown <MF5G 2:20>, d. betw. 14 Apr. 1720 - 23 Jan. 1729 (will & pr.) <MF5G 2:20>. (Mary m.2nd, 10 Sept. 1674, Charlestown, John LONG <Charles-town VR:89> and had 4 chil.) <See MBD 1:292 for 2 chil.> (See CHILTON Probate Appendix for will of Isaac WINSLOW.)

9. **child**, b. pre 1650, d. pre 12 Mar. 1673/4 (fath.will).

10. **Benjamin WINSLOW[3]**, b. 12 Aug. 1653, Plymouth <PCR 8:17; MD 17:70>, d. betw. 12 Mar. 1673/4 (fath.will) - 31 July 1676, unm. (mother's will) <MD 1:65-8>.

CHILTON PROBATE APPENDIX

Will of John BUNDY: <Plymouth Co.PR #3310>
...Apr. 1681, ment. unnamed wf, children & sons; son James BUNDY; unnamed sons by this wf. Pr. 29 Oct. 1681.

==

Estate of **Edward GRAY**: <MDP:145-6 (lengthy); Plymouth Co.Deeds 5:229,301>
...24 Aug. 1681, Division among widow Dorothy & following chil., viz: John GRAY (eldest son), Desire SOUTHWORTH wf of Nathaniel, Elizabeth ARNOLD wf of Seth, Sarah GRAY, Anna GRAY. Division,
28 Jan. 1684 among the 6 younger chil., viz: Edward GRAY, Susanna GRAY, Thomas GRAY, Rebecca GRAY
Lidia GRAY & Samuel GRAY.

Will of **Richard MIDDLECOT**: (merchant) <MD 21:5-6; Suffolk Co.PR 15:299,300>
...22 June 1700, ment. son Edward MIDDLECOT; dau Mary GIBBS wf of Henry; daus Sarah MIDDLECOT &
Jane MIDDLECOT; son in law (step-son) William PAYNE; wf Sarah. Pr. 20 June 1704.

Estate of **Sarah (WINSLOW[3])(Standish)(Payne) Middlecott**: <MDP:149; Suffolk Co.PR #5246, 27:179>
...26 May 1729, Division among children, viz: Sarah BOUCHER, Elisha COOKE in right of wf Jane;
William PAYNE (double portion); heirs of Mary HAGGET dec'd; heirs of Edward MIDDLECOTT dec'd.

Will of **Tobias PAYNE**: <MDP:149; MD 21:4-5; Suffolk Co.PR 6:28>
...11 Sept. 1669, nuncupative will dictated to father in law John WINSLOW..."unto youre daughter
my wife & to our little sonne, to whose care, charge & Education I leave him, enjoyning her in
case shee marries againe that hee may not be abused or wronged but duly taken care for which I
hope also you will mind if it happens during youre life". Pr. 21 Sept. 1669 (ment. son William
PAYNE.)

Will of **Edward WINSLOW[3] (Mary Chilton[2])**: (mariner) <MD 10:53-4; Suffolk Co.PR 6:418>
...8 Nov. 1680, ment. wf Elizabeth; sons John WINSLOW & Edward WINSLOW (both minors). Pr. 1 Feb.
1682.

Will of **Isaac WINSLOW[3] (Mary Chilton[2])**: <MDP:140; Middlesex Co.PR #18085, 3:223 or #25344>
...26 Aug. 1670, ment. wf Mary; dau Parnill WINSLOW; child unborn when he left 12 July 1670. Pr.
29 Aug. 1670. (Note: The unborn child was son Isaac b. 22 July & died 24 Aug., before his fath.)

Will of **John WINSLOW**: <MDP:140; MD 3:129-34; Suffolk Co.PR 5:211-4>
...12 Mar. 1673, ment. wf Mary; son John WINSLOW; minor grandson William PAYNE the son of dau
Sarah MEDDLECOTT; minor granddaughter Parnell WINSLOW the dau of son Isaack WINSLOW; unnamed daus
of dau LATHAM; son Benjamin WINSLOW (under 21); son Edward WINSLOW; granddaughter Susanna LATHAM;
children of dau LATHAM; children of son Edward WINSLOW; children of son Edward GREY that he had
by dau Mary; 2 children of son Joseph WINSLOW; 2 children of grandchild Mercy HARRIS; kinsman
Josiah WINSLOW now Governor of New Plimoth; brother Josiah WINSLOW; kinswoman Eleanor BAKER dau
of brother Kenelm WINSLOW; "my Negro Girle Jane (after she hath served twenty yeares from the
date hereof) shall be free, and that she shall serve my wife during her live/life and after my
wifes decease she shall be disposed of according to the discression of my overseers". Pr. 21 May
1674.

Will of **Mary (CHILTON[2]) Winslow**: <MDP:140; MD 1:65-9; Suffolk Co.PR>
...31 July 1676, ment. son John WINSLOW; grandchild William PAYNE son of dau Sarah MEDDLECOTT;
dau Sarah MEDDLECOTT & her children; dau Susanna LATHAM; granddaughter Ann GRAY; Mary WINSLOW &
Sarah WINSLOW daus of son Edward WINSLOW; children of son Edward WINSLOW; grandchildren Parnell
WINSLOW (minor), Chilton LATHAM (minor), Mercy HARRIS, Mary POLLARD, Susanna LATHAM; Mary WINSLOW
(under 18), dau of son Joseph WINSLOW; children John WINSLOW, Edward WINSLOW, Joseph WINSLOW,
Samuell WINSLOW, Susanna LATHAM, Sarah MIDDLECOTT. Exr. declined 1 May 1679. Pr. 11 July 1679.

Will of **John WINSLOW[3] (Mary Chilton[2])**: (mariner) <MD 10:54-5; Suffolk Co.PR 6:435-37>
...3 Oct. 1683, ment. "each and every" sons of brothers Edward WINSLOW, Joseph WINSLOW & Samuel
WINSLOW; 2 sons of sister Susanna LATHAM dec'd; only son John WINSLOW (under 21); wf Judith. Pr.
12 Oct. 1683.

Will of **Samuel WINSLOW[3] (Mary Chilton[2])**: <MD 10:52-3; Suffolk Co.PR 6:347-8>
...7 Oct. 1680, ment. wf Hannah; son Richard WINSLOW (under 21); dau Mary WINSLOW (under 18);
brother in law Richard MIDDLECOTT; brother in law John BRIGGS. Pr. 26 Jan. 1680/1.

NOTES:

FRANCIS COOKE

Francis COOKE was born after Aug. 1583 <MD 3:95 (he is listed on the Aug. 1643 list of men between 16-60, so was no more than 60 years of age)>, England. He died 7 Apr. 1663, "above 80", Plymouth <PCR 8:23; MD 3:95,17:183; MSR:547>. The date of his marriage to Hester MAHIEU in Leyden,
Holland has often been printed incorrectly (e.g., 30 June 1603 - Stratton:270 & MM:113) with the
source being MD 8:48. However, an article in MD 27:145-55 (New Light On Francis Cooke His Wife
Hester Mahieu And Their Son John) goes to great pains to give an estimated date and states the
date given in MD 8:48 was "erroneous". Marriage intentions were entered 4 July 1603 & 5 July
1603 which means the three banns were proclaimed 6 July, 13 July and 20 July (three successive
Sundays); therefore, the marriage took place on or after 20 July 1603. The marriage intentions
state Hester MAHIEU was from Canterbury, England and she was accompanied by her mother Jennie
MAHIEU and her sister Jennie MAHIEU. In his book, "Hypocrisie Unmasked", Edward WINSLOW stated
she was a "Walloone" and came from the French. MD 27:145 shows she was admitted to the French
Reformed Church in Leiden in 1603. Hester died between 8 June 1666 (agreement of hus. heirs)
<MD 3:103,242; MDP:211; Plymouth Co.Deeds 3:73> and 18 Dec. 1675 (will of grandson John WRIGHT)
<MD 4:128>. (See COOKE Probate Appendix for will & agreement of heirs of Francis COOKE.)

(See also: Mayflower Families In Progress (MFIP), Francis Cooke of the Mayflower and His Descendants for Four Generations, 1994, 3rd Ed., by Robert S. Wakefield, FASG & Ralph Van Wood Jr.;
MD 3:95-105, Francis Cooke and His Descendants; MD 27:145-55 (above); NEHGR 107:61, Hester LeMay-
hieu, Wife of Francis Cooke.)

Francis & Hester had 7 children: <MFIP #1 for 7; MBD 1:316 for 5>

I. John, bpt. betw. 1 Jan. - 31 Mar. 1607, Leyden, Holland
II. child, bur. 20 May 1608, Leyden, Holland
III. Elizabeth, bpt. 26 Dec. 1611
IV. Jane, b. pre 1613, Holland
V. Jacob, b. c1618, Holland
VI. Hester, b. c1620, Holland
VII. Mary, b. c1626 (betw. Mar. 1624 - 22 May 1627, Plymouth

* * * * * * * * * * * * * * * * * *

I. **JOHN COOKE**[2], bpt. betw. 1 Jan. - 31 Mar. 1607, Leyden, Holland <MD 27:147>, d. 23 Nov. 1695,
Dartmouth <Dartmouth VR 3:25; MD 3:33; MSR:147>; m. 28 Mar. 1634, Plymouth **Sarah WARREN**[2] <PCR
1:29; MD 3:98,105,13:83>, (dau of Richard & Elizabeth WARREN - see Warren Family). (See
COOKE Probate Appendix for will of John COOKE.) <See MDP:211 for interesting 1693 petition
of John Cooke regarding his dealings with the Indians.>

5 COOKE Children: <MBD 1:361>

1. **Sarah COOKE**[3], b. c1635, Plymouth, d. aft. 26 Feb. 1712/3 (son's receipt), prob. Dartmouth
<MD 16:112>; m. 20 Nov. 1652, Plymouth, **Arthur HATHAWAY** <PCR 8:14; MD 16:238; MSR:544>, b.
c1620-25, prob. England, d. 11 Dec. 1711, Dartmouth <MD 16:111>. <See MBD 1:373,408 for 7
chil. and PCR 8:15,16 & MD 17:70,71 for 2 chil.> (See COOKE Probate Appendix for will of
Arthur HATHAWAY.)

2. **Elizabeth COOKE**[3], b. pre 1644, Plymouth, d. 6 Dec. 1715, Tiverton MA <RI VR 4:7:115 (in 1747
Tiverton became part of RI)>; m. 28 Nov. 1661, Plymouth, **Daniel WILCOX** <PCR 8:23; MD 16:239,
17:183; MSR:545>, (son of Edward WILCOX & Susanna THOMSON), bpt. 4 Mar. 1632/3, Croft, Lincolnshire, England <NEHGR 147:188-91>, d. 2 July 1702, Tiverton MA/RI <RI VR 4:7:115; MD 16:
243>. <See MBD 1:363 for 8 chil.> (Daniel m.1st (   ) and had sons Daniel & Samuel <MFIP
#8.) (See COOKE Probate Appendix for will of Daniel WILCOX.)

3. **Hester COOKE**[3], b. 16 Aug. 1650, Plymouth <PCR 8:10; MD 16:235>, d. betw. 17 Apr. 1671 (bth.
ch.) - 1672/73 (hus.2nd marr.); m. c1667, **Thomas TABER** <MM:138; MFIP #9>, (son of Philip TAB-
ER & Lydia MASTERS), bpt. Feb. 1646, Yarmouth/Martha's Vineyard <Savage 4:247-8; Little Compton Fam.:645-6>, d. 11 Nov. 1730, Dartmouth <RI Gen.Dict.:195>. <See Dartmouth VR:9, NEHGR
35:32, MSR:156 & MBD 1:363,367 for bth. 2 chil.> (Thomas m.2nd c1672/3, Mary TOMSON[3] (Mary
Cooke[2]) and had 10 chil.) (See COOKE Probate Appendix for will of Thomas TABER.)

4. **Mary COOKE**[3], b. c1651/2, Plymouth, d. betw. 26 Apr. 1708 (receipt) <MD 16:229> - 25 Jan.
1714/5 (agreement of heirs) <MD 16:230>; m.1st c1667, **Phillip TABER** <MD 10:45 (ment. in 1673
deed)>, (son of Philip TABER & Lydia MASTERS), bpt. 8 Feb. 1646, Yarmouth/Martha's Vineyard
<Little Compt.Fam.:645-6>, d. pre 4 Mar. 1692/3 (inv.) <MD 16:226; MSR:44,52>. **Mary** m.2nd,
pre 4 Mar. 1692/3, (   ) DAVIS (she is called Mary DAVIS when she swore to 1st hus. inv.)
<MD 16:226; Bristol Co.PR 1:74>. <See MBD 1:368-9, Dartmouth VR:9 & MSR:160 for bth. 8 chil>

5. **Mercy COOKE**[3], b. 25 July (worn, prob. 1656), Plymouth <PCR 8:16; MD 17:72>, d. 22 Nov. 1733,

77th yr, Dartmouth <Dartmouth VR 3:78>; m. c1683, **Stephen WEST** <MM:139; MFIP #11>, (son of Bartholomew WEST & Katherine ALMY), b. c1654 <MFIP #11>, d. 12 Aug. 1748, 94th yr, Dartmouth <Dartmouth VR 3:78>. <See MBD 1:372, Dartmouth VR:11 & MSR:153 for bth. 9 chil.>

II **JANE COOKE**[2], b. pre 1613, Holland, d. pre 1650, Plymouth (Bradford) <MQ 49:133>; m. aft. 22 May 1627, Plymouth (Cattle Division) <MD 1:149>, **Experience MITCHELL** <MD 3:105>, (poss. son of Thomas MITCHELL of Amsterdam), b. c1609 <Dexter:625>, d. betw. 5 Dec. 1684 (will) - 14 May 1689 (inv.) <MD 4:150,32:97-8>. (Experience m.2nd, Mary (   ) and had children (Mary), Sarah, Jacob, Edward, John & Hannah. Much doubt & contraversy exists as to which wife was the mother of some of these children, particularly Mary. See MDP:248-9 for discussion.)

2 MITCHELL Children: <MBD 1:333>

1. **Elizabeth MITCHELL**[3], b. c1628, Plymouth, d. betw. 1 Nov. 1681 (deed) <MD 15:247,16:249,253> - 5 Dec. 1684 (fath.will) <MD 4:150,32:97-100>; m. 6 Dec. 1645, Plymouth, **John WASHBURN** <PCR 2:94; MD 13:86>, (son of John WASHBURN & Margaret MOORE), bpt. 26 Nov. 1620, Bengeworth, Worcestershire, England <Banks' Planters:154; Stratton:369; Drake:22 (ae 14 on 1635 passenger list to N.E.)>, d. 12 Nov. 1686, Bridgewater <MD 15:251>. <See MBD 1:334 for 11 chil.> (John m.2nd, betw. 7 Nov. 1684 - 30 Oct. 1686, Elizabeth (   ) PACKARD <MD 15:247>, (the widow of Samuel PACKARD who d. 7 Nov. 1684 <MD 15:253>), who d. aft. 27 Oct. 1694 (deed) <MD 15:251>.) (See COOKE Probate Appendix for will of John WASHBURN.)

2. **Thomas MITCHELL**[3], b. c1631, Plymouth <TAG 12:198 says c1636>, d. betw. 6 Mar. 1683/4 (deed) <New Shoreham RI Deeds 1:465> - 6 May 1687, Block Island, RI (the inv. of John WILLIAMS of Newport RI mentions the executors of Thomas MITCHELL at Block Island) <TAG 12:195; Suffolk Co. MA PR 10:341>; m. c1659, Plymouth Colony, (   ) and had 3 or more chil. <MFIP #13>.

III Jacob **COOKE**[2], b. c1618, Holland (ae 56 or there about in 14 July 1674 deposition) <MD 2:45-6; Plymouth Co.Deeds 1:181>, d. betw. 11 Dec. (will) - 18 Dec. 1675 (inv.), Plymouth <MD 3:236>; m.1st aft. 10 June 1646, Plymouth, **Damaris HOPKINS**[2] (the date father Francis COOKE deeds land to his son "upon a conclusion of a marriage between Jacob COOKE of Plymouth & Damaris HOPKINS") <MD 2:27-8,3:105,5:52>, (dau of Stephen HOPKINS - see HOPKINS Family). Jacob m.2nd, 18 Nov. 1669, Plymouth, **Elizabeth (LETTICE) Shurtleff** <PCR 8:32; MD 18:57; MSR:546>, (dau of Thomas & Ann), b. c1637, d. 31 Oct. 1693, 57th yr, Swansea <Plymouth ChR 1:281>. (Elizabeth m.1st, 18 Oct. 1655, Plymouth, William SHURTLEFF/SHIRTLIFFE <MD 17:72; PCR 8:17> who was bur. 24 June 1666 <MD 2:182>; she m.3rd, 1 Jan. 1688/9, Plymouth, Hugh COLE <MD 13:204> who m.1st, 8 Jan. 1654, Plymouth <PCR 8:72,74>, Mary FOXWELL.) (See COOKE Probate Appendix for will of Jacob COOKE.)

9 COOKE Children: (7 by 1st wf, 2 by 2nd wf) <MBD 1:322>

1. **Elizabeth COOKE**[3], b. 18 Jan. 1648/9, Plymouth <PCR 8:5>; MD 5:52,15:27>, d. 21 Nov. 1692, 44th yr, Plymouth <MD 16:63; Plymouth ChR 1:275 ("44th yeare almost finished. Her little dau Martha was baptized Sabbath after")>; m. c1667, Plymouth, **John DOTY**[2] (See DOTY Family.)

2. **Caleb COOKE**[3], b. 29 Mar. 1651, Plymouth <PCR 8:12; MD 5:52,16:237>, d. 13 Feb. 1721/2, 70th yr, Plymouth g.s. <Drew:23; Plymouth ChR 1:191 (smallpox, aged about 70 years)>; m. c1682, Plymouth, **Jane** (   ) <MFIP #15>, b. (   ), d. betw. 8 Apr. (will) - 24 Apr. 1736 (pr.), Kingston <MD 15:139>. <See MBD 1:322, MD 4:111 & Plymouth VR 1:54 for bth. 9 chil.> (See COOKE Probate Appendix for wills of Caleb & Jane COOKE.)

3. **Jacob COOKE**[3], b. 26 Mar. 1653, Plymouth <PCR 8:15; MD 17:70>, d. 24 Apr. 1747, 95th yr, Kingston <MD 7:26,21:42>; m. 29 Dec. 1681, Plymouth, **Lydia MILLER** <MD 21:42>, (dau of John MILLER & Margaret WINSLOW), b. 18 May 1661, Yarmouth <Yarmouth VR 1:128; NEHGR 55:33>, d. 1 Mar. 1727/8, 67th yr, Kingston <MD 7:26,21:42>. <See MBD 1:330, Plymouth VR, MD 2:81,21:42 for bth. 8 chil.> (See COOKE Probate Appendix for will of Jacob COOKE.)

4. **Mary COOKE**[3], b. 12 Jan. 1657/8, Plymouth <PCR 8:17; MD 17:72; MQ 49:122>, d. 28 Aug. 1712, ae 55, Plymouth g.s. <MD 16:64; Drew:150>; m. c1678, Plymouth, **John RICKARD**[3] <MQ 49:122-29>, (son of John RICKARD[2] (Giles[1]) & Hester BARNES), b. 24 Nov. 1657, Plymouth <PCR 8:17; MD 17:72>, d. 25 Apr. 1712, Plymouth g.s. <MD 16:64; Drew:150>. <See MBD 1:333 for bth. 7 chil. and PCR 8:74 (1), 75 (2); MD 1:144 (5).>

5. **Martha COOKE**[3], b. 16 Mar. 1659/60, Plymouth <PCR 8:22; MD 17:182>, d. 17 Sept. 1722, 63rd yr, Plympton <MD 10:112; MD 2:141 (says 65th yr)>; m. 2 Mar. 1683/4, Plymouth, **Elkanah CUSHMAN**[3] <MD 13:203>, (son of Thomas CUSHMAN & Mary ALLERTON[2] - see ALLERTON Family).

6. **Francis COOKE**[3], b. 5 Jan. 1662/3, Plymouth <PCR 8:23; MD 17:183,18:147>, d. betw. 15 May 1736 (codicil) - 18 Sept. 1746 (pr.), Kingston <MD 18:147>; m. 2 Aug. 1687, Plymouth, **Elizabeth LATHAM**[4] <MD 13:204,18:147>, (dau of Robert LATHAM & Susanna WINSLOW[3] (Mary Chilton[2])), b. c1664/5, prob. Bridgewater, d. 16 Nov. 1730, 66th yr, Kingston g.s. <MD 7:26,18:147>. <See

MBD 1:327 for 6 chil.> (See COOKE Probate Appendix for will of Francis COOKE.)

7. **Ruth COOKE**[3], b. 17 Jan. 1665/6, Plymouth <PCR 8:32; MD 18:57>, d. aft. 11 Dec. 1675 (fath. will) <MD 3:236; see MQ 36:189>.

8. **Sarah COOKE**[3], b. 1670/1, Plymouth <PCR 8:32; MD 18:57>, d. 8 Feb. 1744/5, 74th yr, Plymouth g.s. <MD 16:85,20:117; Drew:152>; m. 1 Apr. 1691, Plymouth, **Robert BARTLETT**[4] <MD 13:205,20:117>, (son of Joseph BARTLETT[3] (Mary Warren[2]) & Hannah POPE - see WARREN family), b. c1663, Plymouth, d. 3 Jan. 1718/9, 55th yr, Plymouth g.s. <MD 20:117; Drew:53>. <See MD 1:212 & 20:117 for 12 chil. and MD 20:117-25 for Robert's estate.> (Robert m.1st, 28 Dec. 1687, Plymouth, Sarah BARTLETT[4] (Benjamin[3], Mary Warren[2]) <MD 13:204>, who d. 20 Feb. 1687/8, Plymouth <MD 15:214>.)

9. **Rebeckah COOKE**[3], b. (   ), d. aft. 11 Dec. 1675 (fath.will) <MD 3:236-42>.

———

IV. **HESTER COOKE**[2], b. c1620, prob. Leyden, Holland, d. prob. pre 7 Dec. 1675 (not ment. in will of son John) <MD 24:85; MDP:161 (poss. after 21 May 1669 if she acknowledged a 9 May deed from her hus. to son)>; m. (21 Nov.) 1644, Plymouth, **Richard WRIGHT** <MD 3:101,13:86>, b. c1608, d. 9 June 1691, ae about 83, Plymouth <MD 4:165,16:62; Plymouth ChR 1:271>. (See COOKE Probate Appendix for will of Richard WRIGHT.)

6 WRIGHT Children: <MBD 1:316>

1. **Adam WRIGHT**[3], b. c1645, Plymouth, d. 20 Sept. 1724, 79th or 80th yr, Plympton <Plympton VR: 534; MD 1:178,4:239>; m.1st pre 1680, **Sarah SOULE**[3], (dau of John SOULE[2] & Rebecca SIMMONS - see SOULE Family). Adam m.2nd, c1699, prob. Plymouth, **Mehitable BARROW** <MD 11:242>, (dau of Robert BARROW & Ruth BONUM), b. prob. Plymouth, d. aft. 1744. <See MBD 1:316 for 6 chil. by 1st wf and 4 chil. by 2nd wf.> (Mehitable m.2nd, 13 June (or Dec.) 1744, Plympton, John WASHBURN <Plympton VR.>) (See COOKE Probate Appendix for will of Adam WRIGHT.)

2. **John WRIGHT**[3], b. (   ) <MDP:161 (called 2nd son in 1669 deed from father)>, d. betw. 7 Dec. 1675 (will) - 7 June 1676 (pr.), unm. <MD 24:84-6>. (See COOKE Probate Appendix for will of John WRIGHT.)

3. **Esther WRIGHT**[3], b. betw. Jan.-Mar. 1649, Plymouth <PCR 8:8>, d. 28 May 1717, 68th yr, Middleboro <Middleboro Dths.:201; MD 15:101>; m. c1676/7, Plymouth, **Ephraim TINKHAM**[3] <MD 24:85 (aft. 9 June 1676 when, unmarried, she signed for portion of brother John's estate)>. (See BROWN Family.)

4. **Isaac WRIGHT**[3], b. 26 Aug. 1652, Plymouth <PCR 8:14; MD 16:238>, d. betw. 11 Dec. 1675 (witnessed will of Jacob Cooke) <MD 3:239> - 7 June 1676 (sett. estate) <PCR 5:200; MBD 1:316, 404>, unm.

5. **Samuel WRIGHT**[3], b. (   ), d. betw. 7 Dec. 1675 (ment. in brother John's will) <MD 24:84-6> - 9 June 1676 (did not receipt estate of brother John) <MD 24:84-6>.

6. **Mary WRIGHT**[3], b. c1654 (or later), Plymouth, d. aft. 1 Nov. 1711 <Plymouth Co.PR #16232, 3:95 (adm. est. of son John)>, m. pre 1685, **Hugh PRICE**, b. (   ), d. pre 8 June 1691 <MD 4:165 (she is called widow in fath. will)>. <See Boston Rcd.Com.10:56 for bth. 1 chil. and MD 2:41 for 1 chil.>

———

V. **MARY COOKE**[2], b. c1626 (betw. Mar.-May 1627), Plymouth <MD 1:149,3:98,105>, d. 21 Mar. 1714, 88th yr, Middleboro <Middleboro Dths.:194>; m. 26 Dec. 1645, Plymouth, **John TOMSON** <PCR 2:94; MD 3:101,105,13:86,19:95,30:49; Plymouth Court Orders 2:109,125,147 (On 27 Oct. 1646 John was fined for incontinency with wife before marriage, which indicates their first child was born too soon after marriage)>, b. c1616/7, d. 16 June 1696, 80th yr, Middleboro, Nemasket g.s. <Middleboro Dths:194; MD 2:43,159,4:22,19:95,30:52. His epitah reads: "Death is a debt to nature due/Which I have paid and so must you.">

12 TOMSON Children: <MBD 1:384; MD 14:86,30:51>

1. **Adam TOMSON**[3], b. pre Sept. 1646, Plymouth (the child born too soon), d. c1648, ae about 1y6m, Plymouth <MD 30:49,52>.

2. **John TOMSON**[3], b. (Dec.) 1648, Plymouth <PCR 8:5 (rec. betw. 30 Nov.—26 Dec.); MD 15:27,30:51-2>, d. 11 Feb. 1648/9, Plymouth <PCR 8:5; MD 15:28,30:51-2>.

3. **John TOMSON**[3], b. 24 Nov. 1649, Plymouth <PCR 8:8; MD 16:121,30:51>, d. 25 Nov. 1725, 77th yr, Middleboro <Middleboro Dths:194 (says 5th); MD 14:219 (says 25th)>; m. c1680, **Mary TINKHAM**[3] <MD 30:52>, (See BROWN Family). <See MBD 1:395-6 & Middleboro VR 1:2,3,5,7 for 12 chil.; MD 1:221 (3), 2:41 (8), 2:104 (1).> (See COOKE Probate Appendix for will of John TOMSON.)

4. **Mary TOMSON**[3], b. c1651, Plymouth <MD 19:136,30:52>, d. aft. 15 June 1723 (hus.will), prob.
    Dartmouth <MD 16:231,30:52>; m. c1673, **Thomas TABER** <Torrey:725; MD 30:52>, (son of Philip
    TABER & Lydia MASTERS), bpt. Feb. 1646, Yarmouth/Martha's Vineyard <Little Compt.Fam.:645-6>,
    d. 11 Nov. 1730, Dartmouth <RI Gen.Dict.:195>. <See MBD 1:397-8, Dartmouth VR and MSR:156
    for bth. 10 chil.> (Thomas m.1st, Hester COOKE[3] (John[2]).) (See COOKE Probate Appendix for
    will of Thomas TABER.)

5. **Hester/Esther TOMSON**[3], b. 28 July 1652, Barnstable <MD 14:86,30:51-2>, d. betw. 26 Oct. 1705
    (hus. will) - 12 Sept. 1706 (hus. adm.), Weymouth <MD 23:72-4,30:52>; m. c1675, Middleboro,
    William REED <MD 23:72>, (son of William REED & Avis CHAPMAN), b. 15 Dec. 1639, Weymouth
    <Weymouth VR 1:252>, d. betw. 26 Oct. 1705 - 12 Sept. 1706 (will & adm.), Weymouth <MD 23:72-
    74>. <See MBD 1:388 for bth. 9 chil. and Weymouth VR 1:249 (3), 1:251 (1), 1:252 (1).> (See
    COOKE Probate Appendix for will of William REED.)

6. **Elizabeth TOMSON**[3], b. 28 Jan. 1654, Barnstable <MD 14:86,30:51-2>, d. prob. betw. 14 Jan. -
    21 Sept. 1717 (will of her father-in-law) <Suffolk Co.PR 20:224>; m. aft. 22 Sept. 1687 (mar-
    riage bond), **Thomas SWIFT** <NEHGR 64:189; MD 30:110 mistakenly says she m. William Swift>,
    (son of Thomas SWIFT & Elizabeth VOSE), b. 30 July 1659, Dorchester <Dorchester VR:7>, d. pre
    23 Apr. 1696 (will of his father-in-law) <MD 4:22-4>. <See Weymouth VR 1:286 for bth. 1 chil
    Thomas, 15 Nov. 1687.>

7. **Sarah TOMSON**[3], b. 4 Apr. 1657, Barnstable <MD 14:86, 30:51-2>, d. aft. 19 June 1696 (will)
    <MD 30:52; poss. the Sarah TOMSON who d. 2 Dec. 1730, ae 73, unm., S. Weymouth g.s. <MBD 1:
    384.>

8. **Lydia TOMSON**[3], b. 5 Oct. 1659, Barnstable <MD 14:86,30:51-2>, d. 14 Mar. 1741/2, 83rd yr,
    Middleboro g.s. <MD 16:18; Middleboro Dths.:167>; m. 14 Dec. 1693, Duxbury, **James SOULE**[3]
    (John[2]). See SOULE Family.

9. **Jacob TOMSON**[3], b. 24 Apr. 1662, Barnstable <MD 14:86,24:167,30:51-2>, d. 1 Sept. 1726, 65th
    yr, Middleboro g.s. <Middleboro VR 1:29; Middleboro Dths.:194; MD 14:219,30:52>; m. 28 Dec.
    1693, Middleboro, **Abigail WADSWORTH** <Middleboro VR 1:7; MD 2:43,9:248,24:167,25:38,30:52>,
    (dau of John WADSWORTH & Abigail ANDREWS), b. 25 Oct. 1670, Duxbury <MD 9:172,248,24:167>,
    d. 15 Jan. 1744, 75th yr, Halifax, bur. The Green, Middleboro <Middleboro Dths.:194; MD 3:
    30,14:217,24:167; Halifax VR:1>. <For bth. 10 chil. see MBD 1:392, MD 2:41,42, 105, 201, 3:
    84,25:20 and Middleboro VR 1:5,6,8,13,14.> (See COOKE Probate Appendix for will of Abigail
    (WADSWORTH) Tomson.)

10. **Thomas TOMSON**[3], b. 19 Oct. 1664, Barnstable <MD 14:86,25:175,30:51,53>, d. 26 Oct. 1742, ae
    78, Thompson St. cem., Halifax <Halifax VR:1; MD 3:30,14:9,25:175,30:53; MBD 1:409 #134a (His
    epitaph reads: "His days were spent in doing good/In life & death Faith was his food/Like him
    be pious, just and kind/Then peace & joy at death you'll find."); m. 13 Dec. 1715, Middleboro
    Mary MORTON[4] <Middleboro VR 1:11; MD 2:158,25:175,30:53>, (dau of John MORTON & Mary RING[3]
    (Deborah Hopkins[2]) - see HOPKINS family), b. 15 Dec. 1689, Plymouth <MD 1:209,25:175>, d. 20
    Mar. 1781, 91s yr, Thompson St. cem., Halifax <Halifax VR:5; MD 14:8,25:175>. <See MBD 1:402
    & MD 25:175-6 for bth. 7 chil. and MD 3:85,86,234,4:68,6:228 (2),7:242.>. (See COOKE Probate
    Appendix for will of Mary (MORTON) Tomson & estate of Thomas TOMSON.)

11. **Peter TOMSON**[3], b. c1666-9, Barnstable, d. pre 29 Apr. 1731, prob. Plympton <MD 22:135; MDP:
    246>; m. c1699, **Sarah (   )** <MD 22:135,30:53>, b. c1669/70, d. 24 Oct. 1742, 73rd yr, Thomp-
    son St. cem., Halifax <Halifax VR:1; MD 3:30,14:9,22:135,30:53>. <See MBD 1:402, Plymouth VR
    1:54 and MD 4:111 for bth. 4 chil.> (See COOKE Probate Appendix for estate of Peter TOMSON.)

12. **Mercy TOMSON**[3], b. c1671, prob. Barnstable <MD 30:53>, d. 19 Apr. 1756, 85th yr, unm., Thomp-
    son St. cem., Halifax <MD 14:8,19:135,30:53>. (See COOKE Probate Appendix for estate of Mer-
    cy TOMSON.)

COOKE PROBATE APPENDIX

Will of **Caleb COOKE**[3] (Jacob[2]): <MD 15:136-9; Plymouth Co.PR 4:324>
...10 Feb. 1721, ment. wf Jean; sons John COOKE, Caleb COOKE, James COOKE, Joseph COOKE; grandchildren, chil. of dau Jean HARRIS; daus Ann JOHNSON, Elizabeth JOHNSON, Mary CARVER wf of Robert
Sworn to 31 Mar. 1722.

Will of **Jane COOKE** (widow of Jacob[2]): <MD 15:139>
...8 Apr. 1736, ment. son-in-law Robert CARVER; eldest son John COOKE; heirs of son Caleb COOKE
Jr. dec'd; sons James COOKE, Joseph COOKE; dau Anne JOHNSON, wf of James JOHNSON late of Midleton
in the colony of Connecticut; heirs of dau Jane HARRIS dec'd; dau Mary CARVER wf of Robert; dau
Betty JOHNSON wf of Robert JOHNSON of North Yarmouth in the county of York; grandchild Jane JOHN-
SON alias Morton. Pr. 24 Apr. 1736.

==
Will of **Francis COOKE**[1]: <MD 2:24-7; Plymouth Co.PR 2:2:1-2>
...7 10mth (Dec.) 1659, ment. wf Hester and son John COOKE. Inv. taken 1 May 1663. <MD 3:103> An

agreement of heirs, dated 8 June 1666, ment. wf Hester and children, viz: John COOKE, Jacob COOKE Hester WRIGHT wf of Richard and Mary TOMPSON wf of John.
==
Will of **Francis COOKE³ (Jacob²)**: (yeoman) <MD 18:147-50; MDP:170; Plymouth Co.PR #4874,10:328>
...28 Oct. 1732, ment. son Caleb COOK; chil. of dec'd son Robert COOK; dau Elizabeth COOK; chil. of dec'd son Francis COOK; dau Susanna STERTEVANT; chil. of dau Sarah COLE. Codicil, 15 May 1736 ment. son Caleb and daughters before mentioned. Pr. 18 Sept. 1746.
==
Will of **Jacob COOKE²**: <MD 3:236-42; Plymouth Co.PR 3:2:1-4>
...11 Dec. 1675, ment. wf Elizabeth; 3 youngest daus.; eldest son Caleb COOKE; son Jacob COOKE; brother John THOMSON; land of brother WRIGHT; son Francis COOKE; "6 daus", viz: Mary, (worn)kah; cozen Daniell WILCOCKES. Inv. taken 18 Dec. 1675.
==
Will of **Jacob COOKE³ (Jacob²)**: (yeoman) <MD 21:42-4; MDP:173; Plymouth Co.PR #4883,10:419>
...16 Oct. 1728, "being aged", ment. sons William COOK, Jacob COOK, Josiah COOK, John COOK; daus Damaris COOK (unm.), Lydia, Rebeckah and Margaret. Pr. 21 May 1747.
==
Will of **John COOKE²**: <MD 3:33-6; MSR:65; Bristol Co.PR 1:139-40>
...9 Nov. 1694, ment. wf Sarah; son in law Arthur HATHAWAY & his wf Sarah my dau; son in law Stephen WEST & his wf Mercey my dau; Jonathan DELANO; grandson Thomas TABER; granddau. Hester PERRY. Pr. 16 Apr. 1696. Inv. taken 7 Dec. 1695. (Although MFIP #2 says wf Sarah presented the inv. 7 Dec. 1696, this is an error. First, Bowman states this date is "plainly a mistake of the Register for 1695; and, Sarah did not present the inventory, "Aarther" HATHAWAY & Thomas TABER did. Wf Sarah "being a very antient woman and unable to travile far" made oath to the inventory on 10 Apr 1696.)
==
Will of **Arthur HATHAWAY**: <MD 16:110-2; Bristol Co.PR 3:68>
...9 Feb. 1709/10, ment. sons John HATHAWAY, Thomas HATHAWAY, Jonathan HATHAWAY; daus Mary HAMMOND, Lydia SISSON, Hannah CADMAN; wf Sarah. Pr. 6 Feb. 1711/2. (Interesting note: Receipt of son Jonathan to his mother Sarah, 26 Feb. 1712/3, ment. money he paid Dr. SWEET when his father` had a broken leg in 1709.)
==
Will of **Experience MITCHELL**: <MD 4:150,32:97-101; MDP:176; Plymouth Co.PR 1:44-5>
...5 Dec. 1684, ment. wf Mary; sons Edward MITCHELL, John MITCHELL; grandson Experience MITCHELL the son of son John; daus Mary SHAW, Sarah HAYWARD, Hannah HAYWARD; grandson Thomas MITCHELL; granddau. Mary MITCHELL. Inv. taken 14 May 1689.
==
Will of **William REED/READ**: <MD 23:72-4,30:49-53; Suffolk Co.PR 16:173,174>
...26 Oct. 1705, ment. wf Hester; eldest son William READ; sons John REED, Jacob REED; daus Bashua PORTER, Mercy WHITMARSH, Mary REED, Hester READ, Sarah READ (youngest dau). Pr. 12 Sept. 1706.
==
Will of **John RICKARD**: <MDP:176; Plymouth Co.PR #16907, 3:138>
...20 Apr. 1711, ment. wf Mary; sons John RICKARD (eldest son), James RICKARD (under 21); 4 daus, Mercy CUSHING, Mary RICKARD, Hester RICKARD, Elisabeth RICKARD; negro man Toby "at the expiration of ye term of tenn years...shall have and enjoy his freedom and not any longer be held and kept as a slave". Witnesses made oath 20 June 1712.
==
Estate of **Phillip TABER**: <MD 16:226-31; Bristol Co.Deeds 17:210>
...25 Jan. 1714/5, "Whereas our honoured father Phillip Taber of Dartmouth deceased being suddenly surprised by Death"...Settlement among following chil., viz: Phillip TABER, Thomas EARL & wf Mary, Thomas BROWNELL & wf Ester, Thomas CORY & wf Sarah, Joseph MOSHER & wf Lidia, John MACUMBER & wf Bithiah, John TABER and Abigail TABER.
==
Will of **Capt. Thomas TABER**: (yeoman) <MD 16:231-4; Bristol Co.PR 7:515>
...15 June 1723, ment. wf Mary; sons Thomas TABER, Joseph TABER, John TABER; dau Bethyah BLACKWELL wf of Caleb; sons Jacob TABER, Phillip TABER; daus Esther PERRY (& her hus.), Lidia KINNEY, Sarah HART (& her hus.), Mary MORTON (& her hus.), Abigail TABER (& her hus.). Pr. 20 Mar. 1732/3
==
Will of **Abigail (WADSWORTH) Tomson**: <MD 25:20-25; Plymouth Co.PR 9:411>
...16 Apr. 1739, ment. daus Abigail PACKARD, Mercy BENNET, Lidya PACKARD, Hannah READ, Ester BENNET, Mary TOMSON; grandson Moses the son of dau Abigail; sons Jacob TOMSON, John TOMSON, Barnabas TOMSON, Caleb TOMSON. Pr. 4 Feb. 1744.
==
Will of **Lieut. John TOMSON**: <MD 4:22-9,19:95; Plymouth Co.PR #20588, 1:241-45>
...23 Apr. 1696, ment. wf Mary; sons John TOMSON, Jacob TOMSON, Thomas TOMSON, Peter TOMSON; daus Mary TABOR, Esther READ, Elizabeth SWIFT; grandson Thomas SWIFT (under 21); daus Sarah TOMSON, Lidia SOUL, Mercy TOMSON. Agreement of heirs dated 19 June 1696.
==
Estate of **Mercy TOMSON³ (Mary Cooke²)**: <MD 19:135-6; MDP:236; Plymouth Co.PR #20604,14:67,71>
...Adm. 3 May 1756. Distribution of £81.13.2., sd dec'd leaving no surviving brothers or sisters, the administrator is directed to pay out to the surviving children of several brothers & sisters as follows: to the children of John TOMSON, Jacob TOMSON, Peter TOMSON, all dec'd & brothers of the sd Mercy/Marcy, £10.4.1. and also a like sum to the children of Mary TABOUR, Esther REED, Elizabeth SWIFT & Lydia SOUL, dec'd & sisters of the sd Marcy.
==

Estate of **Peter TOMSON**[3] (**Mary Cooke**[2]): <MD 22:135; MDP:246; Plymouth Co.PR #20625, 6:92>
...23 Sept. 1731, Division of heirs, viz: widow Sarah, eldest son Peter TOMSON, sons James TOMSON & Joseph TOMSON; dau Sarah BOSWORTH/BOZWORTH wf of Nehemiah.

Estate of **Thomas TOMSON**[3] (**Mary Cooke**[2]): <MD 25:177-85; MDP:246; Plymouth Co.PR #20655, 9:202>
...18 Dec. 1743, Divison of heirs, viz: widow Mary and children Ruben TOMSON (eldest son), Ebenezer TOMSON, Zebadiah TOMSON, Thomas TOMSON, Amasa TOMSON, Mary WATERMAN wf of Samuel.

Will of **Mary (MORTON) Tomson:** (widow) <MD 25:185-6; MDP:247; Plymouth Co.PR #20610, 28:182>
...1 May 1756, ment. sons Reuben TOMSON, Thomas TOMSON, Amasa TOMSON, Ebenezer TOMSON, Zebadiah TOMSON and heirs of dau Mary WATERMAN dec'd. Pr. 4 July 1781.

Will of **John WASHBURN Sr.:** <MD 15:248; MDP:177; Plymouth Co.PR 1:84,86>
...30 Oct. 1686, ment. wf Elizabeth; brother Phillip WASHBURN to be taken care of by son John WASHBURN; sons Thomas WASHBURN, Joseph WASHBURN, Samuel WASHBURN, Jonathan WASHBURN, Benjamin WASHBURN, James WASHBURN (minor); dau Mary; dau Elizabeth & her hus.; dau Jane; dau Sarah (minor) brother Edward MITCHEL. Inv. taken 19 Nov. 1686 (states he d. 12 Nov. 1686).

Will of **Daniel WILCOX:** <MD 16:239-43; Bristol Co.PR>
...9 June 1702, ment. wf Elizabeth; eldest son Daniel WILLCOCK & his eldest son Daniel; unnamed chil. of dec'd son Samuel WILCOX; sons Stephen WILLCOCK, John WILLCOCK, Edward WILLCOCK, Thomas WILLCOCK; dau Mary EARLE wf of John; dau Lidiah; dau Sarah BRIGGS wf of Edward; dau Susannah WILCOCK. Inv. 16 July 1702 (states he d. 2 July 1702).

Will of **Adam WRIGHT**[3] (**Hester Cooke**[2]): <MD 4:239-41; Plymouth Co.PR #23497,5:26-29>
...9 Apr. 1723, "grown to old age", ment. sons John WRIGHT, Isaac WRIGHT, Samuel WRIGHT, Moses WRIGHT; grandchildren Joshua PRATT & his sister Sarah, the chil. of dau Esther PRATT dec'd; dau Sarah FULLER wf of Seth; sons James WRIGHT & Nathan WRIGHT (both under 21); dau Mary GIFFORD wf of Jeremiah; dau Rachel BARLOW wf of Ebenezer; wf Mehitable. Inv. 10 Oct. 1724.

Will of **John WRIGHT**[3] (**Hester Cooke**[2]): <MD 24:84-6; MDP:161; Plymouth Co.PR 3:1:177>
...7 Dec. 1675, "being now to goe forth to warr", ment. brothers Isacke WRIGHT, Samuell WRIGHT; father Richard WRIGHT; brother Adam WRIGHT; sisters Ester WRIGHT and Mary. Inv. 8 June 1676.

Will of **Richard WRIGHT:** <MD 4:165-7; Plymouth Co.PR #23539, 1:101-103>
...8 June 1691, ment. three chil., Adam WRIGHT, Esther and Mary PRICE, widow. Inv. 19 June 1691.

NOTES:

JOHN CRACKSTONE

John Crackstone was from Colchester, England <MQ 40:117 (daughter's marr.banns)> but his year of birth is unknown. He died between 11 Jan.-10 Apr. 1621, Plymouth <MD 2:116;MQ 40:118>. The name of his wife and date of marriage is not known. It is possible, though unknown at this time, that he has descendants through his daughter Anna. Bradford:445 states, "John Crackston died in the first mortality, and about some five or six years after, his son died, having lost himself in the woods, his feet became frozen, which put him into a fever of which he died".

John had 2 known children:

I.   John, b. prob. Colchester, Eng., d. aft. 22 May 1627 <MD 1:149 (Cattle Division); 2:116; MQ 40:118>.

II. Anna, b. prob. Colchester, Eng. <MQ 40:117>, d. (   ); m. (banns) 12/22 Dec. 1618, Leiden, Thomas SMITH of Bury, Eng. <MQ 40:117;Stratton:274>

NOTES:

EDWARD DOTY/DOTEN

Edward Doty was born pre 1599 (if age 21 when he signed the Compact) <MD 1:79>. He was called "of London" which may or may not be his place of birth. He died 23 Aug. 1655, Plymouth <MD 3:87, 17:72; PCR 8:17; MSR:548>. According to Bradford's increasings & decreasings he was married twice but nothing is known about the first wife <MD 1:16>. Since a wife is not mentioned with Edward in the 22 May 1627 Cattle Division <MD 1:150 ("Dolton")>, his first marriage probably took place after 1627. Edward m.2nd, 6 Jan. 1634/5, Plymouth, Faith CLARKE <PCR 1:32; MD 13:83>, (dau of Thurston & Faith), b. c1619, prob. Eng. <Banks' Planters:121-4>. Faith was buried 21 Dec. 1675, Marshfield <Marshfield VR:9; MD 2:181,3:87>. (Faith m.2nd, 14 Mar. 1666/7, Plymouth, John PHIL-LIPS <PCR 8:31; MD 3:87,18:56; PCR 4:163-4 (pre-nuptial agreement to ensure her right to care for her children & her property)>, who d. betw. 20 Oct. 1691 (will) - 16 May 1692 (sworn) <Plymouth Co.PR 1:140>. John m.1st, 6 July 1654, Marshfield, Grace (   ) Holloway <VR:1; MD 2:4>, widow of William HOLLOWAY. Grace was killed by lightening with Jeremiah PHILLIPS and William SHURTLEFF and all were buried 24 June 1666 <Marshfield VR:10; MD 2:182; MSR:248>.) (See DOTY Probate Appen-dix for wills of Edward DOTY & Faith (CLARKE)(Doty) Phillips.)

(See: Mayflower Families in Progress, Edward Doty Of The Mayflower and His Descendants for Four Generations, by Marion B. Cushman, Richard Fetzer, Peter B. Hill, Robert S. Wakefield, FASG, 2nd Ed., 1993.)

Edward & Faith had 9 children: <MBD 1:413>

I.   Edward, b. by 1637, Plymouth
II.   John, b. c1640, Plymouth
III. Thomas, b. c1641/2, Plymouth
IV.   Samuel, b. c1643/4, Plymouth
V.   Desire, b. c1645/6, Plymouth
VI.   Elizabeth, b. c1647, Plymouth
VII. Isaac, b. 8 Feb. 1648/9, Plymouth
VIII. Joseph, b. 30 Apr. 1651, Plymouth
IX.   Mary, b. c1653, Plymouth

* * * * * * * * * *

I.   **EDWARD DOTY**[2], b. by 1637 <PCR 8:174,197 (freeman in 1658)>, d. 8 Feb. 1689/90, drowned, Ply-mouth Harbor <MD 5:210,16:62>; m. 25 Feb. 1662/3, Plymouth, **Sarah FAUNCE** <PCR 8:23;MD 13:204, 17:183; MSR:545 (says 26th)>, (dau of John FAUNCE & Patience MORTON), b. c1645, Plymouth, d. 27 June 1695, Plymouth <MD 16:63>. (Sarah m.2nd, 26 Apr. 1693, Plymouth, John BUCK <MD 13: 206,26:38> who d. betw. 4-21 Sept. 1697 <MD 14:128 (will & pr.)>.) (See DOTY Probate Appen-dix for estate of Edward DOTY.)

11 DOTY Children: <MD 1:143>

1. **Edward DOTY**[3], b. 20 May 1664, Plymouth <MD 1:143>, d. betw. 3 Mar. 1689/90 (father is called "Sr.") - 3 Dec. 1696, unm. <MD 5:210-4 (fath. est.)>.

2. **Sarah DOTY**[3], b. 9 June 1666, Plymouth <MD 1:143,25:3>, d. pre 16 Aug. 1759 (adm.) <MD 25:14; Plymouth Co.PR 11:212>; m.1st, 21 June 1687, Plymouth, **James WARREN**[3] <MD 13:204,25:3>, (son of Nathaniel WARREN[2] & Sarah WALKER). See WARREN Family. Sarah m.2nd, 28 Sept. 1726, Ply-mouth, **John BACON** <MD 14:71,25:5,34:117>, (son of Nathaniel BACON & Hannah MAYO), b. "beginn-ing" June 1661, Barnstable <Barnstable VR 1:342; MD 2:214>, d. 20 Aug. 1731, 67th yr, Barns-table <Otis 1:26>. (John m.1st, 17 June 1686, Barnstable, Mary HAWES[4] <MD 2:215; Otis 1:33>, (dau of John HAWES & Desire GORHAM[3] (Desire Howland[2]) - see HOWLAND Family), b. 10 June 1664, Yarmouth <Yarmouth VR 1:126; MD 2:207>, d. 5 Mar. 1725/6, ae 61, Barnstable <Otis 1:33>. They had 8 chil. <MD 2:215; Otis 1:35>.) (See DOTY Probate Appendix for will of John BACON.)

3. **John DOTY**[3], b. 4 Aug. 1668, Plymouth <MD 1:143>, d. 8 Feb. 1689/90, unm. (drowned with father in Plymouth Harbor) <MD 16:62>.

4. **Mary DOTY**[3], (twin), b. 9 July 1671, Plymouth <MD 1:143>, d. pre 6 Apr. 1742 (hus.adm.) <Early CT PR 3:377-8>; m. 21 or 26 Dec. 1699, Plymouth, **Joseph ALLEN/ALLYN** <MD 13:207,14:35>, (son of Samuel ALLYN & Hannah WALLEY), b. 7 Apr. 1671, Barnstable <MD 2:213; Otis 1:9>, d. pre 6 Apr. 1742, Wethersfield CT (adm.) <Early CT PR 3:377-8; MBD 1:421>. <See MBD 1:421 for bth. 7 chil., MD 3:12 (2 at Plymouth) & Wethersfield CT VR 1:75 (4).> (See DOTY Probate Appendix for estate of Joseph ALLYN.)

5. **Martha DOTY**[3], (twin), b. 9 July 1671, Plymouth <MD 1:143>, d. betw. 26 Aug. 1741 - 12 Sept. 1748 (hus. will & pr.) <MD 27:135-40>; m. 23 Dec. 1696, Plymouth, **Thomas MORTON**[3] <MD 13:206>, (son of Ephraim MORTON[2] (George[1]) & Ann COOPER), b. c1667, Plymouth <MD 17:46,48>, d. betw.

26 Aug. 1741 - 12 Sept. 1748 (will & pr.) <MD 27:135-40>. <See MBD 1:420, MD 3:12 & Plymouth VR for bth. 6 chil.> (See DOTY Probate Appendix for will of Thomas MORTON.)

6. **Elizabeth DOTY**[3], b. 22 Dec. 1673, Plymouth <MD 1:143>, d. 16 or 17 Dec. 1745, ae 72, Marshfield g.s. <Marshfield VR:93; MD 9:168 (g.s. says 17th), 22:36 (16th), 31:24>, m. c1696, **Tobias OAKMAN** <MD 22:36, 5:212-3 (pre 3 Dec., her father's est.)>, (son of Samuel OAKMAN & Mary BOARDEN), b. c1664, Maine <ME NH Gen.Dict.:517 (says Saco ME); MBD 1:435, #14 (Marshfield Town Clerk in 1897 says Scarboro ME)>, d. 16 June 1750, 86th yr, Marshfield g.s. <Marshfield VR:98; MD 9:169,22:36>. <See MBD 1:417 for bth. 8 chil. and Marshfield VR:25 (2), 44-5 (4); MD 6:20 (2), 8:177 (1), 179 (3), 31:122 (1) and MD 22:36.> (See DOTY Probate Appendix for will of Tobias OAKMAN.)

7. **Patience DOTY**[3], b. 7 July 1676, Plymouth <MD 1:143>, d. 26 Feb. 1690/1, Plymouth <MD 16:62>.

8. **Mercy DOTY**[3], b. 6 Feb. 1678, Plymouth <MD 1:143>, d. 30 Nov. 1682, Plymouth <MD 1:143>.

9. **Samuel DOTY**[3], b. 17 May 1681, Plymouth <MD 1:143>, d. 26 Jan. 1750, 70th yr, Saybrook CT <MFIP #15; Doty Gen.:36>; m.1st, 3 Dec. 1706, Saybrook, **Anne BUCKINGHAM** <Saybrook CT VR L2: 242>, (dau of Thomas BUCKINGHAM & Hester HOSMER), b. 2 Aug. 1687, Saybrook CT <Saybrook CT VR:10, 2:242>, d. 16 Dec. 1745, 59th yr, Saybrook CT <MFIP #15; Doty Gen.:36>. **Samuel** m.2nd, c1746/7, **Abiah (   )** <Saybrook CT Deeds 7:245>, d. aft. 24 Mar. 1759 <Saybrook CT Deeds 7: 574>. <See Saybroook CT VR L2:242 for bth. 2 chil.> (Abiah m.2nd pre 5 Oct. 1753, Benjamin TOWNER <Saybrook CT Deeds 7:245>.)

10. **Mercy DOTY**[3], b. 23 Sept. 1684, Plymouth <MD 1:143>, d. (   ); m. 24 Nov. 1713, Saybrook CT, **Daniel PRATT** <Saybrook CT VR:32>, (son of John PRATT & Mary ANDREWS), b. 13 Jan. 1680/1, Saybrook CT <Saybrook CT VR:14>, d. pre 11 Mar. 1758 <Saybrook CT Deeds 7:436>. <See Saybrook CT VR:32 for bth. 7 chil.>

11. **Benjamin DOTY/DOTEN**[3], b. 30 May 1689, Plymouth <MD 1:143>, d. pre 25 June 1770 (survey) <Saybrook CT Deeds 8:501>; m. 2 Oct. 1716, Saybrook CT, **Hester BEMEN** <Saybrook CT VR 1:75>, (dau of Samuel BEMEN & Hester BUCKINGHAM), b. (   ) <MFIP #17>, d. pre 19 Mar. 1773 <Saybrook CT Deeds 8:326>. <See MFIP #17 for 11 chil.>

II. **JOHN DOTY/DOTEN/DOUGHTY**[3], b. c1640, Plymouth (prob. 21 in 1661) <Plymouth TR 1:44>, d. 8 May 1701, Plymouth <Plymouth VR:136; Plymouth TR 1:203; MD 6:77,16:63>; m.1st, c1667, Plymouth, **Elizabeth COOKE**[3], (dau of Jacob COOKE[2] & Damaris HOPKINS[2] - see COOKE family). **John** m.2nd, 22 Nov. 1694, Plymouth, **Sarah JONES**[4] <MD 26:37; PN&Q 3:121>, (dau of Joseph JONES & Patience LITTLE[3] (Anna Warren[2]) - see WARREN family), b. 12 Sept. 1671, Hingham <Hist.Hingham 2:387>, d. aft. 10 July 1752 (hus.est.) <MD 6:81; Plymouth Co.PR 12:86,226>. (Sarah m.2nd, 23 Aug. 1704, Joseph PETERSON[3] <MD 14:35>, (son of John PETERSON & Mary SOULE[2] - see SOULE family.)

12 DOTY Children: (9 by 1st wf <MD 1:144>, 3 by 2nd <MD 1:206>; 1st 7 bpt. 1686 <Plymouth ChR 1:258>)

1. **John DOTY/DOTEN**[3], b. 24 Aug. 1668, Plymouth <MD 1:44, 18:57; PCR 8:32>, d. betw. 29 Apr. 1746 (will) - 14 July 1747 (pr.), of Plympton <MD 20:27-30>; m.1st, 2 Feb. 1692/3, Plymouth, **Mehitable NELSON** <MD 13:206,26:36; PN&Q 3:120>, (dau of John NELSON & Sarah WOOD), b. 5 Apr. 1670 <MD 1:141 (Plymouth), 220 (Middleboro)>, d. pre 25 Apr. 1745 (hus.remarr.). **John** m.2nd, 25 Apr. 1745, Plympton, **Hannah SHERMAN** <Plympton VR:308>, (dau of Samuel & Hannah), b. 20 Feb 1688, Marshfield <Marshfield VR:46; MD 9:183>, d. 15 Apr. 1754, 67th yr, Plymouth <MD 15:213, 20:27>. <See MBD 1:426 & MD 2:163 for bth. 6 chil.> (Note: The Plymouth Quarter Sessions, c1718-1723, p.12 state: "1st Tues. Mar. 1719, **John Doty** Sen[r] of Plimton Moving to ye Court Concerning ye Child of Lydia Jackson of Plymouth of which he was Convict to be ye reputed Father at ye Sessions of this Court on ye 1st Tuesday of March 1718" - he moved that the child be boarded out or the weekly payments stopped.) (See DOTY Probate Appendix for wills of John & Hannah DOTY.)

2. **Edward DOTY**[3], b. 28 June 1671, Plymouth <PCR 8:32; MD 1:144,18:57>, d. pre 15 Apr. 1701 (fath will) <MD 6:77-81>.

3. **Jacob DOTY**[3], b. 24 May 1673, Plymouth <PCR 8:32; MD 1:144, 18:57 (says 24th)>, d. pre 15 Apr. 1701 (fath.will) <MD 6:77-81>.

4. **Elizabeth DOTY**[3], b. 10 Feb. 1675/6, Plymouth <MD 1:144>, d. 1772 <MFIP #22; m. 12 Dec. 1698, Plymouth, **Joshua MORSE/MORSS** <MD 13:207>, (son of Joseph & Mary), b. c1675, prob. Beverly, d. 1754 <MFIP #22>. <8 chil., see MBD 1:425 & MD 2:163 (7) and MFIP #22,#136 (1).>

5. **Isaac DOTY/DOTTY/DOTEN**[3], b. 25 Oct. 1678, Plymouth <MD 1:144,25:164>, d. 15 Apr. 1725, 46th yr, Plymouth g.s. <MD 25:164; Drew:135 (says 13th)>; m. 17 Mar. 1702/3, Plymouth, **Martha FAUNCE** <MD 13:207,25:164>, (dau of Thomas FAUNCE & Jean NELSON), b. 16 Dec. 1680, Plymouth <PCR 8:32; MD 1:147,25:164>, d. 9 Sept. 1745, 65th yr, Plymouth g.s. <MD 25:164; Drew:135 (says 63rd yr)>. <See MBD 1:425, MD 2:224-5 and MD 25:164 for bth. 9 chil. (incl.twins).> (See DOTY Probate Appendix for estate of Isaac DOTY.)

6. **Samuel DOTY**[3], b. 31 Jan. 1682/3, Plymouth <MD 1:144,33:114>, d. pre 20 May 1740, Plymouth (adm.) <MDP:259; Plymouth Co.PR #6629,8:189,270>; m. 10 Apr. 1727, Plymouth, **Mercy COBB** <MD 14:72>, (dau of Ebenezer COBB & Mercy HOLMES), b. 1 Jan. 1704/5, Plymouth <MD 2:19>, d. ( ). <See MD 14:240 for bth. 5 chil.> (Mercy m.2nd, 7 June 1743, Plymouth, Cornelius HOLMES <MD 17:3>.)

7. **Elisha DOTY/DOTEN**[3], b. 13 July 1686, Plymouth <MD 1:144,19:176>, d. betw. 24 Dec. 1753 (will) - 17 July 1754 (pr.) <MD 19:178-9>; m. 1 Feb. 1708/9, Marblehead, **Hannah HORTON** <Marblehead VR 2:130; MD 19:177>, b. ( ), d. 19 Jan. 1767, Plymouth <Plymouth ChR 1:396>. <See MD 5: 100, Plymouth TR 1:65 & MBD 1:423 for bth. 9 chil.> (See DOTY Probate Appendix for will of Elisha DOTY.)

8. **Josiah DOTY/DOTEN**[3], b. Oct. 1689, Plymouth <MD 1:144,33:114>, d. 15 Jan. 1767, Plymouth <Plymouth ChR 1:396>; m. c1714, ( ), **Abigail ( )** <MFIP #26>, b. ( ), d. ( ). <See MBD 1:427 & MD 13:171 for bth. 5 chil. and Plymouth ChR 1:221 for bpt. chil.>

9. **Martha DOTY**[3], b. Oct. 1692, Plymouth <MD 1:144>, d. 3 May 1775, Plymouth <Plymouth ChR 1:404> m. 7 Oct. 1718, Plymouth, **Ebenezer CURTIS** <MD 14:38>, (son of Francis CURTICE & Hannah SMITH) b. ( ), d. aft. May 1742 (chairmaker, sued for debt) <Plymouth Co.Court Rec.6:333>. <See MD 7:208 for 4 chil.> (Ebenezer m.1st, 19 Jan. 1709/10, Plymouth, Mary TINKHAM[4] <MD 14:36>, (dau of Helkiah TINKHAM[3] (Mary Brown[2]) - see BROWN family), b. 13 Aug. 1687, Plymouth <MD 4: 110>, d. 17 Mar. 1717/8, 31st yr, Plymouth <Drew:210>; they had 4 chil. <MD 7:208>.)

10. **Sarah DOTY**[3], b. 19 Feb. 1695/6, Plymouth <MD 1:206>, d. aft. 15 Apr. 1701 (fath.will) <MD 6: 77-81>.

11. **Patience DOTY**[3], b. 3 July 1697, Plymouth <MD 1:206>, d. 18 Feb. 1784, 87th yr, Marshfield g.s. <Marshfield VR:399; MD 12:55>; m. 22 Jan. 1718/9, Duxbury, **Kenelm BAKER**[4] <MD 11:25; Duxbury VR:248>, (son of Kenelm BAKER & Sarah BRADFORD[3] (William[2]) - see BRADFORD family), b. 3 Nov. 1695, Marshfield <MD 5:235,24:27>, d. 22 May 1771, 76th yr, Marshfield g.s. <MD 12:55; Marshfield VR:398>. <For bth. 8 chil. see MBD 1:423 & MD 9:186 (3),30:147 (2),154 (2), 31: 164 (1); for 7 chil. see Marshfield VR:49 (3),79 (2),87 (2).> (See DOTY Probate Appendix for will of Kenelm BAKER.)

12. **Desire DOTY**[3], b. 19 Apr. 1699, Plymouth <MD 1:206,33:114>, d. ( ); m. 23 Aug. 1722, Plymouth, **George BARROW/BARROWS** <MD 14:39; 18:143 (int.)>, (son of George BARROWS & Patience SIMMONS), b. 11 Mar. 1698, Plymouth <MD 2:163>, d. ( ) <MD 21:74 (aft. 29 Sept. 1757 if he is the George BARROW Jr. (and not his son) who is mentioned in the estate of Ichabod SOUTHWORTH.)> <See MBD 1:423 & Plympton VR:13,14 for bth. 2 chil.>

III. **THOMAS DOTY/DOTEY**[2], b. c1641/2, Plymouth, d. 4 or 5 Dec. 1678, Plymouth <MD 4:233 (non-cupative will "comitted in writing December the 5th within 24 houres after the Death of the said Thomas DOTEY")>; m.1st, c1674, Plymouth, **Mary CHURCHILL** <MD 1:143 (by Dec. 1675, bth. chil.); TAG 36:1; Stratton:285>, (dau of John CHURCHILL & Hannah PONTUS), b. 1 Aug. 1654, Plymouth <PCR 8:16; MD 17:71>, d. betw. 1676 (bth.chil.) - 1678. (Mary confessed to the Court 17 Jan. 1671/2 that she had become pregnant in July or Aug. 1671 by Thomas DOTEY who shortly afterwards left the colony <PCR 5:83>. She was fined six pounds on 5 June 1672 <PCR 5:94> which indicates her child (Martha) had been born. On 30 Oct. 1672, Mary sued Thomas for having begotten her with child and she was awarded all of his property <PCR 7:173-4>. Thomas returned to Plymouth by 29 Oct. 1673 <PCR 5:133>.) **Thomas** m.2nd, c1678, prob. Plymouth, **Mary ( )** <TAG 36:1; Stratton:285>, b. c1660, d. aft. 18 Oct. 1725 <Plymouth Co.Deeds 19:152>. (Thomas' 2nd wf Mary, m.2nd, 8 Feb. 1687/8, Plymouth, Henry CHURCHILL <MD 13:203; MFIP #3 incorrectly gives the date as "8 Dec. 1687/8">). (Note: You can imagine the confusion that past researchers (incl. Bowman) fell prey to. Thomas' 1st wf was Mary CHURCHILL, his 2nd wf died as "Mary CHURCHILL". MBD 1:433 incorrectly lists Thomas' 1st wf as his only wf and attributes all three children to her, as well as the death date which belongs to the 2nd wf.) (See DOTY Probate Appendix for will of Thomas DOTY.)

3 DOTY Children: (2 by 1st, 1 by 2nd)

1. **Martha DOTY**[3], b. cMay 1672, Plymouth <PCR 5:83,94>, d. aft. 29 June 1748 (hus.will); m. c1695 prob. Plymouth, **John WHITE**[4] <MFIP (Doty) #18>, (son of Samuel WHITE[3] (Resolved[2]) & Rebecca (prob. LAPHAM)), b. 24 Aug. 1669, Sandwich <rec. Rochester VR 1:302>, d. betw. 29 June 1748 - Nov. 1748 (will & pr.), of Rochester <Plymouth Co.PR>. <For bth. 8 chil., see MFIP (Doty) #18 and Rochester VR 1:303-5 (6).> (John m.1st, ( ) and had son John c1689 <MD 30:142>.) (See DOTY Probate Appendix for will of John WHITE.)

2. **Hannah DOTY**[3], b. Dec. 1675, Plymouth <MD 1:143>, d. 12 Apr. 1764, ae 87y4m, Duxbury <Duxbury VR:369>; m. 12 Jan. 1698, Duxbury, **Jonathan DELANO**[3] <Duxbury VR:244; MD 12:33>, (son of Thomas DELANO & Rebecca ALDEN[2]). See ALDEN Family.

3. **Thomas DOTY**[3], b. 22 July 1679, Plymouth <PCR 8:67; MD 21:59>, d. betw. 9 May 1721 - 16 Feb. 1721/2 (will & pr.), of Truro <Barnstable Co.PR>; m.1st 24 Feb. 1702/3, Plymouth, **Elizabeth HARLOW**[5] <MD 14:35>, (dau of William HARLOW[4] (Rebecca Bartlett[3], Mary Warren[2]) and Lydia

CUSHMAN[3] (Mary Allerton[2]) - see WARREN & ALLERTON families), b. 3rd wk Feb. 1683, Plymouth <MD 1:207,29:87>, d. betw. 26 Jan. 1704 (bth.only chil.) - 18 Apr. 1705 (hus.remarr.). **Thomas** m.2nd, 18 Apr. 1705, Sandwich, **Mercy ELLIS** <MD 14:127,30:102>, (dau of Matthias ELLIS & Mercy NYE), b. 17 Aug. 1685, Sandwich <MD 29:24>, d. betw. 2 Sept. 1750 - 30 Oct. 1751 (will & pr.), Sandwich <Plymouth Co.PR 12:400>. <See MD 4:112 for bth. 1 ch. by 1st wf.> (Mercy m.2nd, 25 Aug. 1722, Jonathan BARNES <MD 18:144>; m.3rd, (   ) WILSON; m.4th, 15 Dec. 1737, Kingston, Timothy MORTON <Kingston VR:257>.) (See DOTY Probate Appendix for wills of Thomas and 2nd wf Mercy.)

IV.   **SAMUEL DOTY/DOUGHTEN**[2], b. c1643/4, Plymouth (of age, 5 Mar. 1667/8) <PCR 4:177>, d. betw. 18 Sept. - 9 Nov. 1715 (will & pr.), Piscataway NJ <NJ Wills 1:141>; m. 13 Nov. 1678, Piscataway NJ, **Jane HARMON** <MFIP #5 (Proceedings of the NJ Historical Society (NJHS), new series 4:34)>, (poss. dau of James HARMON & Sarah CLARK of Saco ME), b. c1660 <MFIP #5>, d. aft. 18 Oct. 1717 (will of son Edward) <NJ Wills 1:141>. (See DOTY Probate Appendix for will of Samuel DOTY.)

12 DOTY Children: <1st 11, Piscataway VR (NJHS, 3rd series 2:75-80)>

1. **Samuel DOTY**[3], b. 27 Aug. 1679, Piscataway, NJ <NJHS, 3rd series 2:75-80>, d. aft. 1746 (c1750), prob. Morris Co. NJ (now Warren Co.) <MFIP #30; Doty Gen.:283>; m. 19 Sept. 1700, Piscataway NJ, **Elizabeth HULL** <NJHS, 3rd series, 75-80 (states bth. 1st ch. 12 Dec. 1700 occurred 3 mths after marriage); NJHS, new series, 4:34 (prob. the marr. rec. 19 Sept. 1700 of Elizabeth HULL & Samuel (DRAKE - error for Doty)>, (dau of Samuel HULL & Mary MANNING), b. 14 Nov. 1679, Piscataway NJ <NJHS, new series, 4:38>, d. (   ). <See MFIP #30 & NJHS, 3rd series, 75-80 for bth. 10 chil.>

2. **Sarah DOTY**[3], b. 2 Mar. 1681/2, Piscataway NJ <NJHS, 3rd series, 2:75-80>, d. (   ).

3. **Isaac DOTY**[3], b. 12 Aug. 1683, Piscataway NJ <NJHS, 3rd series, 2:75-80>, d. aft. 1749 (chosen constable), Piscataway NJ <Piscataway NJ TR:45-8>; m. c1716, Piscataway NJ, **Francis (   )**, b. (   ), d. aft. 14 June 1733 (bth.last ch.). <See MFIP #31 & NJHS, 3rd series, 2:75-80 for bth. 7 chil.>

4. **Edward DOTIE/DOTY**[3], b. 14 May 1685, Piscataway NJ <NJHS, 3rd series, 2:75-80>, d. betw. 18 Oct. - 19 Nov. 1717 (will & pr.), of Piscataway NJ <NJ Wills 1:141>; m. c1710, prob. Piscataway, **Sarah (   )**, b. (   ), d. aft. 18 Oct. 1717 (hus.will) <NJ Wills 1:141>. <See MFIP #32 for bth. 3 chil.> (See DOTY Probate Appendix for will of Edward DOTY.)

5. **James DOTY**[3], b. 17 Sept. 1686, Piscataway NJ <NJHS, 3rd series, 2:75-80>, d. poss. pre 1745 <MFIP #33>; m. 16 Sept. 1712, Piscataway NJ, **Phebe SLATER**[5] <NJHS, new series, 4:34>, (dau of Edward SLATER & Elizabeth BONHAM[4] (Hannah Fuller[3], Samuel[2] - see E. FULLER family), b. 28 July 1693, Piscataway NJ <NJHS, 3rd series, 3:14>, d. (   ). <For bth. 7 chil. see MFIP # 33, MF5G 4:112 and NJHS, 3rd series, 2:75-8.>

6. **Jonathan DOTY**[3], b. 24 Feb. 1687/8, Piscataway NJ <NJHS, 3rd series, 2:75-80>, d. aft. 16 Aug. 1739 (lease), poss. Basking Ridge <MFIP #34; Doty Gen.:281>; m. c1717/8, prob. Piscataway NJ, **Mary (   )**, b. (   ), d. (   ). <See MFIP #34 & Doty Gen.:281 for 8 chil.>

7. **Benjamin DOTY/DOUGHTY**[3], b. 14 May 1691, Piscataway NJ <NJHS, 3rd series, 2:75-80>, d. betw. 11 Mar.- 2 May 1746 (will & pr), Princetown NJ <NJ Wills 2:147>; m. (   ), **Abigail WHITEHEAD** <MFIP #35>, (dau of Jonathan WHITEHEAD & Sarah FIELD), b. (   ), Jamaica NY <NYGBR 33:102-3>, d. (   ). <See MFIP #35 & Doty Gen.:289 for bth. 4 chil.> (See DOTY Probate Appendix for will of Benjamin DOTY.)

8. **Elizabeth DOTY**[3], b. 26 Feb. 1695, Piscataway NJ <NJHS, 3rd series, 2:75-80>, d. (   ); m. 9 May 1714, Piscataway NJ, **David MARTIN** <NJHS, new series, 4:34>, (son of Joseph MARTIN & Sarah TROTTER), b. 8 July 1696, Piscataway NJ <NJHS, 3rd series, 2:75-80>, d. pre 12 Mar. 1752, prob. Hunterdon Co. NJ (adm.) <NJ Wills 3:216>. <See MFIP #36 & NJHS, 3rd series, 2: 176 for bth. 3 chil.>

9. **Joseph DOTY**[3], b. 30 Oct. 1696, Piscataway NJ <NJHS, 3rd series, 2:75-80>, d. 10 Sept. 1768, New Providence NJ <MFIP #37 (NJ Gen.Mag.19:43)>; m. c1721/2, prob. New Providence NJ, **Sarah BADGLY** <MFIP #37>, b. (   ), Long Island NY, d. pre 20 Aug. 1785, prob. New Providence NJ (adm.) <NJ Archives, 1st series, 35:123>. <See MFIP #37 for 6 chil.> (See DOTY Probate Appendix for will of Joseph DOTY.)

10. **Daniel DOTY**[3], b. 9 Mar. 1701/2, Piscataway NJ <NJHS, 3rd series, 2:75-80>.

11. **Margaret DOTY**[3], b. 5 Mar. 1704/5, Piscataway NJ <NJHS, 3rd series, 2:75-80>.

12. **Nathaniel DOTY**[3], b. c1706/7, prob. Piscataway NJ <MFIP #38; Doty Gen.:281>, poss. d. Mendham, Morris Co. NJ <MFIP #38>; m. (   ). <See MFIP #38 for 4 chil.>

V. **DESIRE DOTY**[2], b. c1645/6, Plymouth, d. 22 Jan. 1731, ae 86, Marshfield g.s. <Marshfield VR: 409; MD 12:48,13:129,33:5>; m.1st 25 Dec. 1667, Marshfield, **William SHERMAN** <Marshfield VR: 10; MD 2:182,4:171,33:5; MSR:243>, (son of William SHERMAN & Prudence HILL), b. c1640, Marshfield, bur. 17 Nov. 1680, Marshfield <Marshfield VR:9; MD 2:181,4:171,33:5>. On 4 Oct. 1675, Desire was awarded twenty pounds on behalf of her husband, William SHERMAN Jr., "whose fell distracted in the service of the country...being by reason of great charges and necessities in great straightes" <PCR 5:178>. **Desire** m.2nd, 24 Nov. 1681, Marshfield, **Israel HOLMES** <Marshfield VR:16; MD 3:42,4:171,33:5; MSR:243>, (son of William & Elizabeth), bpt. 14 Apr. 1661, Scituate <Scituate VR 1:184; MSR:317>, d. 24 Feb. 1684/5, drowned Plymouth Harbor <MD 3:188,4:171,33:5; MSR:249 (Israel HOLMES & Joseph TRUANT "were cast away saleing into Plimouth harbor & were drowned...& buried at Plimouth")>. **Desire** m.3rd, c1686, **Alexander STANDISH** (See STANDISH Family). <See MD 4:171-4 for estates of William SHERMAN & Israel HOLMES.> (See DOTY Probate Appendix for will of Desire.)

6 SHERMAN Children, 2 HOLMES Children: <MD 6:21> (See STANDISH Family for 3 children)

1. **Hannah SHERMAN**[3], b. 21 Feb. 1668, Marshfield <Marshfield VR:26; MD 6:21>, d. 8 July 1745, 77th yr, Plymouth <MD 15:213>; m. 13 July 1693, Plymouth, **William RING**[3] <MD 13:206>, (son of Andrew RING & Deborah HOPKINS[2]). See HOPKINS Family.

2. **Elizabeth SHERMAN**[3], b. 11 Mar. 1670/1, Marshfield <Marshfield VR:27; MD 6:21>, d. July 1695, unm., Marshfield <Marshfield VR:31; MD 7:118>.

3. **William SHERMAN**[3], b. 19 Apr. 1672, Marshfield <Marshfield VR:27; MD 6:21,25:133>, d. 26 Feb. 1739/40, ae 67, Marshfield g.s. <Marshfield VR:408; MD 13:110,25:133>; m. 3 Feb. 1697, Marshfield, **Mercy WHITE**[3] <Marshfield VR:23; MD 25:133; MSR:244>, (dau of Peregrine WHITE[2] & Sarah BASSETT). See WHITE Family. <For 4 chil. (inc. twins), see MBD 1:415-6; Marshfield VR:24, (1), 32 (2), 44 (1); MD 7:119, 25:133.> (See DOTY Probate Appendix for will of Wm. SHERMAN.)

4. **Patience SHERMAN**[3], b. 3 Aug. 1674, Marshfield <Marshfield VR:27; MD 6:21>, d. pre 30 July 1723 (mother's will) <MD 12:48-52>; m. 15 Jan. 1695, Duxbury, **Josiah WORMALL** <Duxbury VR:340; MD 9:108>, (son of Josiah WORMALL & Remember BROWN), b. c1672 <Sherman Fam.:18-19>, d. pre 3 Nov. 1738 (adm.) <MDP:253; MD 9:249; Plymouth Co.PR #23493, 7:449>. (Josiah m.2nd, 25 Dec. 1723, Middleboro, Grace (WADSWORTH) Sprague <MD 9:249>, (dau of John WADSWORTH & Abigail ANDREWS), b. (   ), d. betw. 13 Jan. 1748 - 3 Apr. 1758 (will & pr.) <MD 9:249>. Grace m.1st, William SPRAGUE, who d. pre 21 Feb. 1712 (adm.) <MD 9:248> and had 4 chil.) <See MFIP #41 for bth. 5 chil.>

5. **Experience SHERMAN**[3], b. 22 or 24 Sept. 1678, Marshfield <Marshfield VR:15 (22nd), 27 (24th); MD 3:42 (22nd), 6:21 (24th)>, d. 31 Mar. 1744, Duxbury <Duxbury VR:427; MD 12:31>; m. pre 5 July 1702, **Miles STANDISH**[3] (codicil of his father's will) <MD 12:102>, (son of Alexander STANDISH[2] & Sarah ALDEN[2] - see STANDISH & ALDEN families). See STANDISH Family.

6. **Ebenezer SHERMAN**[3], b. 21 Apr. 1680, Marshfield <Marshfield VR:27; MD 6:21,20:165>, d. 1 Feb. 1759, 72nd yr, Marshfield g.s. <Marshfield VR:382; MD 9:203,30:165>; m.1st, 18 Sept. 1702, Marshfield, **Margaret DECROW/DECRO** <Marshfield VR:42; MD 8:177; MSR:244; (Ebenezer & Margaret were married a year and a half after the birth of their first child. The Plymouth Quarter Sessions, 1687-1721, dated the third Tues. June 1701 state that Margaret, "...convict by her own confession of having a Bastard child by fornication Is Sentenced to pay a fine of three pound and ten shillings fees & charges or be Publickly whipped ten stripes who chose the former & payd sd fine". See MBD 1:434 #5 for the financial arrangements made by the court to ensure Ebenezer supported the child so it would not be a burden on the town.)>, (dau of Valentine DECROW & Martha BOURNE), b. 10 Jan. 1679/80, Marshfield <Sherman Fam.:21-2>, d. 17 Mar. 1726, ae 46, Marshfield g.s. <Marshfield VR:408; MD 13:110>. <For 10 chil. see MBD 1: 413-4; Marshfield VR:46 (6); MD 9:183 (6).> **Ebenezer** m.2nd, 4 May 1730, Duxbury, **Bathsheba FORD** <Duxbury VR:253; MD 11:240>, (dau of Michael FORD & Bethia HATCH), b. 1 Mar. 1691, Marshfield <Marshfield VR:20; MD 5:234>, d. aft. 11 Apr. 1759 (widow's thirds) <MD 30:169>. <See MBD 1:414 & MSR:374 for bth. 1 ch.> (See DOTY Probate Appendix for will of Ebenezer SHERMAN.)

7. **Israel HOLMES**[3], b. 17 Feb. 1682/3, Marshfield <Marshfield VR:27; MD 6:21,33:6>, d. 8 Sept. 1760, ae 77y6m, Marshfield g.s. <Marshfield VR:404; MD 13:46,33:6>; m. (   ), **Elizabeth TURNER** <MFIP #44>, (poss. dau of Daniel TURNER[2] (Humphrey[1]) & Hannah RANDALL, b. 18 Dec. 1680 Scituate <Scituate VR 1:371>), d. 10 Jan. 1754, 72nd yr, Marshfield g.s. <Marshfield VR:403; MD 13:46>. No known children; Bowman (MBD 1:416) gives them son Israel but proof is lacking.

8. **John HOLMES**[3], b. 15 June 1684, Marshfield <Marshfield VR:27; MD 6:21,33:6>, d. 6 Apr. 1754, 70th yr, Plympton g.s. <Plympton VR:486; MD 10:146>; m. 8 Sept. 1720, Marshfield, **Sarah THOMAS** <Marshfield VR:143; MSR:246; Bowman (MBD 1:416) gives him 1st wf Joanna SPRAGUE, m. 11 May 1710, Marshfield <MM:154; MD 7:132> however, this marriage is now attributed to John HOLMES[3] (Hannah Samson[2])>, (dau of Samuel THOMAS & Mercy FORD), b. c1686/7, Marshfield, d. 15 Sept. 1761, 75th yr, Thompson St. cem, Halifax <MD 13:14>. <For bth. 6 chil. see MBD 1:416; Marshfield VR:79,80; MD 30:147.>

VI. **ELIZABETH DOTY**[2], b. c1647, Plymouth, d. 7 Apr. 1742, Marshfield <Marshfield VR:90; MD 31:21>; m.1st, 13 Jan. 1674/5, Marshfield, **John ROUSE/ROWSE** <Marshfield VR:8; MD 2:180,33:6; MSR:243> (son of John ROWSE & Annis PAYBODY), b. 28 Sept. 1643, Marshfield <Marshfield VR:2; MD 2:4>, d. 3 Oct. 1717, ae 74, Winslow cem., Marshfield <Marshfield VR:388; MD 10:49; MSR:239>. **Elizabeth** m.2nd, 28 Jan. 1718/9, Marshfield, **William CARVER** <Marshfield VR:35,40; MD 8:43; MSR:246>, (son of John CARVER & Millicent FORD), b. 6 Sept. 1659, Marshfield <MD 2:7>, d. 2 Oct. 1760, ae 102, Marshfield <NEHGR 88:218>. (William m.1st, 18 Jan. 1682, Marshfield, Elizabeth FOSTER <Marshfield VR:16; MD 3:43; MSR:243>, (?dau of John, b. 24 Sept. 1664, Marshfield <Marshfield VR:7>) who d. 26 June 1715 <MD 31:121>; they had 9 children <MD 4:125, 126,5:234-5,31:121>.) (See DOTY Probate Appendix for wills of John ROUSE & William CARVER.)

3 ROUSE Children:

1. **George ROUSE**[3], b. c1676, Marshfield, bur. 9 Dec. 1676, Marshfield <Marshfield VR:9; MD 2:182; MSR:248>.

2. **John ROUSE**[3], b. c1678, d. 27 May 1704, ae 26, Winslow cem., Marshfield <Marshfield VR:43,388; MD 8:177,10:49; MSR:239>.

3. **George ROUSE**[3], b. 25 Dec. 1679, Marshfield <Marshfield VR:11; MD 2:249>, bur. 26 Feb. 1682, Marshfield <Marshfield VR:13; MD 2:250; MSR:249>.

VII **ISAAC DOTY/DOTTIE/DOUGHTY**[3], b. 8 Feb. 1648/9, Plymouth <MD 15:27; PCR 8:5 (an error in the dating implies he was born in 1647)>, d. aft. 7 Jan. 1728/9, Oyster Bay NY (deposition, ae about 79) <MBD 1:413>; m. c1673, (   ), **Elizabeth ENGLAND** <MFIP #8>, (dau of William & Elizabeth), b. prob. Portsmouth RI <RI Gen.Dict.:72>.

6 DOTY Children: <Oyster Bay, Long Island NY; MFIP #8, MBD 1:422>

1. **Isaac DOTY**[3], b. c1673, Oyster Bay NY (of age in 1695 deed) <Oyster Bay TR 6:216>, d. (   ); m. c1700, (   ), **Elizabeth (?JACKSON)** <MFIP #49>, b. (   ), d. (   ). <See MFIP #49 for bth. 2 chil.>

2. **Joseph DOTY/DOUGHTY**[3], b. c1680, Oyster Bay NY, d. betw. 7 July 1716 (will) - 15 Aug. 1716 (pr.) <Jamaica NY PR C:75>; m. (   ), **Sarah (   )** <MFIP #50>, b. (   ), d. aft. 29 Jan. 1716/7 (receipt) <Oyster Bay TR 4:421>. <See MBD 1:422 for bth. 4 chil.> (See DOTY Probate Appendix for will of Joseph DOTY.)

3. **Jacob DOTY**[3], b. c1682, Oyster Bay NY (of age in 1704) <Oyster Bay TR 4:165>, d. aft. 19 Oct. 1753 (deed) <Oyster Bay TR 6:130>; m. (   ), **Penelope ALBERTSON** <MFIP #51>, b. c1693/4 (dau of Derrick ALBERTSON & Dinah COLES) <MFIP #51>, d. aft. 19 Oct. 1753 (deed) <Oyster TR 6:130> <See MFIP #51 for bth. 4 chil.>

4. **Solomon DOTY**[3], b. c1683-91, Oyster Bay NY, d. betw. 8 Aug. 1761 (will) - 4 Mar. 1762 (pr.) <NY Wills 6:136>; m. (   ), **Rachel SEAMAN** <MFIP #52>, (dau of David SEAMAN & Temperance WILLIAMS), b. c1695, prob. Oyster Bay NY <MFIP #52>, d. pre 8 Aug. 1761 (hus.will) <NY Wills 6:136>. <See MFIP #52 for bth. 8 chil.> (See DOTY Probate Appendix for will of Solomon DOTY)

5. **James DOTY**[3], b. 21 Dec. 1693, Oyster Bay NY (g.s.), d. 4 Feb. 1773, Oyster Bay NY <g.s., Christ Episcopal Church, Oyster Bay NY>; m. (   ), Oyster Bay NY, **Cathrien/Catherine LATT-ING** <MFIP #53>, (dau of Josias LATTING & Susannah COLES), b. (   ), Oyster Bay NY <MFIP>, d. aft. 15 May 1781 (will of son John) <Doty Gen.:503>. <See MFIP #53 for bth. 7 chil.> (See DOTY Probate Appendix for will of James DOTY.)

6. **Samuel DOTY**[3], b. c1695, d. betw. 6 May 1740 (codicil) - 30 June 1741 (pr.) <NY Wills 3:341>; m. (   ), Oyster Bay NY, **Charity (   )** <MFIP #54 states that although she has been iden-tified as Charity MUDGE, dau of Jarvis MUDGE & Jane HAWXHURST, she is not mentioned in the will or probate records of Jarvis.>, b. (   ), d. aft. 5 May 1740 (hus.will) <NY Wills 3:341> <See MFIP #54 for 8 chil.> (See DOTY Probate Appendix for will of Samuel DOTY.)

VIII **JOSEPH DOTY/DOTEN**[3], b. 30 Apr. 1651, Plymouth <PCR 8:12; MD 16:237 (last of Apr.)>, d. betw 3 May 1731 <Plymouth Co.Court Rec.2:95 (then in 81st yr) - 18 Sept. 1734, prob. Rochester <Plymouth Co.PR #6624 (widow's petition); MQ 47:28; TAG 36:9-11>; m.1st c1674, (   ), **Deborah ELLIS** <MQ 47:28; TAG 36:10-11>, (dau of John ELLIS & Elizabeth FREEMAN), b. c1652 <TAG 36:9-11; NEHGR 119:173>, d. 21 June 1711, Rochester <Rochester VR 2:377>. **Joseph** m.2nd, 5 Mar. 1711/12, Rochester, **Sarah (WOODIN) Edwards** <Rochester VR 2:118>, (dau of John WOODIN & Mary JOHNSON), b. 31 Jan. 1656/7, Salisbury <Salisbury VR:256; TAG 64:73>, d. aft. 18 Sept. 1734 <MBD 1:434 #2 (On this date Sarah petitioned the court as follows, "...That wheras my sd Decased Husband In his lifetime by Reason of old age & adverse Providences was Reduced to such Circumstances as to be obliged to live with & be supported In a measure by his son Jos-eph DOTY & Dyed there, & so all the moveables we had was In our sd sons House and since My sd Husband's Death I Cannot Comfortably Dwell with him but might live with more Comfort with my

own son Joseph EDWARDS, could I obtain such Beding & other necessary household stuff as My Husband & I had at his Decease which he my sd son In Law Joseph DOTY withholds (as I apprehend) very Unjustly from me, Knowing I am through my own Poverty unable to take administration..." <Plymouth Co.PR #6624>) (Sarah m.1st, John EDWARDS <Torrey:244>.) (**Joseph** was accused on 27 Oct. 1674, by Elizabeth WARREN[3] (Nathaniel[2]), of being the father of her unborn child <PCR 5:156>. MFIP #9 suggests this child is poss. Elizabeth, if not, then Joseph had ten children, with the illegitimate unnamed child born c1674/75 and Elizabeth poss. b. c1680.)

9 DOTY Children: (all by 1st wife, except poss. #1 Elizabeth)

1. **Elizabeth DOTY**[3], b. c1674/5, d. (   ); m. 28 Feb. 1705/6, Rochester, **John LEWIS** <Rochester VR 2:118>, b. (   ), d. 24 Jan. 1711/2, Dartmouth <Dartmouth VR 3:46; MSR:147>. (For 4 chil. see Dartmouth VR 1:150 (3) & Rochester VR 1:205 (1).>

2. **Theophilus DOTY**[3], b. 22 Feb. 1674, Sandwich <Sandwich VR; MD 14:108>, d. aft. Mar. 1728/9 <Plymouth Co.Court Rec.2:95 (he & 3 brothers & step-brother, Joseph EDWARDS, were charged with failing to provide for their parents)>; m. c1696, Rochester, **Ruth MENDALL** <PN&Q 2:55; TAG 36:11>, (dau of John), b. 20 Sept. 1675, Marshfield <Marshfield VR:15; MD 3:42>, d. aft. 8 Feb. 1720 <PN&Q 2:55 (fath.will)>. <See MBD 1:428 & Rochester VR 1:119-21 for bth. 7 chil>

3. **Ellis/Elles DOTY**[3], b. 16 Apr. 1677, Sandwich <Sandwich VR; MD 14:108>, d. aft. Mar. 1728/9 <Plymouth Co.Court Rec.2:95 (see Theophilus above)>; m. c1704, (   ), **Elinor (   )**, b. (   ), d. (   ). <See MBD 1:427, Rochester VR 1:119-21 & Rochester General Rcds 1:46 for bth. 6 chil.>

4. **Joseph DOTY**[3], b. 31 Mar. 1683, Rochester <Rochester VR 1:125>, d. aft. 18 June 1749, poss. Sharon CT <NEHGR 124:57-60 (wf dismissed to church at Sharon)>; m. 2 July 1708, Rochester, **Hannah EDWARDS** <Rochester VR 2:118>, (dau of John EDWARDS & Sarah WOODIN), poss. bpt. 1688, Wenham <TAG 64:152-4>, d. aft. 18 June 1749, poss. Sharon CT <NEHGR 124:57-60; Wareham ChR:8 (dismissed to church at Sharon)>. <See MBD 1:428; Rochester VR 1:119-21 & Rochester Gen. Rcds.1:57 for bth. 11 chil.>

5. **Deborah DOTY**[3], b. 31 Mar. 1685, Rochester <Rochester VR 1:125>, d. 13 Jan. 1781, 97th yr, Sharon CT <TAG 36:11>; m. 7 Feb. 1710, Rochester, **Joseph LANDERS** <Rochester VR 2:117>, (son of Thomas & Deborah), b. 14 Feb. 1688/9, Sandwich <MD 29:73>, d. Jan. 1781, 94th yr, Sharon CT <TAG 36:11>. <See Rochester VR 1:198 for bth. 3 chil.>

6. **John DOTY**[3], b. 1 Mar. 1688, Rochester <Rochester VR 1:125>, d. aft. 1749, poss. Sharon CT <NEHGR 124:57-60>; m. c1710, (   ), **Elizabeth (   )** <MFIP #60>, b. (   ), d. aft. 1749, poss. Sharon CT <NEHGR 124:59>. <See MFIP #60 for bth. 2 chil.>

7. **Mercy/Marcy DOTY**[3], b. 12 Jan. 1691, Rochester <Rochester VR 1:125>; nothing further known.

8. **Faith DOTY**[3], b. 18 Jan. 1696, Rochester <Rochester VR 1:125>, d. 18 May 1770, 70th yr, Plympton <Plympton VR:514>; m. 14 Apr. 1719, Rochester, **James SHAW** <Rochester VR 2:270>, (son of Jonathan SHAW & Mehitable PRATT), b. 3 Mar. 1696, Plymouth <MD 3:123>, d. 1745 (French war) <MFIP #61>. <See MFIP #61 for 10 chil.>

9. **Mary DOTY**[3], b. 28 July 1699, Rochester <Rochester VR 1:125>, d. prob. aft. 11 Oct. 1761 (adm. to church), S. Amenia NY <Waterman Gen.1:74>; m. 23 Aug. 1722, Plympton, **Samuel WATERMAN** <MD 2:138; Plympton VR:421>, (son of Samuel & Bethia), b. 23 Sept. 1703, Plymouth <MD 2:19>, d. aft. 11 Oct. 1761 (adm. to church), poss. S. Amenia NY <Waterman Gen.1:74>. <See MFIP #62 for 5 chil. & Plympton VR:220 for 3.>

IX **MARY DOTY**[2], b. c1653, Plymouth, d. pre 13 June 1728 (hus.will) <MD 7:29>; m. betw. 10 July 1677 <MD 3:91 (settlement of mother's est.)> - 10 Nov. 1678 (bth.1st chil.), Scituate, **Samuel HATCH**, (son of Walter HATCH[2] (William[1]) & Elizabeth HOLBROOK), b. 22 Dec. 1653, Scituate <MD 17:73; Scituate VR 1:172>, d. betw. 13 June 1728 (will) - 7 July 1735 (pr.) <MD 7:29-33>. <See MBD 1:435-6, #37 for the possible burial site of Mary & Samuel HATCH.> (See DOTY Probate Appendix for will of Samuel HATCH.)

9 HATCH Children: <Scituate VR 1:172-7, 4:3:53>

1. **Samuel HATCH**[3], b. 10 Nov. 1678, Scituate <MSR:322 (bpt. 4 Aug. 1679)>, d. betw. 23 Oct. 1766 (will) - 2 Feb. 1767 (pr.), of Scituate <Plymouth Co.PR 19:425 or 10:425 (MFIP #63 says 10; the Bowman Files contain a typed transcript in which it appears to be 19 - with the 9 "broken")>; m.1st, 7 Mar. 1704/5, Scituate, **Elizabeth OLDHAM** <Scituate VR 2:222; MD 3:119>, (dau of Thomas OLDHAM & Mary WITHERELL), b. 5 May 1677, Scituate <Scituate VR 1:276; MSR:321 (bpt. 18 Aug. 1678)>, d. betw. 25 Aug. 1723 <MSR:359 (bpt. of son)> - 27 Oct. 1747 (hus.2nd marr.). **Samuel** m.2nd, 27 Oct. 1747, Marshfield, **Mary (   ) Silvester** <Marshfield VR:173>, (   ) d. aft. 23 Oct. 1766 (hus.will). <See MBD 1:433 & Scituate VR 1:175 for 3 chil. by 1st wf.> (See DOTY Probate Appendix for will of Samuel HATCH Sr.)

2. **Josiah HATCH**[3], b. 30 May 1680, Scituate <Scituate VR 1:174; MD 27:97; MSR:322 (bpt.)>, d. 12
   Jan. 1714/5, Rochester <Rochester VR 2:395; MD 27:98>; m. 24 Feb. 1701/2, Yarmouth, **Desire
   HAWES**[4] <Yarmouth VR 1:135; MD 27:97>, (dau of John HAWES & Desire GORHAM[3] (Desire Howland[2]) -
   see HOWLAND family), b. last of Feb. 1681, Yarmouth <Yarmouth VR 1:126; MD 2:207,27:97>, d. 8
   Feb. 1723/4, 40th yr, Provincetown g.s. <MD 8:23,27:98>. (Desire m.2nd, 19 June 1719, Roch-
   ester, John COWING <Rochester VR 2:172>. <See MD 27:97-101 for estate of Josiah HATCH. See
   MBD 1:433 for 7 chil. & Rochester VR 1:170-2 for 5 chil.>

3. **Hannah HATCH**[3], b. 15 or 16 Feb. 1681/2, Scituate <Scituate VR 1:173 (15th); <MD 21:97 (15th
   or 16th); MSR:323 (bpt. 14 May 1682)>, d. 13 Apr. 1771, 91st yr, Nemasket cem., Middleboro
   <MD 15:103,21:97; Middleboro Dths.:212>, m.1st pre 1702, **Japhet TURNER** <MD 21:97>, (son of
   Japheth TURNER[3] (John[2], Humphrey[1]) & Hannah HUDSON), b. 4 Jan. 1682, Duxbury <Duxbury VR:177;
   MD 9:229; MSR:324 (bpt. 24 June 1683, Scituate)>, d. pre 23 Jan. 1710/1 (inv.) <MD 21:97-8>.
   Hannah m.2nd, 9 July 1719, Scituate, **Ebenezer TINKHAM**[4] <Scituate VR 1:302; MD 10:75,21:97>,
   (son of Ebenezer TINKHAM[3] (Mary Brown[2]) & Elizabeth BURROWS - see BROWN family), b. 23 Mar.
   1679, Middleboro <MD 1:221>, d. 31 Mar. 1726, Middleboro <Middleboro Dths.:201>. (Ebenezer
   m.1st, 28 Oct. 1703, Patience PRATT <MD 2:43> who d. 29 Mar. 1718, 37th yr <MD 4:74>; they
   had 6 chil.) **Hannah** m.3rd, 23 Dec. 1729, Middleboro, **Capt. Ichabod TUPPER** <MD 8:250,21:97
   (his 2nd marr.)>, (son of Thomas TUPPER & Martha MAYHEW), b. 11 Apr. 1673, Sandwich <MD 14:
   169>, d. betw. 21 Nov. 1748 (will) - 5 Dec. 1748 (pr.), of Middleboro <MD 21:100-101>. <For
   4 chil. by 1st hus., see: MBD 1:429; Pembroke VR:211,212 (3), Scituate VR 1:375 (1); MD 21:
   97; MSR:339,340,347.> (See DOTY Probate Appendix for wills of Hannah & Ichabod.)

4. **Ebenezer HATCH**[3], b. 6 Apr. 1684, Scituate <Scituate VR 1:172>, d. betw. 7 Jan. 1724 (will) -
   21 Apr. 1724 (inv.), of Pembroke <Plymouth Co.PR #9490>; m. 10 Mar. 1719, Scituate, **Abigail
   JONES**[5] <Scituate VR 2:141; MD 10:76>, (dau of Joseph JONES[4] (Patience Little[3], Anna Warren[2])
   & Sarah FORD), b. 13 Apr. 1694, Hingham <Hist.Hingham 2:383-4>, d. aft. 22 Dec. 1736 (bth.
   last ch.) <Pembroke VR:193>. (Abigail m.2nd, 26 Dec. 1727, Pembroke, Joseph STETSON <Pembroke
   VR:285> & had 3 sons.) <See MBD 1:429 for 2 chil.> (See DOTY Probate Appendix for will of
   Ebenezer HATCH.)

5. **Isaac HATCH**[3], b. 20 Dec. 1687, Scituate <Scituate VR 1:173; MSR:326 (bpt. 1 May 1687)>, d.
   1 Nov. 1759, 73rd yr, Pembroke g.s. <MBD 1:435-6, #37 & #43 (Old Hatch Cemetery, Two Mile,
   Pembroke, "Erected in memory of Mr. Isaac Hatch/He died November 1st 1759 in ye 73rd year of
   his age")>; m.1st 9 Aug. 1716, Scituate, **Lydia CLIFT** <Scituate VR 2:141; MD 9:88>, (dau of
   William CLIFT & Lydia WILLS), b. 13 July 1697, Scituate <Scituate VR 1:66,2:83>, d. betw. 30
   Sept. 1722 <Scituate VR 1:173-7; MSR:358 (bpt. 2 chil.)> - 7 Jan. 1724/5 (hus.2nd marr.).
   Isaac m.2nd, 7 Jan. 1724/5, Scituate, **Penelope EWELL** <Scituate VR 2:141>, (dau of Gershom &
   Mary), b. 11 Apr. 1697, Scituate <Scituate VR 1:149>, d. 13 Jan. 1775, 77th yr, Pembroke g.s.
   <MBD 1:435-6, #37 & #43 (Old Hatch Cemetery, Two Mile, Pembroke, "Erected in memory of Mrs.
   Penelope Hatch/She died Jan. 13 1775 in the 77th year of her age")>. <For 2 chil. by 1st wf
   see Scituate VR 1:173-7; 7 chil. by 2nd wf see MBD 1:432; Scituate VR 173-7 (5), Marshfield
   VR:392 (1), Pembroke VR:102 (1); MSR:364,368,371,374,376,429 (6).> (See DOTY Probate Appen-
   dix for will of Isaac HATCH.)

6. **Elizabeth HATCH**[3], b. 16 June 1690, Scituate <Scituate VR 1:172>, d. pre 26 July 1765 (hus.
   will) <Plymouth Co.PR 19:167-9>; m. 17 Dec. 1713, Pembroke, **John BONNEY** <Pembroke VR:241>,
   (son of John BONNEY & Elizabeth BISHOP), b. 27 June 1690, Pembroke <Pembroke VR:40; NEHGR 89:
   223>, d. betw. 26 July 1763 (will) - 31 Jan. 1765 (inv.) <Plymouth Co.PR 19:167-9>. <See MBD
   1:429 & Pembroke VR:40-6 for bth.5 chil.> (See DOTY Probate Appendix for will of John BONNEY)

7. **Elisha HATCH**[3], b. 7 Nov. 1692, Scituate <Scituate VR 1:172>, d. 15 Apr. 1770, Green River/
   Hillsdale NY <Columbia Co.NY Hist.:372>; m.1st, 30 Oct. 1718, Pembroke, **Patience KEEN** <Pem-
   broke VR:285>, (dau of Matthew KEEN & Martha MacFARLIN), b. 3 Oct. 1699, Pembroke <Pembroke
   VR:131>, d. aft. 1 Jan. 1737 (bth.last ch.) <Rochester VR 1:172>. **Elisha** m.2nd, (   ),
   Isabel (   ), b. (   ), d. 23 July 1767, Green River NY <Columbia Co.NY Hist.:372>. <See
   Rochester VR 1:171-2 for bth. 6 chil. by 1st wf.>

8. **Ezekiel HATCH**[3], b. 14 May 1695, Scituate <Scituate VR 1:173; MD 22:155>, d. betw. 19 June
   1765 (will) - 1 July 1768 (inv.), of Rochester <MD 22:155-6>; m. 25 Sept. 1718, Scituate,
   Ruth CHURCH[5] <Scituate VR 2:141; MD 10:75,22:155>, (dau of Richard CHURCH[4] (Nathaniel Church[3]
   Elizabeth Warren[2] - see WARREN family) & Hannah STOVER), b. 8 Dec. 1701, Scituate <Scituate
   VR 1:71,4:3:72; MD 22:155>, d. aft. 19 June 1765 (hus.will) <MD 22:155-6>. <See MBD 1:429 &
   Rochester VR 1:171-2 for bth. 6 chil.> (See DOTY Probate Appendix for will of Ezekiel HATCH.)

9. **Desire HATCH**[3], b. 25 Sept. 1698, Scituate <Scituate VR 1:172>, d. pre 5 Mar. 1754 (hus.2nd
   marr.); m. 23 Sept. 1731, Scituate, **Joseph LOVELL** <Scituate VR 2:141; MD 1:106>, b. (   ),
   d. pre 13 June 1781, Sharon CT (inv.) <Sharon CT PR E:320>. (Joseph. m.2nd, 5 Mar. 1754,
   Rochester, Mary LEWIS <Rochester VR 2:206>.) <See Rochester VR 2:205 for bth. 3 chil.>

DOTY PROBATE APPENDIX

Estate of **John ALLYN**: <Early CT PR Recs.3:377-8>
...24 Jan. 1743/4, Division of estate among following heirs, viz: Samuel ALLYN; Hezekiah KILBOURN
& wf Elizabeth; James OTIS & wf Mary; Ebenezer WRIGHT & wf Hannah; Nathaniel STILLMAN & wf Sarah;
James KNOWLES & wf Martha; Ephraim BOSTWICK & wf Abigail.
==

Will of **John BACON**: <MDP:317; Barnstable Co.PR 5:1>
...2 Dec. 1730, ment. sons Nathaniel BACON, John BACON, Solomon BACON, Judah BACON; pre-nuptial
agreement dated 27 Sept. 1726 with wf Sarah; negroe Dinah to be sold after wife's decease and
proceeds to be used to buy bibles for grandchildren; dau Desire GREEN; son (son-in-law) GREEN;
dau Hannah MORTON; granddaughter Mary MORTON; granddaughter Mary BACON dau of dec'd son Isaac
BACON. Wit. sworn 2 Sept. 1731.
==

Will of **Kenelm BAKER**: <MDP:90; Plymouth Co.PR 20:496-7>
...13 Apr. 1770, ment. wf Patience; sons John BAKER, Kenelm BAKER, William BAKER; daus Alice LIT-
TLE wf of Ephraim, Sarah LITTLE wf of Thomas, Betty TURNER wf of Abner, Lucy FISHER wf of Daniel.
Pr. 3 June 1771.
==

Will of **John BONNEY**: <Plymouth Co.PR 19:167-9>
...26 July 1763, ment. son John BONNEY; daus Zerviah BONNEY, Rachel CHAMBERLAIN. Pr. 4 Feb. 1765.
==

Will of **William CARVER**: <NEHGR 88:218>
...5 Apr. 1742, ment. sons John CARVER, William CARVER, Josiah CARVER, Joshua CARVER; daus Millicent CARVER, Mary STANDISH, Elizabeth TAYLOR, Sarah TAYLOR. Pr. 10 Oct. 1760.
==

Will of **Benjamin DOTY/DOUGHTY**[3] (**Samuel**[2]): (victualler) <NJ Wills 2:147>
...11 Mar. 1746, ment. wf Abigail and son Benjamin DOUGHTY. Pr. 2 May 1746.
==

Will of **Edward DOTY/DOTTEN**[1]: <MD 3:87-9; Plymouth Co.PR 2:1:14-16>
...20 May 1655, ment. son Edward DOTTEN; unnamed sons (if they live to age 21); unnamed wife. Pr.
5 Mar. 1655/6.
==

Will of **Faith (CLARKE)(Doty) Phillips**: <MD 3:89-91; Plymouth Co.PR 3:2:12>
...12 Dec. 1675, ment. daus Mary, Elizabeth & Desire; son John. Sworn to 8 June 1676.
==

Estate of **Edward DOTY/DOTEY**[2]: <MD 5:210-14; Plymouth Co.PR 1:53,251>
...3 Dec. 1696, Settlement among following heirs, viz: James WARREN & wf Sarah; Martha DOTEY;
Mary DOTEY; Tobias OAKMAN/OAKSMAND & wf Elizabeth; and Thomas FAUNCE & John DOTEY as guardians of
Samuel DOTEY, Benjamin DOTEY & Mercy DOTEY.
==

Will of **Edward DOTY/DOTIE**[3] (**Samuel**[2]): (planter) <NJ Wills 1:141>
...18 Oct. 1717, ment. mother Jane DOTY; sons John DOTY, Jeremie DOTY; wf Sarah; dau Sarah DOTY.
Pr. 19 Nov. 1717.
==

Will of **Elisha DOTY/DOTEN**[3] (**John**[2]): (yeoman) <MD 19:178-9; Plymouth Co.PR 13:312,314>
...24 Dec. 1753, ment. wf Hannah; heirs of dec'd son Elisha DOTEN; heirs of son Samuel DOTEN;
sons Edward DOTEN, Paul DOTEN; dau Lois HARLOW wf of Amaziah; sons Stephen DOTEN, James DOTEN. Pr
17 July 1754.
==

Estate of **Isaac DOTY/DOTEN**[3] (**John**[2]): <MD 25:164-72; MDP:256; Plymouth Co.PR #6621, 6:143,7:183>
...14 Apr. 1730, Division of personal estate to widow Martha DOTEN and following heirs, viz: Jane
DOTEN, Isaac DOTEN, Elizabeth DOTEN, Rebekah DOTEN, Neriah DOTEN, Jabez DOTEN, Ichabod DOTEN and
Mary DOTEN...15 Mar. 1735/6, Divison of real estate to widow Martha DOTEN; eldest son Isaac DOTEN
dau Elizabeth STUDLEY wf of John; Jane PALMER wf of John Jr.; dau Rebekah DOTEN; sons Neriah
DOTEN, Jabez DOTEN & Ichabod DOTEN; dau Mary DOTEN.
==

Will of **James DOTY**[3] (**Isaac**[2]): (yeoman) <NJ Wills 8:177-8>
...13 Jan. 1773, ment. wf Cathrien; sons John DOTY, Zebulon DOTY; dau Jemima TOBIAS; Mary, dau of
Mary GREATMAN and her granddaughter Catherine ROGERS; dau Mary GREATMAN; granddaughter Catherine
ROGERS; sons John & Herman LEFFERTS. Pr. 14 Sept. 1773.
==

Will of **John DOTY/DOTEY**[2]: <MD 6:77-81; Plymouth Co.PR 1:341-43>
...15 Apr. 1701, ment. eldest son John DOTEY; wf Sarah; youngest sons Isaac DOTEY, Samuel DOTEY,
Elisha DOTEY, Josiah DOTEY; dau Elizabeth MOSS; youngest daus Martha, Sarah, Patience, Desire;
brother John RICKARD. Inv. taken 17 May 1701.
==

Will of **John DOTY/DOTEN**[3] (**John**[2]): (husbandman) <MD 20:27-30; Plymouth Co.PR 10:452>
...29 Apr. 1746, ment. wf Hannah; grandson Edward DOTEN eldest son of son John DOTEN; dau Mehitable LUCAS wf of William; son Jacob DOTEN; dau Susanna FINNEY wf of John; dau Lydia LUCAS wf of
John; eldest son John DOTEN. Pr. 14 July 1747.
==

Will of **Hannah (SHERMAN) Doty**: (widow) <MD 20:27-30; Plymouth Co.PR 13:292>
...14 Apr. 1754, nuncupative will ment. brothers Joshua SHERMAN & Caleb SHERMAN. Sworn to 15 Apr.
==

Will of **Joseph DOTY/DOUGHTY**[3] (**Isaac**[2]): <Jamaica NY PR C:75>
...7 July 1716, ment. eldest son Joseph DOUGHTY; son Isaac DOUGHTY; dau Sarah; wf Sarah (who may
be with child). Pr. 15 Aug. 1716.

Will of **Joseph DOTY**[3] (**Samuel**[2]): <NJ Archives (1st series) 33:118>
...3 Sept. 1768, ment. wf Sarah; eldest son George DOTY; sons Anthony DOTY, John DOTY; eldest dau
Elizabeth LUDLOW wf of Jeremiah dec'd; youngest dau Sarah CARL wf of William. Pr. 14 Oct. 1768.

Will of **Samuel DOTY**[2]: <NJ Wills 1:141>
...18 Sept. 1715, ment. wf Jane and son Samuel DOTY. Pr. 8 Nov. 1715.

Will of **Samuel DOTY**[3] (**Isaac**[2]): <NY Wills 3:341>
...5 May 1740, ment. wf Charity; dau Deborah; sons Isaac DOTY, Stephen DOTY, Charles DOTY, Elias
DOTY. Codicil, 6 May 1740, ment. daus Phebe BRANDIGA, Charity DODGE, Elizabeth ALBERTSON. Pr.
30 June 1741.

Will of **Solomon DOTY**[3] (**Isaac**[2]): <NY Wills 6:136>
...8 Aug. 1761, ment. daus Temperance, Elizabeth, Mary; sons Isaac DOTY, Moses DOTY, Stephen DOTY
Samuel DOTY & Seamans DOTY. Pr. 4 May 1762.

Will of **Thomas DOTY**[2]: <MD 4:233-4; Plymouth Co.PR 4:1:33>
...nuncupative will, "did on the fourth Day of December (1678) Declare these following words...
Comitted in writing December the 5th within 24 houres after the Death of the said Thomas Dotey";
ment. wf Mary. Inv. 28 Jan. 1678/9.

Will of **Thomas DOTY/DOTEY**[3] (**Thomas**[2]): (innholder) <MDP:263; Barnstable Co.PR 4:45>
...9 May 1721, ment. wf Mercy; Joseph ABBIT "the child that now lives with me"; son Thomas DOTEY
to maintain his grandmother Mary CHURCHILL. Pr. 8 Feb. 1721/2.

Will of **Mercy (ELLIS)(Doty)(Barnes)(Wilson) Morton**: <Plymouth Co.PR 12:400>
...2 Sept. 1750, ment. brothers Joel ELLIS, Matthias ELLIS & Malachi ELLIS; sister Mehitable MER-
RICK; cousins Benjamin CHURCHELL, Stephen CHURCHELL, Ansel CHURCHELL, Priscilla CHURCHELL; cousin
Hannah CHURCHELL & her dau Hannah; cousin Ruth CHURCHELL; sister Experience CHURCHELL; cousin
Wilson CHURCHELL. Pr. 30 Oct. 1751.

Will of **Ebenezer HATCH**[3] (**Mary Doty**[2]): (yeoman) <MDP:260; Plymouth Co.PR #9460>
...7 Jan. 1724, ment. son Ebenezer HATCH (under 21); dau Sary HATCH (under 18); wf Abigill/Abig-
ail; brother Samuel HATCH. Pr. 4 May 1724.

Will of **Ezekiel HATCH**[3] (**Mary Doty**[2]): (yeoman) <MD 22:155-6; Plymouth Co.PR 20:103,104>
...19 June 1765, ment. only son Isaiah HATCH; unnamed wife & her daus; daus Ruth HATHAWAY, Mary,
Hannah, Lucy & Sarah. Pr. 14 July 1768.

Will of **Isaac HATCH**[3] (**Mary Doty**[2]): (yeoman) <MDP:261; Plymouth Co.PR 15:446>
...11 Dec. 1756, ment. wf Penelope; sons Isaac HATCH, Seth HATCH, Josiah HATCH, Samuel HATCH;
dec'd father Samuel HATCH; Negro Boy named James; daus Penelope HATCH, Lydia HATCH, Sary HATCH
and Mary HATCH wf of Isreal HATCH Jr. Pr. 3 Dec. 1759.

Will of **Samuel HATCH Sr.**: (yeoman) <MDP:260; MD 7:29-33; Plymouth Co.PR 7:143-6>
...13 June 1728, "aged & infirm", ment. sons Samuel HATCH; grandchildren Isaac HAT-
CH & Josiah HATCH, sons of son Isaac; daus Hannah TINCOM, Elizabeth BONNEY, "Desier" HATCH; gran-
dchildren Ebenezer & Sarah, chil. of dec'd son Ebenezer HATCH; grandchildren Edmond HATCH, Jabez
HATCH, Josiah HATCH, "Desier", Zurviah & Mary, chil. of dec'd son Josiah HATCH; sons Elisha HAT-
CH, Ezekiel HATCH. Pr. 7 July 1735.

Will of **Samuel HATCH**[3] (**Mary Doty**[2]): (yeoman) <MDP:262; Plymouth Co.PR 10:425>
...23 Oct. 1766, ment. wf Mary; grandsons John MICHEL, Job MICHEL, Samuel JONES, Amos JONES and
Ezekiel JONES; daus Lidia MITCHEL, Ruth JONES; granddaughters Elizabeth MITCHELL, Betty JONES;
kinsman Benjamin HATCH Jr. Pr. 2 Feb. 1767.

Will of **Thomas MORTON**: <MDP:253; MD 25:133-6; Plymouth Co.PR #18199, 8:172-4>
...26 Aug. 1741, ment. wf Martha; grandchildren Bathshuah MORTON & Martha MORTON daus of dec'd
son Thomas MORTON; sons Lemuel MORTON, Nathaniel MORTON; two unnamed daus (under 18) of dec'd dau
Lydia BARTLETT; daus Sarah BARTLETT, Mary NELSON. Pr. 12 Sept. 1748.

Will of **Tobias OAKMAN**: (yeoman) <MD 22:36; Plymouth Co.PR 12:90,91>
...21 Mar. 1745, ment. son Edward OAKMAN; grandsons Samuel OAKMAN & Tobias OAKMAN sons of dec'd
son Samuel OAKMAN; grandson Jeddediah EAMES; daus Faith FOSTER, Elizabeth FORD, Sarah RANDALL,
Susannah COLLAMER, Mary SHAIRMAN/SHERMAN, Marcy HAMILTON. Appraisers app'td 29 June 1750.

Will of **John ROUSE**: <Plymouth Co.PR 4:34-6>
...1 May 1717, ment. wf Elizabeth; Jedediah BOURNE son of sister Elizabeth; Patience DOTEN neice
of wife; Samuel OAKMAN son of Tobias OAKMAN; John ROUSE son of brother Simon ROUSE. Pr. 24 Oct.
1717.

Will of **Ebenezer SHERMAN**[3] (**Desire Doty**[2]): (laborer)<MDP:253; MD 30:165-71; Plymouth Co.PR 15:263>
...10 Jan. 1759, ment. sons Ebenezer SHERMAN (2nd), Elisha SHERMAN (youngest), William SHERMAN
(eldest), Robert SHERMAN, John SHERMAN; daus Rachel JOYCE, Elisabeth WITHERELL, Abigail CARVER,
Barshaba WALKER. Objections to probate were made 14 Feb. 1759.

Will of **William SHERMAN**[3] (**Desire Doty**[2]): (yeoman) <MDP:253; MD 25:133-36; Plymouth Co.PR #18199,
8:172,174>...30 Nov. 1739, ment. chil. of dec'd dau Thankful POLDEN, viz: John POLDEN (under 21),
Mary POLDEN (under 18); dau Sarah HALL wf of Adam; daus Mary SHERMAN, Abigail SHERMAN. Pr. 12
Sept. 1748.

Will of **Desire (DOTY**[2])**(Sherman)(Holmes) Standish**: <MDP:253; MD 12:48; Plymouth Co.PR 6:177-78-80>
...30 July 1723, ment. sons William SHERMAN (eldest), Ebenezer SHERMAN, Israel HOLMES, John HOL-
MES, Thomas STANDISH, Ichabod STANDISH; daus Hannah RING, Experience STANDISH, Desire WESTON;
granddaughter Desire WORMWALL/WORMALL. Pr. 17 May 1732.

Will of **Ichabod TUPPER**: <MD 21:100-101; Plymouth Co.PR 11:232>
...21 Nov. 1748, ment. son Thomas TUPPER; wf Hannah; unnamed daus; grandson Jabez. Pr. 3 Dec.
1748.

Will of **Hannah (HATCH**[3])**(Turner)(Tinkham) Tupper (Mary Doty**[2]): <MD 21:101; Plymouth Co.PR 21:78>
...26 Aug. 1766, ment. "my 10 grandsons": Isaiah THOMAS, John PRATT, Jedidiah PRATT, Joseph TUR-
NER, Japhet TURNER, Samuel TURNER, Jonathan TURNER, Israel TURNER, Daniel TURNER & Elisha TURNER;
dau Elizabeth PRATT; ensign William THOMAS; "my 15 granddaughters": Betty RENNELS, Hannah LeBARON
Abigail BENSON, Mary TURNER, Thankful THRASHER, Hannah PADDOCK, Ruth ELLIS, Sarah WOOD, Huldah
DARLING, Hannah FULLER, Kezia PRATT, Deborah LORING, Priscilla PHILLIPS, Betty BARKER & Christia-
na SPEARS. Pr. 11 Oct. 1771.

Will of **John WHITE**: <MDP:530; Plymouth Co.PR 11:153,19:125>
...29 June 1748, ment. wf Martha; son Silvenus WHITE; dau Mary; sons Thomas WHITE, Justus WHITE;
daus Elizabeth, Deborah; grandson Nathaniel son of dau Jedidah. Pr. 9 Nov. 1748.

Will of **Grace (WADSWORTH)(Sprague) Wormall**: <MD 9:249; Plymouth Co.PR 14:503>
...13 Jan. 1748, ment. sons Jethro SPRAGUE, Terah SPRAGUE; dau Zerviah CHANDLER; grandchildren,
the chil. of dec'd dau Ruth, viz: William KEEN, Levi KEEN, Abel KEEN, Samuell KEEN, Josiah KEEN &
Grace COLE; granddaughters Silvina SPRAGUE, Grace SPRAGUE; grandsons Reuben CHANDLER, William
SPRAGUE. Pr. 3 Apr. 1758.

NOTES:

FRANCIS EATON

Francis EATON was born in England, date unknown. He was among those who died in the epidemic which swept through Plymouth in 1633, pre 8 Nov. 1633 when his inventory was taken <PCR 1:19; MD 1:198,2:116 (N.S.); MDP:265>. His first wife was Sarah (   ) who was born in England and died in Plymouth in early 1621 (aft. 11 Jan.) <MD 1:15,2:116>. According to Bradford, he had a second wife who died early, probably around 1624. It has been suggested that she was the unnamed maid of the Carver family whom Bradford says "married and died a year or two after" <MD 2:116>. Francis married 3rd, c1624/5, Plymouth, Christian PENN <MD 2:117>, b. c1607, England, d. c1686 (see p.16 within). Christian m.2nd, Francis BILLINGTON (see Billington Family).

See also: Mayflower Families Through Five Generations (MF5G), Francis Eaton of the Mayflower, by Lee Douglas Van Antwerp, M.D.,C.G., 4th Ed., 1988; Mayflower Families In Progress, Francis Eaton Of The Mayflower and His Descendants for Four Generations, rev. 1994 by Robert S. Wakefield FASG.

Francis had one child by wf Sarah and 3 by wf Christian:

I.   Samuel, b. c1620, England
II. Rachel, b. c1625, Plymouth
III. Benjamin, b. cMar. 1627/8, Plymouth
IV. child, living 1651, Plymouth (according to Bradford, "an idiot")

         *   *   *   *   *   *   *   *   *   *   *   *

I. **SAMUEL EATON**[2], b. c1620, England <MD 2:117>, d. pre 29 Oct. 1684, Middleboro (inv.) <MD 2:172 -173>; m.1st, pre 10 Mar. 1646, **Elizabeth (   )** <PCR 12:144; MDP:266 (wf Elizabeth ack. deed)>, b. (   ), d. betw. 5 Oct. 1652 <MD 2:254 (N.S.)> - 1661 (hus. 2nd marr.). **Samuel** m.2nd, 10 Jan. 1660/1, Plymouth, **Martha BILLINGTON**[3] <PCR 8:22; MD 17:183>, (see BILLINGTON Family, p.17). The inclusion of the following two unnamed daughters is based on the phrasing in the settlement of Samuel's estate, see EATON Probate Appendix.

    6 EATON Children: (2 by 1st wf, 4 by 2nd, b. Duxbury or Middleboro)

1. **dau.**, b. pre 1650/1 (Bradford states in 1650/1 Samuel has a child), m. (   ), d. pre 1684.

2. **dau**, b. (   ), m. (   ), d. aft. 1684.

3. **Sarah EATON**[3], b. pre 3 Jan. 1663/4 <Plymouth Co.Deeds 3:47; MDP:57 (she is mentioned in a deed from her grandfather Francis Billington to her parents)>, d. aft. 24 Feb. 1725/6 <MF5G 1:8 (agreement of heirs)>; m. c1685, **Philip BUMPAS/BUMP** <MD 7:128>, (son of Edward & Hannah BOMPASSE), b. pre 1660, poss. Plymouth or Duxbury (if of age in 1681 deed) <MF5G 1:7>, d. 20 Jan. 1724/5, Plainfield CT <VR 1:34>. <See MF5G 1:8,9 for 8 chil.> (See EATON Probate Appendix for estate of Philip BUMPAS/BUMP.)

4. **Samuel EATON**[3], b. c1663 <Plymouth Co.Deeds 3:47,122 (prob. aft. 3 Jan. 1663/4)>, d. 8 Mar. 1723/4, 61st yr, Middleboro <MD 4:74>; m. 24 May 1694, Middleboro, **Elizabeth FULLER**[3] <MD 26:38; PN&Q 3:122>, (dau of Samuel FULLER[2-1] - see S. FULLER Family). <For bth. 4 chil. see MBD 1:442,457; MD 2:42; Middleboro VR. See MD 12:227-29 for Samuel's estate.>

5. **Mercy EATON**[3], b. c1665, d. aft. 27 Feb. 1704 (bth.last ch.); m. 7 Jan. 1685/6, Plymouth, **Samuel FULLER**[3] <MD 13:204>, (son of Samuel FULLER[2-1] - see S. FULLER Family). <See MD 3:14 for bth. 11 chil.>

6. **Bethiah EATON**[3], b. c1668, d. pre 12 Jan. 1735/6 (hus.will); m. 5 Nov. 1691, Taunton, **Joseph BASSETT** <MSR:629>, (son of Joseph BASSETT & Mary LAPHAM), b. c1664, Bridgewater, d. 8 Nov. 1736, Bridgewater <MF5G 1:10>. <See MD 15:46 for bth. 3 chil.> (See EATON Probate Appendix for will of Joseph BASSETT.)

_____

II. **RACHEL EATON**[2], b. c1625, Plymouth <PCR 3:18, MD 36:187 (ae 26 or thereabouts in Oct. 1652 court case); PCR 2:132, MD 36:187 (ae about 23 in Aug. 1648 court case)>, d. betw. 3 June 1656 <PCR 3:102> - Oct. 1661 (hus.2nd marr.); m. 2 Mar. 1645, Plymouth, **Joseph RAMSDEN/RAMSDELL** <PCR 2:94; MD 8:18,13:86,36:187>, b. (   ), d. 25 May 1674 <MD 8:19>. <See MBD 1:448 #22 for an account of the murder trial Rachel testified in (1648) as well as the court records ordering the family to move out of the woods, closer to town. See also MD 36:187-8, The Ramsden Family of Plymouth and MD 8:18-20 for his estate.> (Joseph m.2nd, 16 Oct. 1661, Plymouth, Mary SAVORY <PCR 8:22; MD 8:18,17:183>.)

    1 RAMSDEN Child:

1. **Daniel RAMSDEN**[3], b. 14 Sept. 1649, Plymouth <PCR 8:7; MD 8:18,16:121,36:187>, d. pre 12 Mar. 1721/2 <MD 36:187 (deed)>; m. 1st (   ) <MD 36:188 (Although MF5G & MBD state his five

children are all by wife Hannah, a 1698 court appearance of son Thomas implies he was of age therefore born by 1677 - 13 years before the birth of the other four children. This large gap suggests there was a first wife although she has yet to be identified. A clue into her identity may be found in the births of the four children who are mistakenly recorded as the children of "Daniel & Sarah" - could Sarah have been his first wife?)>. **Daniel** m.2nd, c1689, **Hannah CASWELL** <MD 36:188>, (dau of Thomas & Mary), b. 14 July 1661, Taunton <Taunton VR 1: 83>, d. aft. 10 July 1722 <Bristol Co.Deeds 14:316-7, MD 36:188>. <See MD 36:188 for bth. 1 ch. by 1st wf. and 4 chil. by 2nd wf.; MD 3:14 for bth. 4 chil. See MD 39:1-3 for 6th ch.>

III **BENJAMIN EATON**[2], b. aft. 22 May 1627 (MD 1:153 (Cattle Division), cMar. 1627/8 <Plymouth TR 1:12 (at least 16 in Aug. 1643)>, d. 16 Jan. 1711/2, Plympton, "aged" <MD 2:140,10:113>; m. 4 Dec. 1660, Plymouth, **Sarah HOSKINS** <PCR 8:22; MD 17:183>, (dau of William HOSKINS & Sarah CUSHMAN), b. 16 Sept. 1637 <MF5G 1:7>, d. aft. 31 May 1711 <TG 1:238>.

5 (poss.6) EATON Children:

1. **Benjamin EATON**[3], b. c1664, Plymouth <MBD 1:448, #5, Plymouth Co.Deeds 5:368 (pre 29 Oct. 1664 if 21 when he signed deed 29 Oct. 1685)>, d. betw. 3 or 23 Apr. 1745 (will) - 20 Dec. 1745 (pr.) <MDP:266>; m.1st, 18 Dec. 1689, Plymouth, **Mary COOMBS**[4] <MD 13:205>, (dau of John COOMBS[3] (Sarah Priest[2], Degory[1] - see PRIEST family) & Elizabeth (ROYALL?) Barlow), b. 28 Nov. 1666, Boston <Boston Rcd.Com.9:100>, d. 2 July 1728, Plympton g.s., 63rd yr <MD 10:113>. **Benjamin** m.2nd, 11 Mar. 1728/9, Hingham, **Susanna (LEWIS) Beal** <Hist.Hingham 2:57>, (dau of James LEWIS & Sarah LANE), b. cApr. 1669, poss. Barnstable <Otis 2:126>, d. 13 Apr. 1739, Kingston g.s. "ae 70 (the same month she died)" <MD 7:85>. (Susanna m.1st, 18 Feb. 1689/90, Barnstable, Lazarus BEAL <MFIP #10>.) **Benjamin** m.3rd, (int.) 4 Oct. 1740, Kingston, **Mercy ( ) VAUGHAN** <Kingston VR; MD 42:14 (poss. Mercy (NELSON)(Fuller) Vaughan)>. <See MBD 1: 438 for bth. 11 chil. by 1st wf.; MD 2:78 for bth. 5 & Plymouth VR for 5.> (See EATON Probate Appendix for will of Benjamin EATON.)

2. **William EATON**[3], b. pre July 1669, d. betw. July 1690 (will) - 18 Mar. 1690/91 (inv.), unm., Canada <MDP:266; MD 12:227>. (See EATON Probate Appendix for will of William EATON.)

3. **Sarah EATON**[3], b. pre 1672, prob. Plymouth <MD 43:3>, d. aft. 14 June 1712 (bth.ch.), prob. Plympton <MD 43:3>; m. by 1698 (if bth. of 1st ch. is 1698 and not 1688 as recorded which would leave a 13 yr. gap betw. 1st and 2nd ch.), **Eleazer RICKARD** <MD 43:3>, (son of Giles RICKARD[2-1] & Hannah DUNHAM), b. ( ), d. aft. 23 Jan. 1735/6, prob. Plympton <Plymouth Co. Deeds 30:82; MD 43:4>. <See MD 43:4 for bth. 6 chil.; MD 3:13 (3), 5:207 (3).>

4. **Ebenezer EATON**[3], b. c1674, d. 25 July 1735, N. Yarmouth ME, 72nd yr <N.Yarmouth ME VR:393>; m. 2 Nov. 1701, Plymouth, **Hannah RICKARD** <MD 13:207>, (dau of Giles RICKARD[2-1] & Hannah DUN-HAM), b. ( ), d. 26 Apr. 1755, N. Yarmouth ME <N.Yarmouth ME VR:393>. <See MBD 1:441 & MD 2:165 for bth. 6 chil.; MFIP #12 adds a 7th> (See EATON Probate Appendix for estate of Ebenezer EATON.)

5. **Rebecca EATON**[3], b. c1675, d. 13 Nov. 1770, Plympton g.s., 95th yr <MD 11:116>; m. 21 Nov. 1699, Plymouth, **Josiah RICKARD** <MD 13:207>, (son of Giles RICKARD[2-1] & Hannah DUNHAM), b. c1672, d. 22 Jan. 1765, Plympton g.s., 93rd yr <MD 11:115>. <See MBD 1:441 for bth of 6 chil and MD 3:13 (1), 14 (2), 163 (3).> (See EATON Probate Appendix for will of Josiah RICKARD.)

6. poss. **Experience EATON**[3], (dau), b. ( ), d. aft. 25 Nov. 1731, Plympton <MD 38:189>.

EATON PROBATE APPENDIX

Will of **Joseph BASSETT**: (husbandman) <Plymouth Co.PR 7:265,345>
...12 Jan. 1735/6, ment. eldest dau Bethia BASSETT; 2nd dau Mehetebell HOLLOWAY; 3rd dau Lydia PHILLIPS. Pr. 7 Feb. 1736/7.
===
Estate of **Philip BUMP/BUMPUS**: <Plainfield CT PR 3:115-6>
...Agreement of heirs, 24 Feb. 1725/6, ment. widow Sarah; Samuel BUMP; Philip BUMP; Josiah BUMP; Thomas HERD & wf Lydia; Peleg BALLARD & wf Bethia; dau Sarah BUMP; Thomas SMITH & wf Jemima.
===
Will of **Benjamin EATON**[3] (**Ben.**[2]): (housewright) <MDP:266; Plymouth Co.PR 10:70-74>
...23 Apr. 1745, ment. eldest son William EATON (non compos mentis); sons John EATON, Benjamin EATON, David EATON, Francis EATON, Elisha EATON; chil. of dau Sarah CUSHMAN; dau Mary SOULE; dau Elizabeth STERTEVANT; chil. of dec'd dau Hannah BRYANT. Pr. 7 Dec. 1745.
===
Estate of **Ebenezer EATON**[3] (**Ben.**[2]): (housewright) <York Co.ME PR #4983,4984>
...Agreement of heirs, 27 Dec. 1736, ment. widow Hannah; eldest son Ebenezer EATON; daus Marcy LAKE wf of Benjamin and Joanna EATON; sons Elisha EATON, Gideon EATON.
===

Estate of **Samuel EATON**[2]: <MD 2:172-3; Plymouth Colony Wills 4:1:83>
...Settlement of estate, (ment. in inv. dated 29 Oct. 1684) "the eldest (i.e. son Samuel) shall
have the house and land...the Daughter (i.e. Sarah) provided for by her Grandfather...the Children of the first wife (i.e. two or more unnamed married daus.) to have the sume of twenty shillings a peece & such of them as are Dead the sume to be payed amonge theire Children...twenty
shillings for the two youngest Children" (i.e. Mercy, Bethiah). (Note: It is assumed the unnamed children of the first wife were daughters because they received the same bequest as the two
youngest daughters.)

Will of **William EATON**[3] (**Ben.**[2]): <MDP:266>
...July 1690, "being forth to go against the ffrench I give one cow calf to my father and mother"
Inv. presented 18 Mar. 1690/1. (He died on the expedition to Canada.)
                        ===
Will of **Josiah RICKARD**: <Plymouth Co.PR 19:160>
...17 Dec. 1750, ment. wf Rebecca; sons Giles RICKARD, Benjamin RICKARD, David RICKARD, Josiah
RICKARD; daus Desire FRAZIER, Rebeckah ALLEN; granddau. Elizabeth DOGGETT. Pr. 4 Feb. 1765.

NOTES:

MOSES FLETCHER

Moses FLETCHER was poss. b. St. Peter's, Sandwich, Kent co., England. He died early in 1620/21 in Plymouth. Moses m.1st, 30 Oct. 1589, Sandwich, Eng., Mary Evans by whom he had all his children. He. m.2nd, 21 Dec. 1613, Leyden, Holland, Sarah ( ) Dinbay. Moses FLETCHER is the only Mayflower passenger (known to date) whose family and descendants remained in Holland and did not emigrate to New England. For this reason, little has been written about the Fletchers, therefore the sole source for this family remains the Mayflower Quarterly 41:45-47.

Moses & 1st wf Mary had 10 Children:

I.   Mary. bpt. 4 Jan. 1589/90, Sandwich, Eng.
II.   John , b. c1592, Sandwich, Eng.
III. Catharin, bpt. 1 Sept. 1594, Sandwich, Eng.
IV.   Richard, bpt. 2 Jan. 1596/7, Sandwich, Eng.
V.   Priscilla ' bpt. 24 Mar. 1599/1600, Sandwich, Eng.
VI.   Moyses, bpt. 10 Oct. 1602, Sandwich, Eng., bur. 21 Apr. 1603, Sandwich, Eng.
VII. Elizabeth ' bpt. 8 Apr. 1604, Sandwich, Eng.
VIII. Jayne, bpt. 8 Feb. 1606/7, Sandwich, Eng.
IX.   Judith, b. (   ), bur. 6 Nov. 1609, Sandwich, Eng.
X.   Moses, bpt. 2 Apr. 1609, Sandwich, Eng.

* * * * * * * * * *

II.   JOHN FLETCHER[2], b. c1592, Sandwich, Eng., d. aft. 13 Feb. 1656, Leyden, Holland; m. 5 Dec. 1618, Leyden, **Josina SACHARIAS**, b. (   ), poss. bur. 26 July 1664, Leyden.

4 FLETCHER Children:

1. Mary FLETCHER[3], bpt. 14 Aug. 1622, Leyden, Holland.
2. Sacharias FLETCHER[3], bpt. 12 Jan. 1626, Leyden.
3. Josyna FLETCHER[3], bpt. 8 Oct. 1628, Leyden.
4. Moses FLETCHER[3], bpt. 4 June 1631, Leyden.

V.   PRISCILLA FLETCHER[2], bpt. 24 Mar. 1599/1600, Sandwich, Eng., d. aft. 1652; m.1st 4 Apr. 1626, Leyden, **Thomas COIT/KOET**; m.2nd, 1 June 1637, Leyden, **Help TERRY/TARY**; m.3rd, 4 Aug. 1652, Leyden, **Jan VERMOUT**.

4 COIT/KOET & 1 TERRY/TARY Children:

1. Sarah COIT/KOET[3], bpt. Feb. 1634, Leyden,
2. Jan COIT/KOET[3], bpt. Feb. 1634, Leyden; m. 10 Apr. 1650, **Maartgen JACOBS**.
3. Dirk COIT/KOET[3], bpt. Feb. 1634, Leyden; m. 22 Apr. 1647, **Stijntje/Christine EDUARDS**.
4. Dorothea COIT/KOET[3], b. c1629, Leyden, d. aft. 9 May 1697; m. 21 May 1657, **Jan VAN OUTHUYSEN**, d. aft. 24 Dec. 1705.
5. Maria TERRY/TARY[3], b. 1627/8, Leyden.

VII ELIZABETH FLETCHER[2], bpt. 8 Apr. 1604, Sandwich, Eng., d. aft. 28 Sept. 1677, Leyden; m.1st, (   ), Leyden, **Caspar BARNAART**; m.2nd, 21 May 1636, Leyden, **Michiel VOORSHOREN**, d. aft. 20 Feb. 1678.

4 VOORSHOREN Children:

1. John VOORSHOREN[3], bpt. 22 Mar. 1637, Leyden; m. 13 May 1668, **Magdelena VAN LENSEEL**.
2. Judith VOORSHOREN[3], bpt. 4 Mar. 1640, Leyden.
3. Maria VOORSHOREN[3], bpt. 1 June 1642, Leyden; m. 6 June 1666, **Wynand SMITH**, bpt. 19 Dec. 1638.
4. Michiel VOORSHOREN[3], bpt. 2 Feb. 1645, Leyden.

EDWARD FULLER

Edward FULLER was baptized 4 Sept. 1575, Parish of Redenhall, Norfolk co., England, the son of Robert Fuller & Sarah Dunkhorn <NEHGR 55:411; MF 4:5> and was the brother of Dr. Samuel FULLER. The name of Edward's wife is uknown, she died in early 1621 (aft. 11 Jan.) in Plymouth. <MD 2: 117>.

(See: Mayflower Families Through Five Generations, Edward Fuller of the Mayflower, by Bruce C. MacGunnigle, C.G., Vol.4, 1990.)

Edward & wife had 2 known children:

I.   Matthew, b. pre 1610, prob. England.
II. Samuel, b. c1608, prob. England.

                    * * * * * * * * * * * *

I.   **MATTHEW FULLER**[2], b. pre 1610, prob. England <TAG 61:194-99; Otis 1:381>, d. betw. 25 July - 22 Aug. 1678 (will & inv.), Barnstable <MD 13:7>; m. (   ), **Francis (   )**, b. (   ), d. aft. 26 Oct. 1678 <MD 13:11 (made oath to hus.inv.)>. (See FULLER Probate Appendix for will of Matthew FULLER.)

     ### 5 FULLER Children:

1.   **Samuel FULLER**[3], b. c1630, prob. England, d. 26 Mar. 1675/6, Rehoboth (killed by Indians in King Phillip's War) <MF5G 4:8; MBD 1:451 (Bowman) says 25th; Otis 1:381 says 25th>; m. (   ) **Mary (   )**, b. aft. 1630, d. aft. 7 Aug. 1696 <MD 31:187 (will of son Matthias)>. <See MBD 1:452 & Otis 1:381-2 for bth. 7 chil.> (See FULLER Probate Appendix for will of Samuel FULLER.) <See also MDP:275 for will of son Matthias.)

2.   **Mary FULLER**[3], b. aft. 1630, prob. England, d. aft. 11 May 1691, Barnstable (hus.will) <MD 15: 78>; m. 17 Apr. 1650, Plymouth, **Ralph JONES** <MD 16:235; Otis 2:109>, b. (   ), d. betw. 11 May 1691 (will) - 20 Apr. 1692 (wit.sworn) <MD 15:78-9>. <See Otis 2:110 for 10 chil.; MD 18:201 & PCR 8:45 (3), MD 6:139 (1), 140 (4).> (See FULLER Probate Appendix for will of Ralph JONES.)

3.   **Elizabeth FULLER**[3], b. aft. 1630, prob. England, d. aft. 7 Mar. 1714/5, E. Haddam or Colchester CT <MD 35:130 (deposition)>; m. 22 Apr. 1652, Barnstable, **Moses ROWLEY** <PCR 8:47; MD 12: 153,18:203; Otis 1:381>, b. prob. pre 1630, poss. Eng., d. 14 June 1705, E. Haddam CT <MF5G 4:10>. <See MBD 1:451-2 for bth. 10 chil.; MD 12:153 (8); MD 18:203 (5); PCR 8:47 (5).> (See FULLER Probate Appendix for will of Moses ROWLEY.)

4.   **Anne/Anna FULLER**[3], b. aft. 1640, Plymouth, d. pre 30 Dec. 1691 (hus.est.), Barnstable <MD 12: 189>; m. c1657/8, prob. Barnstable, **Samuel FULLER**[3] (Samuel[2], Edw.[1] - see below).

5.   **John FULLER**[3], b. aft. 1640, Plymouth, d. pre 16 July 1691, Barnstable (inv.) <MD 12:187-88>; m.1st, (   ), **Bethiah (   )** <Otis 1:382>, b. (   ), d. pre Mar. 1686/7 (hus.2nd marr.). John m.2nd, 24 Mar. 1686/7, Plymouth, **Hannah MORTON** <MD 13:203>, b. c1659, Plymouth, d. betw. 7 - 19 Oct. 1738 (will & pr. of 2nd hus.) <Barnstable Co.PR 4:407>. (Hannah m.2nd, 9 Dec. 1695, Capt. John LOTHROP <MD 14:225; Otis 1:382> & had 3 chil. <MD 6:238>.) <See MD 12:188 for 1 ch. by 1st wf; MBD 1:452 & 4:225 for 3 chil. by 2nd wf; Otis 1:382 (4).> (See FULLER Probate Appendix for estate of Dr. John FULLER.)

─────────────────────────────

II. **SAMUEL FULLER**[2], b. c1608, prob. England, d. 31 Oct. 1683, Barnstable <MD 2:237; Otis 1:372>; m. 8 Apr. 1635, Scituate, **Jane LOTHROP** <NEHGR 9:286 (ChR); MSR:602; Otis 1:371,372>, (dau of Rev. John LOTHROP & Hannah HOWES), bpt. 29 Sept. 1614, Edgerton, Kent co., Eng. <MBD 1:450>, d. pre 29 Oct. 1683 (hus.will) <MD 2:237-41>. (See FULLER Probate Appendix for will of Samuel FULLER.)

     ### 9 FULLER Children: <MBD 1:450; Otis 1:372-3>

1.   **Hannah FULLER**[3], b. c1636, Scituate, d. aft. 23 Aug. 1686, Piscataway NJ (hus.est.); m. 1 Jan. 1658/9, Barnstable, **Nicholas BONHAM** <PCR 8:41; MD 2:214,18:198; Otis 1:372>, b. c1630, Eng., d. 20 July 1684, Piscataway NJ <MF5G 4:13>. <See MBD 1:450,452 for bth. 8 chil.> (See FULLER Probate Appendix for will of Nicholas BONHAM.)

2.   **Samuel FULLER**[3], bpt. 11 Feb. 1637/8, Scituate <NEHGR 9:281 (ChR); MSR:597; Otis 1:372-3>, d. pre 29 Dec. 1691 (inv.) <MD 12:189-90; Otis 1:373>; m. c1657/8, Barnstable, **Anne FULLER**[3] (see above). <See Otis 1:373 for 6 chil.> (See FULLER Probate Appendix for estate of Samuel.)

3. Elizabeth FULLER[3], b. (   ), d. aft. 29 Oct. 1683 (fath.will) <MD 2:237>; m. (   ) called Elizabeth TAYLER in fath. will.

4. Sarah FULLER[3], bpt. 1 Aug. 1641, Barnstable, d.y. <NEHGR 9:282 (ChR); MSR:598; Otis 1:372>.

5. Mary FULLER[3], bpt. 16 June 1644, Barnstable <NEHGR 9:283 (ChR); MSR:599; Otis 1:372-3>; d. 11 Nov. 1720, Norwich CT <Norwich CT VR 1:62>; m. 18 Nov. 1674, Haverhill, Joseph WILLIAMS <Otis 1:372>, (son of John & Jane), b. 18 Apr. 1647, Haverhill <Haverhill VR 1:321; Otis 1:373>, d. aft. 4 Jan. 1720/1 (ack.deed) <Norwich CT Deeds 3B:462>. <See MBD 1:450, Haverhill VR 1:321 & Otis 1:373 for bth. 4 chil.>

6. Thomas FULLER[3], b. 18 May 1650, Barnstable <PCR 8:43; MD 4:226,18:199; Otis 1:373; NEHGR 9: 284 & MSR:600 (ChR - bpt. 18 May 1651)>, d. pre 29 Oct. 1683 (fath. will) <MD 2:237>.

7. Sarah FULLER[3], b. 14 Dec. 1654, Barnstable <PCR 8:43; MD 4:226,18:199; Otis 1:373>, d. aft. 29 Oct. 1683 (fath.will) <MD 2:237>; m. (   ), called Sarah CROWE in fath. will.

8. John FULLER[3], b. c1655/6, Barnstable <Otis 1:373>, d. 23 Mar. 1726, E. Haddam CT <MF 4:16>; m. c1678, Barnstable, Mehitable ROWLEY[4] <MF 4:16>, (dau of Moses ROWLEY & Elizabeth FULLER[3] - see p.58), b. 11 Jan. 1660/1, Barnstable <PCR 8:47; MD 18:203>, d. 1732, E. Haddam CT <MF 4: 16>. <See MBD 1:452 #6 for 12 chil. and Otis 1:374 for 8.> (See FULLER Probate Appendix for will of John FULLER.)

9. child, b. 8 Feb. 1658, Barnstable, bur. 23 Feb. 1658 <PCR 8:43; MD 4:226,18:199>.

FULLER PROBATE APPENDIX

Will of Nicholas BONHAM: <New Jersey Hist.Society (1st Series) 1:45>
...6 Feb. 1683/4, ment. wf Hannah; son Hezekiah; unnamed children. Wit. sworn 18 Dec. 1684.
==

Estate of John FULLER[3] (Matthew[2]): (chirurgion) <MD 33:171-3; Barnstable Co.PR 3:135>
...Settlement, 16 Nov. 1713, to widow Hannah LOTHROP and following chil., viz: John FULLER (only son); daus Lydia DIMMOCK (eldest), Bethia LOTHROP, Reliance PRINCE.
==

Will of John FULLER[3] (Samuel[2]): <Hartford CT PR #2081>
...28 Feb. 1725/6, ment. unnamed wf; sons Thomas FULLER, Samuel FULLER, Shubael FULLER, Edward FULLER, John FULLER, Joseph FULLER, Benjamin FULLER; daus Thankfull, Elizabeth, Mehitable. Pr. 21 Apr. 1726.
==

Will of Matthew FULLER[2]: <MD 13:7-11; Plymouth Colony Wills 3:2:127-9>
...25 July 1678, ment. grandchild Shubaell JONES reputed son of Ralph JONES; wf Ffrancis; only son John FULLER; sons of dec'd eldest son Samuel FULLER, viz: Thomas FULLER, Jabez FULLER, Timothy FULLER, Matthias FULLER, Samuel FULLER; Bethyah, wf of son John FULLER; daus Mary JONES wf of Ralph, Anne FULLER wf of Samuel and Elizabeth ROWLEY wf of Moses; Sarah ROWLEY dau of Moses; Jedediah JONES son of Ralph; male & female grandchildren; sons in law Ralph JONES, Samuel FULLER Jr., Moses ROWLEY Sr.; Mary FULLER late wf of dec'd son Samuel FULLER. Inv. taken 22 Aug. 1678.
==

Will of Samuel FULLER[2]: <MD 2:237-41>
...29 Oct. 1683, ment. eldest son Samuel FULLER; son John FULLER; daus Elizabeth TAYLER, Hannah BONHAM, Mary WILLIAMS, Sarah CROWE; Indian "Joell" to go to son John. Pr. 5 June 1684.
==

Will of Lieft. Samuel FULLER[3] (Matthew[2]): <MD 13:8>
...2 Aug. 1675, ment. wf Mary; eldest son Thomas FULLER (under 21); sons Jabez FULLER, Timothy FULLER, Matthias FULLER; daus Abigail, Anne. Inv. taken 3 June 1676. (On 8 June 1676 the widow claimed to be with child.)
==

Estate of Samuel FULLER[3] (Samuel[2]): <MD 12:189>
...Release, 30 Dec. 1691, among sons Matthew FULLER, Barnabas FULLER, Joseph FULLER, Benjamin FULLER and daus Desire FULLER, Sarah FULLER.
==

Will of Ralph JONES: <MD 15:78-9; Barnstable Co.PR>
...11 3mth (May) 1691, "being aged", leaves money to Quakers & asks to be buried in Quaker burying place in Sandwich; ment. unnamed wf; father FULLER; sons Shubael JONES, Jedidiah JONES, Ralph JONES, Samuel JONES, Matthew JONES, John JONES, Ephraim JONES (under 21); daus Mercy, Mary, Hittable. Wit. sworn 20 Apr. 1692.
==

Will of Moses ROWLEY: <Early CT PR 2:107>
...16 Aug. 1704, ment. sons Moses ROWLEY, Matthew ROWLEY; dau Mehetabell FULLER; son John ROWLEY; rest of my chil.; unnamed wf. Inv. taken 15 June 1705.

SAMUEL FULLER

Dr. Samuel FULLER was bpt. 20 Jan. 1580, Parish of Redenhall, Norfolk co., England, the son of Robert Fuller & Sarah Dunkhorn <NEHGR 55:411; MF5G 4:5> and the brother of Edward Fuller (p.58). After lending his invaluable services to others during the epidemic of 1633, he himself succumbed, sometime between 30 July 1633 (will) - 28 Oct. 1633 (pr.) <MD 1:24-8; MF5G 1:50 says betw. 9 Aug. - 26 Sept. 1633>. Samuel m.1st, date unknown, Alice Glascock who died pre 1613, Leyden, Holland <MD 2:117>. He m.2nd, 24 Apr. 1613, Leyden, Agnes Carpenter <MD 8:129-30,22:65-6>, the daughter of Alexander Carpenter, bpt. 16 Dec. 1593, Wrington, Eng. <MF5G 1:49>, died c1615, Leyden. Samuel m.3rd, 27 May 1617, Leyden, Bridget Lee <MD 8:129-30,22:65-6>, who died after 2 May 1667 <MD 39:86>.

(See: Mayflower Families Through Five Generations, Samuel Fuller of the Mayflower (MF5G), by Katharine W. Radasch & Arthur H. Radasch, 1975, vol.1.)

Samuel had 1 child by 2nd wife, 3 children by 3rd wife:

I.   child, bur. 29 June 1615, Leyden, Holland.
II.   child, b. Holland, d.y. Plymouth (Bradford; not ment. in 1627 Cattle Division).
III. Samuel, b. c1628/9, Plymouth.
IV.   Mercy, b. aft. 22 May 1627, Plymouth; living 1651 (Bradford), nothing further known.

*   *   *   *   *   *   *   *   *   *   *   *

III **SAMUEL FULLER**[2], b. c1628/9, Plymouth, d. 17 or 24 Aug. 1695, Middleboro, Nemasket cem. <MD 1: 222 ("sometime in Aug."), 5:65 18:256 (& Middleboro Dths:70 - g.s. says d. 17 Aug. 71st yr), 15:21 (Plymouth ChR - "Mr. Samuel Fuller, the Teacher of the chh at Midlebury a sincere Godly man whom wee had the last yeare dismissed to that service, dyed August 24 being about 66 yeares old a great losse to that place".)> Although his g.s. says he was in his 71st yr at death (b. c1624), this is obviously an error as he is not listed in the 1627 Cattle Division. Although no record has been found, a marriage is assumed due to the approx. date of birth of his first child (c1658); his only known wife was known to have been married to her first husband at least as late as 11 Apr. 1663 when he wrote his will. It is not known if his second child was by the 1st or 2nd wife. Samuel m.2nd, betw. 1663 - 2 May 1667, prob. Plymouth, **Elizabeth (NICHOLS) Bowen** <MD 39:86>, (dau of John NICHOLS), b. c1637, d. 11 Nov. 1713, Plympton <MD 2:140; Middleboro Dths:70 (says 4th). (Elizabeth m.1st, c1660, Thomas BOWEN & had 1 child <MD 39:86>.) (See FULLER Probate Appendix for estate of Samuel FULLER.)

7 FULLER Children: <MD 39:85-7>

1. **Samuel FULLER**[3], b. c1658, Plymouth, d. 6 Sept. 1728, 70th yr, Plympton <MF5G 1:53>; m. 7 Jan. 1685/6, Plymouth, **Mercy EATON**[3] (see p.54). <See MBD 1:461 & MD 3:14 for bth. 11 chil.>

2. **Elizabeth FULLER**[3], b. c1663-66, Plymouth, d. pre June 1724 (div.hus.est.) <MD 12:227-9>; m. 24 May 1694, Middleboro, **Samuel EATON**[3]. See EATON Family p.54.

3. **John FULLER**[3], b. c1667, Plymouth, d. c1710, ae 42 <Middleboro Dths:70; (pre 10 Mar. 1709/10, probate)>; m. c1688, **Mercy NELSON**, (dau of William NELSON & Ruth FOXWELL), b. (   ), d. aft 20 Mar. 1717 (fath.will) <Plymouth Co.PR 4:62>. (Mercy m.2nd, 2 Dec. 1720, Middleboro, Joseph VAUGHAN <MD 4:72> who d. 2 Mar. 1733/4, 81st yr <Middleboro Dths:214>. Did she m.3rd, int. 4 Oct. 1740, Benjamin EATON[3]? - see p.55 within.) <See MBD 1:460,467 for bth. 9 chil. and MD 12:231 (1).> (See FULLER Probate Appendix for estate of John FULLER.)

4. **Experience FULLER**[3], b. c1669, Plymouth, d. betw. 16 Apr. 1725 (deed) - 21 Dec. 1728 (hus. adm.) <MD 18:228-9>; m. 12 Apr. 1693, Middleboro, **James WOOD** <MD 18:227,26:38; PN&Q 3:122>, (son of Henry WOOD & Abigail JENNEY), b. (   ), d. pre 21 Dec. 1728 (adm.) <MD 18:229>. <See MD 18:227 for bth. 7 chil.> (See FULLER Probate Appendix for estate of James WOOD.)

5. **Hannah FULLER**[3], b. c1671, Plymouth, d. betw. 11 June 1707 (ack. deed) <MDP:278> - 1709 (hus. 2nd marr.); m. aft. 27 July 1696, **Eleazer LEWIS** <MF5G 1:55>, (son of Edward LEWIS & Hannah COBB), b. 26 June 1664, Barnstable <MD 10:250>, d. pre 3 Feb. 1727 (adm.) <Plymouth Co.PR 5: 352; MDP:278>. (Eleazer m.2nd by 1709, Mary (   ) & had 3 chil. <MBD 1:459>.) <See MBD 1: 459 for bth. 5 chil.>

6. **Mercy FULLER**[3], b. c1672/3, Plymouth, d. 25 Sept. 1735, 63rd yr, Eastham g.s. <MD 3:180,8:3>; m. pre 1 Oct. 1695 (agreement), **Daniel COLE** <MD 39:87>, (son of Daniel & Ruth), b. c1666/7, d. 15 June 1736, 70th yr, Eastham g.s. <MD 3:180,8:3>. No known issue.

7. **Isaac FULLER**[3], b. c1674/5, Plymouth, d. pe 16 Nov. 1727, Middleboro (adm.) <Plymouth Co.PR 5: 393; MDP:278>; m. 1st 1 Sept. 1709, Plympton, **Mary PRATT** <MD 2:235>, b. (   ), d. aft. 13 Nov. 1734 (ack.deed) <MDP:278; Plymouth Co.Deeds 25:90>. (Mary poss.m.1st Joshua PRATT who

d. 16 Feb. 1697/8, Plymouth <MF5G 1:56>.) <See MBD 1:459 for bth. 7 chil.; MD 7:239 (4), 240 (3).>

FULLER PROBATE APPENDIX

Estate of **John FULLER**[3] (**Samuel**[2]): <Plymouth Co.PR #8260, 3:196; MDP:279>
...Settlement, 19 Sept. 1712, ment. following chil., viz: Ebenezer FULLER, John FULLER and minors Samuel FULLER, Jabez FULLER, Elizabeth FULLER, Joanna FULLER, Mary FULLER, Marcy FULLER & Lydia FULLER.

Will of **Dr. Samuel FULLER**[1]: <MD 1:23-8,2:8-10>
...30 July 1633, ment. 3 children in his care, viz: Sarah CONVERSE, Elizabeth COWLES & George FOSTER; brother <in law> Will WRIGHT & his wife; dau Mercy; sister <in law> Alice BRADFORD; cozen <nephew> Samuel FULLER; son Samuel FULLER "young and tender". Pr. 28 Oct. 1633.

Estate of **Eleazer LEWIS:** <Plymouth Co.PR 48:36; MDP:278>
...Settlement, 12 May 1731, ment. following chil., viz: Edward LEWIS, Susanna LEWIS, Hannah SNELL wf of Tho., Elizabeth LEWIS, Shubael LEWIS, Kezia LEWIS.

Estate of **James WOOD:** <MD 18:229-32; MDP:276>
...Settlement, 15 Mar. 1736, ment. following chil., viz: Jonathan WOOD (eldest son); Benjamin WOOD; chil. of dec'd son Barnabas WOOD; Abell WOOD; Ichabod WOOD; Ledia HOLEMS/HOLMES wf of George; James WOOD.

NOTES:

STEPHEN HOPKINS

Stephen HOPKINS was born in England c1580. He may possibly be the Stephen, son of Stephen Hopkins who was bpt. 29 Oct. 1581, Wortley, Parish of Wotton Underedge, Gloucester co., England <TAG 39:95>. He died between 6 June - 17 July 1644, Plymouth (will & inv.) <MD 2:12; MSR:512; see also MD 4:114 for estate>. Stephen married 1st, c1605, England but despite attempts, his wife's identity has not been proven. (The most popular has been Constance Dudley which seems worth consideration as his daughter by his first wife was named Constance.) Stephen married 2nd, 19 Feb. 1617/8, Whitechapel, London, England, Elizabeth FISHER <Banks 1:61>. Elizabeth's origins are unknown, she died after 4 Feb. 1638/9 <MF5G 6:7 (no reason is given for this date, however it was on this date that Stephen was ordered by the court to provide for his pregnant servant, Dorothy Temple, for the remainder of her two year term <PCR 1:112>. Stephen refused to do so and ultimately on 8 Feb. sold the remainder of her term to John Holmes.)> Elizabeth was deceased by 6 June 1644 when, in his will, Stephen asked to be buried near his wife. See HOPKINS Probate Appendix for the will of Stephen Hopkins.

(See: Mayflower Families Through Five Generations, Stephen Hopkins of the Mayflower, by John D. Austin, F.A.S.G., vol. 6, 1992; MD 5:47-53, Stephen Hopkins and His Descendants.)

Stephen had 2 children by 1st wife, 7 children by 2nd wife:

I.   Constance/Constanta, b. c1607/8, England
II.   Gyles, b. c1610, England
III.   Damaris, b. c1619, England, d.y.
IV.   Oceanus, b. betw. 16 Sept. - 11 Nov. 1620, aboard the Mayflower; d. pre 27 May 1627 (Cattle Division) <MD 1:151> (poss. d. pre 1623 when the land division accounts for the Hopkins family having six members).
V.   Caleb, b. c1622, Plymouth
VI.   Deborah, b. c1624/5, Plymouth
VII.   Damaris, b. c1627, Plymouth
VIII. Ruth, b. (   )
IX.   Elizabeth, b. (   )

* * * * * * * * * * * *

I.   **CONSTANCE HOPKINS**[2], b. c1607/8, England, d. middle Oct. 1677, Eastham <MD 3:167,6:203>; m. pre 27 May 1627, Plymouth, **Nicholas SNOW** <MD 1:151 (Cattle Division), (poss. son of Nicholas bpt. 25 Jan. 1599/1600, Shoreditch, London, England <Banks 1:160>), d. 15 Nov. 1676, Eastham <MD 3:167,6:203>. (See HOPKINS Probate Appendix for will of Nicholas SNOW.)

   9 SNOW Children: <MD 5:47 (Bradford wrote betw. 6 Mar.-3 Apr. 1651 that she had 12 chil.)>

1.   **Mark SNOW**[3], b. 9 May 1628, Plymouth <MF5G 6:10 gives the source MD 7:14 which is incorrect, I have been unable to find the correct source>, d. betw. 23 Nov. 1694 (will) - 9 Jan. 1694/5 (inv.) <MD 18:193-6>; m.1st, 18 Jan. 1654/5, Eastham, **Ann/Anna COOKE** <MD 5:23; PCR 8:15; MSR: 544,547>, (dau of Josiah COOKE & Elizabeth (RING) Deane), b. c1636-9, d. or bur. 24/25 July 1656, Eastham <MD 5:213 (bur.), 7:14 (d.); PCR 8:30 (d. 24th); MSR:547,548 (d. 24th)>. **Mark** m.2nd, 9 Jan. 1660/1, Eastham, **Jane PRENCE** <MD 7:14,17:201; PCR 8:28; MSR:546>, (dau of Thomas PRENCE & Mary COLLIER), b. 1 Nov. 1637, Duxbury <MF5G 6:9 (does not pinpoint source)>, d. betw. late May - 28 June 1712 (inv.) <MD 18:194 (probate records state lodging had been provided from 26 Oct. to latter end May 1712)>. <See MBD 1:16; MD 5:23 & MD 18:55 for 1 ch. by 1st wf.; for 8 chil. by 2nd wf see MBD 2:16 and MD 7:14 (6), 15 (2).> (See HOPKINS Probate Appendix for wills of Mark & Jane SNOW.)

2.   **Mary SNOW**[3], b. c1630, prob. Plymouth, d. 28 Apr. 1704, Eastham, "suddenly" <MD 8:230>; m. pre 3 Apr. 1650/1, **Thomas PAINE** <MD 1:14 (Bradford states Constance has one child married); MSR: 437>, (poss. son of Thomas), b. c1610, England <MSR:437>, d. 16 Aug. 1706, Eastham "aged" <MSR:437; MD 9:50 (mistakenly says 1707)>. <See MBD 2:25 for 10 chil.; see also MD 8:180-84, 227-31,9:49-51,97-99,136-140 for the very interesting journal of son, Deacon John PAINE.> (See HOPKINS Probate Appendix for will of Thomas PAINE.)

3.   **Sarah SNOW**[3], b. c1632, prob. Plymouth, d. aft. 8 Mar. 1697, prob. Eastham (hus.will) <Barnstable Co.PR 2:159-61>; m. 25 Feb. 1654/5, Eastham, **William WALKER** <MD 5:23,6:206; PCR 8:15; MSR:545>, b. c1620, England, d. betw. 8 Mar. 1697 (will) - 23 Oct. 1703 (pr.), prob. Eastham <Barnstable Co.PR 2:259-61>. <See MBD 2:43 & MD 6:206 for bth. 6 chil.> (See HOPKINS Probate Appendix for will of William WALKER.)

4.   **Joseph SNOW**[3], b. c1634, prob. Plymouth, d. 3 Jan. 1722/3, Eastham <MD 3:231>; m. c1670, **Mary ( )**, b. ( ), d. aft. 30 Jan. 1722/3 (hus.est.) <MDP:287>. <See MBD 2:13 & MD 3:230 for bth. 11 chil.> (See HOPKINS Probate Appendix for will of Joseph SNOW.)

5. **Stephen SNOW[3]**, b. c1636, prob. Plymouth, d. 17 Dec. 1705, Eastham <MD 8:15,31:37>; m.1st, 28
    Oct. 1663, Eastham, **Susanna (DEANE) Rogers** <MD 8:15; MD 6:13 (has incorrect date of 13 Dec.
    1665), 31:37-8 (discusses two dates)>, (dau of Stephen DEANE & Elizabeth RING), b. (   ),
    d. pre 9 Apr. 1701 (hus.2nd marr.) <MD 31:38>. (Susanna m.1st, 4 Apr. 1660, Eastham, Joseph
    ROGERS[3] <MSR:545> - see ROGERS Family.) **Stephen** m.2nd, 9 Apr. 1701, Eastham, **Mary (COTTLE)
    BIGFORD/BICKFORD** <MD 6:14,8:15,31:37>, (dau of Edward & Judith), b. 1 Nov. 1653, Salisbury
    <MF5G 6:19>, d. aft. 21 May 1706 (receipt of hus.heirs) <MD 31:38-41>. (Mary m.1st, Samuel
    BICKFORD.) <For 6 chil. by 1st wf see MBD 2:44 & MD 31:38; 4 chil. see MD 8:15,31:37.> (See
    HOPKINS Probate Appendix for will of Stephen SNOW.)

6. **John SNOW[3]**, b. c1638, prob. Plymouth, d. pre 4 Apr. 1692, Eastham (inv.) <MD 12:190>; m. 19
    Sept. 1667, Eastham, **Mary SMALLEY** <MD 7:17>, (twin dau of John SMALLEY & Ann WALDEN), b. 11
    Dec. 1647, Eastham <MD 17:200; PCR 8:27>, d. aft. 7 Dec. 1699, prob. Eastham (will of 2nd
    hus.) <MD 34:56-7>, poss. c1703. <See MD 2:5 & MD 7:17 for bth. 9 chil.> (Mary m.2nd,
    c1692, Ephraim DOANE, (son of John DOANE & Ann PERKINS) who d. 1700, Eastham <MF5G 6:23>.
    Ephraim m.1st, 5 Feb. 1667, Eastham, Mercy/Mary KNOWLES <MD 6:13,19:111; MSR:546> and had 8
    chil. <MD 6:13>.)

7. **Elizabeth SNOW[3]**, b. c1640, Eastham, d. 16 June 1678, Eastham <MD 6:14>; m. 13 Dec. 1665,
    Eastham, **Thomas ROGERS[3]** <MD 6:14>, (son of Joseph ROGERS[2]) See ROGERS Family.

8. **Jabez SNOW[3]**, b. c1642, prob. Eastham, d. 27 Dec. 1690, Eastham <MD 4:32,22:165>; m. c1669,
    prob. Eastham, **Elizabeth (   )**, <MF5G 6:23 (poss. Elizabeth SMITH, dau of Ralph SMITH, b.
    Sept. 1648, Hingham)>, d. aft. 8 Jan. 1732/3 <MDP:301 (inv. of est. of 2nd hus.)>. (Eliza-
    beth m.2nd, William MERRICK - see below under his first wife, Abigail Hopkins[3] (Gyles[2]).)
    <See MBD 2:1-2 for 9 chil.; MD 4:32 (5), 5:22 (4); see MD 14:255 (1).> (See HOPKINS Probate
    Appendix for estate of Jabez SNOW.)

9. **Ruth SNOW[3]**, b. c1644, prob. Plymouth, d. 27 Jan. 1716/7, Eastham <MD 5:197>; m. 10 or 12 Dec.
    1666, Eastham, **John COLE** <MD 5:196 (12th), 19:110 (10th); PCR 8:57 (10th); MSR:546 (10th)>,
    (son of Daniel & Ruth), b. 15 July 1644, Eastham <MD 5:23>, d. 6 Jan. 1724/5, Eastham <MD 5:
    196 (mistakenly says 1714/5)>. <See MBD 2:40 & MD 5:196 for bth. 7 chil.> (See HOPKINS
    Probate Appendix for will of John COLE.)

II. **GYLES/GILES HOPKINS[2]**, b. c1610, England, d. betw. 5 Mar. 1688/9 (codicil) - 16 Apr. 1690 (pr)
    Eastham <MD 1:110,112>; m. 9 Oct. 1639, Plymouth, **Catherine WHELDON** <MD 13:85; PCR 1:134>,
    (dau of Gabriel), b. c1615, d. aft. 5 Mar. 1688/9, Eastham <MD 1:113 (hus.codicil)>. (See
    HOPKINS Probate Appendix for will of Gyles HOPKINS.)

    10 HOPKINS Children: <MBD 2:55; MD 7:236-7>

1. **Mary HOPKINS[3]**, b. Nov. 1640, Yarmouth <MD 7:236>, d. 2 July 1700, Eastham <MD 12:116>; m. 3
    Jan. 1665/6, Eastham, **Samuel SMITH** <MD 8:17,12:112>, (son of Ralph), bpt. 11 July 1641, Hing-
    ham <NEHGR 26:190; Hist.Hingham 3:152>, d. 22 Mar. 1696/7, Eastham, 55th yr <MD 8:18>. <See
    MBD 2:77 & MD 8:18 for bth. 7 chil.> (See HOPKINS Probate Appendix for est. of Samuel SMITH)

2. **Stephen HOPKINS[3]**, b. Sept. 1642, Yarmouth <MD 7:236>, d. 10 Oct. 1718, Harwich <MD 6:56>; m.
    1st, 23 May 1667, Eastham, **Mary MERRICK** <MD 7:16,19:111; PCR 8:58; MSR:546>, (dau of William
    MERRICK & Rebecca TRACY), b. 4 Nov. 1650, Eastham <PCR 8:30; MD 5:23>, d. betw. 15 Apr. 1692
    <MD 7:16 (bth.last ch.)> - 7 Apr. 1701 (hus.2nd marr.). **Stephen** m.2nd, 7/9 Apr. 1701, East-
    ham, **Bethiah (LINNELL) Atkins** <MD 7:16 (7th), 9:9 (9th)>, (dau of Robert LINNELL & Peninah
    HOWES), bpt. 7 Feb. 1640/1, Barnstable <NEHGR 9:282 (ChR); MSR:598>, d. 24 Mar. 1726, Harwich
    <MD 8:35>. (Bethiah m.1st, 25 Mar. 1664, Eastham, Henry ATKINS & had 8 chil. <MD 7:239>.)
    <See MBD 2:83-4 & MD 7:16 for bth. 9 chil. by 1st wf.>

3. **John HOPKINS[3]**, b. 1643, Yarmouth, d. ae 3 mths. <MD 7:236>.

4. **Abigail HOPKINS[3]**, b. Oct. 1644, Yarmouth <MD 7:236>, d. (   ), prob. Eastham; m. 23 May
    1667, Eastham, **William MERRICK** <MD 5:198,19:110; PCR 8:56>, (son of William MERRICK & Rebecca
    TRACY), b. 15 Sept. 1643, Eastham <MD 5:23,18:55; PCR 8:30; MSR:547>, d. 30 Oct. 1732, Har-
    wich, 90th yr, Brewster g.s. <MD 13:70>. (William m.2nd, aft. 22 Apr. 1691, Elizabeth (   )
    SNOW, widow of Jabez SNOW[3] (see above).) <See MBD 2:56 for 9 chil.; MD 5:198 (1), 6:12 (1).>
    (See HOPKINS Probate Appendix for will of William MERRICK.)

5. **Deborah HOPKINS[3]**, b. June 1648, Eastham <MD 7:236>, d. betw. 28 Feb. 1686/7 (bth.last ch.) -
    7 Dec. 1727 (hus.will) <MD 5:185-6>; m. 27 July 1668, Eastham, **Josiah COOKE** <MD 8:88>, (son
    of Josiah COOKE & Elizabeth (RING) Deane), b. c1645, Eastham or Plymouth, d. 31 Jan. 1731/2,
    Eastham <MD 5:185,8:88>. <See MD 8:88 for bth. 8 chil.> (See HOPKINS Probate Appendix for
    will of Josiah COOKE.)

6. **Caleb HOPKINS[3]**, b. Jan. 1650/1, Eastham <MD 7:236,8:240>, d. pre 22 May 1728, prob. Truro
    (adm.) <MD 8:240>; m. (   ), prob. Eastham, **Mary WILLIAMS** <MD 8:240>, (dau of Thomas WIL-
    LIAMS & Elizabeth TART), b. (   ), prob. Eastham, d. betw. 27 May 1709 (bth.last ch.)
    <Truro VR:46> - 5 June 1728 (sett.hus.est.) <MD 8:240>. MF5G 6:31 suggests wf Mary d. pre

1708 and he had a 2nd wife Mary because a child was born in 1709, much later than the first three children (c1680's). If so, Mary (WILLIAMS) Hopkins died pre 1708. <See MBD 2:59 & MD 8:240 for 4 chil.> (See HOPKINS Probate Appendix for estate of Caleb HOPKINS.)

7. **Ruth HOPKINS**[3], b. June 1653, Eastham <MD 7:236>. (MF5G 6:11 suggests the possiblity that Ruth m. 26 May 1681, Eastham, Samuel MAYO the son of Nathaniel MAYO & Hannah PRENCE, but proof is lacking.)

8. **Joshua HOPKINS**[3], b. June 1657, Eastham <MD 7:236>, d. betw. 14 May 1734 (will) - 31 Aug. 1738 (pr.), prob. Eastham <MD 15:175-7>; m. 26 May 1681, Eastham, **Mary COLE** <MD 7:15; MSR:437>, (dau of Daniel & Ruth), b. 10 Mar. 1658, Eastham <PCR 8:27; MSR:437>, d. 1 Mar. 1733/4, Eastham, Orleans g.s. <MD 6:204; MSR:437>. <See MBD 2:75 & MD 7:15 for bth. 8 chil.> (See HOPKINS Probate Appendix for will of Joshua HOPKINS.)

9. **William HOPKINS**[3], b. 9 Jan. 1660/1, Eastham <PCR 8:28; MD 7:237>, d. aft. 5 Mar. 1689, unm. (father's codicil does not mention him specifically, but if he had deceased since writing his will, it would have been mentioned) <MD 1:112>. The wording in his father's will indicates that Gyles did not think his son would marry and have heirs. He asked son Stephen to "take ye care and oversight and maintaine my son William", which implies that William had a mental or physical weakness. The only real estate William was to receive was two acres which went to him and his mother jointly, and after their decease it did not revert to any heirs William might have (which was the customary wording), but to his brother Joshua and his heirs.

10. **Elizabeth HOPKINS**[3], b. Nov. 1664, Eastham, d. ae 1 mth. <MD 7:237>.

III **DAMARIS HOPKINS**[2], b. c1619, England, d.y., poss. betw. 1623-1627, Plymouth. In writing of the Hopkins family in 1651, Bradford gives the increase of children Giles and Constance (who are accounted for separately as Mayflower passengers in their own right) but does not say what became of Damaris or Oceanus, whom he mentions earlier by name. The 1627 Cattle Divison lists a Damaris Hopkins and Plymouth Colony Deeds 2:35, dated 10 June 1646, mentions the upcoming marriage of Damaris Hopkins to Jacob Cooke who had one and possibly two children at the time Bradford wrote in 1651. Bradford states that "4 doughters borne here" - Stephen's will of 1644 mentions 4 daughters, viz: Deborah, Damaris, Ruth and Elizabeth. Bradford goes on to state that one daughter dyed here, 2 are married and one is yet to marry - which matches these four daughters with Ruth the only one who cannot be accounted for in 1651 so is probably the daughter who died. (In speaking of the daughter who died, he appears to be referring to one of these four daughters, not an earlier daughter, e.g. Damaris). The only other explanation would be that the "4 doughters borne here" included an unknown daughter who died before Stephen's will of 1644 - which would leave Ruth alive in 1651 and the first Damaris alive. However, the fact that he does not specifically state (by name) that the first Damaris (as a Mayflower passenger in her own right) was married seems to imply that it was not the first Damaris who married Jacob Cooke. And, if the first Damaris was the one who had one or two children when he wrote, Bradford would have included her increase separately as he did with Giles & Constance. Bradford's writings are not without omission or error, remember, he was recalling events over a 30 year period covering some 27 families. But, if the Mayflower Damaris had married and had recent issue, it is hard to believe he could have overlooked this fact.

So, if we accept the fact that the first Damaris died young, the question now is - when? A Damaris Hopkins is listed in the 1627 Cattle Division whom researchers state is the first Damaris, but I have yet to find their reasoning. In the 1623 Division of land, Stephen Hopkins received 6 acres for his family. It is believed that the allotments were based largely on the number in each family. If this applies to the Hopkins family, who were the six? (The two servants were accounted for separately.) Stephen and his wife account for two, which leaves four children, two of whom were Constance & Giles. We now have two "spots" to fill with three children (Damaris, Oceanus & Caleb) who are known or believed to have been born pre 1623. We know Caleb did not die young, so he would be the third child. Either the first Damaris or Oceanus would account for the fourth child. Since Oceanus was not born under the best of circumstances (during the voyage) and the conditions that first winter felled half their numbers, it might be safe to assume that a newborn baby could not survive, thus the first Damaris could be the fourth child. If we accept this theory, the first Damaris was alive in 1623. The 1627 Cattle Division lists (in order), Stephen, wf Elizabeth, Gyles, Caleb, Debora, Nickolas Snow, Constance Snow. (Note that Gyles, Caleb & Debora are listed in their probable order of birth). Damaris Hopkins is listed with the Fuller group. This also ocurred in the Divison with young Thomas Prence (b. c1624/5) who was listed in a group separate from his parents & baby sister. Would it not seem plausible that, if this was the first Damaris, she would be listed between Gyles & Caleb - with Deborah listed under the Fuller group? The children of those listed in the Cattle Division appear to be listed either in their order of birth, or, the sons first (in order of birth), followed by the daughters (in order of birth). The fact that Damaris appears as she does in the Division, may indicate that she was quite young, therefore I believe it is possible that this was the second Damaris Hopkins who was alive in 1627, not the first.

V. **CALEB HOPKINS²**, b. c1622, Plymouth, d. betw. 30 Nov. 1644 (when he divided his sisters' portions of his father's estate) <MD 4:114-9> - 1651, Barbadoes (when Bradford wrote, pre 3 Apr.
1651 (N.S.) that he was deceased) <MD 1:13>. He was born pre 28 Oct. 1623 if he was of age
(21) in deed dated 28 Oct. 1644 <MDP:285; Plymouth Co.Deeds 1:182>; pre 6 June 1623 if of age
when he served as executor of his father's will, 6 June 1644 <MD 5:50>; he was probably one
of the six in the Hopkins family in the 1623 Land Division (see p.64). No known issue.

VI. **DEBORAH HOPKINS²**, b. c1624/5, Plymouth <MD 1:151 (1627 Cattle Division)>, d. pre 1674, Plymouth (approx. date of hus. 2nd marr.); m. 23 Apr. 1646, Plymouth, **Andrew RING** <MD 5:51,13:
86>, (son of William RING & Mary (?DURRANT)), b. c1618, Leyden, Holland, d. 22 Feb. 1692/3,
Plymouth, 75th yr <Plymouth ChR; MD 4:193>. (Andrew m.2nd, prob. Plymouth, Lettice
(   ) MORTON, b. c1624, d. 22 Feb. 1690/1, Plymouth, ae about 66 <Plymouth ChR 1:269; MD 4:
193; (not the 23rd as stated in MF5G 6:12>. Lettice m.1st, John MORTON, (son of George MOR-
TON & Julianna CARPENTER), b. c1616, d. 3 Oct. 1673, Plymouth <MSR:548> & had 4 chil. <PCR 8:
8,10,15>.)

6 RING Children: <MBD 2:50>

1. **Elizabeth RING³**, b. 19 Apr. 1652, Plymouth <PCR 8:14; MD 5:51,16:238>, d. pre 14 Dec. 1691
(fath.will) <MD 4:195; MD 14:117 (her husband's probate records state she died "in a Short
time after her husband" and on 16 Apr. 1692 her wearing clothes were appraised. When her
father Andrew made his will, 14 Dec. 1691, witnesses testified that he stated his son William "had also bin at considerable charge _for almost a year_ with his dau Elizabeth MAYO
and divers of her children", which would indicate that Elizabeth was a widow for "almost a
year".)>; m. aft. 5 Mar. 1677/8, Plymouth or Eastham, **William MAYO** <MF5G 6:32 (Elizabeth was
still single for on this date Joseph DUNHAM was fined for "laciouiouse carriages used toward
Elizabeth RINGE".)>, (son of John MAYO & Hannah LECRAFT), b. 7 Oct. 1654, Eastham <PCR 8:26;
MD 6:205>, d. pre 16 Oct. 1691, Eastham (inv.) <MD 14:117>. <See MF5G 6:12 for 6 chil.>

2. **William RING³**, b. c1653/4, Plymouth, d. poss. Apr. 1731, Plymouth, 77th yr <Drew:60 (his g.s.
on Burial Hill, Plymouth states he "decd sum time/in April 1729 in ye 77th year of his age",
however the year 1729 is an error as his will was dated June 1730; since it was probated 21
May 1731, he probably died shortly before this); m. 13 July 1693, Plymouth, **Hannah SHERMAN³**
<MD 13:206,22:38>, (dau of William SHERMAN & Desire DOTY²), see DOTY Family. <See MBD 2:55 &
MD 2:78 for bth. 6 chil.> (See HOPKINS Probate Appendix for will of William RING.)

3. **Eleazer RING³**, b. c1655, prob. Plymouth, d. 21 Nov. 1749, Kingston g.s. <Kingston VR:373; MD
7:169,22:160>; m. 11 Jan. 1687/8, Plymouth, **Mary SHAW** <MD 13:204>, (dau of Jonathan SHAW &
Phebe WATSON), b. c1665, d. 28 Nov. 1730, Kingston g.s., 65th yr <MD 7:169>. <See MBD 2:50
for bth. 12 chil.; MD 1:207 (2), 208 (8), 3:166 (1), Plympton VR (1).> (See HOPKINS Probate
Appendix for will of Eleazer RING.)

4. **Mary RING³**, b. c1657/8, prob. Plymouth, d. 31 Oct. 1731, Middleboro, The Green cem., 74th yr
<MD 14:81; Middleboro Dths:117>; m. 4 Mar. 1687/8, Plymouth, **John MORTON** <MD 13:204>, (son of
John & Lettice, see above), b. 21 Dec. 1650, Plymouth <PCR 8:10; MD 16:235>, d. 20 Mar. 1717/
18, Middleboro, The Green cem., 68th yr <MD 5:37,14:81; Middleboro Dths:117>. (John m.1st,
Phebe SHAW, (dau of Jonathan SHAW & Phebe WATSON) who d. 11 or 12 June 1686, ae 28y4m <Ply-
mouth ChR 1:258 (11/12); MD 15:213 (11th)> and had 2 chil. <MBD 2:53; MD 1:209>.) <See MBD
2:53 for 7 chil.; MD 1:209 (6).> (See HOPKINS Probate Appendix for will of John MORTON.)

5. **Deborah RING³**, b. (   ), d. aft. 14 Dec. 1691 (fath. will) <MD 4:193-5>.
6. **Susanna RING³**, b. (   ), d. aft. 14 Dec. 1691 (fath. will) <MD 4:193-5>.

VII **DAMARIS HOPKINS²**, b. poss. c1627 <MD 1:154 (poss. pre 22 May 1627, Cattle Division, see p.64
for discussion of the first and second Damaris)>, d. betw. 20 Oct. 1666 <MDP:164; Plymouth Co
Deeds 3:168 (on this date Jacob Cook & wife ack. a deed dated 18 May 1665)> - 18 Nov. 1669
(hus. 2nd marr.) <MSR:546>; m. soon after 10 June 1646, Plymouth, **Jacob COOKE²** <MD 2:27-8,5:
52>. See COOKE Family, p.37 for issue.

VIII **RUTH HOPKINS²**, b. (   ), d. aft. 30 Nov. 1644 <MD 4:116 (distribution of her portion of
her father's estate)>. Ruth was most probably deceased by 5 Oct. 1659 when the estate of her
sister had been settled upon Gyles Hopkins, Andrew Ring and Jacob Cooke (Andrew & Jacob on
behalf of their wives Deborah & Damaris) <MD 4:116>.. Ruth was probably deceased by this
time as she was not included as an heir of sister Elizabeth. MF5G 6:7 states sister Damaris
was "prob. the dau. reported by Bradford to have 'dyed here'" and then goes on to state that
Ruth probably died before 3 Apr. 1651, "when Governor Bradford indicated that she was dead".
As Bradford was referring to only one daughter I believe it most probable he was speaking of
Ruth (see p.64).

IX **ELIZABETH HOPKINS²**, b. (   ), d. aft. 10 Oct. 1657 <MD 4:118; Plymouth Col.Deeds 2:1:196
(on this date she sold to Jacob Cooke her 10 acres at Jones River)>. What became of Elizabeth is not known. After her father's death in 1644 she was "put out" to Richard Sparrow until the age of 19 or marriage and "in consideracon of the weaknes of the Child and her ina-

billytie to prforme such service as may acquite their charges in bringing of her up and that
she bee not too much oppressed now in her childhood wth hard labour", Sparrow was to have the
use of her portion of her father's estate <MD 4:116; Plymouth Col.Wills 1:65-66>. On 29 Sept.
1659, "the Cattle that goeth under the Name of Elizabeth hopkinses her Cattle and are in the
Custitie of Gyles hopkins" were valued <MD 4:119; Plymouth Col.Wills 2:1:91>. On 5 Oct. 1659
"incase Elizabeth hopkins Doe Come Noe more", the above mentioned cattle were given to brother Gyles as his portion of her estate, with Andrew Ring and Jacob Cooke already having received their portions (on behalf of their wives) <MD 4:119>. On 6 Oct. 1659 "an Inventory of
the estate of Elizabeth hopkins which is in the hands of Jacob Cooke" was taken <MD 4:118-9>;
note that it does not say that Elizabeth is deceased, but her whereabouts were obviously unknown.

HOPKINS PROBATE APPENDIX

Will of John COLE: (yeoman) <MDP:293; Barnstable Co.PR 4:224,226>
...12 Aug. 1717, ment. eldest son John COLE; son Joseph COLE; daus Ruth, Hephzebath, Hannah, Mary
and Sarah. Pr. 13 Jan. 1724/5.
==

Will of Josiah COOKE: (yeoman) <MD 5:185-6; Barnstable Co.PR 5:124-5>
...7 Dec. 1727, ment. sons Josiah COOKE, Richard COOKE, Joshua COOKE, Caleb COOKE; daus Deborah
GODFREY, Elizabeth NEWCOMB; son Benjamin COOKE. Wit. sworn 5 July 1732.
==

Estate of Caleb HOPKINS[3] (Gyles[2]): (yeoman) <MD 8:240-3; Barnstable Co.PR 4:433,440>
...Settlement, 5 June 1728, ment. eldest son Caleb HOPKINS; 2nd son Nathaniel HOPKINS; 3rd son
Thomas HOPKINS; only dau. Thankful HOPKINS.
==

Will of Gyles/Giles HOPKINS[2]: <MD 1:110-3; Barnstable Co.PR 1:32>
...19 Jan. 1682, ment. wf Catorne; son Stephen HOPKINS "shall take ye care and oversight and
maintaine my son William HOPKINS"; sons Caleb HOPKINS, Joshua HOPKINS. Codicil, 5 Mar. 1688/9,
concerns wf & son Stephen. Pr. 16 Apr. 1690.
==

Will of Joshua HOPKINS[3] (Gyles[2]): (yeoman) <MD 15:175-7; Barnstable Co.PR 5:372>
...14 May 1734, "being now arrived to old age", ment. following chil., viz: Elisha HOPKINS, Joshua HOPKINS, Abigal TAYLOR, Mary SMITH, Lydia HOPKINS, Hannah PAINE, Phebe BIXBE; grandsons Joseph
BIXBEE, Ebenezer PAINE, John TAYLOR, Edward TAYLOR. Pr. 31 Aug. 1738.
==

Will of Stephen HOPKINS[1]: <MD 2:12-17; MSR:512; Plymouth Col.Wills 1:65-66>
...6 June 1644, ment. son Giles HOPKINS; Stephen HOPKINS "my sonn Giles his sonne"; dau Constanc
SNOW wf of Nicholas; daus Deborah HOPKINS, Damaris HOPKINS, Ruth HOPKINS, Elizabeth HOPKINS; son
Caleb HOPKINS; he asks to be buried near his deceased wife. Inv. taken 17 July 1644.
==

Will of John MORTON: <MDP:299; MD 20:89-93; Plymouth Co.PR #14303, 4:76,131>
...17 Jan. 1717/8, ment. wf Mary; son Ebenezer MORTON; 3 unmarried daus Phebe MORTON, Hannah MOR-
TON, Deborah MORTON; 5 daus (in order), Johannah, Phebe, Mary, Hannah, Deborah; negro called
Sherper. Pr. 1 May 1718. (Inv. states he d. 20 Mar. 1718.)
==

Will of William MYRICK/MERRICK: (yeoman) <MDP:300-301; Barnstable Co.PR 5:33>
...5 May 1723, ment. wf Elizabeth; sons Benjamin MYRICK, Nathaniel MYRICK, Stephen MYRICK & wf
Deborah, Joshua MYRICK, John MYRICK; chil. of dec'd dau Rebecca SPARROW; dau Ruth SEARS; daughters in law Mercy WITHEREL & Rachael HUGENS. Codicil, 29 Aug. 1729, ment. sons Benjamin, Nathaniel, Stephen & Joshua. Pr. 29 Nov. 1732.
==

Will of Thomas PAINE: <MD 15:189-90; Barnstable Co.PR 3:360-2>
...12 May 1705, "aged & weak", ment. son Nicholas PAINE; dau Mary COLE wf of Israel; sons Samuel
PAINE, Thomas PAINE, Elisha PAINE, John PAINE, Nicholas PAINE, James PAINE, Joseph PAINE; Dorcas
VICKERIE wf of Benjamin; three eldest chil. of dau Mary COLE, viz: James ROGERS, Mary COLE, Abigail YEATS. Pr. 2 Oct. 1706.
==

Will of Andrew RING: <MD 4:193-8; Plymouth Co.PR #16947, 1:163-4>
...14 Dec. 1691, "stricken in years", ment. eldest son William RING; son Eliezer RING; grandson
John MAYO, minor son of dec'd dau Elizabeth; unnamed daus of dec'd dau Elizabeth MAYO; grandson
Andrew RING, son of son Eliezer; granddaughter Mary MORTON, dau of dau Mary MORTON; daus Deborah
& Susannah. Pr. 22 Mar. 1692/3.
==

Will of Eleazer RING[3] (Deborah Hopkins[2]): (yeoman) <MD 17:153-4,22:160-2; Plymouth Co.PR 12:176>
...5 June 1738, ment. sons Samuel RING, Andrew RING, Elkanah RING, Jonathan RING; daus Phebe
STANDISH, Deborah FULLER, Mary SAMSON, Elizabeth CHAGGON/CLAGHORN, Lediah STURDEFANT; granddau.
Deborah BOSWORTH, dau of dau Susanna BOSWORTH. Pr. 1 Jan. 1749/50.
==

Will of William RING[3] (Deborah Hopkins[2]): (husbandman) <MDP:299; MD 17:153-4,22:38-41; Plymouth
Co.PR #16957, 6:34,35>...16 June 1730, ment. wf Hannah; daus Elezabeth PEARSE, Debarah RING; son
Eleazar RING. Wit. sworn 21 May 1731.
==

Estate of **Samuel SMITH**: <MD 12:112-6; Barnstable Co.PR 2:46-7,59>
...Settlement, 22 Apr. 1697, ment. widow Mary; grandsons Samuel SMITH & Joseph SMITH, the sons of eldest son Samuel SMITH; son John SMITH; dau Mary HAMBLETON

==

Estate of **Jabez SNOW³ (Constance Hopkins²)**: <MDP:285; MD 22:165-7; Barnstable Co.PR 1:113>
...Settlement, 8 Apr. 1695, to following chil., viz: eldest son Jabez SNOW, 2nd son Edward SNOW, 3rd son Thomas SNOW; 6 unnamed daus.; unnamed widow.

==

Will of **Joseph SNOW³ (Constance Hopkins²)**: (yeoman) <MDP:287; Barnstable Co.PR 4:101-3>
...23 Nov. 1717, ment. wf Mary; sons Benjamin SNOW, Stephen SNOW, James SNOW, Josiah SNOW; grandsons Nathaniel SNOW, Joseph SNOW; "four daüghters & granddaughters", viz: Sarah YOUNG, Lidia LINCOLN, Ruth BROWN, Rebekah SNOW (mis-copied - should be Deborah SNOW), Rebekah HAMILTON. Pr. 30 Jan. 1732/3.

==

Will of **Mark SNOW³ (Constance Hopkins²)**: <MDP:288; MD 18:193-7; Barnstable Co.PR 1:110-2>
...23 Nov. 1694, ment. sons Nicholas SNOW, Thomas SNOW, Prince SNOW; wf Jane; grandson Jonathan SNOW. Pr. 16 Jan. 1694/5.

==

Will of **Jane SNOW**: (widow) <MDP:288; MD 18:196-7; Barnstable Co.PR 3:271-4>
...21 Dec. 1703, ment. sons Nicholas SNOW, Thomas SNOW, Prince SNOW; grandchildren Jane NICKERSON & Jane SNOW; daus Mary & Sarah; brother Jonathan SPARROW. Inv. taken 28 June 1712. (Executor's account mentions providing lodging for Jane from 26 Oct. to latter end of May following.)

==

Will of **Nicholas SNOW**: <MD 3:167-74; Plymouth Col.Wills 3:2:71-77>
...14 Nov. 1676, ment. wf Constant; sons Marke SNOW, Joseph SNOW, Steven SNOW, John SNOW, Jabez SNOW; son <son in law> Thomas PAINE. Wit. sworn 5 Mar. 1676/7.

==

Will of **Stephen SNOW³ (Constance Snow²)**: <MDP:294; MD 31:37-41; Barnstable Co.PR 3:17-18>
...2 Apr. 1697, ment. sons Micaiah SNOW, Ebenezer SNOW; unnamed wf; dau Mehetabel SNOW. Inv. taken 20 Dec. 1705.

==

Will of **William WALKER**: <Barnstable Co.PR 2:259-61>
...8 Mar. 1697, ment. wf Sarah; sons William WALKER, Jabez WALKER; dau Elizabeth WALKER. Pr. 25 Oct. 1703.

NOTES:

JOHN HOWLAND

John HOWLAND was born c1592 (pre 1593), Fenstanton, Huntingdonshire, England, the son of Henry & Margaret Howland <White 1:1; Stratton:311>. He died 23 Feb. 1672/3 and was buried on Burial Hill in Plymouth <MD 2:70; Drew:56; MSR:548 incorrectly gives the year as 1662/3>. In the Plymouth ChR 1:147, Rev. John Cotton said of him, "He was a good old disciple & had bin sometime a magistrate here, a plaine-hearted christian". Nathaniel Morton wrote, "The 23 of February 1672 Mr John Howland sen^r of the Towne of Plymouth Deceased hee was a Godly man and an ancient professor in the wayes of Christ hee lived untill hee attained above eighty yeares in the world hee was one of the first Comers into this land and proved a usefull Instrument of Good in his place & was the last man that was left of those that Came over in the shipp Called the May Flower that lived in Plymouth hee was with honor Intered att the Towne of Plymouth on the 25 February 1672" <MD 18:69; PCR 8:34>. John married c1624-25, Plymouth, Elizabeth TILLEY <MD 2:118,10:65-66; White 1:1 gives a marriage date of on or about 25 Mar. 1623 (O.S., which would be 4 Apr. 1624 N.S.) but does not give a reason>. Elizabeth was baptized 30 Aug. 1607, Henlow, Bedfordshire, England, the daughter of John TILLEY & Joan (HURST) Rogers <TAG 52:198-208; White 1:3> who both died that first winter in Plymouth. Elizabeth died 21 Dec. 1687, Swansea <MD 2:118 (N.S.), 3:54>. As John's brothers Henry & Arthur HOWLAND later came to Plymouth Colony and had families, care must be taken in determining which family a Howland ancestor belongs to. See HOWLAND Probate Appendix for wills of John & Elizabeth Howland. (Note: Correction to MBD 2:188 under heading "Mayflower Quarterly", the reference should read 46:16-18 not 45:16-18.)

(See also: John Howland Of The Mayflower, Vol. 1, The First Five Generations Documentated Descendants Through his first child Desire Howland and her husband Captain John Gorham and Vol. 2, The First Five Generations Documentated Descendants Through his second child John Howland and his wife Mary Lee, by Elizabeth P. White, 1990, 1993.)

John & Elizabeth had 10 children: <White 1:6>

I.   Desire, b. c1625, prob. Plymouth
II.   John, b. 24 Apr. 1627, prob. Plymouth
III. Hope, b. 30 Aug. 1629, prob. Plymouth
IV.   Elizabeth, b. c1631, poss. Maine
V.   Lydia, b. c1633, poss. Maine
VI.   Hannah, b. c1637, poss. Maine
VII. Joseph, b. c1640, Rocky Nook/Kingston
VIII. Jabez, b. c1644, Rocky Nook/Kingston
IX.   Ruth, b. c1646, Rocky Nook/Kingston
X.   Isaac, b. 15 Nov. 1649, Rocky Nook/Kingston

*   *   *   *   *   *   *   *   *   *   *   *   *   *   *   *

I. **Desire HOWLAND**[2], b. c1625, prob. Plymouth <MD 1:150,10:66>, d. 13 Oct. 1683, Barnstable g.s. <MD 4:217,5:72; Otis 1:413>; m. c1643, prob. Plymouth, **Capt. John GORUM/GORHAM** <MD 5:177,17: 251; Otis 1:413>, b. c1621/2 <MD 5:28, Plymouth Col.Court Orders 5:109 (ae 53 yeares or thereabouts in 1674/5 deposition)>, buried 5 Feb. 1675/6, Swansea, ae 54 yrs <PCR 8:61; Otis 1:413 (says d. Yarmouth); MD 4:153, 5:179 (a Captain in King Phillip's War "and there Was Wownded by having his poudr Horn Shot and Split against his side and Wownded and Dyed att Swansey")>. There are conflicting accounts as to the parentage of John GORUM. Elizabeth P. White, in her above mentioned first volume, states he was the son of Ralph GORUM who was bpt. 28 Jan. 1620/1, Benefield, Northamptonshire, England. In MD 5:174-5, George E. Bowman discusses John's parentage and feels there is a stronger case for John being the son of a John GORUM, based on the writings of Col. John GORHAM, great-grandson of John & Desire. Col. John states in his "Wast Book and Dayly Journal" that the family was from Huntingtunshear <Huntingdonshire>, England and that his "great-great-grandfather had one son nam'd aftr him John GORUM". (Interesting to note that Desire's father, John Howland was from Huntingdonshire.) He goes on to say that the father lived at Marshfield while the son moved to Barnstable. (The 1643 list of men able to bear arms shows a John "Gorame" in Plymouth and a John "Goarum" at Marshfield <Stratton:440,446; MD 5:175>.) Col. John's writings also state that while on a voyage to London in 1737 he had a search made for the family coat of arms and since a fee of seven shillings six pence was paid, Bowman feels the search was succesful which means he was well aware of his family heritage. There was a Ralph GORHAM living in Plymouth between 1637-1642 (he is not on the 1643 list) but no connection has been found between him and Capt. John. Bowman also points out that there was an unidentified John GORUM living at Lynn between 1647-1651. (See HOWLAND Probate Appendix for estates of Capt. John & Desire GORUM/GORHAM.) <See MD 17:251-254 for Capt. John GORHAM's Family Record.>

11 GORUM/GORHAM Children: <MD 5:72,17:253; NEHGR 52:358; Otis 1:413; White:11; MBD 2:104>

1. **DESIRE GORHAM**[3], b. 2 Apr. 1644, Plymouth <PCR 8:44; MD 5:72,17:253,18:200>, d. 30 June 1700, ae 56, Yarmouth <MD 17:252-3 ("My Dear wife Gave up hur Breth to god that gave it to hur the

Last day of June 1700"), 20:74>; m. 7 Oct. 1661, Barnstable, **Capt. John HAWES** <PCR 8:44;
MD 5:72,17:252>, (son of Edmund), b. c1635, prob. Duxbury <White 1:14>, d. 11 Nov. 1701, Yarmouth <Yarmouth VR 1:130; MD 5:177 ("having his Leg Cut of <off> Dyed with It"), 17:252-3,20:
74>. (See HOWLAND Probate Appendix for will of Capt. John HAWES.) <See MBD 2:105; MD 2:207
and Yarmouth VR 1:126 for bth. 11 chil.>

2. **Temperance GORHAM**[3], b. 5 May 1646, Marshfield <MD 5:72,17:253; PCR 8:44 & MD 18:200 err in
    the year - 1648>, d. 12 Mar. 1714/5, 67th yr, Yarmouth <Yarmouth VR 1:133; Otis 1:414>; m.
    1st, c1663, prob. Yarmouth, **Edward STURGIS Jr.** <MD 12:218; MQ 52:33>, (son of Edward STURGIS
    & Elizabeth HINCKLEY), b. 10 Apr. 1642, prob. Charlestown <White 1:15>, d. 8 Nov. 1678, Yar-
    mouth <Yarmouth VR 1:125; Otis 1:414 & MBD 2:121 say Dec.>. **Temperance** m.2nd, 27 Jan. 1679/
    80, Yarmouth, **Thomas BAXTER** <Yarmouth VR 1:127; MD 2:208>, b. c1653, England (he was thought
    to have come from Scotland <MQ 52:33> but Col. John GORHAM's Wast Book (cited within) states
    he was "an old England man" <MD 5:177>), d. 22 June 1713, 60th yr, Yarmouth g.s. <Yarmouth
    VR 1:133>. (See HOWLAND Probate Appendix for wills of Edward STURGIS Jr. and Thomas BAXTER.)
    <See MBD 2:121 and MQ 52:33-36 for bth. 7 STURGIS chil. and 3 BAXTER chil.>

3. **Elizabeth GORHAM**[3], b. 2 Apr. 1648, Marshfield <MD 5:72,17:253>, d. betw. 7 Mar. 1676/7 <MD 4:
    158 (div. fath. est.)> - 5 Mar. 1683/4 <MD 4:220 (div. mother's est.)>; m. pre 5 Mar. 1666/7,
    prob. Barnstable, **Joseph HALLETT** <PCR 4:141 (on this date fined 10 pounds "for committing
    carnal copulation before marriage or contract")>, (son of Andrew & Mary), b. c1630, England,
    d. aft. 30 June 1715 <MDP:275; Plymouth Co.PR #8281, 3:348 (probate rec. of grandson Samuel
    Fuller.)> <See White 1:19 for 2 (poss. 3) chil.>

4. **James GORHAM/GOREHAM**[3], b. 28 Apr. 1650, Marshfield <PCR 8:44; Barnstable VR 1:371; MD 5:72,
    18:200,17:253>, d. betw. 14 Nov.- 9 Dec. 1707 <MD 13:50,52 (codicil & inv.); Otis 1:414,417
    says d. ae 57>; m. 24 Feb. 1673, Barnstable, **Hannah HUCKINS** <Barnstable VR 1:371; MD 5:72;
    Otis 2:63>, (dau of Thomas HUCKINS & Rose (   ) HYLLIER/HILLYER/HOLLIER), b. 14 Oct. 1653,
    Barnstable <PCR 8:45; Barnstable VR 1:385; MD 6:139,18:201,24:179>, d. 13 Feb. 1727/8, ae 74,
    Barnstable <MD 6:139; Otis 1:414,417,2:63>. (See HOWLAND Probate Appendix for will of James
    GORHAM/GOREHAM.) <See MBD 2:112; MD 5:72; Otis 1:417,418 and Barnstable VR 1:371,372 for
    bth. 11 chil.>

5. **John GORHAM**[3], b. 20 Feb. 1651/2, Marshfield <PCR 8:44; MD 5:72,17:253,18:200>, d. 11 Nov.
    1716, 65th yr, Barnstable, bur. Cobb's Hill cem. <MD 5:73; Otis 1:414,421 says 9 Dec. "if I
    rightly decypher the inscription on his tomb">; m. 24 Feb. 1674, Barnstable, **Mary/Mercy OTIS**
    <MD 5:73,5:179>, (dau of John OTIS & Mary JACOBS), b. 14 Mar. 1652/3, Hingham <Lincoln 3:
    102>, d. 1 Apr. 1732, Barnstable, bur. Cobb's Hill cem. <White 1:22; Otis 1:420 says 1733>.
    (See HOWLAND Probate Appendix for wills of Col. John & Mary GORHAM.) <See MBD 2:114-5; MD 5:
    73 and Otis 1:420-421 for bth. 11 chil. Also of interest - MD 5:172-180, "Col. John GORHAM's
    Wast Book And His Dayly Journal". Col. John was the grandson of Col. John GORHAM & Mary/Mer-
    cy OTIS.>

6. **Joseph GORHAM**[3], b. 16 Feb. 1653/4, Yarmouth <PCR 8:44; Yarmouth VR 2:842; MD 5:72,18:200>,
    d. 9 July 1726, ae 72, Yarmouth g.s. <Yarmouth VR 1:154,2:801; Otis 1:415>; m. c1678, prob.
    Yarmouth, **Sarah STURGIS**, (dau of Edward STURGIS & Elizabeth HINCKLEY) <MD 5:180 ("widow Gray,
    sister of Sarah Sturgis")>, b. c1656, d. betw. 1 May 1728 - 3 Feb. 1738/9, Yarmouth <Barns-
    table Co.PR 5:377-8 (will & pr.)>. (See HOWLAND Probate Appendix for wills of Joseph & Sarah
    GORHAM.) <See MBD 2:118; MD 5:160; Yarmouth VR 1:11 and Otis 1:425 for bth. 8 chil.>

7. **Jabez GORHAM**[3], b. 3 Aug. 1656, Barnstable <PCR 8:44; MD 5:72,17:253,18:200>, d. betw. 16 Mar.
    1724/5 - 20 Apr. 1725, Bristol MA (now RI) <MD 17:67; MDP:319 (will & pr.)>; m. c1676, **Hannah
    (STURGIS) Gray** <MD 5:180>, (dau of Edward STURGIS & Elizabeth HINCKLEY), b. c1654 <White 1:
    25>, d. 17 Oct. 1736, Harwich, bur. Brewster <MBD 2:112; White 1:25>. (See HOWLAND Probate
    Appendix for will of Jabez GORHAM.) <See MBD 2:112 for bth. 11 chil. and Arnold's RI VR 6:1:
    80 (9), 136 (1); MD 3:246 (1).> (Hannah m.1st, c1670, John GRAY & had one ch. <White 1:25>.)

8. **Mercy/Mary GORHAM**[3], b. 20 Jan. 1658, Barnstable <PCR 8:44; MD 5:72,17:253,18:200>, d. 24 Sept
    1725, Stonington CT <White 1:27>; m. c1677, prob. Barnstable, **George DENISON** <White 1:26>,
    (son of George DENISON & Ann BORODELL), b. c1653 <White 1:27>, d. 27 Dec. 1711, Westerly RI
    <White 1:27>. (See HOWLAND Probate Appendix for will of George DENISON.) <See White 1:27
    for bth. 9 chil.>

9. **Lydia GORHAM**[3], b. 11 Nov. 1661, Barnstable <PCR 8:44; Barnstable VR 1:371; MD 5:72,17:253,18:
    200>, d. 2 Aug. 1744, 83rd yr, Yarmouth g.s. <Yarmouth VR 1:157,2:820; MD 22:110; Otis 1:416
    (says 82nd yr)>; m. 1 Jan. 1683/4, Yarmouth, **Col. John THACHER** <Yarmouth VR 1:32; MD 2:209,
    13:221,22:110>, (son of Anthony THACHER & Elizabeth JONES), b. 16 Mar. 1638/9, Marblehead
    <Savage 3:271>, d. 8 May 1713, 75th yr, Yarmouth g.s. <Yarmouth VR 1:133,2:820; MD 22:110>.
    (John m.1st, 6 Nov. 1661, Yarmouth, Rebecca WINSLOW <Otis 1:416; MD 22:110>, (dau of Josiah),
    b. 15 July 1643, Marshfield <Marshfield VR:2>, d. 15 July 1683 <MD 13:222>; they had 8 chil.
    <MD 13:221>). (See HOWLAND Probate Appendix for will of Col. John THACHER.) <See MD 13:221
    for bth. 12 chil.>

10. **Hannah GORHAM**[3], b. 28 Nov. 1663, Barnstable <MD 17:253; Otis 1:413>, d. c1728, Cape May, NJ
    <White 1:29>; m. c1682, Yarmouth or Barnstable, **Joseph WHELDON/WHILLDIN** <MD 5:177>, (son of
    John WHILLDIN & Mary FOLLAND), b. c1660, Yarmouth <White 1:29>, d. c1727, Cape May, NJ <White

1:29>. <See White 1:30 for bth. 5 chil.>

11. **Shubael GORHAM**[3], b. 21 Oct. 1667, Barnstable <MD 17:253>, d. betw. 8 July 1749 <MDP:320 (gdn. was appointed as he was judged non compos)> - 7 Aug. 1750 <MDP:320 (pr.); Otis 1:417 says c1750, 83rd yr)>; m. May 1695, Nantucket, **Puella HUSSEY** <Nantucket VR 4:76; Barnstable VR 1: 372; MD 5:73,180 ("he <Shubael> and my Grandfather and all the Weddners In Going over to Nantucket to the wedding with Capt James Gardner Was taken prisoners and Stripped by a Small French Shallop From port Royall betwixt Nantucket & Hyanas")>, (dau of Stephen HUSSEY & Martha BUNKER), b. 10 Oct. 1677, Nantucket <MSR:255; Nantucket VR 2:183>, d. pre 23 Sept. 1748 <MDP:320 (hus.will)>. (See HOWLAND Probate Appendix for will of Shubael GORHAM.) <See MBD 2:119 for bth. 10 chil.; MD 5:73 (8); Barnstable VR 1:372 (8).>

─────────────

II. **JOHN HOWLAND**[2], b. 24 2mth 1627 (24 Apr.) <White 2:17; MD 10:66 (incorrectly gives month as Feb.; in old style dating, March was the first month, not Jan.)>, d. aft. 18 May 1699 <White 2:21, Barnstable West Parish ChR:44; Otis 2:50; PN&Q 5:81-2 (aft. 6 May 1697, ack. deed)>; m. 26 Oct. 1651, Plymouth, **Mary LEE** <PCR 8:13; MD 11:32,16:237; MSR:544>, (dau of Robert LEE & Mary (prob. ATWOOD) <White 2:17; PN&Q 5:82>, b. c1632, d. aft. 6 May 1693 <PN&Q 5:81-2, Plymouth Co.Deeds 6:7> and poss. pre 6 May 1697 <PN&Q 5:81-2 (hus. ack. deed alone)>.

10 HOWLAND Children: <MBD 2:159>

1. **Mary HOWLAND**[3], b. c1652, Plymouth or Marshfield, d. aft. 3 Aug. 1711, prob. Killingly CT <Killingly CT Deeds 1:26 (2 sons agreed to maintain both parents)>; m. c1673/4, Barnstable, **John ALLYN** <MD 2:213; White 2:23, Barnstable West Parish ChR (on 11 8mth 1674 - 11 Oct. 1674 John was brought before the church for fornication, which implies that his first child, b. 3 Apr. 1674, was born too soon after marriage)>, (son of Thomas & Winifred), bpt. 27 Sept. 1646, Barnstable <MBD 2:166; Otis 1:8>, d. betw. 15 Aug. 1715 <Killingly CT Deeds 1:90 (he app'td an attorney)> - 15 Oct. 1716 <Killingly CT Deeds 1:146 (son's deed)>. <For bth. 9 chil. see MD 1:222 (3), 223 (2), 2:213 (4).>

2. **Elizabeth HOWLAND**[3], b. 17 May 1655, Marshfield <MD 2:6>, d. aft. 30 Jan. 1695 <MD 3:53 (bth. last ch.)>; m. Dec. 1673, Barnstable, **John BURSLEY** <MD 3:53; Otis 1:133>, (son of John BURSLEY & Joanna HULL), bpt. 11 Apr. 1652, Barnstable <MSR:600; Otis 1:133>, d. 5 Aug. 1726, 75th yr, Barnstable g.s. <MQ 45:94 (Memorial Inscriptions W. Barnstable Cem.); Otis 1:133>. (In his will dated 1726, John refers to his wife Elizabeth as "mother in law" of his children which implies a second marriage to an unknown Elizabeth.) (See HOWLAND Probate Appendix for will of John BURSLEY.) <See MBD 2:159-160; MD 3:53, Otis 1:134-5 for bth. 10 chil.>

3. **Isaac HOWLAND**[3], b. 25 Nov. 1659, Barntable <MD 5:75>, d. 26 Dec. 1724, 65th yr, Barnstable g.s. <MQ 45:159 (Memorial Inscriptions W. Barnstable Cem.)>; m. 27 Dec. 1686, Barnstable, **Anne TAYLOR** <MD 5:75>, (dau of Edward TAYLOR & Mary MERLL), b. 11 Dec. 1664, Barnstable <MD 14:86>, d. aft. 20 Sept. 1702 <White 2:32, Barnstable West Parish ChR (last ch. bpt.)>. <See MBD 2:162-3 for bth. 7 chil.; MD 5:75 (6).>

4. **Hannah HOWLAND**[3], b. 15 May 1661, Barnstable <MD 5:75>, d. pre 11 Feb. 1710/11, Barnstable (hus.2nd marr.); m. 20 May 1686, Barnstable, **Jonathan CROCKER** <MD 3:150; Otis 1:211>, (son of John CROCKER & Mary BODFISH), b. 15 July 1662, Barnstable <MD 3:150>, d. 24 Aug. 1746, 84th yr, Barnstable g.s. <MQ 45:150 (Memorial Inscriptions W. Barnstable Cem.); Otis 1:211>. (Jonathan m.2nd, 1 Feb. 1710/1, Barnstable, Thankful (TROTT) Hinckley <MD 14:225>, (dau of Thomas), b. (   ), d. betw. 3 Aug. 1748 (will) - 8 Mar. 1748/9 (inv.) <Barnstable Co.PR 8:469-91>. Thankful m.1st, 1 May 1691, Barnstable, John HINKLEY/HINCKLEY <MD 6:98 (& had 6 chil)>, (son of Thomas HINCKLEY & Mary GLOVER), b. 9 June 1667, Barnstable <MD 6:98; Otis 1:36,40>, d. 1706 <Otis 1:41>.) (See HOWLAND Probate Appendix for will of Jonathan CROCKER and 2nd wf Thankful.) <See MBD 2:162 & MD 3:150 for bth. 8 chil.>

5. **Mercy HOWLAND**[3], b. 21 Jan. 1663, Barnstable <MD 5:75; MQ 48:133>.

6. **Lydia HOWLAND**[3], b. 9 Jan. 1665, Barnstable <MD 5:75,20:131; MQ 48:131-2>, d. 6 July 1717, 52d yr, Middleboro, The Green cem. <MD 12:66,14:216,20:131; Wood:182>; m. 25 Feb. 1684, Barnstable, **Jeremiah THOMAS** <MD 1:219 (rec. Middleboro), 20:131>, (son of David & Joanna), b. c1659, poss. Middleboro, d. 2 Feb. 1736, 77th yr, Middleboro, The Green cem. <MD 12:66,14:215>. (Jeremiah m.2nd, 29 Apr. 1720, Taunton, Mary (SANFORD) Durfe <MD 4:71,20:131>, (dau of John SANFORD & Mary GORTON), b. 30 Mar. 1664, Portsmouth RI <White 2:34>, d. 15 Nov. 1749, 85th yr Middleboro, The Green cem. <MD 12:66,20:131,14:216; Wood:183>. Mary m.1st, Robert DURFE.) (See HOWLAND Probate Appendix for will of Jeremiah THOMAS.) <See MBD 2:164; MD 2:107 & Middleboro VR 1:10 for bth. 11 chil.>

7. **Experience HOWLAND**[3], b. 28 July 1668, Barnstable (dau) <MD 5:75; MQ 48:133>.

8. **Anne HOWLAND**[3], b. 9 Sept. 1670, Barnstable <MD 5:75; Barnstable VR 1:375; MQ 49:28>, d. 19 Apr. 1750, 80th yr, Barnstable g.s. <MD 45:95 (Memorial Inscriptions W. Barnstable Cem.), 49:28>; m. 18 Sept. 1691, Barnstable, **Joseph CROCKER** <Barnstable VR 1:355; MD 3:150; MQ 49: 28; Otis 1:212>, (son of John CROCKER & Mary BURSLEY), b. 10 Mar. 1667/8, Barnstable <Barnstable VR 1:354; MD 3:150; Otis 1:212 (says 1 Mar.)>, d. 12 Jan. 1741/2, 74th yr, Barnstable

g.s. <MQ 45:156 (Memorial Inscriptions W. Barnstable Cem.)>. (See HOWLAND Probate Appendix for will of Joseph CROCKER.) <See MBD 2:159; MD 3:150; MQ 49:28-37 for bth. 3 chil.>

9. **Shubael HOWLAND[3]**, b. 30 Sept. 1672, Barnstable <MD 5:75; MSR:613>, d. 17 June 1737, 65th yr, Barnstable g.s. <MQ 45:159 (Memorial Inscriptions W. Barnstable Cem.)>; m. 13 Dec. 1700, Barntable, **Mercy/Mary BLOSSOM** <MD 5:75; Otis 1:77>, (dau of Peter BLOSSOM & Sarah BODFISH), b. Aug. 1678, Barnstable <MD 3:53; Otis 1:77>, d. betw. 24 Nov. 1758 (will) - 6 Mar. 1759 (pr.) <MD 10:87>. (See HOWLAND Probate Appendix for wills of Shubael & Mercy HOWLAND.) <See MBD 2:166; MD 5:75 for bth. 3 chil.>

10. **John HOWLAND[3]**, b. 31 Dec. 1674, Barnstable <MD 5:75; MSR:613>, d. 14 Feb. 1737/8, 63rd yr, Barnstable g.s. <MD 45:159 (Memorial Inscriptions W. Barnstable Cem.)>; m. 1st, 1704, Barnstable, **Joanna SHOVE** <White 2:39>, (dau George SHOVE & Hannah (BACON) Walley), b. 28 Sept. 1678, Taunton <Taunton VR 1:387; MD 22:92>, d. betw. 8 Jan. 1715 (bth. last ch.) - 18 June 1719 (hus.2nd marr.). **John** m.2nd, 18 June 1719, Barnstable, **Mary CROCKER** <MD 32:152,33:121>, (dau of Job CROCKER & Hannah TAYLOR), b. 29 June 1681, Barnstable <MD 3:151; Otis 1:215>, d. 10 Sept. 1759, 79th yr, Barnstable g.s. <MQ 45:159 (Memorial Inscriptions W. Barnstable Cem)> (See HOWLAND Probate Appendix for will of John HOWLAND.) <See MBD 2:163; MD 5:75 for 4 chil. by 1st wf; see MBD 2:163; MD 5:75,33:121 for 2 chil. by 2nd wf.>

III. **HOPE HOWLAND[2]**, b. 30 Aug. 1629, prob. Plymouth <White 1:6 (no source for date)>, d. 8 Jan. 1683/4, ae 54, Barnstable g.s. <MD 3:181,4:121; Otis 1:159>; m. c1646, Plymouth, **John CHIPMAN** <MD 24:129>, b. c1620/1, England <Otis 1:155 (ae about 37 in deposition dated 8 Feb. 1657/8)> d. 7 Apr. 1708, ae 88, Sandwich g.s. <MD 3:181,24:129,29:22>. (John m.2nd, Ruth (SARGENT) (Winslow) Bourne <MBD 2:137>, (dau of William SARGENT), b. 25 Oct. 1642, Charlestown <Otis 1: 159>, d. 4 Oct. 1713, ae 71, Sandwich g.s. <MD 24:129,29:23>. Ruth m.1st, Jonathan WINSLOW (son of Josiah), b. 8 Aug. 1639, Marshfield <Marshfield VR:2>, bur. 8 Sept. 1676, ae 38, Marshfield <Marshfield VR:9; MSR:248>. Ruth m.2nd, 2 July 1677, Sandwich, Richard BOURNE <MD 14:172> who d. 1682 <Otis 1:159>.) (See HOWLAND Probate Appendix for wills of John & Ruth CHIPMAN.)

12 CHIPMAN Children: <MBD 2:137; 2-11, MD 4:121>

1. **Elizabeth CHIPMAN[3]**, b. 24 June 1648, Plymouth <MD 15:27; PCR 8:4 (errs in yr)>, d. aft. 24 Jan. 1711/2 (hus.will); m. pre 1676, Yarmouth, **Hosea JOYCE/JOYSE** <MD 3:37>, b. (   ), d. betw. 24 Jan. 1711/2 - 15 Feb. 1711/2, of Yarmouth <MDP:327 (will & pr.); Otis 1:160>. (Hosea m.1st, Martha (   ) who d. 3 Apr. 1670 and had 2 chil. <MBD 2:140; Otis 1:160>.) (See HOWLAND Probate Appendix for will of Hosea JOYCE.) <See MBD 2:140 for bth. 8 chil.; MD 3:37 for bth. 3.>

2. **dau,** stillborn, bur. 9 Sept. 1650 <MSR:602; NEHGR 9:286; Otis 1:160>.

3. **Hope CHIPMAN[3]**, b. 13 or 31 Aug. 1652, Barnstable <PCR 8:42 & MD 18:199 (13th); MD 4:121 & Otis 1:160 (31st)>, d. 25 July 1728, about 76th yr, Middleboro, The Green cem. <MD 12:144>; m.1st, 10 Aug. 1670, Barnstable, **John HUCKINS/HUCKENS** <MD 6:139,24:179; Otis 2:63,65>, (son of Thomas HUCKINS & Rose (   ) HYLLIER/HILLYER/HOLLIER), b. 2 Aug. 1649, Barnstable <PCR 8:45; MD 6:139,18:201,24:179>, d. 10 Nov. 1678, ae 28, Barnstable <MD 6:139,24:179; Otis 1: 160,2:63,65>. **Hope** m.2nd, 1 Mar. 1682/3, Barnstable, **Jonathan COBB** <MD 3:149,24:179; Otis 2:63,65>, (son of Henry COBB & Sarah HINCKLEY), b. 10 Apr. 1660, Barnstable <PCR 8:42; MD 3:73,18:199; Otis 1:160>, d. 5 Aug. 1728, about 68th yr, Middleboro, The Green Cem. <MD 5:38, 12:144>. (See HOWLAND Probate Appendix for estate of John HUCKINS.) <See MBD 2:142 & MD 6: 139 for bth. 5 Huckins chil., MBD 2:142 & MD 3:150 for bth. 6 Cobb chil.>

4. **Lydia CHIPMAN[3]**, b. 25 Dec. 1654, Barnstable <PCR 8:42; MD 4:121,18:199; Otis 1:161>, d. 2 Mar 1730, ae 76, Malden <Malden VR; Otis 1:161>; m. c1674, **John SARGEANT** <MD 24:9>, (son of William), b. c1639/40, poss. Charlestown, d. 9 Sept. 1716, ae 76y9m, Malden, Bell Rock cem. <MBD 2:148>. (John m.1st, int. 19 Mar. 1662/3, Barnstable, Deborah HYLLIER/HILLIER <MD 12:154 (& 2 chil.), 18:201,24:9>, (dau of Hugh & Rose), b. 30 Oct. 1643, Yarmouth <MD 6:139>, d. (   ) Malden. John m.2nd, Mary BENSE who d. 1670 (no issue).) (See HOWLAND Probate Appendix for will of John SARGEANT.) <See MBD 2:148 & MD 24:10 for bth. 11 chil.>

5. **John CHIPMAN[3]**, b. 2 Mar. 1656/7, Barnstable, d. 29 May 1657 <PCR 8:43; MD 4:121,18:199>.

6. **Hannah CHIPMAN[3]**, b. 14 Jan. 1658/9, Barnstable <PCR 8:43; MD 4:121,18:199>, d. 4 Nov. 1696, ae 37, Barnstable <MD 6:139; Otis 1:161,2:63,65>; m. 1 May 1680, Barnstable, **Thomas HUCKINS/HUCKENS** <MD 6:139; Otis 1:161,2:63,65>, (son of Thomas HUCKINS & Rose (   ) HYLLIER/HILLYER/HOLLIER), b. 25 Apr. 1651, Barnstable <PCR 8:45; MD 6:139;18:201,24:179; Otis 2:64>, d. pre 5 Oct. 1714 (inv.) <MD 10:12; MDP:327 (says 15th)>. (Thomas m.2nd, 17 Aug. 1698, Barnstable, Sarah (POPE) Hinckley <MD 6:139, 10:12 (& had 1 ch.)>, (dau of Thomas), b. (   ), d. betw. 5 Jan. 1726/7 (will) - 5 July 1727 (pr.) <MD 10:12>. Sarah m.1st, 13 Nov. 1676, Barnstable, Samuel HINCKLEY <Otis 2:38,39; MD 6:98 (& had 11 chil.)>, (son of Thomas HINCKLEY & Mary RIC-HARDS), b. 14 Feb. 1652, Barnstable <MD 6:98,18:200; PCR 8:44>, d. 19 Mar. 1697, ae 46, Barnstable <MD 6:98,10:11; Otis 2:38>. See MD 10:11-16 for wills of Samuel HINCKLEY & Sarah (POPE)(Hinckley) Huckins.) (See HOWLAND Probate Appendix for estate of Thomas HUCKINS.)

<See MBD 2:141; MD 6:139 for bth. 9 chil.>

7. **Samuel CHIPMAN**[3], b. 15 Apr. 1661, Barnstable <PCR 8:43; MD 4:121,18:199; Otis 1:161>, d. betw. 31 Aug. 1722 (will) – 17 June 1723 (wit.sworn) <MD 16:65-7; MQ 45:95 (Memorial Inscriptions W. Barnsstable Cem., d. 1723 ae 63)>; m. 27 Dec. 1686, Barnstable, **Sarah COBB** <MD 4: 121; Otis 1:161,172>, (dau of Henry COBB & Sarah HINCKLEY), b. 10 Mar. 1662/3, Barnstable <MD 3:73; Otis 1:172>, d. 8 Jan. 1742/3, 81st yr, Barnstable g.s. <MQ 45:95 (Memorial Inscriptions W. Barnstable Cem.); Otis 1:161 says ae 79>. (See HOWLAND Probate Appendix for will of Samuel CHIPMAN.) <See MBD 2:150,151; MD 4:121 for bth. 10 chil.>

8. **Ruth CHIPMAN**[3], b. 31 ("last of") Dec. 1663, Barnstable <MD 4:121; Otis 1:161>, d. 8 Apr. 1698 ae 34, Barnstable <MD 4:120; Otis 1:161>; m. 7 Apr. 1682, Barnstable, **Eleazer CROCKER** <MD 4: 120; Otis 1:161>, (son of William & Alice), b. 21 July 1650, Barnstable <PCR 8:43; MD 3:150, 18:199>, d. pre 6 Sept. 1723, Barnstable (inv.) <MD 18:158>. (Eleazer m.2nd, Mercy PHINNEY[4] <MD 18:158>, (dau of John PHINNEY[2-1] & Mary ROGERS[3] (Joseph[2]) – see ROGERS Family), b. 10 July 1679, Barnstable <MD 11:131> and had one ch. <MBD 2:149>.) (See HOWLAND Probate Appendix for estate of Eleazer CROCKER.) <See MBD 2:149; MD 4:120,18:158 for bth. 10 chil.>

9. **Bethiah CHIPMAN**[3], b. 1 July 1666, Barnstable <MD 4:121; Otis 1:161>, d. aft. 12 Nov. 1702 <MD 3:183 (fath.will)>. It has been extremely difficult to identify Bethiah's husbands. Her father's will (cited within), dated 12 Nov. 1702 mentions daughter Bethiah as well as two grandchildren, Mary GALE and Jabez DIMMOCK who cannot be otherwise identified and have been attributed to Bethiah. Bowman states she married 1st, ( ) GALE and 2nd, Timothy DIMMOCK <MBD 2:137> who m.2nd, 17 Mar. 1702/3, Abigail DOANE. According to this data, Bethiah would have died betw. 12 Nov. 1702 – 17 Mar. 1702/3. Otis 1:161 states Bethiah "married as I have noted, Shubael DIMMOCK" and goes on to state Shubael m.2nd, 4 May 1699, Tabitha LOTHROP. There are two problems with his statement, first, although he states he has noted this marriage elsewhere in his book, it is nowhere to be found; second, Bethiah was alive in 1699 (as shown by her father's will), so her husband could not have remarried. Another piece which does not add up can be found in the Barnstable ChR as printed in MSR:617 & NEHGR 10:351 where Bethia, wf of Shubal DIMOCK was baptized on 1 Sept. 1700. Since Shubael was married to Tabitha in 1699, is this an error for "Tabitha wf of Shubael" or "Bethia wf of Timothy"? Otis mentions Shubael's marriage to Tabitha in two other places in his book, 1:341,2:165 and in neither does he mention Bethiah. Otis 1:341 also mentions Timothy DIMMOCK (who is Shubael's brother) and says only that his wife was Abigail, unfortunately he does not give an account of his children so there is no mention of a Jabez DIMMOCK. It would appear from the above that Bethiah married, date unknown, **Timothy DIMMOCK**, (son of Shubael DIMMOCK & Joanna BURSLEY), b. Mar. 1668 <MD 4:221>, d. c1733, Ashford CT <Otis 1:341> who m.2nd, 17 Mar. 1702/3, Abigail DOANE. (The other "contender", brother Shubael DIMMOCK, b. Feb. 1673, Barnstable <MD 4:221>, d. 16 Dec. 1728, Barnstable <Otis 1:341>, m. 4 May 1699, Barnstable, Tabitha LOTHROP <MD 4:222 (& 3 chil. b.1702-1712)>, (dau of Melatiah LOTHROP & Sarah FARRAR), b. 3 Apr. 1671, Barnstable <MD 6:237>, d. 24 July 1727, Barnstable <Otis 1:341>.)

10. **Mercy CHIPMAN**[3], b. 6 Feb. 1668, Barnstable <MD 4:121; Otis 1:161>, d. 12 June 1724, Chilmark g.s. <Chilmark VR:94; MSR:100 (citing diary of Rev. William HOLMES, under date of 21 June he states she died "Friday last", i.e. 19 June.)>; m. 13 Dec. 1699, Sandwich, **Nathan SKIFFE/ SKIFF** <Sandwich VR:44,72; MD 29:31>, b. c1655 (?son of James & Mary SKEFF, b. 27 May 1658, Sandwich <MD 14:167>), d. 12 Feb. 1725/6, ae 71, Chilmark g.s. <Chilmark VR:94; Diary of Rev. William HOLMES as cited in MSR:110, under date 13 Feb. 1725/6, "On Wednesday morning last, being the 9th instant Mr. Nathan Skiffe departed this life. He was, I hope, a good man and died well. He had been some months in a languishing condition and died in the 68th year of his age">. (Nathan m.1st, ( ), Hephzibah CODMAN, (dau of Robert), d. 19 July 1696 <MBD 2:148 (& 5 chil.).) <See MBD 2:148,149 & Chilmark VR:29 for bth. 5 chil.>

11. **John CHIPMAN**[3], b. 3 Mar. 1670/1, Barnstable <MD 4:121; Otis 1:161,163>, d. 4 Jan. 1756, Newport RI <NEHGR 91:161>; m.1st, c1691 or 1693, **Marcy/Mary SKIFF**[4] <Otis 1:164 gives a first son John who d.y., if so, they were married c1691>, (dau of Stephen SKEFF & Lydia SNOW[3] (Abigail WARREN[2] – see WARREN family), b. 13 Nov. 1671, Sandwich <MD 29:21>, d. 12 Mar. 1711, ae 40, Sandwich <Otis 1:164 (yr. only)>. **John** m.2nd, c1716, Dartmouth, **Elizabeth (HANDLEY)(Pope) Russell** <Otis 1:164; NEHGR 91:159-76>, (dau of Capt. Thomas HANDLEY), b. ( ), d. 30 Jan. 1725, Dartmouth <MBD 2:146; MSR:110 (Rev. William HOLMES diary, under date 6 Feb. 1725/6, "Mrs Chipman departed this life last Saturday night, about midnight. She died in Dartmouth at Capt. Popes. She was a pious good woman and died well, with a rational assurance of her future well being. She had long been in a languishing condition. She went in the fall to visit Capt. Pope and sickened there. She was buryed the Tuesday following in Dartmouth".)> **John** m.3rd, c1725, Newport RI, **Hannah (HOXIE/HUXLEY)(Griffin) Case** <NEHGR 91:159-76>. (See HOWLAND Probate Appendix for will of John CHIPMAN.) <See MBD 2:146 for 9 (poss. 10) chil. by 1st wf (incl. 2 sets of twins); MD 29:70 (5), 71 (4); see MBD 2:146 for 2 (poss. 3) chil. by 2nd wf; MD 29:71 (2)>

12. **Desire CHIPMAN**[3], b. 26 Feb. 1673/4, Barnstable <MD 4:121; Otis 1:161>, d. 28 Mar. 1705, ae 31, Sandwich <MD 29:70; Otis 1:161>; m. 23 Feb. 1692/3, Sandwich, **Melatiah BOURNE** <MD 29:70>, (son of Shearjashub BOURNE[2] (Richard[1]) & Bathsheba SKIFFE), b. 12 Jan. 1673/4, Sandwich <MD 14:169; Otis 1:114>, d. 24 Nov. 1742, Sandwich <MBD 2:138>. (Melatiah m.2nd, Abigail ( ) SMITH, widow of Thomas. (See HOWLAND Probate Appendix for will of Melatiah BOURNE.) <See MBD 2:138; MD 29:70; Otis 1:116 for bth. 8 chil.>

IV. **ELIZABETH HOWLAND**[2], b. c1631, poss. Maine, d. 1691, Oyster Bay, Long Island, NY <MQ 45:150>;
m.1st 13 Sept. 1649, Plymouth, **Ephraim HICKS** <PCR 8:8; MSR:544>, b. (   ), d. 12 Dec. 1649,
Plymouth <PCR 8:8; MSR:547; MQ 45:150>. **Elizabeth** m.2nd, 10 July 1651, Plymouth, **John DICK-
ENSON** <PCR 8:13; MQ 45:150>, b. (   ), d. Oct. 1682, Oyster Bay, Long Island, NY <MQ 45:150;
NYGBR 3:185; MBD 2:103 (Bowman) states she d.1683>. (John m.1st, (   ).)

9 DICKENSON Children: <MBD 2:127>

1. **Elizabeth DICKENSON**[3], b. 11 Oct. 1652, prob. MA, d. 1695; m. (   ), **Caleb WRIGHT**, b. 1645,
d. 1695 of Oyster Bay NY. <See MBD 2:127 for 1 ch.>

2. **Joseph DICKENSON**[3], b. 24 Dec. 1654, prob. MA <MQ 45:152>, d. c1721, Long Island NY <MQ 45:
152>; m. c1675, Oyster Bay NY, **Rose TOWNSEND** <MQ 45:152>, (dau of Henry TOWNSEND & Ann COLES)
b. c1648, prob. RI <MQ 45:152>, d. aft. 1720, Long Island NY <MQ 45:152>. <See MQ 45:152 &
MBD 2:128 for 4 chil.>

3. **Mercy DICKENSON**[3], b. 23 Apr. 1657, (   ) <MQ 45:150>, d. (   ); m. (   ), **Benjamin HAR-
COURT** <MQ 45:150>, (son of Richard HARCOURT & Elizabeth POTTER), b. c1660 <MQ 45:150>, d.
(   ). <See MQ 45:150 for bth. 2 chil.>

4. **Jabez DICKENSON**[3], b. 29 Sept. 1660, (   ).

5. **Lydia DICKENSON**[3], b. 5 Oct. 1662, Oyster Bay NY <MQ 45:150>, d. (   ); m. pre 1693, Musketa
Cove NY, **Ephraim CARPENTER** <MQ 45:150>, (son of William), b. (   ), d. (   ). (This was
Ephraim's 3rd marriage.)

6. **Samuel DICKENSON**[3], b. 26 Mar. 1665, (   ).

7. **Mehitabel DICKENSON**[3], b. Apr. 1667, Oyster Bay NY <MQ 45:150>, d. (   ); m. (   ), **Thomas
CHESHIRE** <   >, b. (   ), d. (   ).

8. **Hannah DICKENSON**[3], b. 6 Mar. 1671, (   ), d. (   ); m. 22 Oct. 1696, (   ), **Isaac GIBBS**
<   >, b. (   ), d. (   ). <See MBD 2:128 for 1 ch.>

9. **James DICKENSON**[3], b. 27 July 1675, (   ) <MQ 45:153>, d. (   ); m. (   ), **Sarah (   )**
(poss. dau of Abraham & Sarah UNDERHILL) <MQ 45:153>, b. (   ), d. (   ).

V. **LYDIA HOWLAND**[2], b. c1633, poss. Maine, d. aft. 11 Jan. 1710/11 <MD 7:166 (hus.pr.)>; m. c1654
(   ), **James BROWN** <MD 7:163;MQ 49:109>, (son of John & Dorothy), b. (   ), d. 29 Oct.
1710, Swansea <MD 7:165>. (Note that there are 11 years between their first and second child.
This normally indicates either two marriages (for James) or infants who died young. However,
as the will of her mother (1686) mentions daughter Lydia and grandchildren James, Dorothy &
Jabez Brown, we know Lydia was the only mother.) <See HOWLAND Probate Appendix for will of
James BROWN.)

4 BROWN CHILDREN:

1. **James BROWN**[3], b. 4 or 21 May 1655, Rehoboth <Rehoboth BMD, 1648-1939:14>, d. 15 Apr. 1718,
60th yr, Attleboro <MSR:626 (Rehoboth/Seekonk g.s.)>; m. 5 June 1678, Swansea, **Margaret DENI-
SON** <MQ 50:8 (no date)>, (dau of George), b. c1656, d. 5 May 1741, 85th yr, Attleboro <MSR:
626 (Rehoboth/Seekonk g.s.)>. <See MBD 2:175, Swansea VR for bth. 12 chil.> (See p.78)

2. **Dorothy BROWN**[3], b. 29 Aug. 1666, Swansea <Swansea VR A:1>, d. 2 June 1727, Rehoboth <Rehoboth
VR:843,2:238>; m. 12 Nov. 1690, Swansea, **Joseph KENT Jr.** <Swansea VR A:94; MD 7:163>, (son of
Joseph), b. (   ), d. 20 Mar. 1734/5, Rehoboth <Rehoboth VR:843,2:243>. (Joseph m.2nd,
Mary (   ).) (See HOWLAND Probate Appendix for will of Joseph KENT Jr.) <See MBD 2:174
for bth. 8 chil.; Swansea VR (3), Rehoboth VR (5).>

3. **Jabez BROWN**[3], b. 9 July 1668, Swansea <Swansea VR>, d. betw. 12 May 1747 <MDP:342 (deposition
dated 12 May 1747 "in the eightieth year of his age")> - 7 July 1747, of Barrington/Rehoboth
<MDP:342 (pr.)>; m.1st **Jane (   )** <MBD 2:175>, b. (   ), d. aft. 30 Mar. 1708
<MDP:342; Bristol Co.Deeds 5:352>. **Jabez** m.2nd, (   ), **Abijah (   )**, b. (   ), d. pre
5 Apr. 1766 (inv.) <MDP:343; Bristol Co.PR 20:552 (The account of the admr. of her estate
(step-son John BROWN) mentions providing for her for 18 years, which would refer to the time
from her husband's death to her own, therefore she d. c1765/6.)> (See HOWLAND Probate Appendix for will of Jabez BROWN.) <See MBD 2:175 for 6 chil. by 1st wf.>

4. **Joseph BROWN**[3], b. 9 July 1668, Swansea <Swansea VR>, d. pre 17 Dec. 1686 <MD 3:54 (not ment.
in will of grandmother, cited above)>.

VI. **HANNAH HOWLAND**[2], b. c1637, poss. Maine, d. (   ); m. 6 July 1661, prob. Swansea, **Jonathan
BOSWORTH** <MM:214>, b. (   ), d. (   ).

9 BOSWORTH Children: <MBD 2:128-9; Swansea VR>

1. **Mercy BOSWORTH[3]**, b. 30 May 1662, Swansea.

2. **Hannah BOSWORTH[3]**, b. 5 Nov. 1663, Swansea <Swansea VR A:17; MD 20:177 (Jenckes Family Bible); MBD 2:182, #77 cites PCR 8:8 which should read 8:48; PCR 8:48 (printed in MD 19:21) incorrectly gives the year as 1673)>, d. aft. 31 July 1723, prob. Providence RI (hus.codicil) <MBD 2:128 (Bowman does not give a source for Nathaniel's will but states only that he mentions grandchildren Jonathan & Mary JENCKS, chil. of son Jonathan JENCKES "now with me")>; m. 4 Nov 1686, Swansea, **Nathaniel JENCKES** <MD 20:175> (son of Joseph), b. 29 Jan. 1662/3, Providence RI <MD 20:177>, d. 11 Aug. 1723, Providence RI <MBD 2:134 (note: Nathaniel's name should be added to the index.)>. <See MBD 2:134; MD 20:177 for bth. 4 chil.>

3. **Elizabeth BOSWORTH[3]**, b. 6 June 1665, Swansea, d. 31 July 1676.

4. **Jonathan BOSWORTH[3]**, b. 24 Dec. 1666, Swansea, bur. 16 July 1676.

5. **David BOSWORTH[3]**, b. 15 Sept. 1670, Swansea, d. 12 June 1747, 77th yr, Halifax g.s. <MD 9:152> m.1st, 18 Aug. 1698, Plymouth, **Mary/Mercy STURTEVANT** <MD 13:207,27:79>, (dau of Samuel STURTEVANT[2-1] & Mercy CORNISH), b. c1676, d. 23 Apr. 1707, 31st yr, Plympton g.s. <MD 8:153,27:80>. **David** m.2nd, (   ), **Patience (   )** <MD 27:80>, b. c1668, d. 10 Sept. 1758, 90th yr, Halifax g.s. <MD 9:152>. (See HOWLAND Probate Appendix for will of David BOSWORTH.) <See MD 2:80,27:79; MBD 2:129 for 4 chil. by 1st wf.>

6. **John BOSWORTH[3]**, b. 6 Apr. 1671, Swansea <Swansea VR A:21>, d. pre 10 Nov. 1719, of Barrington <MDP:325 (inv.)>; m. 10 or 16 June 1702, Swansea, **Elizabeth TOOGOOD** <Swansea VR A:79,95>, (dau of Nathaniel & Elizabeth), b. 25 July 1682, Swansea <PCR 8:84; Swansea VR A:6>, d. aft. 7 Nov. 1733 (ack.deed) <MDP:325; Bristol Co.Deeds 23:399; MDP:326, Bristol Co.Deeds 33:289 (13 Jan. 1740/1 son David quit claimed his rights in mother's thirds and 2 Oct. 1741 son Nathaniel mentions land bounded by mother's thirds - she is not called deceased in either.)>. **Elizabeth** m.2nd, int. 19 Dec. 1723, Rehoboth, James THURBER <Rehoboth VR:429> who poss. d. 26 Mar. 1736 <Bowman Files>. (See HOWLAND Probate Appendix for estate of John BOSWORTH.) <See MBD 2:136 for 9 chil.>

7. **Jabez BOSWORTH[3]**, b. 14 Feb. 1673, Swansea, prob. the son who d. 22 June 1678 <MBD 2:182 #78>.

8. **Ichabod BOSWORTH[3]**, b. 18 Mar. 1676, Swansea, d. (   ); m. (   ), **Sarah STACEY**, b. (   ) d. (   ).

9. **Jonathan BOSWORTH[3]**, b. 22 Sept. 1680, Swansea <Swansea VR A:24>, d. pre 3 Apr. 1759, Rehoboth (adm.) <MDP:326>; m. 26 Nov. 1703, Swansea, **Sarah ROUNDS** <Swansea VR A:95>, b. (   ), d. aft. 1 Apr. 1760 (hus.acc't, called "ancient") <MDP:326>. (See HOWLAND Probate Appendix for estate of Jonathan BOSWORTH.) <See MBD 2:136 for 2 chil.>

VII JOSEPH HOWLAND[2], b. c1640, Rocky Nook/Kingston <MQ 48:132>, d. Jan. 1703/4, Plymouth <MD 6:86; Plymouth ChR; MQ 48:132>; m. 7 Dec. 1664, Plymouth, **Elizabeth SOUTHWORTH** <PCR 8:25>, (dau of Thomas SOUTHWORTH[2] (Edward[1]) & Elizabeth REYNER), b. c1645 <MQ 48:132; Stratton:356>, d. Mar. 1717, Plymouth <Plymouth ChR; MQ 48:132>.

9 HOWLAND Children: <MBD 2:167; MD 6:87>

1. **Thomas HOWLAND[3]**, b. (   ), d. 2 Dec. 1739, Plymouth g.s. <MD 16:85,27:82; Drew:58 (1739 is all that remains of the broken stone)>; m. pre 1700, (   ), **Joanna COLE** <MD 27:42>, (dau of James COLE & Abigail DAVENPORT), b. (   ), d. 4 Jan. 1760, Plymouth <Plymouth ChR 1:390>. (See HOWLAND Probate Appendix for will of Thomas HOWLAND.) <See MBD 2:173, MD 4:112 for bth. of 8 chil.>

2. **James HOWLAND[3]**, b. (   ) <MBD 2:168 (Bowman states he was born pre 29 Dec. 1669 which would imply a deed dated 29 Dec. 1690 in which James was of legal age (21) but I have been unable to find a reference to such a deed)>, d. aft. 23 Dec. 1703 <MD 6:88 (fath.codicil); note he had a ch. b. in 1713)>; m. 8 Sept. 1697, Barnstable, **Mary LOTHROP** <MD 14:225>, (dau of John LOTHROP & Mary COLE), b. 27 Oct. 1675, Barnstable <MD 6:238; Otis 2:164>, d. 26 May 1723, Plymouth <Plymouth ChR>. <See MBD 2:168; MD 4:111 for bth. 6 chil.>

3. **Nathaniel HOWLAND[3]**, b. c1670, d. 20 Dec. 1746, 76th yr, Plymouth g.s. <Drew:95>; m.1st, 16 Mar. 1696/7, Plymouth, **Martha COLE** <MD 13:206,27:41>, (dau of James COLE & Abigail DAVENPORT) b. c1672, d. 11 or 15 Aug. 1718, ae about 46, Plymouth g.s. <Drew:95 (11th); MD 27:41 (11th); Plymouth ChR 1:219 (15th)>. **Nathaniel** m.2nd, 25 Jan. 1725/6, Plymouth, **Abigail (CHURCHILL) Billington** <MD 14:71,27:41>, (dau of Eleazer CHURCHILL & Mary (?BRYANT)), b. c1680, Plymouth, d. (   ). (Abigail m.1st, 17 May 1702, Plymouth, Francis BILLINGTON[4] <MD 13:207; Plymouth ChR 1:196-7 (On 27 Jan. 1702/3, Abigail was brought before the church for fornication before marriage with husband Francis)>, (son of Joseph BILLINGTON[3] (Francis[2]) & Grace (   ) - see BILLINGTON family), b. c1676, poss. Block Island RI <MF 5:49>, d. betw. 3 Dec. 1719 <MDP:58; Plymouth Co.Deeds 14:255> - 29 July 1724 <Plymouth ChR 1:228 (Abigail is called widow)>; see

MBD 1:106, MD 13:33 for bth. 7 BILLINGTON chil.>) <See MBD 2:171,186 for bth. 8 chil. by 1st wf; MD 2:80 (4).>

4. **Sarah HOWLAND**[3], b. c1673, d. betw. 24 Mar. 1698/9 - 23 Dec. 1703 <MD 6:88 (fath.codicil)>. Sarah does not appear to have married, yet according to the records she bore two children. Plymouth ChR 1:273 state, "13 Dec. 1691, Sarah HOWLAND, a child of the church, was called before the whole Congregation to answer for the sin of fornication, she confessed her sin against God & his people, and desired forgiveness and prayers, by the vote of the church she was by the Pastour laid under the solemne ordinance of Admonition with severe rebukes. The Bretheren exprest that they would proceed thus farre at present and not put hereby a finall issue to dealing with her case afterward further guilt and aggravations of her sin should appear, but then to act accordingly". (Her daughter Mary was born, probably in 1692.) Seven years later, 21 Mar. 1698/9, she was fined "for ye like Transgression" <Plymouth Quarter Sessions:147>. Apparently the child had been found dead, on 24 Mar. 1698/9 she was brought before the Superior Court and "tried" <Suffolk Co.Superior Court 2:246>. <See MQ 45:138-43.>

5. **Lydia HOWLAND**[3], b. c1674 <MQ 48:132>, d. aft. 25 Jan. 1733 (hus.will) <MDP:338>; m. Oct. 1694 Barnstable, **Joseph JENKINS** <MD 6:236,20:131; MQ 48:132>, (son of John JENKINS & Mary EWER), b. 31 Mar. 1669, Barnstable <MD 6:236; MQ 48:132; Otis 2:92>, d. 13 Oct. 1734, 66th yr, Barnstable g.s. <MQ 45:221 (Memorial Inscriptions W. Barnstable Cem.). (See HOWLAND Probate Appendix for will of Joseph JENKINS.) <MBD 2:168-9 for bth. 9 chil.; MD 6:236 (7).>

6. **Elizabeth HOWLAND**[3], b. (   ), d. aft. 15 Feb. 1723/4 <MDP:338 (sett.1st hus.est.)>; m.1st, 14 Sept. 1698, Barnstable, **Isaac HAMBLIN/HAMBLEN** <MD 6:137; Otis 1:533; MQ 48:132>, (son of Eleazer HAMBLIN & Mehitable JENKINS), b. 20 Aug. 1676, Barnstable <MD 6:137; Otis 1:527,533>, d. pre 8 Feb. 1709/10 <MDP:338 (adm.)>. **Elizabeth** m.2nd, 9 Nov. 1711, prob. Barnstable, **Timothy CANNON** <Otis 1:533; MQ 48:132>; they apparently had children.> (See HOWLAND Probate Appendix for estate of Isaac HAMBLIN.) <See MBD 2:167; MD 6:137 for bth. 3 chil.>

7. **Mercy HOWLAND**[3], b. (   ), d. aft. 21 May 1721 (bth. last ch.); m. 27 Apr. 1704, Barnstable, **Joseph HAMBLIN/HAMLIN** <MD 6:137; MQ 48:132; Otis 1:534 (says 27 May)>, (son of Eleazer HAMBLIN & Mehitable JENKINS), b. 20 Nov. 1680, Barnstable <MD 6:137; MQ 48:132; Otis 1:534>, d. 27 Aug. 1766, 86th yr, Barnstable g.s. <MQ 45:158 (Memorial Inscriptions W. Barnstable Cem.); Otis 1:534>. <See MBD 2:171; MD 6:137; Otis 1:534-5 for bth. 5 chil.>

8. **Joseph HOWLAND**[3], b. (   ), d. 8 July 1689 <MD 16:62>.

9. **Benjamin HOWLAND**[3], b. 1689, d. 7 Sept. 1689 <MD 16:62>.

VIII **JABEZ HOWLAND**[2], b. c1644, Rocky Nook/Kingston, d. betw. 14 May 1708 (will) - 6 Feb. 1711/2 (inv.), Bristol MA (now RI) <MD 7:198-200>; m. c1688, Plymouth, **Bethiah THACHER** <   >, (dau of Anthony), b. (   ), d. aft. 26 Nov. 1714 <MD 7:207-8 (agreement of heirs of hus.est.); I have an unconfirmed death date of 19 Dec. 1725)>. (See HOWLAND Probate Appendix for will of Jabez HOWLAND.)

11 HOWLAND Children: <MBD 2:157>

1. **Jabez HOWLAND**[3], b. 15 Nov. 1669, Plymouth <PCR 8:35; MD 18:70,21:145>, d. 17 Oct. 1732, 64th yr, Bristol MA (now RI) <MD 21:145 (both he and his wife were buried in the cemetery near St. Michael's Church, Bristol but the older gravestones were later moved to the Juniper Hill Cemetery)>; m. c1699, (   ), **Patience STAFFORD**, b. (   ), bur. 1 June 1726, Bristol g.s. <MBD 2:158>. (See HOWLAND Probate Appendix for estate of Jabez HOWLAND.) <See MBD 2:158 for bth. 9 chil.>

2. **John HOWLAND**[3], b. about 15 Jan. 1672/3, Plymouth, d. same month. <PCR 8:35; MD 18:70>.

3. **Bethiah HOWLAND**[3], b. 3 June 1674, Plymouth <PCR 8:35; MD 18:70>, d.y.

4. **Josiah HOWLAND**[3], b. 6 Aug. 1676, Plymouth <PCR 8:68>, d. (   ); m. 24 Nov. 1709, Barnstable **Yetmercy SHOVE** <MD 14:88>, (dau of George SHOVE & Hannah WALLEY), b. 7 Nov. 1682, Taunton <PCR 8:85>, d. (   ). <See MBD 2:158,185 for 6 chil.>

5. **John HOWLAND**[3], b. 26 July 1679, Plymouth <PCR 8:68>, d. pre 14 May 1708 (fath.will).

6. **Judah HOWLAND**[3], b. 7 May 1683, (   ) <MBD 2:157>, d. pre 14 May 1708 (fath.will).

7. **Seth HOWLAND**[3], b. 5 Jan. 1684/5, (   ) <MBD 2:157>, bur. 12 Apr. 1685 <MBD 2:157>.

8. **Samuel HOWLAND**[3], b. 16 May 1686, Bristol MA (now RI) <MBD 2:157>, d. 15 May 1748, Bristol RI <MBD 2:157>; m.1st 6 May 1708, Bristol MA, **Abigail CARY** <MM:226>, (dau of John & Abigail), b. 31 Aug. 1684, Bristol MA <MBD 2:158>, d. 6 Aug. 1737, Bristol <MBD 2:158; Bristol VR>. **Samuel** m.2nd, int. 19 Feb. 1741/2, Barrington RI, **Rachel (   ) ALLEN** <MM:226; Barrington RI VR>. <See MBD 2:159 for 8 chil. by 1st wf.>

9. **Experience HOWLAND**[3], b. 19 May 1687, Bristol MA (now RI) <MBD 2:157> d. pre 14 May 1708 (fath will) <MD 7:198-200>.

10. **Joseph HOWLAND**[3], b. 14 Oct. 1692, Bristol MA <MBD 2:157>, d. 16 Aug. 1737, (   ) <MBD 2:157>; m. c1714, (   ), **Bathsheba CARY** <MM:226>, (dau of David & Elizabeth), b. 14 Aug. 1693 (   ) <MBD 2:158>, d. 16 Aug. 1775, (   ) <MBD 2:158>. <See MBD 2:158 for 3 chil.>

11. **Elizabeth HOWLAND**[3], b. (   ), d. pre 26 Nov. 1714, of Newport RI <MD 7:205-7 (the agreement of her father's heirs states she is dec'd with one son living; she was poss. dec'd pre 14 May 1708 as she was not mentioned in her father's will)>; m. (   ), **Nathan TOWNSEND** <MD 7:199>, b. (   ), d. (   ).

IX. **RUTH HOWLAND**[2], b. c1646, Rocky Nook/Kingston, d. betw. 29 May 1672 (fath.will) - 16 Oct. 1679 (hus.2nd marr.); m. 17 Nov. 1664, Plymouth, **Thomas CUSHMAN**[3] <PCR 8:25; MSR:547; MBD 1:84,102 (PCR 4:83 states they were fined 7 Mar. 1664/5 for committing "carnal coppulation" before marriage but after contract. Note approx. birth date of first child.)>, (son of Thomas CUSHMAN & Mary ALLERTON[2], see ALLERTON Family)

3 CUSHMAN Children: <MBD 1:84; MFIP (Allerton) #10>

1. **Robert CUSHMAN**[3], b. c4 Oct 1664, Plymouth (the date of birth (derived from his age at death) would mean he was born one month before his parents' marriage. Although one would assume this to be in error, the above mentioned reference to his parents suggests this date is possible), d. 7 Sept. 1757, ae 92y11m3d, Kingston <MD 7:28; MQ 57:330>; m.1st c1697, prob. Plymouth, **Persis (?LEWIS)** <MQ 57:330-5>, (poss. dau of Thomas), poss. b. 15 June 1671, Swansea <Swansea VR A:45; MQ 57:330-5>, d. 14 Jan. 1743/4, 73rd yr, Kingston <MD 7:28; MQ 57:330>. **Robert** m.2nd, 2 Feb. 1744, Marshfield, **Prudence SHERMAN** <Marshfield VR:172>, (dau of Samuel SHERMAN & Sarah DOGGETT), b. c1674 <MFIP (Allerton) #38>. (See HOWLAND Probate Appendix for will of Robert CUSHMAN.) <See MD 4:111 for bth. 7 chil. by 1st wf; Plymouth ChR 1:218 for baptisms.>

2. **Desire CUSHMAN**[3], b. c1668, Plymouth, poss. d. 8 Feb. 1762, ae about 94, Barrington RI, Tylers Point g.s. <MBD 1:84,102 (Bowman), "Mrs. Desire Kent, wife of Mr. Samuel Kent of Barrington, was English woman, Daughter on New England, died Feb. 1762, aged about 94 years"- no source>; poss. m. c1700, (   ), **Samuel KENT** <MM:28 (Bowman) and MFIP (Allerton) #38A indicate proof for this marriage is needed>, (son of Joseph KENT & Susanna GEORGE), b. c1668, Swansea <MFIP #38A>, d. 15 May 1737, Barrington RI <MFIP #38A>. <See MFIP (Allerton) #38A for 2 chil>

3. **Thomas CUSHMAN**[3], b. c1670, Plymouth, d. 9 Jan. 1726/7, ae 57, Lebanon CT <MBD 1:84>; m. pre 1703, poss. Lebanon CT, **Sarah STRONG** <MM:30>, (dau of Jedidiah STRONG & Freedom WOODWARD), b. c1674, Coventry CT <MFIP (Allerton) #39>, d. 25 Dec. 1726, ae 52, Lebanon CT g.s. <MBD 1:89>. (See HOWLAND Probate Appendix for will of Thomas CUSHMAN.) <See MFIP #39 for 6 chil.>

X. **ISAAC HOWLAND**[2], b. 15 Nov. 1649, Rocky Nook/Kingston <White 1:6 (no source for date)>, d. 9 Mar. 1723/4, 75th yr, Middleboro, The Green cem. <MD 5:38,6:147,13:27,17:187,219; Wood:90>; m. c1676, prob. Middleboro, **Elizabeth VAUGHN** <MD 17:187,219,18:115>, (dau of George), b. 8 Apr. 1653, Marshfield <Marshfield VR:4>, d. 29 Oct. 1727, 75th yr, Middleboro, The Green cem. <MD 5:38,6:147,13:27,17:187,219; Wood:90>. (See HOWLAND Probate Appendix for wills of Isaac & Elizabeth HOWLAND.)

8 HOWLAND Children: <MBD 2:153>

1. **Seth HOWLAND**[3], b. 28 Nov. 1677, Middleboro <MD 1:220,21:179>, d. 26 Oct. 1729, 52nd yr, Middleboro, The Green cem. <MD 5:38,13:27,21:179; Wood:90>; m. 24 May 1728, Middleboro, **Elizabeth DELANO** <MD 5:40,21:179>, b. (   ), d. aft. 27 Mar. 1732 <MD 21:184 (hus.est.)>. No issue. (See HOWLAND Probate Appendix for estate of Seth HOWLAND.)

2. **Isaac HOWLAND**[3], b. 6 Mar. 1678/9, Middleboro <Middleboro VR 1:2; MD 1:220>, d. 26 Feb. 1723/4 45th yr, Middleboro, The Green cem. <MD 13:27,17:188; MQ 45:70; Wood:90>; m. c1712, (   ), **Sarah THOMAS**[4] <MD 17:188>, (dau of Jeremiah THOMAS & Lydia HOWLAND[3] (John[2])), b. 25 Dec. 1687 Middleboro <Middleboro VR 1:10; MSR:253>, d. 30 Apr. 1756, Middleboro, 68th yr, The Green cem <MD 14:224; Wood:90,232>. (Sarah m.2nd, 7 Aug. 1730, Middleboro, Samuel WOOD <MD 9:46>, (son of Samuel[2] (Henry[1]), b. 19 Sept. 1684, Middleboro <MD 1:222>, d. (   ).) <See MBD 2:153 for bth. 4 chil.>

3. **Priscilla HOWLAND**[3], b. 22 Aug. 1681, Middleboro <MD 1:221>, d. 3 Mar. 1746, 65th yr, Middleboro, The Green cem. <MD 12:70,21:171; Wood:16>; m. 30 Oct. 1700, Bridgewater, **Capt. Peter BENNETT** <MD 2:146,21:171; Plymouth Court Quarterly Sessions, 1687-1721,:179 (they were fined on 16 Sept. 1701; note that their first ch. was b. 5 mths after marr.)>, b. Sept. 1674, d. 22 Oct. 1749, ae 75y1m4d, Middleboro, The Green cem. <MD 12:70,21:171; Wood:16>. (See HOWLAND Probate Apendix for will of Capt. Peter BENNETT.) <See MBD 2:154 for bth. 11 chil.; MD 1:220 (3), 2:102 (2), 201 (1), 3:84 (1), 85 (1), 86 (1), 234 (1), 5:40 (1).>

4. **Elizabeth HOWLAND**[3], b. 2 Dec. 1682, Middleboro <MD 1:221>, d. 1 Apr. 1685 <MD 1:222>.

5. **Nathan HOWLAND**[3], b. 17 Jan. 1687, Middleboro <Middleboro VR 1:3; MD 1:223>, d. pre July 1759 <Plymouth Co.CT Rcds.7:419>; m. betw. 15 May 1711 - 2 Feb. 1712 <MDP:356 (her fath.est.)>, prob. Middleboro, **Frances COOMBS/COMBES**[4] <MM:224>, (dau of Francis COOMBS[3] (Sarah Priest[2]) & Mary BARKER - see PRIEST family), b. 6 Jan. 1682, Middleboro <MD 1:221>, d. aft. Oct. 1762 <Plymouth Co.CT Rcds.8:65>. <See MBD 2:153 for bth. 6 chil.; MD 3:235 (4), 6:226 (1), 8:28 (1); Middleboro VR 1:21 (4), 35 (1), 42 (1).>

6. **Jael HOWLAND**[3], b. 13 Oct. 1688, Middleboro <MD 1:223>, d. 9 Nov. 1745, 67th yr, Middleboro, Nemasket cem. <MD 15:7; Wood:171>; m. c1709, prob. Middleboro, **Nathaniel SOUTHWORTH**[5], (son of Desire Gray[4] (Mary Winslow[3], Mary Chilton - see Chilton family) & Nathaniel SOUTHWORTH[3] (Constant[2], Edward[1]), b. 18 May 1684, Plymouth <MD 1:142>, d. 8 Apr. 1757, 72nd yr, Middleboro, Nemasket cem. <MD 15:8; Wood:171>. <See MBD 1:298 for bth. 6 chil.; MD 1:207 (1), 3:84 (2), 234 (1), 6:180 (1), 7:242 (1).>

7. **Susannah HOWLAND**[3], b. 14 Oct. 1690, Middleboro <MD 1:223>, d. 1 Oct. 1720, ae 30, Middleboro, Nemasket cem. <MD 15:109 (not 15:100 as in MBD 2:153); Wood:232>; m. c1709, prob. Middleboro, **Ephraim WOOD** <MM:225>, (son of Samuel[2] (Henry[1])), b. Jan. 1679, Middleboro <MD 1:221>, d. 9 July 1744, 65th yr, Middleboro <Wood:232>. (Ephraim m.2nd, c1723, Patience (NICHOLS) Holmes, prob. Middleboro <MM:225; MBD 2:156>; poss. dau of Thomas NICHOLS & Sarah WHISTON, b. 25 Feb. 1685/6 <Scituate VR 1:272; MBD 2:156>, d. aft. 20 May 1738 (hus.will) and had 2 chil. <MD 6: 228, 7:242>. Patience m.1st, Experience HOLMES, b. c1681, d. 1715, ae 34, Dartmouth and had 5 chil. <MBD 2:156>.) (See HOWLAND Probate Appendix for will of Deacon Ephraim WOOD.) <See MBD 2:156 for bth. 5 chil.; MD 2:201 (1), 3:84 (1), 85 (1), 233 (1), 234 (1).>

8. **Hannah HOWLAND**[3], b. 6 Oct. 1694, Middleboro <MD 1:224>, d. 25 Mar. 1792, 98th yr, Middleboro, Nemasket cem. <MD 15:101; Wood:201>; m. 11 Dec. 1716, Middleboro, **John TINKHAM**[4] <Middleboro VR 1:24; MD 4:70>, (son of Ephraim TINKHAM[3] (Mary Brown[2]) & Esther WRIGHT[3] (Hester Cooke[2]) - see BROWN & COOKE families), b. 22 Aug. 1680, Middleboro <MD 1:221>, d. 14 Apr. 1766, 86th yr Middleboro, Nemasket cem. <MD 15:102; Wood:201>. (See HOWLAND Probate Appendix for will of John TINKHAM.) <See MBD 1:273 for bth. 10 chil.; MD 3:86 (1), 233 (1), 234 (1), 4:69 (1), 6:228 (1), 229 (1), 7:242 (1), 8:249 (1), 9:48 (1), 12:232 (1); Middleboro Vr 1:4,17,18,20, 23,36,38,41,45,48,54.>

HOWLAND PROBATE APPENDIX

Will of Thomas BAXTER Sr.: (yeoman) <MD 12:218-21; Barnstable Co.PR 3:303-6,4:358,4:503>
..."about" 2 June 1713, ment. wf Temperance; son John BAXTER; son Thomas BAXTER and "his Two Children att Coneicticut, Timothy ye son & the Daughter"; son Shoball BAXTER. Pr. 9 July 1713. (On 30 Mar. 1727, grandson Timothy BAXTER receipted. On 28 Mar. 1729, granddaughter Elizabeth BAXTER receipted.) The inventory mentions negro slaves and molatto servants.

==

Will of Capt. Peter BENNETT/BENNET: <MDP:333-4; Plymouth Co.PR #1844, 11:382,385>
...5 Oct. 1749, ment. son Isaac BENNET; brother Seth HOWLAND dec'd; grandsons John BENNET & Samuel BENNET, sons of dec'd son Joseph BENNET; minor grandchildren Peter BENNET, Anna BENNET & Jael BENNET, chil. of dec'd son Peter BENNET; granddaughters Priscilla BENNET & Susanna BENNET, daus of dec'd son Nathan BENNET & his widow Jemima BENNET; daus Elizabeth DARLING, Susanna DREW, Priscilla MILLER; grandson Abiezer EDSON son of dec'd dau Jael EDSON; dau Deborah THACHER. Pr. 6 Nov. 1749.

==

Will of David BOSWORTH: (yeoman) <MD 27:80-1; Plymouth Co.PR 11:396>
...27 Oct. 1740, ment. wf Patience; sons David BOSWORTH, Nehemiah BOSWORTH, Jonathan BOSWORTH; dau Hannah. Codicil, 8 May 1743, states son Jonathan BOSWORTH is dec'd. Pr. 14 July 1747.

==

Will of Melatiah BOURNE/BOURN: <MD 19:36-40; Barnstable Co.PR 6:262>
...11 Aug. 1742, ment. wf Abigail and her chil. Samuel SMITH, John SMITH & Rebecca; Mary & Isaac, chil. of wife's son Shoble <SMITH>; wife's grandson Dr. Thomas SMITH; eldest grandson Melatiah; sons Silvanus BOURN, Silas BOURN, John BOURN, Shearjashob BOURN; dau Bathsheba RUGGLES, wf of William NEWCOMB dec'd and their minor chil.; "my Negro man Nero be manumitted and Sett free from his Servitude...upon Condition that he faithfully Serve my Son Silas one year". Codicil, 7 Sept 1742, ment. wf Abigail, son Silas and "rest of my children" Codicil, 24 Sept. 1742, ment. son Silas and "rest of my children". Pr. 15 Feb. 1742/3.

==

Estate of John BOZWORTH[3] **(Hannah Howland**[2]**):** <MDP:325; Bristol Co.PR 5:135>
...Division, 2 Mar. 1724/5, to the "late widow (viz) the wife of James THURBER" and foll. chil.: Nathaniel BOZWORTH (eldest son), John BOZWORTH (2nd son), David BOZWORTH (3rd son), Oliver BOZWORTH (4th son), Elizabeth THOMAS wf of John (eldest dau), Mary BOZWORTH (2nd dau), Anna BOZWORTH (3rd dau), Lydia BOZWORTH (4th dau).

==

Will of Jabez BROWN[3] **(Lydia Howland**[2]**):** <MDP:342-3; Bristol Co.PR 11:281,292>
...11 Apr. 1746, "being aged", ment wf Abijah; son John BROWN; dau Jane BOSWORTH wf of Nathaniel; Rebecca BROWN & Ann BROWN (both under 18), daus of son Oliver BROWN; Jerusha PECK & Winchester PECK, (both under 18), chil. of dau Rebeccah PECK; son Hezekiah BROWN; son John BROWN "to take

good care & provide sutably for my dau Elizabeth...& give her a decent buriall." Pr. 7 July 1747.

==

Will of **James BROWN**: <MD 7:163-66; Bristol Co.PR 3:6-8>
...25 Oct. 1694, "being about seventy one years of age", ment. wf Lidia; sons James BROWN, Jabez BROWN; dau Dorothy KENT; "Matte my Negro". Inv. taken 29 Oct. 1710.

==

Will of **James BROWN[3] (Lydia Howland[2])**: <MD 17:193-6; Bristol Co.PR 3:557>
...28 June 1717, ment. eldest son James BROWN; wf Margrett; sons William BROWN, Benjamin BROWN, Issace <Isaac> BROWN; daus Mary ANGELL, Ann HILL, Margrett CARPENTER, Dorrotha BROWN, Mercy BROWN Wit. sworn 4 May 1719.

==

Will of **Margaret (DENISON) Brown**: (widow) <MD 17:197-9; Bristol Co.PR 10:159-60>
...6 Feb. 1733/4, ment. unnamed chil. of dec'd son James BROWN; unnamed chil. of dec'd son William BROWN; grandson William CARPENTER; unnamed chil. of dec'd son Isaac BROWN; son Benjamin BROWN & his son Nathan BROWN; daus Mary ANGEL, Ann HILL, Dorothy MEDBURY, Mercy CARPENTER. Wit. sworn 18 May 1742.

==

Will of **John BURSLEY**: <MDP:336; Barnstable Co.PR 4:326,329>
...18 July 1726, ment. wf Elizabeth; sons John BURSLEY, Jabez BURSLEY; son Joseph BURSLEY "shall be kind to his mother in law"; daus Mary, Joannah, Abigail, Elizabeth; dau Temperance "being weakly" to have same liberty in the house with her "mother in law". Pr. 29 Aug. 1726.

==

Will of **Elder John CHIPMAN**: <MD 3:181-5; Barnstable Co.PR 3:228-31>
...12 Nov. 1702, ment. compact made with wf Ruth at their marriage; sons Samuel CHIPMAN, John CHIPMAN; grandchildren Mary GALE, Jabez DIMMOCK; daus Elizabeth, Hope, Lydia, Hannah, Ruth, Mercy, Bethia and Desire. Pr. 17 May 1708. Inv. gives his death date.

==

Will of **Ruth (SARGENT) Chipman**: (widow) <MD 3:185-6; Barnstable Co.PR 3:258-9>
...6 Dec. 1710, ment. brother John SERJANT & his unnamed chil. incl. son William SERJANT; kinswoman Hanna SERGEANT; kinsman Joseph BREAD & his daus. Sarah & Elizabeth "and to the other children of my sister BREAD"; daus of sister FELCH; kinsman Seath TOBY; Bathshebe, dau of Melatiah BOURNE; Jabez DIMOK; sister Lydia SERGEANT; kinswoman Deborah WEIGHT. Pr. 8 Oct. 1713.

==

Will of **John CHIPMAN[3] (Hope Howland[2])**: <MDP:331; Newport RI Town Council, 1756-60, p.11>
...17 Oct. 1749, ment. sons James CHIPMAN, Handley CHIPMAN, John CHIPMAN; dau Lydia SWIFT; grandchildren Isaac SMITH, Mary SMITH; dau in law Mary CHIPMAN & her son William CHIPMAN; children Perces, Bethia & Deborah; Perces CHIPMAN son of son James CHIPMAN; dec'd dau Rebecca MOORE (her husband & children living); son in law David MOORE. Pr. 2 Feb. 1756.

==

Will of **Samuel CHIPMAN[3] (Hope Howland[2])**: <MD 16:65-7; Barnstable Co.PR 4:125>
...31 Aug. 1722, ment. wf Sarah; sons Samuel CHIPMAN, Jacob CHIPMAN, Thomas CHIPMAN, John CHIPMAN, Joseph CHIPMAN, Seth CHIPMAN, Barnabas CHIPMAN; grandsons Elamuel JACKSON, Nathaniel JACKSON; dau Hannah LOTHROP. Wit. sworn 17 June 1723.

==

Will of **Sarah (COBB) Chipman**: (widow) <MD 16:67-8; Barnstable Co.PR 6:433>
...27 Nov. 1733, ment. sons Samuell CHIPMAN, Jacob CHIPMAN; granddaughter Sarah, the dau of son Jacob; dau Hannah LOTHROP; sons Thomas CHIPMAN, John CHIPMAN, Seth CHIPMAN, Barnabas CHIPMAN; chil. of dec'd dau Abigail JACKSON. Wit. sworn 8 Mar. 1743.

==

Estate of **Eleazer CROCKER**: <MD 18:158-65; Barnstable Co.PR 4:142,145,216-9>
...Inventory taken 6 Sept. 1723, "leaveing a widow and one smale child...Mercy CROCKER a minor". Settlement, 19 Nov. 1724 among following chil., viz: Nathan CROCKER (eldest son), Theophilus CROCKER, Able CROCKER, Eleazer CROCKER, Bethiah WHITEING, Sarah BURSLEY, Ruth FULLER, Rebacca ROBINS and Mercy CROCKER (youngest dau.)

==

Will of **Jonathan CROCKER**: <Barnstable Co.PR 8:10-11>
...10 June 1746, ment. wf Thankful; sons Isaac CROCKER, James CROCKER; daus Lydia BODFISH, Hannah FULLER; chil. of dec'd dau Reliance SMITH; unnamed eldest son of son James CROCKER; kinsman Jabez HOWLAND; son in law Benjamin BODFISH. Pr. 9 Oct. 1746.

==

Will of **Thankful (TROTT) Crocker**: (widow) <Barnstable Co.PR 8:469-91>
...3 Aug. 1748, ment. son John HINCKLEY; granddaughter Thankful COBB; heirs of dec'd son James HINCKLEY; heirs of dec'd dau Abiah CHIPMAN; granddaughters Mary CHIPMAN, Hannah CHIPMAN; grandson Nathaniel CHIPMAN; dau Thankful SMITH. Inv. taken 8 Mar. 1748/9.

==

Will of **Joseph CROCKER**: <MDP:336; Barnstable Co.PR 6:154,157>
...27 Apr. 1741, ment. wf Anne; son Benjamin CROCKER; dec'd brother Nathaniel CROCKER; dau Prudence GORHAM & her son Joseph GORHAM; unnamed minor male & female grandch. Pr. 11 Feb. 1741/2.

==

Will of **Robert CUSHMAN[3] (Ruth Howland[2])**: <MDP:46; Plymouth Co.PR #5883, 14:410>
...9 Feb. 1746/7, ment. wf Prudence and follow. chil., viz: Robert CUSHMAN, Thomas CUSHMAN, Joshua CUSHMAN, Jonathan CUSHMAN, Ruth PERKINS, Abigail LEONARD, Hannah WASHBURN. Codicil, 9 May 1749. Pr. 7 Nov. 1757.

==

Will of **George DENISON**: <White 1:27>
...4 Dec. 1711, ment. wf Mercy; eldest sons Edward DENISON, Joseph DENISON, Samuel DENISON; two
eldest daus Mercy DUNBAR, Elizabeth CHAMPLIN; youngest son George DENISON; youngest daus Desire
DENISON, Thankful DENISON. Pr. 10 Mar. 1712.
==

Will of **Jabez GORHAM³ (Desire Howland²)**: (yeoman) <MD 17:67; Bristol Co.PR 5:75>
...16 Mar. 1724/5, "under much pain and bodily ilness", ment. wf Hannah; sons Jabez GORHAM (eldest son), Isaac GORHAM, Joseph GORHAM; dau Elisabeth BAXTER wf of Shobael; grandsons Edward
DOWNS, William DOWNS, Samuel DOWNS; son Benjamin GORHAM; negro named Niell. Pr. 20 Apr. 1725.
==

Will of **James GORHAM/GOREHAM³ (Desire Howland²)**: <MD 13:51-2; Barnstable Co.PR 3:254,256,674>
...4 Nov. 1707, ment. wf Hannah; sons John GOREHAM, Thomas GOREHAM, James GOREHAM, Joseph GORE-
HAM, Jabez GOREHAM, Selvanus GOREHAM, Ebenezer GOREHAM; daus Desier SPRINGER, Experience LOTH-
ROP and Mehittable; 5 unnamed grandchildren. Codicil, 10 Nov. 1716 (concerning land). Inv. taken
9 Dec. 1707.
==

Estate of **Capt. John GORHAM/GORUM**: <MD 4:153-8; Plymouth Col.Wills 3:1:162-4>
...Division, 7 Mar. 1676/7, among wf Desire and foll. chil., viz: James GORUM, John GORUM, Joseph
GORUM, Jabez GORUM, Mercye GORUM, Lydia GORUM, Hannah GORUM and Shubaall GORUM. (states 3 daus
are married and have already received their portions.)
==

Estate of **Desire (HOWLAND²) Gorham/Gorum**: <MD 4:217-20; Plymouth Col.Court Orders 6:2:2>
...Settlement, 5 Mar. 1683/4, ment. follow. chil., viz: James (eldest son), John, Joseph, Jabez,
Shuball (minor, youngest son), Desire, Temperance, chil of Elizabeth dec'd, Marsy, Lidia, Hannah.
==

Will of **Col. John GORHAM³ (Desire Howland²)**: <MD 13:53-4; Barnstable Co.PR 3:389,391-2>
...8 Nov. 1716, ment. wf Mary; sons Stephen GORHAM, Shubal GORHAM, John GORHAM, Job GORHAM; daus
Temperance, Mary, Thankfull & Marcy. Codicil, 10 Nov. 1716, "in case my son Job shuld Dye with
out any heir". Inv. taken 28 Nov. 1716.
==

Will of **Mary (OTIS) Gorham**: (widow) <MD 13:54-5; Barnstable Co.PR 5:110>
...7 Nov. 1727, "advanced in years", ment. sons Stephen GORHAM, John GORHAM, Job GORHAM, Shubael
GORHAM; grandson John GORHAM son of son Shubael; daus Temperance CLAP, Mary HINCKLEY, Thankfull
FULLER, Mercy BOURNE; son in law Silvanus BOURNE. Pr. 20 Apr. 1733.
==

Will of **Joseph GORHAM³ (Desire Howland²)**: <MDP:319; Barnstable Co.PR 4:309-11>
...27 July 1723, ment. wf Sarah; sons Josiah GORHAM, Joseph GORHAM; dau Desire BAXTER; grandchildren Sarah SEARS, Thomas HOWES, Ebenezer HOWES & Elizabeth HOWES, the chil. of dec'd dau Sarah
HOWES. Pr. 20 July 1726.
==

Will of **Sarah (STURGIS) Gorham**: (widow) <Barnstable Co.PR 5:377-8>
...1 May 1728, ment. son Joseph GORHAM; son Josiah GORHAM & his minor dau Rebecca by his 1st wf;
grandsons Thomas HOWES, Ebenezer HOWES; granddaughters Sarah SEARS, Lydia CROSBY <error for Elizabeth CROSBY>, the chil. of dec'd dau Sarah HOWES; dau Desire BAXTER & hus. John BAXTER. Pr. 3
Feb. 1738/9.
==

Will of **Shubael GORHAM³ (Desire Howland²)**: (yeoman) <MDP:320; Barnstable Co.PR 7:181,8:265-6>
...23 Sept. 1748, ment. son George GORHAM; daus Abigail, Lydia, Hannah, Theodate, Desire, Ruth &
Deborah. Pr. 7 Aug. 1750. (On 8 July 1749 a guardian was app'td for Shubael as he was judged
to be non compos.)
==

Estate of **Isaac HAMBLIN/HAMBLEN**: <MDP:338; Barnstable Co.PR 3:87>
...Settlement, 15 Feb. 1723/4, "the former widow Elizabeth CANNON having resigned her right of
dower in sd lands, the real estate is settled on the eldest son Eleazer HAMLIN, he to pay his
brother Joseph HAMLIN and sister Elizabeth."
==

Will of **Capt. John HAWES**: <MD 20:73-5; Barnstable Co.PR 2:134>
...15 Oct. 1701, ment. son Isaac HAWES; daus Desire HAWES, Experience HAWES; sons Ebenezer HAWES,
Joseph HAWES, John HAWES, Benjamin HAWES; daus Mary BACON, Elizabeth DOGGET; brothers Major John
GOREHAM, John THACHER. Pr. 19 Nov. 1701. (Order of daus appears to be Elizabeth, Mary, Desire,
Experience.)
==

Will of **Isaac HOWLAND²**: <MD 6:147-52; Plymouth Co.PR 4:408>
...6 Feb. 1718, ment. wf Elisabeth; sons Seth HOWLAND, Isaac HOWLAND, Nathan HOWLAND; daus Priscilla BENNETT, Jael SOUTHWORTH, Susannah WOOD, Hannah TINKHAM. Wit. sworn 6 Apr. 1724.
==

Will of **Elizabeth (VAUGHN) Howland**: (widow) <MD 17:188,219; Plymouth Co.PR 5:391>
...13 Oct. 1725, ment. follow. chil., viz: Nathan HOWLAND, Seth HOWLAND, Priscilla BENNETT, Jael
SOUTHWORTH, Hannah TINKHAM. Wit. summoned 15 Dec. 1727.
==

Will of **Jabez HOWLAND²**: (blacksmith) <MD 7:199-200; Bristol Co.PR 3:82>
...14 May 1708, "haveing had Repeated warnings (by the paines of my body offten Returning upon
me) of the approches of Death", ment. wf Bethiah; 4 unnamed sons; son Jabez HOWLAND. Inv. taken
6 Feb. 1711/2. Agreement of heirs, 26 Nov. 1714, ment. wf Bethiah, sons Jabez HOWLAND (eldest
son), Josiah HOWLAND, Samuel HOWLAND, Joseph HOWLAND (youngest son), Nathan TOWNSEND (under 21),

only son of dec'd dau Elizabeth TOWNSEND.

Estate of **Jabez HOWLAND**[3-2]: <MD 21:150-1; Bristol Co.PR 8:115>
...Division, 18 Apr. 1734, ment. eldest son Jabez HOWLAND, son Thomas HOWLAND and daus Bethiah
DAVIS, Mercy MARTINDALL, Elisabeth LITTLE, Sarah LAWTON and Patience.

Will of **John HOWLAND Sr.**: <MD 2:70-7; Plymouth Col.Wills 3:1:49-54>
...29 May 1672, "being now Grown aged", ment. eldest son John HOWLAND; son Jabez HOWLAND; youngest son Isacke HOWLAND; wf Elizabeth; son Joseph HOWLAND; daus Desire GORUM, Hope CHIPMAN, Elizabeth DICKENSON, Lydia BROWNE, Hannah BOSWORTH, Ruth CUSHMAN; granddaughter Elizabeth HOWLAND dau
of son John. Inv. taken 3 Mar. 1672.

Will of **Elizabeth (TILLEY) Howland**: (widow) <MD 3:54-7; Bristol Co.PR 1:13-4>
...17 Dec. 1686, "being 79 yeares of Age", ment. eldest son John HOWLAND; sons Joseph HOWLAND,
Jabez HOWLAND, Isaack HOWLAND; dau Lidia BROWNE & son in law James BROWNE; daus Elisabeth DICKEN-
SON, Hannah BOSWORTH; granddaughter Elizabeth BURSLEY; grandson Nathaniel HOWLAND son of son Jos-
eph; grandsons James BROWNE, Jabez BROWNE; granddaughters Dorothy BROWNE, Desire CUSHMAN. Pr. 10
Jan. 1687/8.

Will of **John HOWLAND**[3] (**John**[2]): (yeoman) <MD 10:87-8; Barnstable Co.PR 5:326-8>
...8 Feb. 1737/8, ment. wf Mary; daus Mary HOWLAND & Joanna HOWLAND "goods that came by their own
mother"; sons George HOWLAND, John HOWLAND, Job HOWLAND; dau Hannah. Wit. sworn 23 Feb. 1737/8.

Will of **Capt. Joseph HOWLAND**[2]: <MD 6:86-91; Plymouth Co.PR 2:43-5>
...Jan. 1691/2, ment. wf Elizabeth; sons Thomas HOWLAND, James HOWLAND, Nathaniel HOWLAND; daus
Sarah, Lydia, Elizabeth, Marcy. (Note: Sarah's name was crossed out, probably at the time of the
codicil). Codicil, 23 Dec. 1703, ment. dau Mercy HOWLAND; Mary, the dau of dec'd dau Sarah HOW-
LAND (her legacy to be paid by son James HOWLAND); daus Lydia HOWLAND, Elizabeth HOWLAND, Mercy
HOWLAND. Pr. 10 Mar. 1703.

Estate of **Seth HOWLAND**[3] (**Isaac**[2]): <MD 21:179-84; Plymouth Co.PR 6:150>
...Settlement, 27 Mar. 1732, among the brothers & sisters of dec'd, viz: Nathan HOWLAND; chil. of
Susannah WOOD, dec'd wf of Ephraim; Jael SOUTHWORTH wf of Nathaniel; chil of Isaac HOWLAND dec'd;
Priscilla BENNETT wf of Capt. Peter; Hannah TINKHAM wf of John.

Will of **Shubael HOWLAND**[3] (**John**[2]): (yeoman) <MD 10:86-7; Barnstable Co.PR 5:370-1>
...14 June 1737, ment. wf Mercy; sons Zacheus HOWLAND, Jabez HOWLAND; grandson James HOWLAND; dau
Mercy JENKENS. Pr. 31 Aug. 1737.

Will of **Mercy (BLOSSOM) Howland**: (widow) <MD 10:87; Barnstable Co.PR 9:417>
...24 Nov. 1758, ment. son Jabez HOWLAND; dau Mercy JENKINS & her unnamed late husband; granddaughters Elisabeth WOOD, Mercy HOWLAND, Mary HOWLAND. Pr. 6 Mar. 1759.

Will of **Thomas HOWLAND**[3] (**Joseph**[2]): <MD 27:82-7; Plymouth Co.PR 8:135>
...1 Oct. 1739, ment. wf Joanna; son Consider HOWLAND; brother Nathaniel HOWLAND; sons Thomas
HOWLAND, Joseph HOWLAND; daus Experience LOTHROP wf of Benjamin, Elizabeth HOWLAND, Hannah DYRE
wf of William, Joanna HOWLAND; grandson Southworth HOWLAND (under 21). Pr. 29 Dec. 1739.

Estate of **John HUCKINS**: <MD 24:180-1; Plymouth Col.Wills 4:1:8-9>
...Settlement, 7 Mar. 1678/9, ment. wf Hope and minor chil., Elizabeth, Mary, Experience, Hope &
Mehittable.

Estate of **Thomas HUCKINS**: (yeoman) <MDP:327; Barnstable Co.PR 3:161>
...Settlement, 11 Dec. 1714, to foll. chil., viz: John HUCKINS, Thomas HUCKINS, Samuel HUCKINS,
Hope HAMBLEN wf of Benjamin, Hannah HUCKINS.

Will of **Joseph JENKINS**: <MDP:338; Barnstable Co.PR 5:233>
...25 Jan. 1733, ment. wf Lidia; daus Abigail HINCKLEY, Lidia CROCKER, Prudence BAKER, Hannah
JENKINS; sons Joseph JENKINS, Benjamin JENKINS. Pr. 8 Nov. 1734.

Will of **Hosea JOYCE**: (yeoman) <MDP:327; Barnstable Co.PR 3:346,349>
...24 Jan. 1711/2, ment. wf Elizabeth; sons John JOYCE, Samuel JOYCE, Thomas JOYCE, Hosea JOYCE;
daus Martha GODFREE, Dorcas HOWSE/HOWES, Mary GORHAM, Lydia HOWES, Mehitable & Dorothy. Inv.
taken 15 Feb. 1711/2.

Will of **Joseph KENT**: <MDP:342; Bristol Co.PR 8:217,224>
...12 Mar. 1734/5, ment. wf Mary, "the ten pounds due by contracte...(to be paid) fifty shillings
yearly"; son Joseph KENT; daus Lidia BOSWORTH, Dorethea NEWMAN, Susanna BOWEN, Mary KENT; sons
John KENT, Hezekiah KENT, James KENT. Inv. taken 7 Apr. 1735.

Will of **John SARGEANT**: <MD 24:9; Middlesex Co.PR 14:451>
...20 May 1708, ment. wf Lydia; sons Joseph SARGEANT, John SARGEANT, William SARGEANT, Samuell
SARGEANT; daus Hannah, Lydiea, Deborah, Hope, Ruth, Sarah, Mehittebell (states some daughters are
under 18 & unmarried); estate of brother Samuel SARGEANT; grandchildren Seth TOBE & Deborah IVERY
the chil. of dau Mary; estate of son Jabiz SARGEANT; sons Jonathan SARGEANT, Ebenezer SARGEANT.
Pr. "12 9th 1716" (Nov.). Widow agrees to probate 9 Nov. 1716.

Will of **Edward STURGIS Jr.**:   <MDP:320-21; Plymouth Co.Wills 4:1:26>
...Nuncupative will, 15 Nov. 1678, ment. unnamed wf., son Joseph STURGIS, dau Desire and unnamed
children. Inv. taken 24 May 1679. <Barnstable Co.PR 1:98; MD 23:61-4>...Division of land, 12
Apr. 1694, ment. sons Joseph STURGIS (eldest son), Samuel STURGIS, James STURGIS, Edward STURGIS.

===

Will of **Col. John THACHER**:   <MDP:319-20; MD 22:110-13; Barnstable Co.PR 3:295,298-9>
...25 Apr. 1713, ment. wf Lydia; sons Peter THACHER, John THACHER; male heirs of dec'd son Josiah
THACHER; minor sons Judah THACHER, Joseph THACHER, Benjamin THACHER & Thomas THACHER; daus Rebecca STURGIS, Bethiah PAINE; unnamed chil. of dec'd dau Elizabeth HATCH; daus Lydia FREEMAN, Mary
GORHAM; unnamed 4 youngest daus by his present wife; "to ye two drummers of Yarmouth if they beat
at my funeral 5s apeice...thou I had much rather be decently buried without any military ceri-
mony". Pr. 19 June 1713.

===

Will of **Jeremiah THOMAS**:   <MDP:337; MD 20:131; Plymouth Co.PR 7:267>
...29 Sept. 1735, ment. wf Mary; sons Nathaniel THOMAS (eldest son), Jeremiah THOMAS, Jedediah
THOMAS; daus Sary WOOD, Elizabeth THOMSON, Mary BLUSH, Lydia HACKETT, Thankfull COBB, Bethiah
CHIPMAN, Priscilla THOMAS; son Ebenezer THOMAS. Pr. 7 Feb. 1736. <Note: MDP:337 - add eldest
son Nathaniel to will.>

===

Will of **John TINKHAM**:   <MDP:131; Plymouth Co.PR #20870, 19:370>
...13 Feb. 1766, ment. wf Hannah; sons John TINKHAM, Abisha TINKHAM, Amos TINKHAM; daus Esther
VAUGHAN, Hannah WESTON, Susannah COBB, Mary WESTON, Zilpah MILLER; dec'd brother Seth HOWLAND.
Pr. 23 May 1766. <Note: Correction to MDP:131, John's will ment. dec'd brother Seth HOWLAND,
not TINKHAM as stated.>

===

Will of **Deacon Ephraim WOOD**:   <MDP:335; Plymouth Co.PR 9:269-70>
...20 May 1738, ment. wf Patience; sons Josiah WOOD, Samuel WOOD, Ephraim WOOD, Manassa WOOD (under 18); daus Rebecca BARTLETT, Barsheba WOOD (under 18); Ephraim Jr. and Rebecca must confirm
father's sale of estate of their uncle Seth HOWLAND. Pr. 12 July 1744.

NOTES:

RICHARD MORE

Richard MORE was baptized 13 Nov. 1614, Shipton, Shropshire, England, the son of Katherine MORE <MD 5:256,22:77>. Although Katherne was married to her cousin, Samuel MORE, at the time, apparently Jacob BLAKEWAY was Richard's father. (It is not certain if Samuel MORE fathered some or any of the children, viz: Richard, Jasper, Ellen, Mary.) Jacob BLAKEWAY was prob. bpt. 25 July 1583, Stanton Long Parish, the son of Edward BLAKEWAY <MD 44:11; see the excellent 3 part article in MD 43 & 44>. The Royal Descent of 500 Immgrants, p.350 gives Katherine More's ancestry back to Henry II (continuing back, his line also includes among others, William I (The Conqueror), Alfred the Great and Duncan I (King of Scots)). Richard's date of death has not been found. He was alive 19 Mar. 1693/4 when he witnessed a bond <MD 22:77> and called deceased in a deed dated 20 Apr. 1696 <MD 22:77,78,84-5>. His gravestone in the Charter St. cem., Salem states he died age 84. Around 1918 someone erroneously added 1692 as his year of death (this would give him a 1608 year of birth). A more accurate estimate can be found in the various records. In 1635 when he returned from England, his age is given as 20 (he could have turned 21 that year) <Drake:35> and in a deposition dated 27 Sept. 1684 he states he is 70 or thereabouts <MD 3:194-5; NEHGR 50:203>. However, as he grew older Richard became less than accu- rate regarding his age. In four separate depositions made between 1 Apr. - 25 Nov. 1690, he states he is about 78 - he seems to have added two years onto his actual age <MDP:347>. Perhaps this is why his gravestone states he died age 84 (being two years older than he actually was). If we use his age given in 1635 and 1684, a year of birth of c1614 can be assumed and if we agree that the age given him at death was two years off, then we can safely assume Richard died in 1696 age 82. Richard m.1st, 20 Oct. 1636, Plymouth, Christian HUNTER <TAG 40:77>. Christian was born c1614/5, England <Drake:40 (age 20 in 1635 passenger list)> and died 18 Mar. 1676, ae 60, Salem <MD 3:198>. Richard m.2nd, date unknown, Jane (   ) CRUMPTON who was born c1631 <MF5G 2:123 (ae 44 in 1675 when she adm. est. of 1st hus.)> and died 8 Oct. 1686, ae 55, Salem <MD 3:198>. (Jane m.1st, Samuel CRUMPTON who died 18 Sept. 1675, Deerfield <MF5G 2:123>. Bowman states she was the daughter of Richard HOLLINGSWORTH as Richard calls him father in law in a deed <MFP:347>, however his first wife, Christian, came to Plymouth in 1635 with the Hollingsworth family so the family connection could be through her, not Jane.) Richard and both wives (with son Caleb and two grandchildren) are all buried in the Charter St. cem., Salem <MD 3:197-9>.

Stratton:329 cites the records of the First Church in Salem, p.166 and states that for many years Capt. More was "under suspicion and a common fame of lasciviousness" and because of lack of proof was only spoken to by the Elders. In 1688 he was finally convicted of "gross unchastity" with a married woman. Stratton states this "tends to confirm" a parish record from St. Dunstan's, Stepney, Middlesex, England which states a Richard More of Salem, New England, mariner, married 23 Oct. 1645, Elizabeth WOOLNO. Could this be our Richard who was married to Christian at the time? In reviewing the births of his children, assuming they were born within a week of their baptisms, his fourth child would have been conceived in late July 1645, therefore it is conceivable that he could have made a voyage to England in time for an October wedding. Given his reputation with women, the time frame and the coincidence that he happened to be a mariner of Salem, it is entirely possible that he had another wife across the sea. (There was one other Richard Moore/Mower of Salem in 1661, called husbandman & innholder in deeds <MDP:346>, who died in 1689, prob. Lynn <MBD 2: 190,194>, but I have been unable to ascertain if he was in Salem in the 1640's.)

(See also: Mayflower Families For Five Generations: Richard More of the Mayflower (MF5G), vol. 2, by Robert S. Wakefield, F.A.S.G. and Lydia R.D. Finlay, C.A.L.S., repr. 1986; MD 3:193-201, The Only Mayflower Gravestone; MD 5:256, Parentage of Richard More; MD 22:49-51, Capt. Richard More of Salem MA Can Now Be Added To The List of Proved Mayflower Ancestors; MD 22:74-85, The Recent Desecration of The Only Mayflower Gravestone; NEHGR 114:163, The Origin of the Mayflower Children: Jasper, Richard & Ellen More; NEHGR 123:85, The Royal Descent of a Mayflower Passenger; TAG 40:77, Notes on the Hollingsworth, Hunter, More & Woodbury Families of Salem MA.)

Richard and Christian had 7 children: (Salem) <MBD 2:190; Essex Inst.Hist.Coll.6:238-43>

I.   Samuel, bpt. 6 1mth (Mar.) 1642, d. betw. 1650/1 <Bradford> - 5 May 1675 (fath.deed) <Essex Co.Deeds 4:114,300>.
II.   Thomas, bpt. 6 1mth (Mar.) 1642, d. betw. 1650/1 - 5 May 1675.
III. Caleb, bpt. 31 1mth (Mar.) 1644, d. 4 Jan. 1678/9, ae 34, Salem g.s., unm. <MD 3:199>.
IV.   Joshua, bpt. 3 3mth (May) 1646, d. betw. 1650/1 - 5 May 1675.
V.   Richard, bpt. 2 11mth (Jan.) 1647/8.
VI.   Susanna, bpt. 12 3mth (May) 1650.
VII. Christian, bpt. 5 7mth (Sept.) 1652.

          *   *   *   *   *   *   *   *   *   *   *   *

V. RICHARD MORE[2], bpt. 2 11mth (Jan.) 1647/8, Salem, d. aft. 1 May 1696 (ment. in deed) <MF5G 2: 126>; m. c1672, prob. Salem, **Sarah** (   ) <MD 22:50>, b. (   ), d. aft. 19 June 1691, Salem (ack. deed) <MD 22:83>. <Note: in MBD 2:191, footnote <10> assigned to Richard belongs to Samuel Dutch directly below.>

6 MORE Children: <MF5G 2:190; Salem 1st ChR>

1. **Samuel MORE**[3], b. 15 Nov. 1673, d. 24 Nov. 1673, ae 9 days, Charter St. cem., Salem <MD 3:199>

2. **child,** bpt. Dec. 1674, Salem.

3. **Thomas MORE**[3], bpt. 1 June 1679, Salem.

4. **Christian MORE**[3], bpt. Aug. 1681, Salem.

5. **Sarah MORE**[3], bpt. Jan. 1683/4, Salem.

6. **Caleb MORE**[3], bpt. 15 Apr. 1688, Salem.

VI. **SUSANNA MORE**[2], bpt. 12 3mth (May) 1650, Salem, d. aft. 30 Oct. 1728, poss Ipswich <MD 22:51 (receipted for portion of 3rd husband's est.)>; m.1st, c1675, prob. Salem, **Samuel DUTCH** <MD 3:200,22:50>, (son of Osmond DUTCH & Grace PRATT) <MDP:349>, b. c1645, d. pre 19 Mar. 1693/4 <MDP:348-9; Essex Co.PR #8420; MBD 2:191 (footnote <10> refers to Samuel, not Richard More); <MDP:349 (On 6 Jan. 1695/6 the widow incl. expenses for bringing up a child for two and a half years - the time since her husband's death? (i.e. July 1693)); who is the Samuel Dutch buried 27 Apr. 1691, St. Michael's Church, Bridgetown, Barbadoes? <NEHGR 67:370>.) **Susanna** m.2nd, betw. 19 Mar. 1693/4 (called Susanna Dutch) - 3 Dec. 1694 (called Susanna Hutton), **Richard HUTTON** <MDP:348 (est. of 1st hus.); MD 3:200,22:50>, b. c1617 (based on age at dth.) or c1621 <MDP:349; Essex Co.7:54 (based on 12 Dec. 1657 deposition in which he states he is 57)>, d. poss. 22 June 1713, 96th yr, Wenham <Wenham VR:205>. Richard is called blind in a deed dated 20 May 1707 <MDP:347>. (Richard m.1st, Elizabeth KILLAM <MF5G 2:126> & had 5 or 6 chil. <MBD 2:191; Wenham VR:47 (4), 205 (1), Beverly VR 1:189 (1)>). **Susanna** m.3rd, int. 11 Apr. 1714 Wenham, **John KNOWLTON Sr.** <MD 22:50 (yr only)>, (son of William KNOWLTON & Elizabeth BALCH), b. poss. Ipswich, d. 14 Aug. 1728, Ipswich <MDP:351 (dth. date given in probate records)>. (John m.1st, c1669, Bethiah EDWARDS & had 11 chil. <MF5G 2:127>, one of whom marr. Susanna's daughter below.) (See MORE Probate Appendix for will of John KNOWLTON Sr.)

4 DUTCH Children: <MF5G 2:127; MBD 2:191>

1. **Barbara DUTCH**[3], bpt. 2 Dec. 1677, Salem, d. 10 Apr. 1678, ae 8 mths, Charter St. cem., Salem <MD 3:197,199>.

2. **Susanna DUTCH**[3], bpt. 28 Sept. 1679, Salem, d. pre 1683.

3. **Susanna DUTCH**[3], bpt. 22 Sept. 1683, Salem, d. aft. 18 Aug. 1762 <MDP:350; Essex Co.Deeds 111: 182 (ack. deed)>; m. 26 Dec. 1705, Beverly, **Benjamin KNOWLTON** <Ipswich VR 2:262>, (son of John KNOWLTON & Bethiah EDWARDS - see above), b. c1674, Ipswich Hamlet (now Hamilton) <MF5G 2:128>, d. betw. 18 Aug. 1762 <MDP:350; Essex Co.Deeds 111:182 (ack. deed)> - 17 Dec. 1764 <MDP:350; Essex Co.PR #16055 (pr.)>. <See MBD 2:191,194; MF5G 2:128; MD 22:51 for 3 chil.> (See MORE Probate Appendix for will of Benjamin KNOWLTON Sr.)

4. **Christian DUTCH**[3], bpt. June 1689, Salem, d.y.?

VII **CHRISTIAN MORE**[2], bpt. 5 7mth (Sept.) 1652, Salem, d. 30 May 1680, ae 28, Salem, Charter St. cem. <MD 3:200>; m. 31 Aug. 1676, Salem, **Joshua CONANT** <Salem VR; MD 3:200>, (son of Joshua CONANT & Seeth GARDNER), b. 15 4mth (June) 1657 <MF5G 2:127>, d. betw. 11 July 1702 (defendant at Salem court) - 7 June 1705, Salem (widow Sarah's petition for dec'd husband's unpaid service) <MF5G 2:127>. (Joshua m.2nd, 9 Jan. 1690/1, Sarah NEWCOMB & had 4 chil. <MD 3:200>.)

1 CONANT Child:

1. **Joshua CONANT**[3], b. 12 May 1678, Salem <MD 3:200; Essex Inst.Hist.Coll.2:42>.

MORE PROBATE APPENDIX

Will of **Benjamin KNOWLTON Sr.**: (yeoman) <MDP:350; Essex Co.PR #16055, 342:7>
...5 Aug. 1759, ment. wf Susanna; daus Susanna DODGE, Elizabeth BROWN; son Benjamin KNOWLTON. Pr. 17 Dec. 1764.

==

Will of **John KNOWLTON Sr.**: (housewright) <MDP:351; Essex Co.PR #16078, 316:349,318:16>
...29 Feb. 1713/4, ment. eldest son John KNOWLTON; sons Rice KNOWLTON, Benjamin KNOWLTON (& his wf), Thomas KNOWLTON (& his wf), Timothy KNOWLTON; daus Abigail GIDDINGS, Miriam KNOWLTON, Hannah POTTER wf of Nathaniel, Bethiah WOODEN, Susanna CORNING, Elizabeth CORNING and heirs of dec'd dau Mary PATCH. Pr. 24 Aug. 1728. (Wf is not ment., but she receipted 10 & 30 Oct. 1728.)

WILLIAM MULLINS

William MULLINS came from Dorking, co. Surrey, England and was born c1572, the son of John MULLY-NS & Joane BRIDGER <MD 44:42>; he died 21 Feb. 1620/1, Plymouth <MD 30:3,44:43>. His wife was Alice (   ), her origins remain unknown <MD 44:44>. She died after 21 Feb. 1620/1, the date her husband's will is thought to have been written, and probably after 2 Apr. 1620/1 when Bowman states the will was copied to return to England on the Mayflower with nothing added to indicate any named in the will were deceased <MD 1:230-2,44:43>. Alice and son Joseph were deceased pre Nov. 1621 when the ship Fortune arrived <Stratton:331>. <See MD 44:39-45, The Mullins Family.> (See MULLINS Probate Appendix for will of William MULLINS.)

William had 4 known children: <MD 44:43>

I.   William, b. (   ), prob. Dorking, co. Surrey, England.
II.   Sarah, b. (   ), England, d. (   ); called Sarah BLUNDEN in father's probate.
III. Priscilla, b. c1602, England. See ALDEN Family.
IV.   Joseph, b. (   ), England, d. betw. Apr.-Nov. 1621, Plymouth.

* * * * * * * * * * * * * * *

I. **WILLIAM MULLINS**[2], b. (   ), d. 12 Feb. 1672/3, Braintree <Braintree VR 1:25; MD 7:180>; m. c1617, England (   ). Bowman <MD 7:181> questions if he remarried 7 May 1656, Boston, Ann BELL who prob. d. 4 Dec. 1661, Boston and married 1st Thomas BELL who d. 7 June 1655, Boston.

   3 MULLINS Children: <MD 44:44>

1. **Elizabeth MULLINS**[3], bpt. 26 Mar. 1618, Dorking, co. Surrey, England.

2. **Ruth MULLINS**[3], bpt. 31 Oct. 1619, Dorking, co. Surrey, England.

3. **Sarah MULLINS**[3], bpt. 5 May 1622, Dorking, England <MD 7:182 (age 73 in 1694 will); d. betw. 13 Aug. 1694 (will) - 25 Nov. 1697 (pr.), Braintree <MD 7:181-2>; m.1st, (   ), **Thomas GANNATT/GANNETT** of Duxbury <MD 7:37>, b. (   ), d. betw. 19 June - 10 July 1655, Bridge-water <MD 7:38-39,180 (will & inv.)>. **Sarah** m.2nd, 9 Aug. 1655, Braintree, **William SAVILL** <Braintree VR 1:125; MD 7:180>, b. (   ), d. 6 Apr. 1669, Braintree <Braintree VR 1:25; MD 7:43,180>. **Sarah** m.3rd, 5 Sept. 1670, Braintree, **Thomas FAXON** <Braintree VR 1:126>, b.   , d. 23 Nov. 1680, Braintree <MD 7:180>. No known issue (although Faxon & Savil had issue so were married previously). (See MULLINS Probate Appendix for wills of Sarah FAXON, Thomas GANNNAT/GANNETT & William SAVILL/SAVEL Sr. and estate of Thomas FAXON.)

MULLINS PROBATE APPENDIX

Estate of Thomas FAXON: <MD 7:45-8; Suffolk Co.PR 9:19>
...23 Dec. 1680, adm. granted to widow Sarah and only dau. Joannah FISHER, widow, until his grandson Thomas FAXTON/FAXON comes of age. On 19 Dec. 1683, Sarah petitioned the court that the grandson Thomas FAXEN/FAXON, son of Richard FAXEN/FAXON was now of full age.

Will of Sarah (MULLINS[3]**) Faxon**: <MD 7:182-3; Suffolk Co.PR>
...13 Aug. 1694, "aged seaventy three years", ment. cousin Ruth WEBB wf of Peter; daughter in law Lidia SAVELL wf of Benjamin and her dau Sarah SAVELL; son in law Benjamin SAVELL executor. <11: 372> Pr. 25 Nov. 1697.

Will of Thomas GANNATT/GANNET: <MD 7:38-9; MSR:520; Plymouth Co.Wills 2:1:12,13>
...19 June 1655, ment. unnamed wife and brother Mathew GANNATT. Inv. taken 10 July 1655.
===
Will of William MULLINS: <MD 1:230-2,44:39; NEHGR 42:62>
...nuncupative, 21 Feb. 1620/1, ment. wf Alice; son Joseph MULLINS; dau Priscilla; unnamed eldest son; unnamed eldest dau.; son William MULLINS if he comes to "Virginia". 23 July 1621, adm. granted to dau Sarah BLUNDEN.
===
Estate of William MULLINS[2]: <MD 7:37-8; Suffolk Co.PR 8:356-7>
...28 Mar. 1674, adm. granted to Thomas FAXTON "in the Right of his wife the sd Mullins beeing his wifes Father".
===
Will of William SAVEL/SAVILL Sr.: <MD 7:41-43; Suffolk Co.PR 7:36>
...19 Feb. 1668, ment. wf Sarah; sons John SAVEL, Samuel SAVEL, Benjamin SAVEL, William SAVEL (under 21); daus Hannah SAVELL, Sarah SAVELL (under 21); bro. Samuel BASS. Wit.sworn 29 July 1669

DEGORY PRIEST

Degory PRIEST was born c1579, England. <Dexter:630 (age 40 in Apr. 1619 deposition); "of London" in Leyden marriage record>. He is possibly the Digorius, son of Peter Prust, bpt. 11 Aug. 1582, Hartland, Devonshire, England <NEHGR 111:320>. He died 1 Jan. 1620/1, Plymouth <MD 1:87 (N.S.), 4:136>. Degory married 4 Nov. 1611, Leyden, Holland, Sarah (ALLERTON) Vincent <MD 2:118 (N.S.), 7:129-30,22:15-6 (she is also called "of London")>. Sarah was the sister of Mayflower passenger Isaac ALLERTON, her birth date and parentage are unknown. (NEHGR 44:290 suggests the parents of Isaac and Sarah may be Edward ALLERTON & Rose DAVIS who were married 14 Feb. 1579/80, St. Dionis, Backchurch, London, England.) Sarah died pre 24 Oct. 1633, Plymouth <MD 1:154-7; MD 4:136 (inv)> She m.1st, John VINCENT; 3rd, 13 Nov. 1621, Leyden, Holland, Cuthbert CUTHBERTSON/Godbert GODBERTSON <MD 4:136> who died pre 24 Oct. 1633 <MD 1:154-7; MD 4:136 (inv.)>, they had one son.

See: Mayflower Families Through Five Generations (MF5G), Degory Priest, vol. 8, by Mrs. Charles D. Townsend, Robert S. Wakefield, F.A.S.G. & Margaret H. Stover, ed. by Robert S. Wakefield, 1994

Degory and Sarah had two children:

I.   Mary, b. c1613, Leyden, Holland.
II. Sarah, b. c1615, Leyden, Holland.

* * * * * * * * * * * * * *

I.   **MARY PRIEST**[2], b. c1613, Leyden, d. betw. 7 Mar. 1686/7 <MD 4:137, Charlestown Town Orders 4: 56 (town provided for her support)> - 22 July 1689 <MD 4:136 (order to appraise est.)>; m. betw. 22 May 1627 (cattle division) - 24 Oct. 1633 <MD 4:136 (her mother's inv.)>, **Phineas PRATT**, b. c1593, prob. England <MD 2:46 (ae 81 or thereabouts in deposition 30 June 1674), 4: 91 (ae about 30 in 1622), 136>, d. 19 Apr. 1680, Charlestown, Old Phipps St. cem. <MD 2:46,4: 136,6:1 (although his g.s. says he d. ae 90, credence must be given to the age he gives when alive, not the age given him at his death)>. (See PRIEST Probate Appendix for will of Phineas PRATT.)

8 PRATT Children: <MBD 2:195>

1. **John PRATT**[3], b. c1631, Plymouth, d. betw. 14 Mar. 1697/8 <MD 3:3-6 (deed)> - 5 Feb. 1713/14, prob. Oyster Bay, Long Island NY <MD 3:2, Oyster Bay TR D:169 (sons' deed)>; m. c1663/4, **Ann BARKER** <MD 4:138,17:109>, (dau of John BARKER & Ann WILLIAMS) <MD 4:138>, b. c1643, Marshfield, d. aft. 27 Apr. 1695 <MD 3:5,6 (deed)>. <See MBD 2:196; MD 3:6; VR RI 7:70 for bth. of 8 chil.>

2. **Mary PRATT**[3], b. c1632, Plymouth, d. 11 Feb. 1702, 70th yr, Cambridge, Harvard Sq. cem. <Cambridge Epitaphs:32>; m. 1 Mar. 1655/6, Cambridge, **John SWAN** <Cambridge VR 2:314,380>, b. c1620 England, d. 5 June 1708, 88th yr, Cambridge, Harvard Sq. cem. <Cambridge Epitaphs:32>. (John m.1st, 1 Jan. 1650/1, Cambridge, Rebecca PALFREY and had 2 chil. <MF5G 8:7>.) <See MBD 2:197 & Cambridge VR 1:685 (3), 686 (5) for bth. 8 chil.>

3. **Samuel PRATT**[3], b. c1636, Plymouth, d. 26 Mar. 1676, Rehoboth, "Pawtucket Fight" <MBD 2:195; MFIP #6 cites a letter from his widow Mary Pratt, probably written around 1690, in which she asks that her son Samuel Pratt not be "pressed a souldier" because "my first husband, was slain by the heathen in Captain Pierce's fight...and I shall take it very unkindly, Iff he that is the only son of his father that was slain in the former warr should be compelled to go out againe">; m. betw. 19 Dec. 1667 <MD 17:109 (she is single in will of grandf. John WILLIAMS)> - 2 Nov. 1668 <MD 17:111; TAG 4:31 (receipt for father's est.)>, poss. Scituate, **Mary BARKER**, (dau of John BARKER & Anna WILLIAMS) <MD 3:128; Gen.Adv.4:31-2>, b. c1647, Marshfield, d. aft. 15 May 1711 <MDP:356; Plymouth Co.Deeds 9:101 (div. of 2nd hus. est.)>. (Mary m.2nd, c1678, Francis COOMBS[3] (Sarah Priest[2] - see within); m.3rd, 5 Mar. 1684/5, Middleboro, David WOOD <MD 1:219; Middleboro VR 1:1>; see MD 1:224 for 3 WOOD chil.) <See MBD 2:199 for 2 chil (note: MBD 2:199, reference to Mary Barker should read "see p.200" not p.201)>

4. **Daniel PRATT**[3], b. c1640, Plymouth, d. betw. 23 June 1680 <Providence Early Rec.6:24 (inv. of Stephen Harding Jr.)> - 2 June 1690, Providence RI <Providence RI Deeds 2:245 (wife's deed)>; m. (   ), **Anna/Anne** (   ), b. (   ), d . aft. 12 Feb. 1718/9 <Providence RI Deeds 4:19-20>. (Anna m.2nd, int. 27 Jan. 1690/1, Providence RI, William TURPIN <Providence Early Rec. 8:176> who m.1st, Elizabeth HOARE <Torrey:760>.) <MF5G 8:9 (only one known child, Rachel).>

5. **Mercy PRATT**[3], b. c1642, Plymouth, d. betw. 14 Dec. 1691 <Middlesex Co.Deeds 10:424> - 14 Mar. 1694/5 <Middlesex Co.Deeds 17:649>; m. c1662, **Jeremiah HOLMAN** <MM:238>, (son of William & Winifred), b. c1629, England <MF5G 8:8>, d. 30 Nov. 1709, Cambridge <Cambridge VR 2:605>. (Jeremiah m. 2nd, pre 6 May 1703, Susanna (   ) <Middlesex Co.Deeds 23:265-6> who d. 4 Dec. 1709 <MF5G 8:9>.) <See MF5G 8:10 for 5 or 6 chil. & Cambridge VR 1:364 (2), 2:605 (1).>

6. **Joseph PRATT**[3], b. c1645, Plymouth, d. 24 Dec. 1712, Charlestown <Charlestown VR:230>; m. 12
    Feb. 1674/5, Charlestown, **Dorcas FOLGER** <Charlestown VR:89>, (dau of Peter FOLGER & Mary MOR-
    RILL), b. (   ), d. aft. 8 July 1728 <Charlestown TR 7:106 (town provided for her)>. (See
    PRIEST Probate Appendix for will of Joseph PRATT.) <For bth. 9 chil., see Charlestown VR:
    106,109,115,121,122,132,143; Nantucket VR 2:394; Charlestown 1st ChR:256 (bpt.); MBD 2:197
    (gives a 10th ch. Rachel but points out the date does not fit.)>

7. **Peter PRATT**[3], b. c1647, prob. Charlestown, d. 24 Mar. 1688, Lyme CT <Lyme CT VR:255>; m. 5
    Aug. 1679, Lyme CT, **Elizabeth (GRISWOLD) Rogers** <Lyme CT VR:255>, (dau of Matthew GRISWOLD &
    Anna WOLCOTT), b. (   ), d. ?pre 1700 <MF5G 8:11; MFIP #10 said July 1727>. <See MBD 2:199
    for one ch.> (Elizabeth m.1st 17 Oct. 1670, New London CT, John ROGERS <VR 1:7> whom she
    divorced 12 Oct. 1676 <MF5G 8:11>; she m.3rd, betw. 1689-1691, prob. Lyme CT, Matthew BECK-
    WITH & had 1 ch. <MF5G 8:11>.)

8. **Aaron PRATT**[3], b. c1649, Charlestown, d. 23 Feb. 1735/6, ae 87, Hingham, Cohasset g.s. <Hing-
    ham VR 1:277>; m.1st, c1684, Woburn, **Sarah PRATT** <MM:237>, (dau of Joseph PRATT & Sarah JUD-
    KINS), b. 31 May 1664, Weymouth <Weymouth VR 1:239>, d. 22 July 1706, ae 42, Hingham <Lincoln
    3:116>. **Aaron** m.2nd, 4 Sept. 1707, Charlestown, **Sarah (WRIGHT) Cummings** <Charlestown VR; MM:
    237; MF5G 8:12 says Reading VR:423>, (dau of Joseph/Josiah WRIGHT & Elizabeth HASSELL), b. 25
    Feb. 1670, Woburn <Woburn VR:283>, d. 13 Dec. 1752, Hingham <Hingham VR 2:68>. (Sarah m.1st,
    28 Feb. 1687, Woburn, Abraham CUMMINGS <Woburn VR:66>.) (See PRIEST Probate Appendix for
    will of Aaron PRATT.) <For 11 chil. by 1st wf see MBD 2:195 & Hingham VR 1:97; for 4 chil.
    by 2nd wf see MBD 2:195 & Hingham VR 1:144 (1), 148 (1), 155 (1).>

II. **SARAH PRIEST**[2], b. c1615, Leyden, Holland, d. aft. 1 Aug. 1648, poss. England <PCR 2:131-3,12:
    137 (15 Oct. 1646, William SPOONER mentions a child Mrs. Coombs left with him when she went
    to England; 1 Aug. 1648 he was ordered to keep the children of Mrs. Combe and not dispose of
    them)>; m. c1631?, Plymouth, **John COOMBS**, b. pre 1612 <PCR 1:3 (if at least 21 when a free-
    man)>, d. prob. pre 15 Oct. 1646. <MBD 2:204 #29, should read "John Coombs was alive 5 June
    1644 <PCR 2:71>...">.

    2 COOMBS Children: <MF5G 8:5; MBD 2:200>

1. **John COOMBS**[3], b. c1632?, Plymouth, d. pre 29 May 1668, Boston <Suffolk Co.PR 5:91 (adm.)>; m.
    24 Feb. 1661/2, Boston, **Elizabeth (Royall?) BARLOW** <Boston Rcd.Com.9:82>, b. (   ), d. Jan.
    1671/2, Boston <MF5G 8:13>. (Elizabeth m.1st, c1656, Boston, Thomas BARLOW who d. 23 Oct.
    1661 <Boston Rcd.Com.9:81> & had 2 chil. <Boston Rcd.Com.9:60,69>; m.3rd, c1669, Boston, John
    WARREN & had 1 son <MF5G 8:13>.) <See MBD 2:200 & Boston Rcd.Com.9:83,92,100 for bth. 3 chil>

2. **Francis COOMBS**[3], b. c1635?, Plymouth, d. 31 Dec. 1682, Middleboro <MD 1:222; Wood:45>; m.1st,
    c1672, prob. Plymouth, **Deborah MORTON** <MM:238>, (dau of John & Lettice), b. poss. c1652, Ply-
    mouth, d. betw. 3 Jan. 1674/5 (bth.last ch.) - c1678 (hus.2nd marr.). **Francis** m.2nd, c1678,
    Mary (BARKER) Pratt <MD 3:138; TAG 4:31>, she m.1st Samuel PRATT, see p.85. (See PRIEST Pro-
    bate Appendix for estate of Francis COOMBS.) <For 2 chil. by 1st wf see MBD 2:200 & MD 1:
    221; for 3 chil. by 2nd wf see MBD 2:200 & MD 1:221 (2), 224 (1).>

PRIEST PROBATE APPENDIX

Estate of Francis COOMBS/COMBS: <MDP:356; Plymouth Co.Deeds 9:101,11:164>
...Division, 15 May 1711, ment. following heirs, viz: widow Mary WOOD; Ralph JONES & wf Deborah;
Frances COMBS; Samuel BARROWS & wf Mercy; John MILLER & wf Lydia; Ebenezer BENNETT & wf Ruth.
Additional division, 2 Feb. 1712, ment. Samuel BARROWS & wf Mercy; John MILLER Jr. & wf Lydia;
Ebenezer BENNETT & wf Ruth; Nathan HOWLAND & wf Frances.
==
Will of Aaron PRATT[3] **(Mary Priest**[2]**):** (yeoman) <MDP:352; Suffolk Co.PR #6701, 32:383>
...1 June 1730, ment. wf Sarah; dec'd dau Sarah WEBB; daus Elizabeth PRATT, Mercy ORCUT, Hannah
PRATT, Abigail PRATT; sons Benjamin PRATT, Henry PRATT (eldest), Daniel PRATT, Aaron PRATT, Jona-
than PRATT, John PRATT, Moses PRATT, Phenies/Phineas PRATT, Nathaniel PRATT. Pr. 9 Mar. 1735.
==
Will of Joseph PRATT[3] **(Mary Priest**[2]**):** <MDP:353; Middlesex Co.PR #17902, 13:197>
...23 July 1712, ment. wf Dorcas; son Joshua PRATT; daus Mary, Bethiah, Sarah; chil. of son Joseph PRATT. Inv. taken 17 Jan. 1712/3.
==
Will of Phineas PRATT: (joyner) <MD 4:139; Middlesex Co.PR #17922>
...8 Jan. 1677, "very aged", ment. wf Mary; son Joseph PRATT; unnamed children. Inv. 21 3mth
(May) 1680. (On 31 July 1738 the distribution of real estate mentions the following chil., viz:
John PRATT, Peter PRATT, Samuel PRATT, Daniel PRATT, Mary, Mercy, Aaron PRATT, Joseph PRATT. Al-
though only John & Peter are called dec'd they were all dec'd. Sureties: Samuel PRATT, William
SWAN, William THOMAS, James PERRY.)

THOMAS ROGERS

Thomas ROGERS was probably born in England, his date & place of birth and parentage are unknown. He died the first winter in Plymouth, sometime after the signing of the Mayflower Compact on 11 Nov. 1620. His wife was Elsgen/Elizabeth who was living in Leiden, Holland in 1622, a widow with children John, Lysbeth/Elizabeth and Grietgen/Margaret. Bradford states that "the rest of Thomas Rogers' <children> came over and are married and have many children". Son Joseph came with his father and it is known from the records that son John came to Plymouth c1630. Although proof has not yet been found in the records, Bradford's statement implies that his daughters came over as well. He states the children who came over had <u>many</u> children; son Joseph had only four children which would not be considered "many" in those days. Therefore it is very likely that some day researchers will "find" daughters Elizabeth and Margaret which will result in new Mayflower lines being opened up.
(See: Mayflower Families Through Five Generations, Thomas Rogers of the Mayflower (MF5G), Vol.2, by Alice W.A. Westgate, 1978.)

Thomas & Elizabeth had four known children:

I.   Joseph, b. c1610 (or earlier), England or Holland
II. John, b. c1614, England or Holland
III. Lysbeth/Elizabeth, b. (   ), living 1622, Leiden, Holland
IV. Grietgen/Margaret, b. (   ), living 1622, Leiden, Holland

* * * * * * * * * * * * * * *

I.   **JOSEPH ROGERS**[2], b. c1610, d. betw. 2-15 Jan. 1677/8, Eastham <MD 3:67-9 (will & inv.)>; m. c1632, (   ), **Hannah** (   ), b. (   ), d. aft. 2 Jan. 1677/8 <MD 3:67-9 (hus.will)>. <Note: in MBD 2:214, footnote <60> refers to Jonathan Higgins below, not Joseph Rogers.> (See ROGERS Probate Appendix for will of Lt. Joseph ROGERS.)

   8 ROGERS Children: <PCR 8:14 (rec. Sandwich); MD 16:238; MBD 2:214>

1. **Sarah ROGERS**[3], b. 6 Aug. 1633 (prob. Duxbury), d. 15 Aug. 1633 <MD 16:238; PCR 8:14>.

2. **Joseph ROGERS**[3], b. 19 July 1635 (prob. Duxbury) <MD 16:138>, d. 27 Dec. 1660, Eastham <MD 6:202; MF5G 2:158 (court records of 5 Mar. 1660/1 state John Hawes was found not guilty of "takeing away the life of Josephth Rogers of Eastham by giveing him a most deadly fall, on the 25 of Dec. 1660...whereof he...about 48 hours after died")>; m. 4 Apr. 1660, Eastham, **Susannah DEANE** <MD 15:34,6:13-4>, (dau of Stephen DEANE & Elizabeth RING), b. c1634, Plymouth <MD 15:34>, d. pre 9 Apr. 1701, prob. Eastham <MD 6:13-4 (2nd hus. remarried)>. <Susannah m. 2nd, 28 Oct. 1663, Eastham, Stephen SNOW[3] <MD 6:13-4> - see HOPKINS family.> No known issue.

3. **Thomas ROGERS**[3], b. 29 Mar. 1638 (prob. Duxbury) <MD 16:238>, d. betw. 5 Mar. 1677/8 <MD 3:67 (fath.inv.)> - 7 Aug. 1678, prob. Eastham <MD 11:179 (his inv.)>; m. 13 Dec. 1665, Eastham, **Elizabeth SNOW**[3] <MD 6:14> - see HOPKINS family. <See MBD 2:234 and MD 6:14 for bth. 7 chil.> (See ROGERS Probate Appendix for estate of Thomas ROGERS.)

4. **Elizabeth ROGERS**[3], b. 29 Sept. 1639 (prob. Duxbury) <MD 16:238>, d. betw. 2 Jan. 1677/8 <MD 3:67-9 (fath.will)> - 4 July 1679, Eastham <PCR 6:20; MBD 2:241 #70 (on 4 July 1679, Jonathan Higgins was fined for his relationship with his deceased wife's sister whom he soon after married)>; m. 9 Jan. 1660, Eastham, **Jonathan HIGGINS** <MD 6:15,7:16>, (son of Richard HIGGINS & Lydia CHANDLER), b. July 1637, Plymouth <PCR 8:27; MD 5:23,17:200>, d. poss. pre 28 May 1711 <MDP:372 (on this date Joseph Higgins Sr. sold to Jonathan Higgins Jr. & Elisha Higgins land given to "our" dec'd mother Elizabeth Higgins by "our" dec'd grandfather Lt. Joseph Rogers); MF5G 2:161 says Jonathan d. aft. 21 May 1711 but refers only to this deed dated 28 May which does not mention him but his son Jonathan>. (Jonathan m.2nd, Hannah ROGERS[3].) <See MBD 2:214 for bth. 6 chil. and MD 6:15 (3).>

5. **John ROGERS**[3], b. 3 Apr. 1642 (prob. Duxbury) <MD 16:238>, d. betw. 27 Apr. 1713 - 10 Aug. 1714, of Eastham <MD 11:180 (will & inv.)>; m. 19 Aug. 1669, Eastham, **Elizabeth TWINING** <MD 8:90>, (dau of William TWINING & Elizabeth DEAN), b. (   ), d. 10 Mar. 1724/5, Eastham <MD 8:91>. <See MBD 2:219 for bth. 9 chil.; MD 8:90 (6), 91 (3).> (See ROGERS Probate Appendix for will of John ROGERS Sr.)

6. **Mary ROGERS**[3], b. 22 Sept. 1644 (prob. Duxbury) <MD 16:238>, d. aft. 19 Apr. 1718, Barnstable <MD 20:143 (hus.will)>; m. 10 Aug. 1664, Barnstable, **John PHINNEY** <VR 11:130; MD 11:130, 20:142 (says 16th)>, (son of John FINNEY & Christian PATTEN), b. 24 Dec. 1638, Plymouth <MD 11:130; NEHGR 148:325; Barnstable VR 11:130; Otis 2:225>, d. betw 19 Apr. 1718 - 9 Mar. 1718/19, Barnstable <MD 20:143 (will & inv.)>. <See MBD 2:225 for bth. of 12 chil. & MD 11:130 (2), 11:131 (10).> (See ROGERS Probate Appendix for will of John PHINNEY.) <See NEHGR 148:315-27, The Finney Family of Lenton, Nottinghamshire And Plymouth, Mass.>

7. **James ROGERS[3]**, b. 18 Oct. 1648, Eastham <MD 16:238>, d. 13 Apr. 1678, Eastham <MD 6:203>; m. 11 Jan. 1670, Eastham, **Mary PAINE[4]** <MD 5:195; PCR 8:58>, (dau of Thomas PAINE & Mary SNOW[3] - see HOPKINS family), b. c1650, prob. Eastham, d. betw. 12 May 1705 <MD 15:189-90 (fath.will)> - 20 Jan. 1723/4 <MDP:292 (2nd hus.will)>. <See MBD 2:217 for bth. 3 chil.; MD 5:195 (1), 196 (2).> (Mary m.2nd, 24 Apr. 1679, Eastham, Israel COLE <MD 5:195>, (son of Daniel & Ruth) b. 8 June 1653, Eastham <MD 5:23>, d. betw. 20 Jan. 1723/4 - 23 July 1724 <MDP:292 (will & pr.)>, and had 2 chil. <MBD 2:217; MD 5:195>.) (See ROGERS Probate Appendix for will of Isreal COLE.)

8. **Hannah ROGERS[3]**, b. 8 Aug. 1652, prob. Eastham <MD 16:238>, d. aft. 18 Oct. 1690 <MD 6:15 (bth of last ch.)>; m. prob. cJuly 1679, Eastham, **Jonathan HIGGINS** <PCR 6:20; MBD 2:241 #70 (4 July 1679, Jonathan was fined for his relationship with Hannah who was his dec'd wife's sister; their first child was b. Feb. 1680/1)>; see under Elizabeth ROGERS[3]. <See MBD 2:216 and MD 6:15 for bth. 5 chil.>

II. **JOHN ROGERS[2]**, b. c1614, England or Holland, d. betw. 26 Aug. 1691 - 20 Sept. 1692, of Duxbury <MD 5:205-6 (will & wit.sworn)>; m. 16 Apr. 1639, Plymouth, **Anna CHURCHMAN** <Plymouth Col. Court Orders 1:198; MD 13:85>, b. (   ), d. aft. May 1664 <MF5G 2:159 (deed; aft. 23 Aug. 1670 if she is the unnamed wife who ack. a deed with John)>. The order of the following children is based on the ages given to John & Abigail at their death (b. c1640 & c1641) which, if correct, means they were the eldest.(See ROGERS Probate Appendix for will of John ROGERS Sr.)

4 ROGERS Children: <MBD 2:206>

1. **John ROGERS[3]**, b. c1640, prob. Duxbury, d. 28 June 1732, 92nd yr, Barrington MA (now RI) <MD 20:2>; m.1st, Nov. 1666, Duxbury, **Elizabeth PABODIE[3]** <MD 8:232>, (dau of William PABODIE & Elizabeth ALDEN[2] - see ALDEN family). John m.2nd, 21 Oct. 1679, (   ), **Hannah (HOBART) Browne** <MD 19:187,192,20:1>, (dau of Rev. Peter), b. 15 May 1638, Hingham <Lincoln 3:335>, d. 11 Sept. 1691, Bristol MA (now RI) <MD 20:1 (d. 1691)>. (Hannah m.1st, John BROWNE[2-1] of Salem <MD 19:187> who d. pre 10 Aug. 1677 <MD 19:188 (inv.)>.) John m.3rd, betw. 22 Mar. 1692/3 <MD 20:3 (pre-nuptial agreement)> - 16 Apr. 1696 <MDP:371 (deed)>, **Marah (COBHAM) Browning/Bruning** <MD 19:192>, (dau of Josiah COBHAM & Mary HAFFIELD), b. 21 May 1652, Salisbury <MF5G 2:164>, d. betw. 25 Sept. 1733 <MD 20:10 (her statement that she was innocent of embezzeling money from her husband's est.)> - 8 Dec. 1739 <MD 20:2 (petition to adm. her est.)>. (Marah m.1st, Joseph BROWNING/BRUNING of Boston <MD 20:1>.) <See MBD 2:213 for 5 chil. by 1st wf; MD 9:172 (2), 173 (3).> (See ROGERS Probate Appendix for estate of John ROGERS & wf Marah and will of wf Hannah.)

2. **Abigail ROGERS[3]**, b. c1641, prob. Duxbury, d. 1 Aug. 1727, ae 86, Taunton, Summer St. cem. <MD 20:192>; m. c1662, (   ), **John RICHMOND** <MD 20:192>, (son of John), b. c1629 <MDP:361 (ae about 67 in deposition 6 Jan. 1696/7); the age given him at death makes him 2 yrs. older than the age he gives himself>, d. 7 Oct. 1715, ae 88, Taunton, Summer St. cem. <MD 20:192>. (John m.1st, c1653, Bridgewater, Susanna HAYWARD & had 4 chil. <MBD 2:206; MSR:636; MD 9:58.> <See MBD 2:206, MD 9:58 & MSR:636 for bth. 7 chil.; MD 20:52 (1), 21:57 (1), 22:94 (1).>

3. **Anna ROGERS[3]**, b. (   ), d. betw. 24 July 1710 <MDP:362 (deed), aft. 11 Sept. 1710 if she ack.> - 29 June 1737 <MDP:362 (div. of dower)>; m.1st, 23 Nov. 1664, Taunton, **John TISDALE Jr** <MD 19:108,21:29>, (son of John TISDALE & Sarah WALKER), b. (   ), prob. Duxbury, d. "about the last of" Dec. 1677, Taunton <MD 21:29,35 (dth. given in inv.)>. Anna m.2nd, aft. 5 Mar. 1677/8 <MD 21:34 (adm.1st hus. est.), **Thomas TERRY** <MD 21:29>, b. c1631 (ae 60 or thereabouts in 1691 will), d. betw. 10 Aug. 1691 (will) - 30 Oct. 1691, of Freetown (refused probate as he didn't sign will) <MDP:362>. Anna m.3rd, (   ), **Samuel WILLIAMS** <MM:241>, (son of Richard WILLIAMS & Frances DIGHTON), b. c1637/8, Taunton, d. betw. 6-31 Aug. 1697 <MDP:362 (will & pr.)>. (Samuel m.1st, Mary GILBERT <MF5G 2:166>, (?dau of Thomas GILBERT & Jane ROSSITER) and had 6 chil.) <4 Tisdale chil., see MBD 2:208 & MD 21:29; MD 19:108 (2), 20:52 (1), 21:61 (1); 3 Terry chil., see MBD 2:208.> (See ROGERS Probate Appendix for estate of Anna WILLIAMS and wills of Thomas TERRY & Samuel WILLIAMS.)

4. **Elizabeth ROGERS[3]**, b. (   ), d. aft. 5 Oct. 1709 <MDP:362 (agreement)>; MBD 2:239 #1a (Bowman) gives dth. date of 11 May 1724 with no source>; m. 17 Nov. 1668, Taunton, **Nathaniel WILLIAMS** <MF5G 2:167; MD 22:60>, (son of Richard WILLIAMS & Frances DIGHTON), b. 17 Nov. 1639, Taunton <MF5G 2:167; MBD 2:211 (Bowman) says 7 July 1641 - another Nathaniel?>, d. 16 Aug. 1692, Taunton <MD 22:60 (says Aug. 1692)>. <See MBD 2:211 for 3 chil.; Taunton VR 1:161 (1), PCR 8:66 (1).> (See ROGERS Probate Appendix for estate of Deacon Nathaniel WILLIAMS. Note: MBD 2:240 #36 - his division (not will) is dated 25 July 1698.)

III. **LYSBETH/ELIZABETH ROGERS[2]**, b. (   ), living 1622, Leiden, Holland; poss. came to Plymouth c1630 with brother John and as Bradford implies, married and had children. Stratton:287-8 suggests she could be the Elizabeth (   ), wf of Samuel Eddy. Elizabeth Eddy died 24 May 1689, at the end of her 82nd year <Plymouth ChR 1:265>, thus her birth date of c1606 fits the time frame of the birth of the Rogers children. Samuel is included in a 1662 list of "first born children" to receive grants of land. All those who received land were either in Ply-

mouth pre 1627 or married someone who was (the only exception was William Pontus who was a
member of the Leiden group). Since it is known that Samuel Eddy arived in 1630 in the ship
"Handmaid", the fact that he is included indicates it was in right of his wife Elizabeth,
the daughter of an "Old Comer" family. Bradford's statement that the children who came over
had "many" children fits the Eddy family whom the records show had many children (born before
Bradford's writings), some of whom they had to "put out" because of their "many wants" <PCR
2:82,2:112; MD 2:30>. Since Bradford states that the rest of the Rogers children came over,
one could assume they came together and, as it is known that brother John came to Plymouth
c1630 (between 1627-1633), is it possible that, along with Samuel Eddy, John and his sisters
Elizabeth & Margaret were among the sixty passengers of the Handmaid?

IV. GRIETGEN/MARGARET ROGERS[2], b. (   ), living 1622, Leiden, Holland; poss. came to Plymouth
   and as Bradford implies, married and had children. See above.

ROGERS PROBATE APPENDIX

Will of **Israel COLE**: <MDP:292; Barnstable Co.PR 4:204>
...21 Jan. 1723/4, ment. son Israel COLE and grandchildren Israel HIGGENS, Theoder HIGGENS, Jacob
HIGGENS, Samuel HIGGENS. Pr. 23 July 1724.
==

Will of **John PHINNEY**: (weaver) <MD 20:143; Barnstable Co.PR 3:595>
...19 Apr. 1718, ment. unnamed wf; daus Mary EASTLAND, Mercy CROCKER, Reliance MORTON; sons John
PHINNEY, Joseph PHINNEY, Thomas PHINNEY, Ebenezer PHINNEY, Samuel PHINNEY, Benjamin PHINNEY, Jonathan PHINNEY. Inv. taken 9 Mar. 1718/9.
==

Will of **John ROGERS Sr.**[2]: <MD 5:205-6; Plymouth Co.PR 1:145>
...26 Aug. 1691, ment. grandson John ROGERS & his sisters Elibeth/Elizabeth ROGERS, Hannah BRAD-
FORD, Ruth ROGERS & Sarah ROGERS; grandson John TISDALL & his mother Anne TERREY; dau Elizabeth
WILLIAMS; dau Abigail RICHMOND; grandsons Joseph RICHMOND, Edward RICHMOND; son John ROGERS. Wit
sworn 20 Sept. 1692.
==

Estate of **John ROGERS**[3] (John[2]): <MD 20:5-10; Bristol Co.PR>
...30 Aug. 1732, Petition of Peleg RICHMOND, Perez RICHMOND, Ichabod RICHMOND, Nathaniel FISHER,
Ephraim ATWOOD & Peleg HEATH that "our" Brother William RICHMOND assist "our" Aunts Mrs. Bradford
and Mrs. Searl in administering estate of "our" grandfather, John Rogers. (The records contain
many petitions and complaints against John's widow, Marah, by Peres BRADFORD, William RICHMOND &
Nathaniel SEARLE Jr. who state 30 Nov. 1732, "we have Grate Reason to Suspect that Divers bonds
of Considerable sums...& Money & Other personall Estate of the sd Deceased is Concealed Imbezell-
ed & Conveyd Away whereby the Complainants Have Grate Reason to suspect that Marah Rogers the
Widdow of sd Deceased And John Peirce...Are Guilty...we Have Divers Evidence". <8:50> On 25 Sept
1733, Marah stated she was innocent.)

Will of **Hannah (HOBART)(Browne) Rogers**: <MD 20:2-3; Bristol Co.PR>
...9 June 1691, "I Hannah Rogers formerly Browne", ment. brothers Gershom HOBART & Nehemiah HOB-
ART. Inv. taken 31 Oct. 1691.

Estate of **Marah (COBHAM)(Browning) Rogers**: (widow) <MD 20:11; Bristol Co.PR>
...(no date), Petition of Mary NEWEL "akin unto Marah Rogers", being in advanced age asks that
her sons John NEWEL & Moses NEWEL administer "my Ant Marah Rogers estate"; they were app'td. 20
Feb. 1739. Petition, dated 8 Dec. 1739 by Joseph SIMPSON Jr. & Jonathan BLAKE "being near relations to Marah Rogers". Petition, dated 5 Mar. 1739, by John NEWEL & Moses NEWEL, who com-
plained "that they have Grait Reason Suspect that" John PEARCE, Peleg RICHMOND & wf Mary "have
Concealed Embezled or Conveyed away Considerable of the moneys Goods or Chattles" of Marah Rogers
==

Will of **John ROGERS Sr.**[3] (Jos.[2]): <MD 11:180-1; Barnstable Co.PR 3:166>
...27 Apr. 1713, "now stricken in years", ment. son John ROGERS Jr.; dec'd father Joseph ROGERS;
sons Judah ROGERS, Joseph ROGERS, Eleazer ROGERS, Nathaniel ROGERS; daus Elizabeth ROGERS, Mehitable ROGERS, Hannah ROGERS; grandson John ROGERS; wf Elizabeth. Inv. taken 10 Aug. 1714.
==

Will of **Lt. Joseph ROGERS**[2]: <MD 3:67-71; Plymouth Col.Wills 3:2:103-5>
...2 Jan. 1677/8, ment. sons Thomas ROGERS, John ROGERS, James ROGERS; dau Elizabeth HIGGENS wf
of Jonathan; grandchild Beriah/Benjah HIGGENS; dau Hannah ROGERS; wf Hannah. Inv. taken 15 Jan.
1677/8.
==

Estate of **Thomas ROGERS**[3] (Jos.[2]): <MD 11:179-80; Barnstable Co.PR 2:167,169>
...8 July 1704, Complaint was made that the estate had not been settled in 26 years; ment. dau
Hannah HARDING wf of Amasiah; sons Joseph ROGERS (eldest), Thomas ROGERS, Eleazer ROGERS.
==

Will of **Thomas TERRY**: <MDP:362; Bristol Co.PR>
...10 Aug. 1691, aged about 60 years; ment. minor sons Thomas TERRY (eldest), John TERRY, Benjamin TERRY; wf Anna. Wit. made oath 30 Oct. 1691.

Estate of **Anna (ROGERS[3])(Tisdale)(Terry) Williams (John[2])**: <MDP:362; Bristol Co.Deeds 27:27>
...29 June 1737, Division of dower to following heirs, viz: son Thomas TERRY, son Benjamin TERRY, grandson John TERRY, great-great-granddau. Remember TERRY the only dau of Silas & Sarah TERRY (Sarah TERRY who is now Sarah DAVIS.)

Will of **Samuel WILLIAMS**: <MDP:362; Bristol Co.PR 1:199-200>
...6 Aug. 1697, ment. eldest son Seth WILLIAMS; son Daniel WILLIAMS; daus Sarah DEAN, Mary ANDROS & Hannah BUN; unnamed wf. Inv. taken 31 Aug. 1697.
===
Estate of **Deacon Nathaniel WILLIAMS**: <MDP:366; MD 22:60; Bristol Co.PR 1:223>
...25 July 1698, Division among following heirs, viz: widow Elizabeth WILLIAMS; sons John WILL-IAMS (eldest) and Nathaniel WILLIAMS (2nd son) to pay their Grandmother Williams during her life; only dau Elizabeth WILLIAMS (under 18). Inv. states he d. "sum time in ye month of August".

NOTES:

HENRY SAMSON

Henry SAMSON was baptized 15 Jan. 1603/4, Henlow, Bedfordshire, England the son of James Samson & Martha Cooper <TAG 52:198> and died 24 Dec. 1684, Duxbury <MD 8:231,12:31>. Bradford called both he and Humility Cooper the "cousins" of Edward & Ann (Cooper) Tilley. He married 6 Feb. 1635/6, Plymouth, Ann PLUMMER <PCR 1:36; MD 13:84>. Ann's birth and parentage are unknown; she is called cousin in the 1668 will of John Barnes <MD 4:98-100; Plymouth Col.Wills 3:1:31; Stratton:447-56> and was probably the sister or cousin of his wife, Mary Plummer. Ann died between 24 Dec. 1668 <MD 4:128 (ack. deed)> - 24 Dec. 1684 <MD 2:142-3 (hus. will)>.

(See also: Mayflower Families In Progress, Henry Samson Of The Mayflower and His Descendants for Four Generations (MFIP), by Robert M. Sherman, FASG and Ruth W. Sherman, FASG, ed. by Robert S. Wakefield, FASG, 1992; TAG 18:1, The Early Sampsons; TAG 52:198, The English Ancestry of Seven Mayflower Passengers: Tilley, Sampson & Cooper; TAG 56:141, Henry Samson's Paternal Grandfather; TG 6:166, The Baronial Ancestry of Henry Samson, Humility Cooper & Ann (Cooper) Tilley.)

Henry & Ann had 9 children: (The order of births is unknown, the order of the daughters & sons are given as they appear in Henry's will. Bradford stated he had 7 children in 1650/1; possibly born in Duxbury.)

I.   Elizabeth, b. (   )
II.   Hannah, b. (   )
III.   dau., b. (   )
IV.   Stephen, b. (   )
V.   Mary, b. (   )
VI.   Dorcas, b. (   )
VII.   John, b. (   )
VIII. James, b. (   )
IX.   Caleb, b. (   )

* * * * * * * * * * * * * * * *

I. **ELIZABETH SAMSON**[2], b. (   ), d. betw. 23 Nov. 1711 <MD 6:9 (if she is the unnamed wf)> - 12 Dec. 1719 <MD 25:69-70 (called dec'd in deed)>; m. c1661, (   ), **Robert SPROUT** <MD 6:8; MM:255>, b. (   ), d. betw. 6 June 1712 <MDP:390, Plymouth Co.Deeds 10:2:28> - 11 Dec. 1712 <MD 6:8-11 (pr.), 25:69>. (See SAMSON Probate Appendix for will of Robert SPROUT.)

8 SPROUT Children: <Scituate VR 4:3:24>

1. **Mercy SPROUT**[3], b. 15 July 1662, Scituate <VR>, d. betw. 6 Sept. 1725 <MDP:393, Plymouth Co. Deeds 19:513> - 8 Oct. 1728 <MDP:393, Plymouth Co.Deeds 37:178 (called dec'd)>; m. 27 June 1683, Scituate, **Thomas OLDHAM Jr.** <MD 2:87,21:186; MSR:621>, (son of Thomas OLDHAM & Mary WITHERELL), b. 30 Oct. 1660, Scituate <PCR 8:29; Scituate VR 1:276>, d. betw. 21 Feb. 1733 - 24 Jan. 1734 <MDP:393 (will & wit. made oath)>. <See MBD 2:257 & Scituate VR 1:276 for bth. 10 chil.> (See SAMSON Probate Appendix for will of Thomas OLDHAM.)

2. **Elizabeth SPROUT**[3], b. July 1664, Scituate <VR; MD 25:69>, d. betw. 28 Jan. 1724/5 <MD 25:69; Plymouth Co.Deeds 19:153 (ack. deed)> - 8 Nov. 1726, unm. <MD 25:69-71 (adm.)>.

3. **Mary SPROUT**[3], b. 1 May 1666, Scituate <VR; MD 25:69>, d. betw. 28 Jan. 1724/5 <MD 25:69; Plymouth Co.Deeds 19:153 (ack. deed)> - 8 Nov. 1726, unm. <MD 25:69-71 (adm.)>.

4. **Robert SPROUT**[3], b. Apr. 1669, Scituate <VR>, d. June 1690, unm., expedition to Canada <Scituate VR 2:442>.

5. **Anna SPROUT**[3], b. Mar. 1671/2, Scituate <VR; MD 21:186>, d. aft. 7 Dec. 1739 <MDP:390,Plymouth Co.Deeds 33:122 (ack. deed)>; m. c1700, (   ), **Ebenezer RICHMOND**[4] <MD 21:186>, (son of John RICHMOND & Abigail ROGERS[3] (John[2]) - see ROGERS family), b. 12 May 1676, Newport RI <PCR 8:65; MD 21:186>, d. betw. 14 Apr. 1729 <MDP:390, Plymouth Co.Deeds 25:50 (ack. deed)> - 12 May 1729, Middleboro <MD 21:186 (agreement of heirs)>. <See MBD 2:206 for bth. 6 chil. and MD 2:43 (3), 105 (1), 106 (1), 201 (1), 21:57 (1).> (See SAMSON Probate Appendix for will of Ebenezer RICHMOND.)

6. **James SPROUT**[3], b. Feb. 1673/4, Scituate <VR>, d. aft. 13 July 1752, of Middleboro <MD 38:71 (deposition)>; m.1st, 5 June 1712, Scituate, **Elizabeth SOUTHWORTH**[5] <MD 9:87,21:24>, (dau of Nathaniel SOUTHWORTH & Desire GRAY[4] (Mary Winslow[3], Mary Chilton[2]) - see CHILTON family), bpt. 1687, Plymouth <MD 21:24; Plymouth ChR 1:260>, d. pre 8 Jan. 1728/9, poss. Middleboro (hus.2nd marr.). **James** m.2nd, 8 Jan. 1728/9, Scituate, **Rachel (BUCK) Dwelly** <Scituate VR; MM:256>, (dau of John), b. 22 Aug. 1674, Scituate <VR; MSR:320 (bpt. 4 Oct. 1674)>, d. pre 31 May 1738, prob. Scituate <MDP:391, Plymouth Co.PR #19142, 7:416 (adm.)>. (Rachel m.1st, 4 Jan. 1692/3, Scituate, John DWELLY <MD 2:87> & had 11 chil.) <See MBD 2:255-6 for bth. of 4 chil.

and Scituate VR (1), MD 3:235 (1), 6:180 (1).>

7. **Ebenezer SPROUT**[3], b. May 1676, Scituate <VR; MD 25:126>, d. 28 Sept. 1726, 52nd yr, Middle-
    boro, The Green cem. <MD 14:135,25:101,126; Wood:174 ("cancer")>; m. 1 Mar. 1703/4, Yarmouth,
    Experience HAWES[4] <Yarmouth VR 1:136; MD 25:101,126>, (dau of John HAWES & Desire GORHAM[3]
    (Desire Howland[2] - see HOWLAND family), b. 24 Sept. 1686, Yarmouth <Yarmouth VR 1:126>, d. 19
    Nov. 1758, 74th yr, Middleboro, The Green cem. <Wood:112,174; MD 13:119,25:102,126>. (Exper-
    ience m.2nd, 22 Nov. 1731, Middleboro, Francis MILLER[5] <MD 13:249,25:101,126>, (son of John
    MILLER & Lydia COOMBS[4] (Francis Coombs[3], Sarah Priest[2] - see PRIEST family), b. 11 Jan. 1702/
    3, Middleboro <MD 25:102>, d. betw. 29 Oct. 1746 - 6 Apr. 1747 <MD 25:101-4 (will & pr.)>.)
    <See MBD 2:255 for bth. 5 chil. and Scituate VR (4), Yarmouth VR 1:126 (1).> (See SAMSON
    Probate Appendix for wills of Lt. Ebenezer SPROUT and Francis MILLER.)

8. **Hannah SPROUT**[3], b. Aug. 1680, Scituate <VR>, d. prob. pre 12 Sept. 1729 <MDP:390, Plymouth Co
    Deeds 28:29 (she is not ment. when hus. sold her fath. land)>; m. 1 Apr. 1703, Scituate,
    Ephraim KEEN <MD 3:119,21:186>, (son of Josiah KEEN & Hannah DINGLEY), b. (   ) <MD 19:128>
    d. aft. 29 Oct. 1731 <MDP:390, Plymouth Co.Deeds 28:29 (ack. deed); MFIP #14 says prob. after
    23 Jan. 1738/9 when his son is still called Ephraim Jr. in a deed - MDP:390, Plymouth Co.
    Deeds 33:122>. <See MBD 2:255 for bth. 7 chil. and Pembroke VR:127 (1), 128 (2), 130 (2),
    132 (1); MD 6:180 (1); MFIP #14 adds an 8th ch.>

────────────────

II. **HANNAH SAMSON**[2], b. (   ), d. aft. 24 Dec. 1684 <MD 2:143 (fath. will); poss the Hanna HOL-
    MES who d. 9 Jan. 1715 - Pembroke VR>; m. 20 Mar. 1665/6, Duxbury, **Josiah HOLMES** <MD 8:232;
    Torrey:385>, (son of William & Elizabeth), b. (   ), d. aft. 8 May 1721 <Plymouth Co.Deeds;
    MFIP #3 (ack. deed)>.

6 HOLMES Children:

1. **Hannah HOLMES**[3], b. 11 Oct. 1667, Duxbury <MD 9:172>, d. (   ). MFIP #15 states she married
    either 1/ Thomas LAMBERT, (son of Thomas), bpt. 1 July 1660, Scituate (poss. b. 6 Nov. 1659,
    son of Thomas & Mary <Boston Rcd.Com.9:70> who m.2nd, 3 May 1709, Scituate, Joanna TERRY) and
    had one child, or 2/ John LAMBERT (brother of Thomas) who had a wife "Anna" and d. 1 Jan.
    1752, Hanover and had 9 children.

2. **Dorcas HOLMES**[3], b. 4 Aug. 1669, Duxbury <MD 9:172>.

3. **Josiah HOLMES**[3], b. 13 Aug. 1672, Duxbury <MD 9:172>.

4. **Mary HOLMES**[3], b. 5 Nov. 1674, Duxbury <MD 9:174>.

5. **John HOLMES**[3], b. 28 May 1678, Duxbury <MD 9:174>, d. 16 Feb. 1756, Hanover <Hanover 1st ChR:
    187>; m.1st, 11 May 1710, Marshfield, **Joanna SPRAGUE** <Marshfield VR:36,39; MD 7:132,8:42;
    MSR:245; MBD 1:416 (Bowman) attributes this marriage to John HOLMES[3] (Desire Doty[2])>, (dau of
    Samuel SPRAGUE & Sarah CHILLINGSWORTH), b. (   ), d. 1 Aug. 1713, Pembroke <MFIP #19>. **John**
    m.2nd, 25 Nov. 1714, Pembroke, **Susanna (RANDALL) Stetson** <Pembroke VR>, (dau of Isaac RANDALL
    & Susanna BARSTOW), b. 15 Nov. 1687, Scituate <Scituate VR>, d. 22 Oct. 1732, Pembroke <Pem-
    broke VR>. (Susanna m.1st, 28 July 1710, Scituate, Nathaniel STETSON <MD 8:206> & had two
    chil.) <See MFIP #19 for 1 ch. by 1st wf, 8 by 2nd.>

6. **William HOLMES**[3], b. 18 Jan. 1679, Duxbury <MD 9:174>, d. 13 May 1760, 81st yr, Halifax g.s.
    <MD 9:154,20:166>; m. 22 Nov. 1715, Pembroke, **Bathsheba STETSON** <Pembroke VR 1:330>, (dau of
    Joseph STETSON & Hannah OLDHAM), b. 29 Sept. 1693, Scituate <Scituate VR 1:330>, d. 30 Mar.
    1763, 70th yr, Halifax g.s. <MD 9:154,20:166>. <See MBD 2:260 for bth. 9 chil.; MD 9:154 for
    dths. of 2.> (See SAMSON Probate Appendix for estate of William HOLMES & will of wife.)

────────────────

III. (   ) **SAMSON**[2], b. (   ), d. (   ); m. (   ), **John HANMER/HANMORE** <MD 6:245>, (son of
     John & Hannah), b. (   ), d. pre 22 Feb. 1703, Rochester <MDP:383, Plymouth Co.Deeds 5:140
     (deed of son John - "John Hanmer, eldest son of John Hanmer late of Rochester dec'd who was
     eldest son of John Hanmer late of Scituate dec'd")>. He poss. d. aft. 19 Sept. 1702 if he is
     the John Hanmer of Rochester (& not his son) who bought land 10 Mar. 1700/01 and is called of
     Middleboro when he sold it 19 Sept. 1702. Both deeds were ack. 8 Sept. 1711 but it is not
     clear by whom <MDP:383, Plymouth Co.Deeds 10:2:75,93>.

2 HANMER Children:

1. **John HANMER/HANDMER**[3], b. pre 22 Feb. 1682 <MDP:383 (at least 21 to sell land in 1703)>, d.
    aft. 17 Jan. 1737, of Halifax <Plymouth Co.Deeds 31:168>; m. (   ), **Mary (   )**, b. (   )
    d. aft. 17 Mar. 1727 <Plymouth Co.Deeds 21:202>. <See MFIP #21 for 1 known ch.>

2. **William HANMER/HANDMOR**[3], b. (   ), d. betw. 17 Jan. 1737 <Plymouth Co.Deeds 31:168 (wit. to
    brother's deed)> - 5 Oct. 1741 <Plymouth Co.Deeds 42:33 (wf is called widow)>; m. (   ),
    Elizabeth KINGMAN <MFIP:22>, (dau of Henry KINGMAN & Bethiah HOWARD), b. 22 Mar. 1695,

Bridgewater <MD 15:47>, d. aft. 3 Jan. 1742/3 <Plymouth Co.Deeds 44:20>. <See MFIP #22 for 3 chil.>

IV. **STEPHEN SAMSON**[2], b. (   ), d. betw. 22 Jan. 1711/2 <Bristol Co.Deeds 12:24; Gen.Adv.4:84> - 31 Jan. 1714/5, prob. Duxbury <MD 6:114 (adm.)>; m. pre 1686, (   ), **Elizabeth** (   ), b. (   ), d. aft. 12 Mar. 1723/4 <MDP:396, Plymouth Co.Deeds 18:89; Suffolk Deeds 60:87 (poss. aft. 19 Sept. 1740, Bellingham if she is the Elizabeth Samson who wit. deed of Jonathan & Elizabeth Thayer)>. (See SAMSON Probate Appendix for estate of Stephen SAMSON.)

8 SAMSON Children:

1. **Benjamin SAMSON**[3], b. c1686, prob. Duxbury, d. 19 Apr. 1758, 72nd yr, Kingston g.s. <MD 7:170> m. 19 Mar. 1716, Plymouth, **Rebecca COOKE**[4] <MD 14:37>, (dau of Jacob COOKE[3] (Jacob[2]) (Damaris Hopkins[2]) & Lydia MILLER - see COOKE & HOPKINS families), b. 19 Nov. 1688, Plymouth <MD 2:81> d. 14 Apr. 1769, 81st yr, Kingston g.s. <MD 7:171>. <See MBD 2:262 for bth. 6 chil. and MD 7:171 (2), Kingston VR 1:16 (2), Duxbury ChR (1).> (See SAMSON Probate Appendix for wills of Benjamin & Rebecca SAMSON.)

2. **John SAMSON**[3], b. 17 Aug. 1688, Duxbury <MD 9:231,18:244>, d. 26 Jan. 1770, ae 81y5m6d, Duxbury <Duxbury VR:420; MD 18:244>; m. 31 Dec. 1718, Duxbury, **Priscilla BARTLETT**[5] <MD 11:25,18:244>, (dau of Benjamin BARTLETT[4] (Benjamin[3], Mary Warren[2]) (Sarah Brewster[3], Love[2]) & Ruth PABODIE[3] (Elizabeth Alden[2]) - see ALDEN, BREWSTER & WARREN families), b. Jan. 1696/7, Duxbury <MD 9:231,18:244>, d. 7 July 1758, ae near 61, Duxbury <Duxbury VR:411; MD 18:244>. <See MBD 2:264 & MD 11:237 for bth. 9 chil. incl. twins.>

3. **Cornelius SAMSON**[3], b. (   ), d. prob. pre 12 Mar. 1723/4 <MDP:396, Plymouth Co.Deeds 18:189 (not ment. in deed of father's heirs)>.

4. **Hannah SAMSON**[3], b. (   ), prob. Duxbury, d. aft. Nov. 1753, of Mendon <Worcester Co.Deeds 32:414 (ack. deed)>; m. 13 Dec. 1721, Duxbury, **Robert TYLER** <Duxbury VR; MD 11:239>, (son of John TYLER & Hannah PARKER), b. 19 July 1689, Andover <Andover VR>, d. aft. 25 Aug. 1756 <Worcester Co.Deeds 41:243>. <See MBD 2:264 & Mendon VR for bth. 5 chil.>

5. **Mary SAMSON**[3], b. (   ), prob. Duxbury, d. aft. 20 Aug. 1764 <Worcester Co.PR #A58793 (adm. hus. est.)>; m. 13 Aug. 1716, Mendon, **Samuel THAYER** <Mendon VR; MM:259>, (son of Thomas THAYER & Mary POOLE), b. 28 Mar. 1696, Mendon <Mendon VR>, d. 21 June 1764, 70th yr, Mendon g.s. <MFIP #35>. <See MFIP #35 & Mendon VR for bth. 9 chil.> (See SAMSON Probate Appendix for will of Samuel THAYER.)

6. **Elizabeth SAMSON**[3], b. (   ), prob. Duxbury, d. aft. 19 Mar. 1762, of Bellingham <Suffolk Co Deeds 97:182 (ack.deed)>; m. 21 Feb. 1722/3, Duxbury, **Jonathan THAYER** <Duxbury VR; MD 11:240> (son of Josiah & Sarah), b. 28 Feb. 1701/2, Mendon <Mendon VR>, d. 12 Apr. 1747, Bellingham <Bellingham VR; MBD 2:263>. <See MBD 2:263 for 8 chil. and Bellingham VR (5); MFIP #37 gives a 9th child.>

7. **Dorcas SAMSON**[3], b. (   ), prob. Duxbury, d. aft. 24 May 1754, of Brookfield <Worcester Co. PR #A33056 (will of 2nd hus.)>; m.1st 15 Apr. 1723, Mendon, **John PLUMBLY/PLUMLY** <Mendon VR>, (son of Alexander PLUMBLY & Elizabeth DREW), b. 5 Sept. 1702, Mendon <Mendon VR 364,475>, d. 11 July 1740, Upton <Upton VR>. <See MBD 2:263 & Mendon VR for one known ch.> **Dorcas** m.2nd, 11 Jan. 1742, Upton, **Jonathan JENNINGS** <Upton VR; Torrey:419>, (son of Stephen JENNINGS & Hannah (DICKINSON) Gillett), b. 24 Nov. 1692, Hatfield <MFIP #37>, d. 19 July 1754, Brookfield <MFIP #37>. (He poss.m.1st, (   ), **Joanna** (   ) who d. 13 Jan. 1727 <MFIP #37>; m.2nd, 17 July 1727, Marlboro, Esther RICE <VR>, poss. dau of Jacob & Mary, b. 26 Jan. 1700/01, Marlboro <VR> and had 5 chil.) **Dorcas** prob. m.3rd, 18 May 1758, Brookfield, **Daniel SNOW** <MFIP #37>. (See SAMSON Probate Appendix for will of John PLUMBLY.)

8. **Abigail SAMSON**[3], b. c1702, prob. Duxbury, d. 20 July 1794, 93rd yr, Grafton <Grafton VR>; m. 11 July 1727, Mendon, **George BRUCE** <Mendon VR; Boston Rcd.Com.28:303; MM:258>, (son of Joseph & Hannah), b. 20 Sept. 1703, Woburn <Woburn VR>, d. 15 Feb. 1768, Mendon <Mendon VR; MBD 2: 262>. <See MFIP #38 for 4 chil.>

V. **MARY SAMSON**[2], b. (   ), d. betw. 24 Dec. 1684 (fath.will) - c1686 (hus.2nd marr.); m. pre 24 Dec. 1684, (   ), **John SUMMERS** <MD 2:143 (fath. will), 6:245>, b. (   ), d. pre 1 Feb. 1721/2, of Rochester <Plymouth Co.PR 4:299,327-8 (adm.)>. No known issue. (John m.2nd, pre 1686, (   ), Elizabeth BRANCH <MFIP #5>, (dau of John BRANCH & Mary SPEED), b. 14 Oct. 1656 Marshfield <Marshfield VR:4; MD 2:7>, d. 29 Nov. 1715, 60th yr, Rochester <Rochester VR; they had 7 children <MD 5:235 (4); Rochester VR (3); Marshfield VR:21 (4). John m.3rd, 26 Nov. 1716, Scituate, Elizabeth BOOTH <Scituate VR>, (dau of John), b. 5 Oct. 1657, Scituate <Scituate VR>, d. aft. 9 Feb. 1721/2 (dower set off) <Plymouth Co.PR 4:299,327-8>.)

VI **DORCAS SAMSON**[2], b. (   ), d. pre 18 July 1695 (hus.2nd marr.); m. pre 24 Dec. 1684, (   ) **Thomas BONNEY** <MD 2:143 (fath.will)>, (son of Thomas & Mary), b. pre 1665, d. betw. 29 July

1735 - 19 Aug. 1735 <MDP:388-9 (will & wit.sworn)>. (Thomas m.2nd, 18 July 1695, Duxbury, Sarah STUDLEY <Duxbury VR; MD 9:108> who d. aft. 29 July 1735 (hus.will).)

3 BONNEY Children:

1. **Ebenezer BONNEY**[3], b. (   ), prob. Duxbury, d. 25 Nov. 1712, Duxbury, unm. <Boston News Obits 2:106; MBD 2:253; Winsor:86 (drowned from whale boat off Gurnet Beach)>.

2. **Elizabeth BONNEY**[3], b. (   ), prob. Duxbury, d. aft. 10 May 1748, of Duxbury <MFIP #24>; m. 30 Jan. 1712/3, Marshfield, **Ephraim NORCUT** <MD 7:132,8:42; Marshfield VR:37,39; MSR:245>, (son of William NORCUT & Sarah CHAPMAN), b. 4 Nov. 1683, Marshfield <Marshfield VR:40; MD 8:43>, d. aft. 26 Apr. 1757 <Plymouth Co.PR #14693 (adm. son's est.)>. <For 6 chil. see Marshfield VR:37 (1), 40 (2), 84 (1), 87 (1), Duxbury VR (1) and MD 7:133 (1), 8:43 (2), 10:185 (1), 30:151 (1), 155 (1).>

3. **Mercy BONNEY**[3], b. (   ), prob. Duxbury, d. aft. 28 Apr. 1755 <MFIP #25, Plymouth Co.PR (est of son)>; m.1st, 14 Oct. 1714, Duxbury, **Nathaniel DELANO** <Duxbury VR:245; MD 11:24>, (son of John DELANO & Mary WESTON), b. c1685, d. pre 29 Apr. 1731 (wf's 2nd marr.). **Mercy** m.2nd, 29 Apr. 1731, Kingston, **John CURTIS** <Kingston VR>, b. (   ), d. betw. 3 Mar. 1754 (wf is not called widow in son's est.) - 28 Apr. 1755 (wf is called widow) <MFIP #25, Plymouth Co.PR>. <See MQ 49:136 for 5 chil. by 1st hus.>

VII **JOHN SAMSON**[2], b. (   ), d. betw. 27 May 1702, of Dartmouth (ack.deed) <MD 7:226-7; Gen.Adv. 4:83; Bristol Co.Deeds 3:446 (21 May, he gave his brother James all his lands in return for James providing for him for life)> - 10 Jan. 1715/16, unm. <MD 7:225-7 (will of brother James who did not mention him nor make any provision for him)>.

VIII **JAMES SAMSON**[2], b. pre 1657 <MFIP #7 (at least 21 when proposed as a freeman)>, d. betw. 10 Jan. 1715/6 - 7 July 1718, Dartmouth <MD 6:184,7:226 (will & pr.)>; m. pre 21 May 1679 (deed) **Hannah (   ) WAIT** <NEHGR 73:293; MDP:394; Gen.Adv.4:83; Bristol Co.Deeds 13:368>, b. (   ) d. aft. 31 Dec. 1718 (released dower, son's deed) <Gen.Adv.4:86; Bristol Co.Deeds 12:445>, (did she d. aft. 24 July 1726 when son James quitclaimed "all manner of Action...which by Law or Equity may now or hereafter Arise Concerning Mother Hannah Samson's thirds of the Estate of our father James"; another from dau Ann is dated 7 July 1726 <Gen.Adv.4:85; Bristol Co. Deeds 9:440-1>) (Hannah m.1st, Samuel WAIT and had 3 chil. <MFIP #7>.) (See SAMSON Probate Appendix for will of James SAMSON.)

7 SAMSON Children:

1. **James SAMSON**[3], b. c1680, prob. Dartmouth <MFIP #26 (age 74 in 1754)>, d. betw. 10 July 1755 <Gen.Adv.4:86; York ME Co.Deeds 32:141 (gave power of attorney)> - 6 May 1761 <Gen.Adv.4:86; York ME Co.Deeds 37:111 (wf called widow)>; m. c1708, (   ), **Ruth SAWYER** <MM:258>, (dau of William SAWYER & Sarah (LITTLEFIELD) Wells), b. 26 May 1687, Wells (now in ME) <MFIP #26>, d. aft. 5 Apr. 1762, of Arundel <York Co.ME Deeds 37:112>. <See MFIP #26 for 8 chil. and Dartmouth VR (3).>

2. **Henry SAMSON**[3], b. (   ), prob. Dartmouth, d. pre 22 Feb. 1750, unm., of Dartmouth (petition for adm.) <MD 23:42; Gen.Adv.4:87; Bristol Co.PR 12:513,543>.

3. **Joseph SAMSON**[3], b. (   ), prob. Dartmouth, d. pre 26 Feb. 1738/9, Dartmouth <MD 23:175 (appraisers sworn)>; m. 6 May 1719, Duxbury, **Sarah SAMSON**[4] <MD 11:25,23:174-5; Duxbury VR>, (dau of Abraham SAMSON & Lorah STANDISH[3] (Alexander Standish[2]) (Sarah Alden[2] –see ALDEN & STANDISH families), b. (   ), d. aft. 8 July 1757 <Bristol Co.PR 15:78-80,509-11 (div. 2nd hus.est)> <See MBD 2:261 & MD 23:175 for bth. 6 chil. (incl. twins) and Dartmouth VR:174 (4).> (Sarah m.2nd, 18 Nov. 1739, Dartmouth, John ROUSE <MD 23:176>, (son of Simeon & Christianna), b. c1690, d. pre 4 May 1756, Dartmouth and had one or more chil. <MFIP (Samson) #27, (Standish) #26>. John m.1st, 29 June 1720, Duxbury, Anne LATHLY <MD 11:79; Marshfield VR:349 ("Anna Cashly")> and had 3 chil.) (See SAMSON Probate Appendix for estate of Joseph SAMSON.)

4. **Anne SAMSON**[3], b. (   ), prob. Dartmouth, d. aft. 10 Feb. 1734, of Chilmark (hus.will); m. 12 Oct. 1725, Dartmouth, **Shubael SMITH** <Chilmark VR:71,73; MD 23:174 (no date)>, (son of John SMITH & prob. Susanna HINCKLEY), b. Mar. 1653/4, Barnstable <MD 12:154; Otis 2:237 says 13 Mar.>, d. 5 Apr. 1734, Chilmark <Chilmark VR; MSR:100 says 24 Apr.>. No known issue. (Shubael m.1st, 6 Feb. 1678, Sandwich, Mara/Mary SWIFT <MD 14:172>, (dau of William), b. 7 Apr. 1659, Sandwich <MD 14:169>, d. 1 Mar. 168(worn - prob. 2 or 3), Sandwich <MD 14:173>; they had 3 chil. <MD 14:172>. Shubael m.2nd, 3 Dec. 1684, Sandwich, Abigail SKIFF who d. 1718 <MFIP #28>; they had 5 chil. <Sandwich VR 2:46>.) (See SAMSON Probate Appendix for will of Shubael SMITH.)

5. **Penelope SAMSON**[3], b. c1686, prob. Dartmouth, d. aft. 23 Nov. 1727, Duxbury <MD 6:187-8 (receipted to fath.est.)>; m. c1712, (   ), **Abraham SAMSON**[4] <MD 6:188,23:174>, (son of Abraham SAMSON & Lorah STANDISH[3] (Alexander[2]) (Sarah Alden[2]) - see ALDEN & STANDISH families), b. c1686, Duxbury, d. 16 Nov. 1775, ae 89, Duxbury <Duxbury VR>. (Abraham m.2nd, Mary (   ),

who d. aft. 22 May 1764 (his will).) <See MBD 2:261 for bth. 8 chil. and MD 10:185 (3), 186 (4), 12:119 (1).> (See SAMSON Probate Appendix for will of Abraham SAMSON.)

6. **Susanna SAMSON**[3], b. (   ), prob. Dartmouth, d. aft. 5 Apr. 1757 <Dukes Co.PR 4:48-40 (div. son's estate); Banks' Martha's Vineyard 3:196 says d. 1761>; m. 15 May 1722, Dartmouth, **Benjamin HILLMAN** <Dartmouth VR; MD 23:174 (no date)>, (son of John HILLMAN & Hannah COTTLE), b. c1690, prob. Chilmark, d. 22 Apr. 1745, Chilmark <MSR:101; NEHGR 48:452>. (He had an un-known first wife and one ch.) <See MFIP #30 for 6 chil.> (See SAMSON Probate Appendix for will of Benjamin HILLMAN.)

7. **Priscilla SAMSON**[3], b. (   ), d. aft. 6 Dec. 1727, of Dartmouth <MD 6:189 (receipted to fat-her's est.; her husband is called Solomon - see MD 7:254 for explanation)>; m. pre 27 Dec. 1712, (   ), **Samuel HAMMOND Jr.**[5] (deed) <MDP:396; MD 7:254,24:174>, (son of Samuel HAMMOND & Mary HATHAWAY[4] (Sarah Cooke[3], John[2]) - see COOKE family), b. 8 Mar. 1685, Rochester <VR>, d. aft. 12 July 1728 <Plymouth Co.PR 5:475 (his fath.will); MDP:523 (poss. d. aft. 24 Jan. 1731/2 if he is the Samuel HAMMOND who witnessed the will of Lettice JENNEY of Dartmouth)>. <See MFIP #31 for one or more chil.>

IX. **CALEB SAMSON**[2], b. (   ), d. aft. 9 July 1744 <MD 8:34; Plymouth Co.Deeds 37:5>; m.1st, c1684, (   ), **Mercy STANDISH**[3] <MD 12:101>, (dau of Alexander STANDISH[2] & Sarah ALDEN[2] - see STANDISH & ALDEN families), see STANDISH family. **Caleb** m.2nd, 30 Jan. 1728/9, Duxbury, **Rebecca (BARTLETT**[4]**) (Bradford) Stanford** <MD 11:80>, (dau of Benjamin BARTLETT[3] (Mary Warren[2]) & Sarah BREWSTER[3] (Love[2]) - see BREWSTER & WARREN families), b. pre 1663, prob. Duxbury, d. 14 Dec. 1741, Duxbury <MD 12:125>. (Rebecca m.1st, c1679, William BRADFORD[3-2] & had 3 chil. - see BRADFORD family. Rebecca m.2nd, betw. 21 Aug. 1691 (her fath.will) <MD 6:44-9> - Aug. 1692, Robert STANFORD who d. betw. 15 May 1721 - 7 Mar. 1721/2 (deeds) <MFIP #50>; they had one child. Robert was accused Mar. 1678/9 by Lydia HANMORE wf of Isacke of fathering her recently born child <MFIP #50>. Robert m.1st, 22 Jan. 1679, Marshfield, Mary (HOWLAND) Wil-liamson <Marshfield VR:16> who d. 26 Aug. 1690, Marshfield <Marshfield VR:17>. Mary HOWLAND m.1st, June 1653, Marshfield, Timothy WILLIAMSON <Marshfield VR:1> who was bur. 6 Aug. 1676, Marshfield <Marshfield VR:9>; they had 6 chil. <Marshfield VR:4 (2), 5 (1), 7 (2), 8 (1).)

9 SAMSON Children: (by 1st wf) <See TAG 28:1-11>

1. **David SAMSON**[3], b. c1686, prob. Duxbury, d. 10 May 1772, ae 85y3m or 87th yr, Duxbury, Dingley cem. <Duxbury VR; MD 11:57>; m. 5 June 1712, Marshfield, **Mary CHAFFIN/CHAPIN** <Marshfield VR: 37; MD 7:132,8:42; MSR:245>, (dau of Ebenezer CHAFFIN & Elizabeth ADAMS), b. 1 July 1694, Boston <Boston Rcd.Com.9:214>, d. 11 Nov. 1780, ae 87, Duxbury <Duxbury VR:411; MFIP #43 also attributes this death date to Mary, wf of Joshua SAMSON below>. <See MBD 2:250 & MD 31:116-17 for bth. 10 chil.> (See SAMSON Probate Appendix for will of David SAMSON.)

2. **Lora SAMSON**[3], b. (   ), prob. Duxbury, d. betw. 16 Dec. 1715 (bth. last ch.) - c1717 (hus. 2nd marr.); m. 3 Jan. 1705/6, Duxbury, **Benjamin SIMMONS**[4] <MD 9:108>, (son of John SIMMONS & Mercy PABODIE[3] (Elizabeth Alden[2]) - see ALDEN family), b. c1678, Duxbury, d. pre 2 May 1748, of Duxbury <MDP:12; Plymouth Co.PR 11:50 (adm.)>. <See MBD 1:15 & MD 12:162 for bth. 5 chil> (Benjamin m.2nd, c1717, prob. Duxbury, Priscilla DELANO[4], (dau of Samuel DELANO & Elizabeth STANDISH[3] (Alexander[2]) - see STANDISH family), b. c1686, Duxbury, d. 7 Feb. 1746/7, Duxbury <MD 12:32>; they had 5 chil. <MBD 1:15; MD 12:162>. Benjamin m.3rd, aft. Feb. 1746/7, Hannah (   ), who d. aft. 5 June 1749 <MDP:12; Plymouth Co.PR 11:206 (div.hus.est.).) Note: MBD 1:64 #40 (Bowman) states Lora was the dau. of "?Abraham SAMSON not Caleb". (See SAMSON Pro-bate Appendix for estate of Benjamin SIMMONS.)

3. **Joshua SAMSON**[3], b. (   ), prob. Duxbury, d. 4 Aug. 1741, Duxbury <MD 12:31>; m. 23 May 1724 Marshfield, **Mary OAKMAN** <Marshfield VR:144; MSR:246; Plymouth Co.Court Rcds.2:57 (Mar. 1724/5 Joshua & wf were fined for fornication>, b. (   ), d. aft. 2 Apr. 1753 (acc't of hus.est.) <MDP:388; Plymouth Co.PR #17580, 13:77; MFIP #39 & #43 attributes a death date of 11 Nov. 1780, ae 87 to this Mary as well as to Mary SAMSON the wf of Joshua's brother David above>. <See Duxbury VR & MD 11:238 for bth. 4 chil.>

4. **Sarah SAMSON**[3], b. (   ), d. aft. 14 July 1721, unm. <MD 8:31 (brother to maintain her for life)>.

5. **Caleb SAMSON**[3], b. (   ), prob. Duxbury, d. 17 Oct. 1750, Duxbury <MD 12:167>; m. 12 Feb. 1729/30, **Mehitable FORD** <Marshfield VR:146>, (dau of Michael FORD & Bethiah HATCH), b. 18 Sept. 1698, Marshfield <Marshfield VR:42; MD 8:177>, d. aft. 1 July 1751 (swore to hus.inv.) <Plymouth Co.PR #17467, 12:236>. <See MBD 2:249 & Duxbury VR for bth. 5 chil.; MD 12:124 (2), 125 (3).>

6. **Priscilla SAMSON**[3], b. c1697, d. 7 July 1758, ae 61, Duxbury, unm. <Duxbury VR>.

7. **Rachel SAMSON**[3], b. 5 Dec. (worn), Duxbury <MD 9:26; 11:122 (bpt. 20 Apr. 1701, Marshfield)>, d. aft. 3 Aug. 1761 (hus.pr.) <MDP:10>; m. 26 Mar. 1718, Duxbury, **Moses SIMMONS**[4] <MD 11:25>, (son of John SIMMONS & Mercy PABODIE[3] (Elizabeth Alden[2]) - see ALDEN family), b. cFeb. 1690/91, Duxbury <MD 9:26 (rec. as Feb. 1680)>, d. 21 June 1761, ae 70y4m, Duxbury <Duxbury VR:

417>. <See MBD 1:12 for bth. 10 chil; MD 12:121 (4), 122 (6).> (See SAMSON Probate Appendix
for will of Moses SIMMONS.)

8. **Ruth SAMSON**[3], b. c1702, prob. Duxbury, d. betw. c1742 (bth.last ch.) - 17 Apr. 1746 (hus.2nd
   marr.); m. 13 Oct. 1720, Marshfield, **John FULLERTON** <Marshfield VR:143>, (son of Alexander &
   Mary), b. 30 Sept. 1696, Boston <Boston Rcd.Com.9:226>, d. June 1780, Marshfield <MFIP #44>.
   (John m.2nd, 17 Apr. 1746, Marshfield, Rebecca DELANO <Marshfield VR:160>, (dau of Joseph &
   Hannah; poss. Joseph DELANO & Hannah (BARTLETT[5]) Arnold (Samuel[4], Benjamin[3], Mary Warren[2])
   (Hannah Pabodie[3], Elizabeth Alden[2]) (Sarah Brewster[3], Love[2]) - see ALDEN family), b. 17 Oct.
   172(0?), Duxbury <MD 12:165> & had 4 or more chil. <MFIP #44>.) <See MFIP #44 for 8 (poss.
   more) chil.; MD 9:185 (2), 186 (1), 30:153 (1), 154 (1), 155 (2); Marshfield VR:48 (2), 49
   (1), 86 (2), 87 (2); MQ 46:133 (poss. a 9th); for baptisms see MD 31:163 (1), 164 (1), 165
   (1), 168 (1), 170 (1), 32:14 (1), 16 (1).>

9. **Jerusha SAMSON**[3], b. c1705, prob. Duxbury, d. 2 June 1778, ae 73, Duxbury <Duxbury VR; MBD 2:
   397>; m. 8 Oct. 1730, Duxbury, **Ebenezer BARTLETT**[5] <MD 11:80>, (son of Ebenezer BARTLETT[4]
   (Benjamin[3], Mary Warren[2]) & Hannah (   ) - see WARREN family), b. c1694, Duxbury, d. 24 Oct
   1781, ae 87y4m, Duxbury <Duxbury VR:350; MBD 2:397>. (Ebenezer m.1st, 3 July 1718, Plymouth,
   Mary RIDER <MD 14:38>, (dau of Samuel[2-1]) b. 10 Oct. 1694, Plymouth <MD 1:210> & had 3 chil.
   <MD 13:115; Plymouth VR; MBD 2:397>.) <See MBD 2:397 & MD 11:237 for one child.>

SAMSON PROBATE APPENDIX

Will of **Thomas BONNEY**: (husbandman) <MDP:388-9; Plymouth Co.PR #2280, 7:156>
...9 July 1735, "aged & in daily expectation of dissolution by reason of many infirmities", ment.
dau Elisabeth NORCUTT wf of Ephraim; chil. of dau Mercy CURTIS (now wf of John) which she had by
her late husband Nathaniel DELANOE dec'd, viz: Nathaniel DELANOE, Mercy DELANOE, Lydia, Zerviah &
Mary; son in law Ephraim NORCUT. Wit. made oath 19 Aug. 1735.

Will of **Benjamin HILLMAN**: <Dukes Co.PR 3:178>
...26 Mar. 1745, ment. wf Susannah; eldest son Seth HILLMAN; youngest son James HILLMAN; sons
Benjamin HILLMAN, Henry HILLMAN, Silas HILLMAN; dau Hannah HATCH. Pr. 7 May 1745.

Estate of **William HOLMES**[3] **(Hannah Samson**[2]**)**: (husbandman) <MD 20:166-7; Plymouth Co.PR 15:577>
...1 Sept. 1760, Account, ment. shares to the following, viz: the widow; William HOLMES; Simeon
HOLMES; Hezekiah HOLMES; Joseph BARSE for his wife; Ephraim HOLMES for his wife; Zilpha HOLMES.

Will of **Bathsheba (STETSON) Holmes**: (widow) <MD 20:167-8; Plymouth Co.PR 10:436>
...25 Dec. 1762, ment. sons William HOLMES, Simeon HOLMES, Hezekiah HOLMES; chil. of dec'd dau
Lydia TILDEN; dau Hannah BEARS wf of Joseph; dau Zilpha HOLMES; dau Elizabeth HOLMES wf of son
William; dau Jane HOLMES wf of Capt. Ephraim. Pr. 4 Apr. 1763.

Will of **Francis MILLER**: (yeoman) <MD 25:102-3; Plymouth Co.PR 10:440>
...29 Oct. 1746, ment. wf Experience; brothers John MILLER, David MILLER, Elias MILLER. Pr. 6
Apr. 1747.

Will of **Thomas OLDHAM**: <MDP:393; Plymouth Co.PR #14876, 7:121>
...21 Feb. 1733, "being aged and weak",ment. sons Joshua OLDHAM, Thomas OLDHAM, Caleb OLDHAM;
daus Mercy, Mary, Elizabeth, Abigal, Ann, Desire & Grace. Wit. made oath 24 Jan. 1734.

Will of **John PLUMBLY**: <Worcester Co.PR #A47157>
...7 June 1740, ment. wf Dorcas; 6 unnamed married sisters; brothers Daniel PLUMBLY, Joseph PLUM-
BLY. Pr. 20 Aug. 1740.

Will of **Ebenezer RICHMOND**: <MD 21:187-89; Plymouth Co.PR>
...7 Apr. 1729, ment. wf Annah; eldest son Ebenezer RICHMOND; sons Roberd/Robert RICHMOND, Silvester RICHMOND; daus Annah RICHMOND, Rachel RICHMOND, Elizabeth WORSHBON/WASHBURN wf of Edward.
Agreement of heirs 12 May 1729.

Will of **Abraham SAMSON**: <MDP:441; Plymouth Co.PR #17434>
...22 May 1764, ment. wf Mary; children: Abraham SAMSON, Stephen SAMSON, Henry SAMSON, Hannah
HOLMES, Rebeckah BLACKMORE, Penelopy SAMSON; granddau. Rhoda CHANDLER wf of Thomas; chil. of
dec'd dau Ruth DELANO wf of Amaziah. Codicil, 30 May 1765 (regarding choice of exr.). Warrant to
appraise, 8 Mar. 1776.

Will of **Benjamin SAMSON**[3] **(Stephen**[2]**)**: (merchant) <MDP:397; Plymouth Co.PR #17457, 14:523-6>
...20 Feb. 1750/1, ment. wf Rebecca; minor grandson Micah SAMPSON; eldest son Cornelius SAMPSON;
son Benjamin SAMPSON; dau Deborah VEAZIE wf of Rev. Samuel. Pr. 14 Mar. 1759.

Will of **Rebecca (COOKE) Samson**: (widow) <MDP:397; Plymouth Co.PR #17631, 20:226>
...6 Jan. 1769, ment. son Cornelius SAMSON & wf Desire; son Benjamin SAMSON & wf Deborah; grandchildren Micha SAMSON, John VEAZIE, Samuel VEAZIE, Deborah VEAZIE, Rebecca VEAZIE. Pr. 15 May
1769.

Will of **David SAMSON**[3] **(Caleb**[2]**)**: (yeoman) <MDP:385; Plymouth Co.PR #17490, 21:164>
...26 Mar. 1767, ment. wf Mary; eldest son Charles SAMSON; son David SAMSON "who is labouring under bodily weakness & indisposition"; sons Ebenezer SAMSON, Jonathan SAMSON, Chaphen SAMSON,
David SAMSON; daus Lidia BOZWORTH wf of Nathaniel, Mary LITTLE wf of John, Mercy HUTCHINSON wf of
Timothy, Elizabeth PENEO/PINEO wf of Peter, Eleanor FARNUM wf of Joseph. Pr. 17 June 1772.
==
Will of **Henry SAMSON**[1]: <MD 2:142-3; Plymouth Col.Wills 4:2:94-5>
...24 10mth (Dec.) 1684, ment. sons Stephen SAMSON, John SAMSON, James SAMSON, Caleb SAMSON; daus
Elizabeth SPROUT wf of Roberd/Robert, Hannah HOLMES wf of Josias, unnamed dau the wf of John HAN-
MORE, Mary SUMMERS wf of John, Dorcas BONY wf of Thomas. Wit. made oath 5 Mar. 1684/5.
==
Will of **James SAMSON**[2]: (yeoman) <MD 6:184-6; Gen.Adv.4:84-5; Bristol Co.PR 3:447-8>
...10 Jan. 1715/6, "being well stricken in years", ment. wf Hannah; sons James SAMSON, Henry SAM-
SON, Joseph SAMSON; daus Anna, Penelopy, Susannah, Pricilla. Wit. made oath 7 July 1718.
==
Estate of **Joseph SAMSON/SAMPSON**[3] **(James**[2]**)**: <MDP:394; MD 23:176-81; Bristol Co.PR 11:393-4>
...5 May 1747, Division ordered (carried out 23 June 1747), to widow and following chil., viz:
Joseph SAMPSON, Ruhama SAMPSON, Sarah SAMPSON, Lois GRAY.
==
Estate of **Stephen SAMSON**[2]: <MD 6:119-20; Plymouth Co.PR 3:421>
...1716, Settlement, ment. widow; eldest sons Benjamin SAMSON & John SAMSON; children: Cornelius
SAMSON, Hannah, Mary, Elizabeth, Dorcass, Abigall. (undated, prob. 21-22 June 1716)
==
Estate of **Benjamin SIMMONS**: <MDP:12; Plymouth Co.PR 11:206>
...5 June 1749, Division, ment. widow Hannah; unnamed chil of dec'd eldest son Zachariah SIMMONS;
sons Aaron SIMMONS, Benjamin SIMMONS; daus Mercy SIMMONS, Content SIMMONS, Hannah RICHARDS wf of
William, Betty SIMMONS, Priscilla SIMMONS, Abiah SIMMONS.
==
Will of **Moses SIMMONS**: <MDP:10; Plymouth Co.PR #18376, 16:208-9>
...10 Apr. 1758,ment. wf Rachel; eldest son Ichabod SIMMONS; son William SIMMONS; daus Mercy SIM-
MONS wf of Nathaniel, Lydia DELANO wf of Judah, Deborah WESTON wf of Jacob and Anna. Codicil, 24
Feb. 1761. Pr. 3 Aug. 1761.
==
Will of **Shubael SMITH**: <Dukes Co.PR 5:50>
...10 Feb. 1734, ment wf Anne; son Shubael SMITH; daus Lydia SKIFF, Dorcas BURGES, Abigail GIBBS;
great-granddau. Mercy, the granddau. of dec'd dau Mercy NEWCOMB & William NEWCOMB; two unnamed
granddaus, the daus of dau "JENNINGS". Pr. 7 May 1734.
==
Will of **Lt. Ebenezer SPROUT**[3] **(Elizabeth Samson**[2]**)**: (gent.) <MD 25:127-8; Plymouth Co.PR>
...8 Sept. 1726, ment. eldest son Ebenezer SPROUT (under 21); son James SPROUT (under 21); daus
Thankfull BENNET, Abigall SPROUT (under 18) and Mary SPROUT (under 18); brother James SPROUT; wf
Experience. Wit. made oath 7 Nov. 1726.
==
Will of **Robert SPROUT**: <MD 6:8-11; Plymouth Co.PR 3:222-4>
...23 Nov. 1711, ment. daus Mercy OLDHAM, Anna RICHMOND, Hannah CANE/KEEN, Elisabeth SPROUT, Mary
SPROUT; sons James SPROUT, Ebenezar SPROUT; unnamed wife. Pr. 11 Dec. 1712.
==
Will of **Jonathan THAYER**: (physician) <MDP:399; Suffolk Co.PR #8751>
...31 Mar. 1747, ment. wf Elizabeth; sons Curnelues/Cornelius THAYER, Ezra THAYER, Micah THAYER;
daus Sarah THAYER, Hopstill THAYER and Elizabeth THAYER (under 14). Pr. letter 11 May 1747.
==
Will of **Samuel THAYER**: <MDP:399; Worcester PR #A:58793, 8:425>
...17 Oct. 1761, ment. wf Mary; dau Abigail PARTRIDGE; son Samuel THAYER; four unnamed chil. of
dec'd dau Zilpah HOLBROOK (when they reach 21); dau Thankfull HOLBROOK; granddau. Olive FARNUM
(under 18); dau Susanna THAYER; son Stephen THAYER; dec'd father Thomas THAYER; dau Mary THAYER
to be provided for; granddau. Fern THAYER (under 18). Pr. 20 Aug. 1764.

NOTES:

GEORGE SOULE

George SOULE was born c1595-1600, probably in England although his origins are unknown. He died between 20 Sept. 1677 (codicil) and 22 Jan. 1679/80 (inv.), Duxbury <MD 2:81-4>. The 1627 Cattle Division shows him with wife Mary and a child <MD 1:152>, so he probably married c1624-25. His wife is thought to be Marie/Mary Bucket/Becket who is listed in the 1623 Land Division <PCR 12:4-6>. Mary's origins are also unknown, she died Dec. 1676, Duxbury <MD 2:81,84>. (See SOULE Probate Appendix for will of George SOULE.)

(See also: Mayflower Families in Progress, George Soule of the Mayflower and His Descendants for Four Generations, rev. by Robert S. Wakefield, FASG, 1992 (note that this is a revision of Mayflower Families Through Five Generations (MF5G), George Soule, Vol. 3, pub. 1980); TG 1:225-48, Mayflower Families: A Critical Examination; NGSQ 69:59-60 (Review of Mayflower Families, Vol.3 with errors and corrections.)

George & Mary had 9 children: (order uncertain as are approx. yrs. of bth.; the span of 6 years betw. 1st and 2nd indicates one or more chil. should be moved up)

I.   Zachariah, b. pre 22 May 1627 (Cattle Division).
II.   John, b. c1632 (ae about 74 in 1705/6)
III.   Nathaniel, b. c1637
IV.   George, b. c1639 (ae about 34 in 1673)
V.   Susanna, b. c1642
VI.   Mary, b. c1644
VII.   Elizabeth, b. c1645
VIII. Patience, b. c1648
IX.   Benjamin, b. c1651, d. 26 Mar. 1676, Pawtucket RI (King Phillip's War) <MFIP #1>

* * * * * * * * * * * * * * *

I. **ZACHARIAH SOULE[2]**, b. c1625-26 (pre 22 May 1627) <MD 1:152,5:110>, d. pre 11 Dec. 1663, Duxbury <MD 5:110 (inv.)>; m. (   ), **Margaret** (   ) who d. aft. 2 Mar. 1663/4 <MD 5:110 (adm hus.est.)>. MFIP #1 and Stratton:293 both suggest she was the dau. of William FORD Sr.; the 12 Sept. 1676 will of William Ford mentions (among others) dau Margaret and her unnamed husband <Plymouth Col.PR 3:2:22>. Since Zachariah had been dead for 13 years, this is either the wrong Margaret, or she remarried. No known issue.

II. **JOHN SOULE[2]**, b. c1632, Plymouth (ae about 74 in deposition dated 8 Mar. 1705/6) <MD 5:46>, d. betw. 11 July 1701 (ack.deed) <MD 8:186> - 14 Nov. 1707, Duxbury (adm.) <MD 4:159>; m.1st, c1654, prob. Duxbury, **Rebecca SIMMONS** <MD 19:96 (On 30 Dec. 1674, Moses SIMMONS "in Consideration of a Marriage heretofore Consumated between John Soule...and my eldest Daughter Rebeckah" deeded land to John Soule.)>. **John** m.2nd, c1678, prob. Duxbury, **Hester/Esther (   ) SAMPSON** <MBD 2:303-4, #31; TAG 15:165-7; originally thought to have been a dau of Samuel NASH (MM:263, MD 25:72, etc.) proof has not been found>, b. c6 Mar. 1640 (based on dth), d. 12 Sept. 1735, ae 95y6m6d, Duxbury, Centre St. cem. <MD 10:169>. (Esther m.1st, Samuel SAMPSON & had 2 chil.) <Note: MBD 2:310, under MD 19:96 should read John Soule[2] not Soule[3].> (See SOULE Probate Appendix for estate of John SOULE.)

  12 SOULE Children: (9 by 1st, 3 by 2nd; see MD 8:184-6 for deeds to sons)

1. **Rebecca SOULE[3]**, b. c1656/7, Duxbury, d. 18 Nov. 1732, 76th yr, Plympton g.s. <MD 1:245,11:195,23:20>; m. 13 Dec. 1688, Plymouth, **Edmond WESTON** <MD 13:204,24:19>, (son of Edmund), b. c1660/1, Duxbury, d. 23 Sept. 1727, 67th yr, Plympton g.s. <MD 1:178,11:194,23:20>. <For bth 6 chil. see MBD 2:293, MD 3:166, 23:19; MD 2:80 (5), Plympton VR (1).> (See SOULE Probate Appendix for estate of Edmund WESTON.)

2. **James SOULE[3]**, b. 4 Oct. 1659, Duxbury <   >, d. 27 Aug. 1744, 85th yr, Middleboro, The Green cem. <MD 16:18,23:49; Wood:167 (error, says Thomas)>; m. 14 Dec. 1693, Duxbury, **Lydia TOMSON[3]** <MD 26:37; PN&Q 3:121>, (dau of John TOMSON & Mary COOKE[2] - see COOKE family). On 9 Oct. 1690 James received a fine & imprisonment by the Council of War at Plymouth for refusing to serve on the Canadian expedition <PCR 6:238> (smart move considering the heavy losses which incl. his brother Zachariah). <See MD 2:41 and Middleboro VR 1:5 for bth. 5 chil.> (See SOULE Probate Appendix for will of James SOULE.)

3. **Sarah SOULE[3]**, b. c1660, Duxbury, d. betw. 16 Mar. 1690/1, Plymouth (deed) <MD 11:242,244; MDP:160> - c1699 (hus.2nd marr.); m. pre 1680, Duxbury or Plymouth, **Adam WRIGHT[3]** <MD 11:242>, (son of Richard WRIGHT & Hester COOKE[2] - see COOKE family).

4. **Rachel SOULE[3]**, b. c1662, Duxbury, d. 18 Sept. 1727, 65th yr, Middleboro, The Green cem. <MD

12:144; Wood:39>; m. 5 or 7 Sept. 1688, Plymouth, **John COBB** <MD 2:43 & 13:204 (7th); Middleboro VR 1:7 (5th); MD 24:35>, (son of John COBB & Martha NELSON), b. 24 Aug. 1662, Plymouth <PCR 8:23; MD 1:141>, d. 8 Oct. 1727, 66th yr, Middleboro, The Green cem. <MD 12:144; Wood: 39>. <See MBD 2:291 & MD 2:42 for bth. 5 chil.; Middleboro VR 1:5 (3), 6 (2).> (See SOULE Probate Appendix for will of John COBB.)

5. **Aaron SOULE**[3], b. c1664, Duxbury, d. aft. 23 Mar. 1752, of Pembroke <MDP:411,412; Plymouth Co. Deeds 43:249,51:156>; m. c1697-8, poss. Duxbury, **Mary WADSWORTH** <MD 9:248,11:39 (1st ch.b. 1699)>, (dau of John WADSWORTH & Abigail ANDREWS), b. 18 Dec. 1668, Duxbury <Duxbury VR; MD 9:172,248>, d. 9 May 1741, 73rd yr, Pembroke g.s. <Pembroke VR; MD 9:248>. <See MBD 2:273 for 4 chil.; MD 11:39 (bpt.1st ch.).>

6. **Benjamin SOULE**[3], b. c1665/6, Duxbury, d. 1 Dec. 1729, 64th yr, Plympton g.s. <MD 11:162>; m. c1694, prob. Plymouth, **Sarah STANDISH**[3] <MM:264; MD 4:113 (bth.1st ch.)>, (dau of Alexander STANDISH[2] & Sarah ALDEN[2] - see STANDISH family). <See MBD 2:275 & MD 25:72-3 for bth. 6 chil and MD 4:113 (5), 5:182 (1); see MD 15:193-4 for children's deed.> (See SOULE Probate Appendix for will of Benjamin SOULE.)

7. **Moses SOULE**[3], b. c1669, Duxbury, d. betw. 9 May 1748 (list of Proprietors) <MD 18:233> - 25 Jan. 1748/9, Duxbury (adm.) <MD 18:233>; m.1st, c1700/01, Duxbury, **Mercy SOUTHWORTH**[4] <MM:269> (dau of Edward SOUTHWORTH & Mary PABODIE[3] (Elizabeth Alden[2]) - see ALDEN family) <MD 18:246>, b. c1675-80, d. betw. 11 June 1719 (fath.will) <MD 18:246> - 15 Jan. 1729/30, prob. Duxbury (hus.2nd marr.) <MD 11:240>. **Moses** m.2nd, 15 Jan. 1729/30, Duxbury, **Sarah CHANDLER** <Duxbury VR; MD 11:240>, b. (   ), d. (   ).; <MF5G 3:16 gives a dth. date of 28 Apr. 1737, Yarmouth ME g.s. (with no source); MFIP #15 does not.> <See MBD 2:288-9 for 9 chil. by 1st wf; MD 12:164 (1).> (See SOULE Probate Appendix for estate of Moses SOUL/SOULE.)

8. **Zachariah SOULE**[3], b. pre 1670, Duxbury, d. pre 16 Mar. 1690/1 (inv.) <MD 8:186; MDP:411; Plymouth Co.PR 1:87 (inv. ment. wages due for the "Canada Expedition" where he prob. died c1690, see under his brother James.)>.

9. **John SOULE**[3], b. c1675, Duxbury, d. 19 May 1743, 69th yr, Middleboro, The Green cem. <MD 14:134; Wood:168>; m. 8 Dec. 1701, Middleboro, **Martha TINKHAM**[4] <Middleboro VR 1:1; MD 1:220; Plymouth Co.Quarter Sessions, 1687-1721, p.197 (3d Tues. June 1702, John & Martha were fined "being Convict upon Confession", apparently because their first ch. was born 4 mths after marriage)>, (dau of Ephraim TINKHAM[3] (Mary Brown[2]) & Esther WRIGHT[3] (Hester Cooke[2]) - see BROWN & COOKE families), b. c1678, d. 16 Feb. 1758, 80th yr, Middleboro, The Green cem. <MD 14:134; Wood:168>. <See MBD 2:282 for bth. 9 chil.; Middleboro VR 1:8 (4), 10 (1), 13 (2), 15 (1), 19 (1); MD 2:105 (4), 107 (1), 201 (2), 3:84 (1), 233 (1).> (See SOULE Probate Appendix for wills of John & Martha SOULE Sr.)

10. **Joseph SOULE**[3], b. 31 July 1679 (twin), Duxbury <   >, d. 11 July 1763, ae 83y11m10d, Duxbury, Centre St. cem. <Duxbury VR; MD 10:169 (ae 84 wanting 20 days)>; m. c1710/11, Duxbury, **Mary PETERSON**[3] <MM:267>, (see under Mary SOULE[2]). <See MBD 2:283 for bth. 5 chil.; MD 11:235 (4), 236 (1).> (See SOULE Probate Appendix for will of Joseph SOULE.)

11. **Josiah SOULE**[3], b. 31 July 1679 (twin), Duxbury <   >, d. 25 Jan. 1764, ae 84y6m, Duxbury, Centre St. cem. <Duxbury VR; MD 10:170 (85th yr)>; m. 25 May 1704, Duxbury, **Lydia DELANO** <MD 9:109>, (dau of John DELANO & Mary WESTON), b. cMar. 1679/80, prob. Duxbury, d. 23 or 24 Nov. 1763, ae 83y8m, Duxbury, Centre St. cem. <Duxbury VR (23rd); MD 10:170 (24th)>. <See MBD 2:286 & MD 11:25 for bth. 6 chil.> (See SOULE Probate Appendix for will of Josiah SOUL/SOULE.)

12. **Joshua SOULE**[3], b. 12 Oct. 1681, Duxbury <MD 11:235>, d. 29 May 1767, ae 85y7m6d, Duxbury, Centre St. cem. <Duxbury VR; MD 10:170,11:133>; m. 15 Feb. 1704/5, Duxbury, **Joanna STUDLEY** <MD 9:108>, b. (   ), d. pre 8 May 1767 (hus.will) <MDP:418>. <See MBD 2:283 & Duxbury VR for bth. 9 chil.; MD 11:235 (6), 236 (1), 237 (2).> (See SOULE Probate Appendix for will of Joshua SOULE.)

III **NATHANIEL SOULE**[2], b. c1637, prob. Plymouth, d. pre 12 Oct. 1699, Dartmouth (inv.) <MD 7:74>; m. (   ), **Rose (   )**, b. (   ), d. aft. 15 May 1702 (div.hus.est.) <MD 7:75; Bristol Co PR 2:56>. On 4 Mar. 1673/4, Nathaniel was charged with adultry with an Indian woman and they were both sentenced to be whipped on 1 Mar. 1674/5; he was also ordered to pay 10 bushels of corn towards the support of the child <PCR 5:163>. (Bowman notes (MD 7:72) the curious coincidence of the name Rose and naming a son Myles, but admits he had been unable to find a connection between Rose and the Standish family.) (See SOULE Probate Appendix for estate of Nathaniel SOULE.)

4 SOULE Children:

1. **Nathaniel SOULE**[3], b. 12 Jan. 1681, Dartmouth <Dartmouth VR 1:55>, d. betw. 12 Mar. 1764 - 26 May 1766, Dartmouth (will & warrant to appraise) <MDP:429; NEHGR 129:32>; m.1st, 20 July 1708, Dartmouth, **Meribah GIFFORD** <Dartmouth VR 1:55; MSR:146; NEHGR 129:32>, (dau of Christopher GIFFORD & Deborah PERRY), b. 31 Oct. 1687, Sandwich <MD 29:33; NEHGR 129:32>, d. c1732 Dartmouth <NEHGR 129:32>. **Nathaniel** m.2nd, 13 Feb. 1732/3, Dartmouth, **Hannah MACOMBER** <Dart-

mouth VR 2:303>, (dau of William MACOMBER[2-1] & Elizabeth RANDALL), b. 8 Nov. 1703, Dartmouth
<MSR:142; MBD 2:297>, d. pre 17 July 1759, Dartmouth <MBD 2:297, MFIP #20 (reason for date?)>
<See MBD 2:297 for 4 chil. by 1st wf; Dartmouth VR 1:55 (2); see MBD 2:197 for 1 ch. by 2nd.>
(See SOULE Probate Appendix for will of Capt. Nathaniel SOULE.)

2. **Sylvanus SOULE[3]**, b. c1684, Dartmouth, d. aft. 27 May 1749 (mother-in-law's will) <Bristol Co.
PR 17:535-6; MF5G 3:20 says aft. 9 June 1754, prob. Tiverton RI - no reason given>; m. c1705,
poss. Swansea, **Sarah SLADE** <MM:272>, (dau of William SLADE & Sarah HOLMES), b. 1 June 1687,
Swansea <Swansea VR; TG 1:239>, d. aft. 27 May 1749 (mother's will) <Bristol Co.PR 17:535-6>.
<See MFIP #21 for 5 poss. chil.; see also TG 1:229,250 #22.>

3. **Jacob SOULE[3]**, b. c1687, Dartmouth, d. betw. 12 Aug. 1747 (will) - 2 Mar. 1747/8 (inv.), prob.
Dartmouth <MDP:429; NEHGR 129:222 says cFeb. 1747/8>; m. 22 Jan. 1709/10, Dartmouth, **Rebecca
GIFFORD** <Dartmouth VR; NEHGR 129:222>, (dau of Robert GIFFORD & Sarah WING), b. c1689 <NEHGR
129:222>, d. pre 12 Aug. 1747 (hus.will) <MDP:429>. <See MBD 2:297, Dartmouth VR & MSR:159
for bth. 8 chil.> (See SOULE Probate Appendix for will of Jacob SOULE.)

4. **Myles SOULE[3]**, b. c1690, Dartmouth, d. aft. 27 Feb. 1719/20, prob. unm. <Bristol Co.Deeds 31:
188 (on this date his brothers mention their past & continuing care of Myles, "an idiot"; he
prob. d. pre 6 June 1740 when the brothers ack. the deed)>.

IV GEORGE SOULE[2], b. c1639, prob. Duxbury <MBD 2:269; Newport Court Files 1:16 (ae about 34 on 10
Apr. 1673)>, d. betw. 25 Mar. 1697 (will) - 17 May 1704, Dartmouth (inv.) <MD 7:210; MSR:145
("George Soule, d. May 12 (   )" - 1704?)>; m. (   ), **Deborah (   )**, b. (   ), d. betw.
24 Jan. 1708/9 (will) - 1 Mar. 1709/10 (pr.) <MD 7:210,217>. (See SOULE Probate Appendix for
wills of George & Deborah SOULE.)

8 SOULE Children:

1. **George SOULE[3]**, b. pre 1665 (if at least 21 when a freemen 24 Mar. 1686) <MFIP #23>, d. pre 25
Mar. 1697, prob. Dartmouth (fath.will) <MD 7:211-2,216>; m. c1694, Dartmouth, (   ).
<See Dartmouth VR, MD 7:216 & MSR:151 for bth. 1 ch.>

2. **William SOULE[3]**, b. pre 1671, Dartmouth, d. betw. 6 Oct. 1722 <MDP:409; Bristol Co.Deeds 15:
14> - 25 Apr. 1723, Dartmouth (inv.) <MDP:409; Bristol Co.PR 4:180>; m. c1691, prob. Dartmouth, **Hannah (   )** <MFIP #24>, b. (   ), d. betw. 3 Apr. 1729 - 1 July 1734, Dartmouth
<MFIP #24 (no reason given for dates)>. <For bth. 11 chil. see MBD 2:271, Dartmouth VR and
MSR:158-9,161; NEHGR 34:198 (6), 34:406 (4), 35:33 (1).> (See SOULE Probate Appendix for estate of William SOULE.)

3. **John SOULE[3]**, b. c1671-75, Dartmouth, d. 11 May 1704, Dartmouth <Dartmouth VR; MSR:145>.

4. **Nathan SOULE[3]**, b. c1675-80, Dartmouth, d. 10 Sept. 1736, Dartmouth <MBD 2:269; NEHGR 129:222>
m. 12 June 1704, Dartmouth, **Mary GIFFORD** <Dartmouth VR; NEHGR 129:222>, (poss. dau of Robert
GIFFORD & Sarah WING), b. c1683, prob. Dartmouth <NEHGR 129:222>, d. betw. 7-13 Jan. 1772,
Dartmouth (will & exr.declined) <MDP:408; Bristol Co.PR 22:99,105>. <See MBD 2:271 & Dartmouth VR for bth. 6 chil.> (See SOULE Probate Appendix for wills of Nathan & Mary SOULE.)

5. **Deborah SOULE[3]**, b. aft. 1679 (under 18 in fath.will), Dartmouth, d. betw. 25 Mar. 1697 (fath.
will) - 24 Jan. 1708/9 (moth.will).

6. **Mary SOULE[3]**, b. aft. 1679 (under 18 in fath.will), Dartmouth, d. aft. 10 May 1732 <MDP:409;
Bristol Co.Deeds 23:214 (aft. 6 Mar. 1732/3 if she ack.)>; m. c1700, prob. Dartmouth, **Joseph
DAVOL/DAVIL/DEVOL/DEVIL,** (son of Jonathan DEVOL & Hannah AUDLEY), b. (   ), Dartmouth or
Newport RI <MFIP #26>, d. pre 14 Nov. 1726, Dartmouth (adm.) <MDP:407; Bristol Co.PR 5:323>.
<See MFIP #26 for bth. 7 chil.; MSR:152 (4).>

7. **Lydia SOULE[3]**, b. aft. 1679 (under 18 in fath.will), Dartmouth, d. aft. June 1720, prob. Little Compton RI (bth.last ch.); m. c1704, (   ), **William BROWNELL**, (son of William BROWNELL
& Sarah SMITON), b. 11 Aug. 1682, Little Compton RI <MFIP #27>, d. (   ), prob. Little Compton RI. <See MBD 2:270-1 for bth. 7 chil.; Dartmouth VR 1:241 (6).>

8. **Sarah SOULE[3]**, b. aft. 1679 (under 18 in fath.will), Dartmouth, d. aft. 9 Nov. 1768, prob.
Dartmouth (will of nephew John Soule) <Bristol Co.PR 22:5>; m. 19 Apr. 1726, Dartmouth, **John
TIBBETTS** <Dartmouth VR>, (son of Henry TIBBETTS & Sarah STANTON), b. (   ), E. Greenwich,
RI <MFIP #28>, d. 19 Apr. 1755, Carteret co. NC <MFIP #28>. (John m.1st, 7 June 1705, Kings-
town RI, Elizabeth HALL and had 7 chil. <MFIP #28>.) (See SOULE Probate Appendix for will of
John TIBBETTS.)

V. SUSANNA SOULE[2], b. c1642, prob. Duxbury, d. aft. Sept. 1684, prob. Kingstown RI (bth.twins)
<RI VR (N.Kingstown)>; m. prob. c1660, (   ), **Francis WEST/WAST** <MD 26:1>, b. prob. England
<MD 26:10 "came from Europe">, d. aft. 6 Sept. 1687 (Kingstown RI tax list) <NEHGR 35:125-6>.
<See MD 26:1-11 for Samuel West's Memmorandum Book.>

9 WEST Children: <MD 26:10; MBD 2:299; MFIP #5>

1. **Francis WEST[3]**, b. c1662, poss. Duxbury, d. pre 13 Oct. 1724, N. Kingstown RI <Kingstown RI PR
    6:160,162>; m. 12 May 1699, E. Greenwich RI, **Sarah (   )** <TG 1:233; MFIP #29>, b. (   ),
    d. (   ), prob. N. Kingstown RI. <See MFIP #29 for 7 chil.> (See SOULE Probate Appendix
    for will of Francis WEST.)

2. **Richard WEST/WAST/WASTE[3]**, b. c1664, poss. Duxbury, d. pre 1 Apr. 1728 (adm.) <Plymouth Co.PR
    5:319,370>; m.1st, 26 Oct. 1693, Duxbury, **Mary SAMSON** <Duxbury VR; MD 26:37; PN&Q 3:121>,
    (poss. dau of Abraham) <TAG 63:207-10>, b. (   ), d. pre Oct. 1706 (hus.2nd marr.). **Richard**
    m.2nd, 21 Oct. 1706, Plymouth, **Elizabeth CONNADAY/CANEDY** <MD 14:34>,(dau of Alexander CANNEDY
    & Elizabeth LISNOR), b. 6 Aug. 1682, Plymouth <MD 1:208>, d. 7 Feb. 1750, 68th yr, Taunton
    g.s. <Taunton VR>. (Elizabeth m.2nd, 16 Sept. 1730, Middleboro, Benjamin LEONARD <Middleboro
    VR 1:47; MD 9:46; Gen.Adv.1:4>, (son of Benjamin LEONARD & Sarah THRASHER), b. 25 June 1689,
    Taunton <MSR:639>.) <See MFIP #30 for 1 ch.>

3. **Peter WEST[3]**, b. c1688/9, N. Kingstown RI.

4. **John WEST[3]**, b. c1672, N. Kingstown RI.

5. **Susanna WEST[3]**, b. c1674, N. Kingstown RI, d. betw. 21 Sept. 1755 (will) - 4 Apr. 1758 (pr.)
    <Charlestown RI PR 1:292>; m. 24 Mar. 1691/2, Kingstown RI, **Moses BARBER** <TAG 52:101-2>, b.
    c1652 <MFIP #31 (ae 70 & upwards in deposition dated 17 Mar. 1722)>, d. betw. 15 Apr. 1728
    <Westerly RI Deeds 4:267> - 13 Dec. 1733 (pr.) <Kingstown RI PR (1723-35) 2:238>. (Moses had
    3 chil. by a 1st wf <MFIP #31>.) <For 14 chil., see MBD 2:300-301 and VR RI (N. & S. Kings-
    town) 5:1:57.> (See SOULE Probate Appendix for wills of Moses & Susanna BARBER.)

6. **Martha WEST[3]**, b. c1676, N. Kingstown RI, d. 2 Dec. 1764, 88th yr, N. Kingstown RI g.s. <MFIP
    #32>; m.1st, 4 Mar. 1702/3, N. Kingstown RI, **James CARD** <VR RI (N. Kingstown) 1:44>, (son of
    Richard & Rebecca), b. c1650, Newport RI <MFIP #32>, d. pre Mar. 1704/5 (adm.) <N. Kingstown
    RI PR 5:52; MDP:432>. (James had 2 chil. by a 1st wf <MFIP #32>.) **Martha** m.2nd, 9 Nov. 1710
    Jamestown RI, **Jeremiah FONES** <VR RI (Jamestown) 4:5:8 (Martha's maiden name is not stated)>,
    b. c1664, d. 29 Apr. 1747, 84th yr, N. Kingstown RI g.s. <MFIP #32>. (Jeremiah m.1st, 30 May
    1694, Jamestown RI, Elizabeth (   ) & had poss. 5 chil. <MFIP #32; MBD 2:300,309 #188; VR
    RI (Jamestown) 4:5:21>.) <See MBD 2:309 #188 for discussion of Martha's 1741 testimony in
    which she states she was a widow living with her brother Francis West in <u>1711</u>.> <See MFIP #32
    MBD 2:300 & VR RI (N. Kingstown) 5:1:62 for 2 chil. by 1st hus.; see MFIP #32, MBD 2:300,309
    #188 for poss. 6 chil. by 2nd hus.> (See SOULE Probate Appendix for will of Jeremiah FONES.)

7. **William WEST[3]**, b. 31 May 1681, N. Kingstown RI <N. Kingstown RI VR 1:30>, d. aft. July 1742
    <Charlestown RI Town Rec.Book (1738)>; m.1st, c1709, (   ), **Abiah SPRAGUE** <MFIP #33>, (dau
    of William SPRAGUE & Deborah LANE), b. 27 Jan. 1688/9, Hingham <Lincoln 3:165>, d. pre Apr.
    1721 (fath.will) <Providence RI PR 2:158>. **William** m.2nd, pre 1723, (   ), **Jane TANNER**
    <MD 26:10>, (dau of Francis TANNER & (   ) BABCOCK) <MD 26:10>, b. (   ), d. aft. 1741 if
    she is the unnamed wf ment. in Charlestown RI Town Rec.Book. <See MFIP #33 for 4 chil. by
    1st wf; see MFIP #33, MBD 2:309 #191 for 8 chil. by 2nd wf.>

8. **Thomas WEST[3]**, b. 18 Sept. 1684, N. Kingstown RI <VR RI (N. Kingstown) 1:1:110>, d. (   );
    m. 20 Sept. 1716, New Shoreham RI, **Dorcas RATHBORN** <VR RI (New Shoreham)>, (dau of William &
    Sarah), b. 14 Jan. 1695, New Shoreham RI <TG 1:239; VR RI (New Shoreham)>, d. aft. 18 Sept.
    1727 (fath.will) <Westerly RI PR 2/3:233>. <See VR RI (New Shoreham) & TG 1:239 for 2 chil.>

9. **Clement WEST[3]**, b. 18 Sept. 1684, N. Kingstown RI <N.Kingstown RI VR 1:30; although the date
    is the same as brother Thomas, they are not entered together as twins in the records>, d. aft
    5 Jan. 1746/7 (ack.deed) <MFIP #35>; m. c1725, (   ), **Sarah (   )** <MFIP #35>, b. (   ),
    d. aft. 23 July 1745 (bth.last ch.) <MFIP #35 (aft. 5 Jan. 1746/7 if she ack. deed)>. <For
    bth. 9 chil. see MBD 2:300, VR RI (Charlestown) 5:5:28.>

VI **MARY SOULE[2]**, b. c1644, prob. Duxbury <PCR 2:27 (in Jan. 1652 she was "placed" with John WIN-
    SLOW for 7 years)>, d. aft. 29 Apr. 1718 (hus.will); m. c1666, prob. Duxbury, **John PETERSON**
    <MM:271>, b. c1636, d. betw. 29 Apr. 1718 (will) - 16 Mar. 1719/20 (inv) <MDP:426-7; Plymouth
    Co.PR #15782, 4:232>.

9 PETERSON Children:

1. **John PETERSON[3]**, b. (   ), prob. Duxbury, d. pre 29 Mar. 1690, unm. (inv.) <Gen.Adv.1:114;
    Plymouth Co.PR #15781, 1:62>.

2. **Joseph PETERSON[3]**, b. (   ), prob. Duxbury, d. pre 1 Apr. 1751, prob. Duxbury (adm.) <MDP:
    428; Plymouth Co.PR 12:86>; m. 23 Aug. 1704, Plymouth, **Sarah (JONES[4]) Doty** <MD 14:35>, (dau
    of Joseph JONES & Patience LITTLE[3] (Anna Warren[2]) - see WARREN family), b. 12 Sept. 1671,
    Hingham <Lincoln 2:387-8>, d. aft. 10 July 1752 (acc't of hus.est.) <MDP:428; Plymouth Co.PR
    12:86,226>. (Sarah m.1st, 22 Nov. 1694, Plymouth, John DOTY[2] <MD 1:206,26:37; PN&Q 3:121> -
    see DOTY family.) <See MFIP #36 for 2 chil.>

3. **Benjamin PETERSON**[3], b. Sept. 1669, prob. Duxbury (based on dth), d. 11 Feb. 1760, ae 90y5m, Duxbury <Winsor:289>; m. 9 Feb. 1698/9, Duxbury, **Hannah WADSWORTH** <MD 9:108,248>, (dau of John WADSWORTH & Abigail ANDREWS) <MD 9:248>, b. (   ), d. 7 Feb. 1732/3, Duxbury <Duxbury VR:166; MD 12:32 ("night following the 6th day")>. <See MFIP #37 for 7 chil.; MBD 2:296 (1); MD 8:233 (1).>

4. **Martha PETERSON**[3], b. c1672, prob. Duxbury, d . aft. 29 Apr. 1718 (fath.will).

5. **Jonathan PETERSON**[3], b. c1674, prob. Duxbury, d. betw. 20 Feb. 1744/5 - 24 May 1745 (will & pr.), prob. Pembroke <MDP:427; Plymouth Co.PR #15783, 9:509>; m. c1700, poss. Duxbury <MD 9:249 (aft. 23 Apr. 1700, her fath.will)>, **Lydia WADSWORTH** <MD 9:249>, (dau of John WADSWORTH & Abigail ANDREWS), b. c13 Feb. 1678/9 (based on dth), d. 26 May 1756, ae 77y3m3d, S. Duxbury g.s. <Duxbury VR; MD 9:161,250>. <See MFIP #38 for 6 chil.; MBD 2:296 (5); MD 8:233 & 9:250 (4).> (See SOULE Probate Appendix for will of Jonathan PETERSON.)

6. **David PETERSON**[3], b. 1 Oct. 1676, prob. Duxbury (based on dth), d. 30 Sept. 1760, ae 84 wanting a day, S. Duxbury g.s., unm. <MD 9:161>. (See SOULE Probate Appendix for will.)

7. **Isaac PETERSON**[3], b. c1678, prob. Duxbury, d. pre 27 Jan. 1741/2 (adm.) <MDP:427>; m. 28 Mar. 1711 or 10 Sept. 1712, Hingham, **Mary HOBART** <Lincoln 2:337>, (dau of Daniel HOBART & Elizabeth WARREN), b. 19 Aug. 1686, Hingham <Lincoln 2:337; Savage 2:433>, d. 22 Mar. 1763, 74th yr, S. Duxbury g.s. <MD 9:161>. <See MFIP #39 for 4 chil.> (See SOULE Probate Appendix for estate of Isaac PETERSON.)

8. **Mary PETERSON**[3], b. c1680, prob. Duxbury, d. pre 16 Jan. 1755, prob. Duxbury (hus.will) <MDP:418>; m. c1710/1, Duxbury, **Joseph SOULE**[3] (See p.99).

9. **Rebecca PETERSON**[3], b. c1682, prob. Duxbury, d. 4 Apr. 1761, 79th yr, Plympton g.s. <Plympton VR; MD 11:195>; m. 1 Oct. 1717, Duxbury, **John WESTON** <Duxbury VR; MQ 46:57>, (son of Edmund), b. c1662, d. pre 18 Nov. 1736, Duxbury (adm.) <MQ 46:57; Plymouth Co.PR 7:238,255-6>. (John m.1st, c1695-7, Deborah DELANO[3] (Rebecca Alden[2]) & had 6 chil. <MQ 46:58>; see ALDEN family.) <See MFIP #40 & TG 1:231 for 1 child.>

VII **ELIZABETH SOULE**[2], b. c1645, prob. Duxbury (if at least 18 in 1663), d. (   ), poss. Middleboro. On 3 Mar. 1662/3 she and Nathaniel CHURCH were fined for fornication <PCR 4:34>; she sued him for failure to marry her and won partial judgement in Oct. 1663 <PCR 7:111-12>. Elizabeth was before the court again on 2 July 1667 when she was sentenced to be whipped for fornication <PCR 4:162>. She m. betw. this date and 23 July 1668 <MDP:406; MD 27:39-40; Plymouth Co.Deeds 3:126 (called Elizabeth Walker in deed from father)>, **Francis WALKER**, b. (   ) d. betw. 10 May 1698 - 30 Oct. 1701, prob. Middleboro <MQ 50:35-36>. <See MQ 50:31-40, Elizabeth Soule, Wife of Francis Walker And Their Posterity.> <Note: MDP:406, bottom of page - the last line is missing, it should read "land in Middleboro of his honoured father, Francis Walker".>

1 WALKER Child:

1. **Isaac WALKER**[3], b. 1660's, prob. Plymouth Col. (if he was the reason for his mother's 2nd court appearance, he may have been born cDec. 1667 - Jan. 1667/8) <MQ 50:37>, d. aft. 31 May 1705, of Swansea <MDP:407; Plymouth Co.Deeds 12:17>; m. 8 July 1692, Woodbridge NJ, **Desire SHELLEY** <MFIP #41; MQ 50:36>, b. (   ), d. (   ). <See MFIP #41 for 1 child.>

VIII **PATIENCE SOULE**[2], b. c1648, prob. Duxbury, d. 11 Mar. 1705/6, Middleboro <MD 2:160; Wood:82>; m. Jan. 1666, Middleboro, **John HASKELL** <MD 1:219,27:39>, (son of Roger HASKELL & Elizabeth HARDY), b. c1640, Salem <MFIP #8>, d. 15 May 1706, 67th yr, Middleboro <MD 2:159; Wood:82>. (What a land deal - On 29 Sept. 1721, John exchanged his 100 acres in Middleboro for 500 acres in Killingly CT <MDP:430>.)

8 HASKELL Children: <MBD 2:297; MD 1:222; see MDP:430 for deeds which identify chil.>

1. **John HASKELL**[3], b. 11 June 1670, Middleboro <MD 1:222>, d. 17 Feb. 1728, Killingly CT <MFIP #42>; m. 2 Mar. 1699/1700, Middleboro, **Mary SQUIRE** <Middleboro VR 1:1; MD 1:220>, (dau of John SQUIRE & Sarah FRANCIS), b. 18 Oct. 1681, Cambridge <MBD 2:298; NEHGR 87:153-6>, d. aft. 25 Feb. 1724/5, prob. Killingly CT <MFIP #42>. <For 12 chil. see Middleboro VR 1:4 (2), 8 (2), 9 (1), 10 (1), 14 (1), 15 (2), 17 (1), Killingly CT VR 1:28 (1), 29 (1); for 10 chil. see MD 1:224 (2), 2:104 (2), 107 (2), 3:84 (2), 86 (2).>

2. **Elizabeth HASKELL**[3], b. 2 July 1672, Middleboro <MD 1:222>, d. aft. 1717 (2nd marr.); m.1st, c1699, poss. Middleboro, **Thomas DRINKWATER** <MM:272; MFIP #43>, b. (   ), England, d. betw. 10 Sept. 1711 <MDP:430; Plymouth Co.Deeds 11:77> - 25 June 1715 (adm.), Taunton or Dighton <MFIP #43; see MDP:431 for deed of heirs>. **Elizabeth** m.2nd, 2 May 1717, Dighton, **John DUDLEY** <Dighton VR>. <See MFIP #43, MBD 2:298 for 8 chil.>

3. **William HASKELL**[3], b. 11 June 1674, Middleboro <MD 1:222>, d. aft. 27 May 1740, of Middleboro (ack.deed) <Plymouth Co.Deeds 33:145>.

4. **Patience HASKELL**[3], b. 1 Feb. 1679, Middleboro <MD 1:222>, d. 14 Feb. 1705/6, 27th yr, unm., Middleboro <MD 2:160; Wood:82>.

5. **Bethiah HASKELL**[3], b. 15 Jan. 1681, Middleboro <MD 1:222>, d. aft. Mar. 1738/9 <Plymouth Co. Court Rec.5:187,6:154>; m.1st, 10 May 1715, Dighton, **Richard WESTCOTT/WASCOTT** <Dighton VR 1:31>, b. (   ), poss. Middleboro, d. (   ). **Bethiah** m.2nd, 29 Aug. 1727, Rochester, **Thomas CHILDS/CHILES** <Rochester VR>, b. (   ), d. pre Mar. 1738/9 (wf is called widow). <For bth. 1 child see MD 8:28 & Middleboro VR 1:42.> (Is she the Bethiah Haskell who recorded the birth of son William Sherman, 5 Apr. 1710? <Rochester VR>.)

6. **Mary HASKELL**[3], b. 4 July 1684, Middleboro <MD 1:222>, d. aft. May 1706 (the court record cited under sister Bethiah above states that when their parents died all the children were living except Patience. Proof has not yet been found to show she was the Mary Haskell who m. 17 Apr. 1706, Rochester, Scotto/Scottoway Clark; see TAG 57:77-81.

7. **Josiah HASKELL**[3], b. 18 June 1686, Middleboro <MD 1:222>, d. (   ), prob. Freetown; m.1st, 26 Mar. 1718, Middleboro, **Sarah CANNEDY/KANADY** <Middleboro VR 1:25; MD 4:71>, (dau of Alexander CANNEDY & Elizabeth LISNOR), b. 11 Nov. 1693, Plymouth <MD 1:209>, d. betw. June 1726 (bth.last ch.) - Mar. 1729 (hus.2nd marr.). **Josiah** m.2nd, 27 Mar. 1729, Middleboro, **Sarah BRAYLEY** <Middleboro VR 1:31; MD 5:39; Gen.Adv.1:3>, (dau of Roger & Alice), b. 25 Mar. 1707, Portsmouth RI <VR RI (Portsmouth)>, d. (   ). <For 5 chil. by 1st wf see MBD 2:298-9, MD 7:240, Middleboro VR 1:39; for 4 chil. by 2nd wf see MFIP #45, MD 8:29 (1).>

8. **Susanna HASKELL**[3], b. 15 Jan. 1690/1, Middleboro <MD 2:43>, d. betw. 11 Oct. 1723 (bth.last ch.) - 29 Aug. 1731, Freetown (hus.2nd marr.); m. 21 Feb. 1711/2, Taunton, **Thomas PAIN/PAINE** <MSR:632; MM:272>, (son of Ralph & Dorothy), b. (   ), d. betw. 27 Oct. 1752 (will) - 6 Nov. 1759 (pr.) <Bristol Co.PR 16:420; MDP:431, Bristol Co.Deeds 43:555 (betw. 14 Jan. 1754 - 23 Apr. 1759 if he is the Thomas Pain who sold to Job Pain and ack.)> (Thomas m.2nd, 19 Aug. 1731, Freetown, Annable CANNEDY <Gen.Adv.4:35; Freetown VR; NEHGR 15:235>, (dau of Alexander CANNEDY & Elizabeth LISNOR), b. 8 May 1698, Plymouth <MD 1:209>, d. aft. 27 Oct. 1752 (hus. will).) <See SOULE Probate Appendix for will of Thomas PAIN/PAINE.>

SOULE PROBATE APPENDIX

Will of **Moses BARBER Sr.**: <Kingstown RI PR (1723-35) 2:238>
...29 Mar. 1728, ment. wf Susannah; sons William BARBER, Moses BARBER, Samuel BARBER, Thomas BARBER, Joseph BARBER, Benjamin BARBER, Ezekiel BARBER, Daniel BARBER; youngest dau Ann BARBER; heirs of dec'd dau Lydia MOWRY; unnamed married daus. Pr. 13 Dec. 1733.

Will of **Susannah (WEST**[3]**) Barber (Susanna Soule**[2]**)**: (widow) <Charlestown RI PR 1:292>
...21 Sept. 1755, ment. daus Dinah WILCOCKS, Susanna PERRY (widow), Martha PARKER, Ruth BENTLEY, Marcy TIFT, Ann KENYON; son Benjamin BARBER. Pr. 4 Apr. 1758.
===

Will of **John COB/COBB Sr.**: <MD 24:35-7; Plymouth Co.PR>
...29 May 1727, ment. wf Rachell; son John COB & his two sons Gershom COB & John COB; son James COB; daus Martha SIMONS, Patience TINKHAM, Rachell STANDISH. Codicil, 28 Sept. 1727, ment. his wife's decease "the other day"; daus Martha, Patience & Rachell; son James; "my sons". Wit. sworn 16 Nov. 1727.
===

Will of **Jeremiah FONES**: <MDP:432; N. Kingstown RI PR 8:156>
...12 Dec. 1727, ment (worn) FONES the dau of son (worn) when she come to the age of 18; sons Joseph FONES, John FONES; grandson John DAVIS (under 21) the son of dec'd dau Margaret DAVIS; son Daniel FONES (under 21); sons Samuel FONES, Thomas FONES. Wit. sworn 13 July 1747.
===

Will of **Thomas PAIN/PAINE**: (husbandman) <MDP:431; MD 37:84; Bristol Co.PR 16:420,422>
...27 Oct. 1752, ment. wf Annable; sons Ralph PAIN, Job PAIN, Charles PAIN, Peter PAIN; daus Mary FARROW, Betty WINSLOW, Patience WINSLOW, Thankfull PAIN. Pr. 6 Nov. 1759.
===

Will of **David PETERSON**[3] **(Mary Soule**[2]**)**: <MDP:427; Plymouth Co.PR #15748, 16:45,46>
...7 July 1760, ment. sister Rebecca WESTON; kinsman Jonathan PETERSON & his son David PETERSON; the following are ment. with no relationship stated: Hannah SOULE, Rebecca SOULE, Priscilla WESTON wf of Eliphas, Faith DREW wf of Samuel, Jael PETERSON, John PETERSON, Jonathan PETERSON Jr., Turner PETERSON. Pr. 2 Mar. 1761.
===

Estate of **Isaac PETERSON**[3] **(Mary Soule**[2]**)**: (yeoman) <MDP:427; Plymouth Co.PR #15774, 9:519>
...4 Apr. 1744, Division of real estate to widow Mary and chil., viz: Joel PETERSON, Faith and Priscilla; granddaus. Mary PETERSON & Orphan PETERSON, daus of son Daniel PETERSON.
===

Will of **John PETERSON**: <MDP:426-7; Plymouth Co.PR 4:232>
...29 Apr. 1718, "of old age", ment. wf Mary and chil., viz: Joseph PETERSON (eldest son), Jona-

than PETERSON, David PETERSON, Isaac PETERSON, Martha PETERSON, Mary SOULE wf of Joseph, Rebecca
WESTON wf of John, Benjamin PETERSON. Inv. taken 16 Mar. 1719/20.

Will of **Jonathan PETERSON**[3] **(Mary Soule**[2]): (Practitioner) <MDP:427; Plymouth Co.PR #15783, 9:409>
...20 Feb. 1744/5, ment. wf Lydia; eldest son John PETERSON; sons Jonathan PETERSON, Ruben PETER-
SON; daus Hopestill DELANO, Lydia SOUL. Pr. 24 May 1745.

Will of **Benjamin SOULE**[3] **(John**[2]): (yeoman) <MD 25:72-86; Plymouth Co.PR 5:617>
...2 Nov. 1729, ment. wf Sarah; son Zachariah SOLE; dau Hannah SAMSON wf of George; sons Benjamin
SOLE, Ebenezer SOLE. Wit. sworn 12 Dec. 1729.

Will of **George SOULE Sr.**[1]: <MD 2:81-4; Plymouth Col.Wills 4:1:50>
...11 Aug. 1677, ment. sons Nathaniel SOULE, Gorge/George SOULE; daus Elizabeth, Patience, Susa-
nah, Mary; "and forasmuch as my Eldest son John SOULE and his family hath in my extreame old age
and weaknes bin tender and carefull of mee and very healpfull to mee..." Codicil, 20 Sept. 1677,
concerning son John and dau Patience. Inv. taken 22 Jan. 1679.

Will of **George SOULE**[2]: <MD 7:210-17; Bristol Co.PR 2:93>
...25 Mar. 1697, ment. sons William SOULE (eldest), John SOULE, Nathan SOULE; daus Deborah SOULE,
Mary SOULE, Lydia SOULE & Sarah SOULE (all under 18); wf Deborah. Inv. taken 17 May 1704. (On 5
Aug. 1719, Mary COGGESHALL wf of Joshua and dau of George SOULE[3], the son of George[2], petitioned
that her father had deceased before her grandfather's will and as his heir, neither she nor her
father had received anything in the will; her petition was dismissed <2:586>.)

Will of **Deborah (   ) SOULE**: (widow) <MD 7:217-20; Bristol Co.PR 2:275>
...24 Jan. 1708/9, ment. dau Sarah SOULE; sons William SOULE, Nathan SOULE; daus Mary DIVEL, Lediah BROWNIELL; Mary SOULE dau of dec'd son George SOULE. Pr. 1 Mar. 1709/10.

Will of **Jacob SOULE**[3] **(Nathaniel**[2]): (yeoman) <MDP:429; Bristol Co.PR 11:451>
...12 Aug. 1747, ment. sons Stephen SOULE, Joseph SOULE, Nathaniel SOULE, Benjamin SOULE; daus
Elizabeth TRIP, Rosamond POTTER; grandchildren Phebe WAIT, Jeremiah WAIT. Inv. taken 2 Mar.
1747/8.

Will of **James SOULE**[3] **(John**[2]): <MD 23:49-54; Plymouth Co.PR 9:341>
...30 Nov. 1736, ment. wf Lydia; dau Martha FAUNCE wf of Joseph & her 5 chil.; dau Rebecca SOULE;
son Jacob SOULE. Codicil, 22 Aug. 1744 states wf & son Jacob are dec'd and ment. Jacob's unnamed
widow & chil. Pr. 20 Sept. 1744.

Estate of **John SOULE**[2]: <MD 4:159-161; Plymouth Co.PR 2:91>
...5 Mar. 1707, Settlement, ment. unnamed sons (who have already received their portions); chil.
of dec'd dau Sarah WRIGHT wf of Adam; daus Rachel COB wf of John and Rebecka WESTON wf of Edmund.

Will of **John SOUL/SOULE Sr.**[3] **(John**[2]): <MDP:417; MD 19:137-8; Plymouth Co.PR #18813, 9:84>
...1 Mar. 1743, ment. wf Martha and following chil., viz: John SOUL, James SOUL, Martha TOMSON,
Sarah SNOW, Ester/Esther SOUL, Mary SAMSON, Rebecca SOUL, Rachel SOUL. Pr. 6 June 1743.

Will of **Martha (TINKHAM) SOUL/SOULE**: (widow) <MDP:417; MD 19:138-9; Plymouth Co.PR #18836, 15:29>
...19 Nov. 1751, ment. heirs of son John SOUL; son James SOUL; heirs of dec'd dau Sarah SNOW;
daus Easter/Esther SOUL, Rebeccah SOUL, Martha THOMSON, Mary SAMSON, Rachal VAUGHAN. Bond 1 May
1758.

Will of **Joseph SOULE**[3] **(John**[2]): (yeoman) <MDP:418; MD 11:108-11; Plymouth Co.PR #18819, 16:483>
...16 Jan. 1755, "by reason of old age", ment. unnamed chil. of dec'd dau Mary CUSHMAN wf of
Joshua; grandson Joseph CUSHMAN son of Joshua; dec'd dau Alethea CUSHMAN wf of Allerton & her
chil.; daus Hannah SOULE, Rebeccah SOULE. Pr. 1 Aug. 1763.

Will of **Joshua SOULE**[3] **(John**[2]): (yeoman) <MDP:418; MD 11:133-7; Plymouth Co.PR #18822, 20:73>
...8 May 1767, ment. sons Ezekiel SOULE, Joseph SOULE, Nathan SOULE; grandson Samuel SOULE; daus
Zurviah SAMSON wf of Ebenezer, Abigail DREW wf of Perez, Sarah BISBEE wf of Aaron; granddau.
Lidia SIMMONS wf of Jedediah. Pr. 20 Oct. 1767.

Will of **Josiah SOUL/SOULE**[3] **(John**[2]): (yeoman) <MD 11:107-8; Plymouth Co.PR 19:56>
...5 Nov. 1762, ment. wf Lidia; sons Jonathan SOUL (eldest), Abisha SOUL, Micha SOUL, Nathaniel
SOUL (youngest); daus Mary SOUL (eldest), Lidia SIMMONS (youngest) wf of Ichabod. Pr. 14 Feb 1764

Estate of **Moses SOUL/SOULE**[3] **(John**[2]): (yeoman) <MD 18:233-41; Plymouth Co.PR 11:505-11>
...23 Aug. 1749, Division of real estate, among following chil., viz: Isaac SOUL (eldest son),
Cornelius SOUL, Barnabes SOUL, Abigal SOUL the only dau of son Ichabod SOUL, Gideon SOULE, Jedediah SOUL, Ruth SOULE, Else PERRY wf of Barnabas, Deborah HUNT wf of John.

Will of **Nathan SOULE**[3] **(George**[2]): <MDP:408; Bristol Co.PR 8:416>
...15 Nov. 1735, ment. wf Mary; eldest son John SOULE; youngest son Timothy SOULE; son George
SOULE; dec'd father George SOULE; son Cornelius SOULE; daus Content & Mary. Appraisers sworn 13
Oct. 1736.

Will of **Mary (GIFFORD) Soule**: (widow) <MDP:408; Bristol Co.PR 22:99,105>

...7 Jan. 1772, ment. "grandson otherwise called my great-grandson, Nathan DAVIS son of Job DAVIS"; sons George SOULE, Cornelius SOULE (& his wf Sarah); grandson Joseph SOULE son of dec'd son Timothy SOULE; grandson Abner SOULE son of son Cornelius; granddau. Ellefell TABER dau of son Cornelius; granddaus. Margret DAVEL, Content SHELDON; granddaus Alice SOULE & Anne SOULE, daus of son George; grandson Joseph DAVIS (under 21), son of dec'd dau Mary DAVIS; son in law Joseph DAVIS. 13 Jan. 1772 one of exrs. declined.

===

Estate of **Nathaniel SOULE²**: <MD 7:72-6; Bristol Co.PR 2:56>
...15 May 1702, Division of personal estate, ment. widow Rose; Nathaniel SOUL (eldest son), Silvanus SOUL (2nd son), Jacob SOUL (3rd son), Miles SOUL (4th son).

===

Will of **Capt. Nathaniel SOULE³ (Nathaniel²)**: <MDP:429; Bristol Co.PR 19:417>
...12 Mar. 1764, ment. youngest son Wesson SOULE; son Henry SOULE & his wf Barbrey & their son Nathaniel SOULE; grandson Henry SOULE; son James SOULE & his wf Mary; grandson James SOULE, son of son Wesson; ment. what Wesson's mother (his wife) brought when he married her; son Jonathan SOULE. Warrant to appraise, 26 May 1766.

===

Estate of **William SOULE³ (George²)**: <MDP:409; Bristol Co.PR 4:180-3>
...26 Mar. 1725, Division of real estate among widow Hannah and following chil., viz: eldest son William SOLE, 2d son George SOLE, 3d son Benjamin SOLE, 4th son Joseph SOLE, 5th son Samuel SOLE 6th son Jonathan SOLE, eldest dau Hannah HOLLEY wf of Joseph, 2d dau Mary PAGE wf of William, 3d dau Sarah HOWLAND wf of Samuel, dau Allis SOLE, youngest dau Deborah SOLE.

===

Will of **John TIBBITTS**: <MFIP #28; N. Carolina Hist. & Gen. Reg. 1:496>
...4 Apr. 1755, ment. wf Sarah; sons Henry TIBBITTS, George TIBBITTS; daus Mary HOPKINS, Aves SOLE, Ann BALA, Alse HILL. Pr. June 1755.

===

Will of **Francis WEST/WAST³ (Susanna Soule²)**: <MDP:432; N. Kingstown RI PR 6:160,162>
...(date is worn), ment. wf Sarah; 2 eldest sons Peter WAST (under twenty---) & (worn); eldest daus Susannah WAST, Sarah WAST, Mary WAST (all under 18). Wit. sworn 13 Oct. 172(4).

===

Estate of **Edmund WESTON**: <MD 24:19-24; Plymouth Co.PR 5:350>
...6 Nov. 1727, Settlement, ment. widow Rebeckah and chil.: Nathan WESTON, Zachariah WESTON, John WESTON, Edmund WESTON, Benjamin WESTON, Rebeckah DARLING wf of Thomas.

NOTES:

MYLES STANDISH

Myles STANDISH was born poss. c1584, prob. Isle of Man, England. In his will he mentions lands in England which has resulted in much research carried out in an attempt to locate his origins. (see reference list below). It is also interesting to note that the will of his son Alexander mentions searches made in old England to recover the family lands. Capt. Standish died 3 Oct. 1656, Duxbury <MD 3:153>. His burial site was exhumed in 1890 and found to contain the remains of an older well built man with red & gray hair, two young women (one under 18) and two boys, aged about five and nine <MQ 36:58>. His will requested that he be buried near his daughter Lora and daughter in law Mary, the two boys are probably his sons Charles and John who died young. Myles first wife, Rose, origins unknown, died 29 Jan. 1620/1, Plymouth <MD 30:3>. He married 2nd, betw. July 1623 (when she arrived) - 24 Mar. 1623/4 (land division), Plymouth, Barbara (   ), origins unknown who d. aft. 6 Oct. 1659 when she was mentioned in the inventory of Elizabeth Hopkins <MD 4:119>. (See STANDISH Probate Appendix for will of Capt. Myles STANDISH.)

(See also: Mayflower Families In Progress, Myles Standish Of The Mayflower and His Descendants for Five Generations (MFIP), by Russell L. Warner, ed. by Robert S. Wakefield, FASG, 2nd ed., 1992; Pilgrim Myles Standish: First Manx American, by G.V.C. Young, 1984; MQ 52:109-14, Standish Lands in England; NEHGR 87:149, The Children and Grandchildren of Capt. Myles Standish; NEHGR 68:339, Some Recent Investigations Concerning the Ancestry of Capt. Myles Standish.)

Myles & Barbara had 7 children: <3 chil. by 22 May 1627 Cattle Division; MBD 2:311>

I.   Charles, b. c1624, Plymouth, d.y. betw. 22 May 1627 - c1634 (How do we know there were two sons named Charles? The Cattle Division, which appears to list children in order of birth, lists sons Charles, Alexander & John, yet in his will Myles states Alexander is the eldest with Charles named last, indicating he was the youngest. Bradford wrote in 1650/1 that "4 sons are living & some are dead".)
II.   Alexander, b. c1625, Plymouth
III.   John, b. c1626, Plymouth, d.y. aft. 22 May 1627
IV.   Myles, b. c1628, Plymouth
V.   Lora, b. c1630, Plymouth or Duxbury (her order of birth unknown), d. pre 7 Mar. 1655/6 (fath.will) and prob. pre 1650/1 as Bradford does not ment. any daughters; prob. pre 1648 if she is the young woman under 18 found in the burial site.
VI.   Josiah, b. c1632, Plymouth or Duxbury
VII.   Charles, b. c1634, Plymouth or Duxbury, d. aft. 7 Mar. 1655/6 (fath.will).

* * * * * * * * * * * * * * *

II. **ALEXANDER STANDISH[2]**, b. c1625, Plymouth, d. 6 July 1702, ae about 76, Duxbury <MD 12:99>; m. 1st, aft. 7 Mar. 1655/6 (he is single in fath.will), **Sarah ALDEN[2]** <MD 12:99>, (dau of John ALDEN & Priscilla MULLINS); see ALDEN family. **Alexander** m.2nd, c1688, poss. Duxbury, **Desire (DOTY[2])(Sherman) Holmes** <MD 12:99>, (dau of Edward DOTY & Faith CLARK); see DOTY family. (See STANDISH Probate Appendix for will of Alexander STANDISH.)

11 STANDISH Children: <MBD 2:311; 8 by 1st wf, 3 by 2nd; order unknown>

1. **Lora/Lorah STANDISH[3]**, b. (   ), prob. Duxbury, d. aft. 2 Aug. 1725 (hus.will) <Plymouth Co.PR 5:477-80>; m. c1680, (   ), **Abraham SAMSON** <MD 12:101,177; MQ 52:146>, (son of Abraham SAMSON & (   ) NASH, b. c1658 <MFIP #5>, d. betw. 2 Aug. 1725 - 4 Sept. 1727 (will & pr.), prob. Duxbury <Plymouth Co.PR 5:477-80>. <See MBD 2:318 for 7 chil.> (See STANDISH Probate Appendix for will of Abraham SAMSON.)

2. **Lydia STANDISH[3]**, b. (   ), prob. Duxbury, d. aft. 30 Apr. 1734 <MD 23:161 (est. of son Josiah); is she ment. in 1748 will or est. of son Isaac?>; m. betw. 26 Oct. 1686 <Plymouth Col.Court Rec.1:189 (fined for "comitting carnall copilation")> - Apr. 1688 (bth.1st ch.) <MD 3:122>, Duxbury or Plymouth, **Isaac SAMSON** <MD 12:101,177,23:161>, (son of Abraham SAMSON & (   ) NASH), b. c1660/1 <MFIP #6>, d. 3 Sept. 1726, 66th yr, Plympton g.s. <MD 11:118,23:161>. See MD 23:161-4 for estate. <See MBD 2:320 for bth. 8 chil.; Plymouth VR; MD 3:122 (5), 123 (3 - incl. twins).>

3. **Mercy STANDISH[3]**, b. (   ), prob. Duxbury, d. (   ) <MFIP (Standish) #8 and (Samson) #9 state she d. aft. 17 May 1722 with no supporting evidence. On 14 Jul 1721, Caleb deeded to their son David the 80 acre homestead where he (Caleb) was living. As wife Mercy did not release dower, consent or ack. the deed, I assume she was dec'd <MD 8:31-2>.>; m. c1684, **Caleb SAMSON[2]** - see SAMSON family.

4. **Elizabeth STANDISH[3]**, b. (   ), prob. Duxbury, d. aft. 1731 <Plymouth Co.Deeds 29:28>; m. c1683, (   ), **Samuel DELANO** <MD 12:101,184>, (son of Philip DELANO & Mary PONTUS), b. c1659, d. pre 9 Aug. 1728, Duxbury (inv.) <Plymouth Co.PR #6318, 5:424>. <See MBD 2:317, 326 for 9 chil.> (See STANDISH Probate Appendix for estate of Samuel DELANO.)

5. **Myles STANDISH[3]**, b. (   ), prob. Duxbury, d. 15 Sept. 1739, Duxbury <MD 12:31,23:133,29:178>; m. pre 5 July 1702 (his fath.codicil), (   ), **Experience SHERMAN[3]** <MD 23:133>, (dau of William SHERMAN & Desire DOTY[2]), see DOTY family. <See MBD 2:322, MD 9:232, Duxbury VR for bth. 5 chil.> (See STANDISH Probate Appendix for will of Myles STANDISH.)

6. **Sarah STANDISH[3]**, b. c1666/7, prob. Duxbury, d. 4 Mar. 1740, 74th yr, Plympton g.s. <Plympton VR; MD 25:73>; m. c1693, (   ), **Benjamin SOULE[3]** <MD 12:177,25:72>, (son of John SOULE & Rebecca SIMMONS), see SOULE family.

7. **Ebenezer STANDISH[3]**, b. c1672, prob. Duxbury, d. 19 Mar. 1755, 83rd yr, Plympton g.s. <MD 5:184,11:163>; m. c1697, (   ), **Hannah STURTEVANT** <MFIP #11>, (dau of Samuel[2-1] & Mercy), b. c1679/80, d. 23 Jan. 1759, 80th yr, Plympton g.s. <MD 5:184,11:163>. <See MBD 2:311 & Plympton VR for bth. 6 chil.; MD 5:183 (1), 184 (5).>

8. **David STANDISH[3]**, b. (   ), prob. Duxbury, d. pre 14 Feb. 1689 (inquest) <Plymouth Col. Court Rec. 1:191>.

9. **Desire STANDISH[3]**, b. 5 May 1689, Marshfield <Marshfield VR:38; MD 7:134>, d. 20 June 1766, 77th yr, Plympton g.s. <Plympton VR; MD 11:194>; m. 21 Feb. 1715, Plympton, **Nathan WESTON[4]** <Plympton VR; MD 2:236,15:187>, (son of Edmund WESTON & Rebecca SOULE[3] (John[2]) - see SOULE family), b. 8 Feb. 1688/9, Plymouth <MD 2:80>, d. 11 Oct. 1754, 66th yr, Plympton g.s. <Plympton VR; MD 11:195>. <See MBD 2:311 & Plympton VR for bth. 4 chil.; MD 1:245 (2), 246 (2).>

10. **Thomas STANDISH[3]**, b. 29 Jan. 1690/1, Marshfield <Marshfield VR:38; MD 7:134>, d. aft. 13 June 1774 (ack.deed) <MDP:446; Plymouth Co.Deeds 58:73>; m. 20 Jan. 1717/8, Marshfield, **Mary CARVER** <Marshfield VR:40; MD 7:132,8:43; MSR:245 (says 30th)>, (dau of William CARVER & Elizabeth FOSTER), b. 20 Mar. 1695, Marshfield <Marshfield VR:21>, d. aft. 5 Apr. 1742 (fath. will) <MFIP #13 says aft. 25 Dec. 1769 with no supporting evidence>. <See MBD 2:323-4 & Pembroke VR for bth. 7 chil. (note the 8 yr gap betw. 4th & 5th ch.).>

11. **Ichabod STANDISH[3]**, b. 10 June 1693, Marshfield <Marshfield VR:38; MD 7:134>, d. 29 Feb. 1772, 79th yr, Halifax g.s. <MD 3:158,13:219>; m. 26 Nov. 1719, Plympton, **Phebe RING[4]** <MD 3:91>, (dau of Eleazer RING[3] (Deborah Hopkins[2]) & Mary SHAW), b. 26 Jan. 1691, Plymouth <MD 1:208>, d. 15 May 1756, 65th yr, Halifax g.s. <MD 13:219>. <See MBD 2:317-18 for bth. 4 chil; Middleboro VR 1:23 (1), 37 (1), 41 (1), 42 (1); MD 6:228 (1), 8:28 (1), 4:69 (1), 7:242 (1).> (See STANDISH Probate Appendix for will of Ichabod STANDISH.)

IV **MYLES STANDISH[2]**, b. c1628, Plymouth, d. aft. 20 Mar. 1661 <MD 21:3, Plymouth Co.Deeds 3:22-3 (on this date he gave Edward Gray his power of attorney to sell land); MD 20:1 (sailed for England a few months after marriage and was not heard of again); MFIP #3, Mass.Archives 60:125 (aft. 19 Aug. 1661 bond for delivery made to England)>; m. 19 July 1660, Boston, **Sarah WINSLOW[3]** <Boston Rcd.Com.9:76; MD 21:1>, (dau of John WINSLOW & Mary CHILTON) - see CHILTON family. No known issue.

VI **JOSIAH STANDISH[2]**, b. c1632, Plymouth or Duxbury, d. 19 Mar. 1690, Preston CT <Preston CT Deeds 3:48 (dth. date given in sons' deed)>; m.1st 19 Dec. 1654, Marshfield, **Mary DINGLEY** <Marshfield VR:1; MSR:242>, (dau of John), b. (   ), d. 1 July 1655, Marshfield, bur. Duxbury <Marshfield VR:2; MD 2:5; MSR:248 (error, says 1665)>. **Josiah** m.2nd, aft. 7 Mar. 1655/6 (fath.will), (   ), **Sarah ALLEN** <MD 3:153-5>, (dau of Samuel & Ann), b. 30 Mar. 1639, Braintree <MFIP #4>, d. aft. 16 Sept. 1690 (hus.adm.) <MFIP #4>.

8 STANDISH Children: (by 2nd wf) <MFIP #4>

1. **Mary STANDISH[3]**, b. c1660, Duxbury, d. aft. 16 Apr. 1731 (deed) <MFIP #4>; m. 4 Jan. 1681, Bridgewater, **James CARY** <MD 2:90 (wife's name not given); NEHGR 21:225-8 says the marriage rcd. gives the wife's name as Mary SHAW>, (son of John CARY & Elizabeth GODFREY), b. 28 Mar. 1652, Braintree <MD 2:91>, d. 20 Nov. 1706, Bridgewater <MD 14:45>. <See MD 14:45 for bth. 6 chil.; MD 2:90 (1).> (See STANDISH Probate Appendix for will of James CARY.)

2. **Martha STANDISH[3]**, b. (   ), prob. Duxbury, d. betw. 22 June 1730 - 16 Apr. 1731, unm. (deed) <MFIP #4>.

3. **Myles STANDISH[3]**, b. (   ), prob. Duxbury, d. pre 9 Apr. 1728, Preston CT (adm.) <MDP:447; New London CT PR 3:79>; m.1st, 5 Dec. 1700, Bristol MA/RI, **Mehitabel (CARY) Adams** <RI VR (Bristol)>, (dau of John CARY & Elizabeth GODFREY), b. 24 Dec. 1670, Bridgewater <Bridgewater VR; MD 2:90>, d. pre 8 July 1724 (hus.2nd marr.). **Myles** m.2nd, 8 July 1724, Lebanon CT, **Elizabeth (THATCHER) Fuller** <Lebanon CT VR 1:279>, b. (   ), d. aft. 8 May 1729 <MDP:447; Mansfield CT Deeds 2:394>. No known issue. (Elizabeth m.1st, 3 Oct. 1700, Mansfield CT, Samuel FULLER <Mansfield CT VR:D24> & had 7 chil. <Mansfield CT VR D82-3>.)

4. **Josiah STANDISH[3]**, b. (   ), prob. Duxbury, d. 26 Mar. 1753, Stafford CT <Stafford CT VR 1:

45,2:168>; m. (   ), **Sarah (   )** <MD 2:90 (poss. the Sarah CARY, b. 2 Aug. 1667, Bridge-
gewater, dau of John CARY & Elizabeth GODFREY)>, d. 16 June 1741, Stafford CT <Stafford CT VR
1:45,2:168>. <See MBD 2:324-5 for 7 chil.>

5. **Israel STANDISH[3]**, b. (   ), prob. Duxbury, d. pre 26 Jan. 1729/30, prob. Preston CT <Pres-
    ton CT Deeds 4:657>; m. 8 Feb. 1703/4, Preston CT, **Elizabeth RICHARDS** <Preston CT VR 1:29>,
    (dau of William RICHARDS & Mary WILLIAMS) <MFIP #19>, b. (   ), d. prob. pre 26 Jan. 1729/
    30 <Preston CT Deeds 4:657>. <See Preston CT VR 1:29 for bth. 4 chil.>

6. **Lois STANDISH[3]**, b. (   ), prob. Duxbury, d. aft. 16 Apr. 1731 (deed) <MFIP #4>; m.1st, 29
    Nov. 1706, Norwich CT, **Hugh CALKINS** <Norwich CT VR 1:46>, (son of John CALKINS & Sarah ROYCE)
    b. June 1659, New London CT <MFIP #20>, d. 15 Sept. 1722, 63rd yr, Norwich CT <Norwich CT VR
    1:46>. (Hugh m.1st, May 1689, Norwich, Sarah SLUMAN & had 6 chil. <MFIP #20>.) **Lois** m.2nd,
    21 Mar. 1726, Lebanon CT, **John SPRAGUE** <Lebanon CT VR 1:280 (she is called Lois Abel>, (son
    of John SPRAGUE & Ruth BASSETT), b. (   ), prob. Duxbury, d. 6 Mar. 1728, Lebanon CT <MFIP
    #20>. (John m.1st, Lydia (   ) & had 2 sons <MFIP #20>.) No known issue.

7. **Samuel STANDISH[3]**, b. c1680, prob. Duxbury, d. pre 4 Aug. 1753, prob. Preston CT <Norwich Co.
    Deeds 12:436-7>; m.1st, 1 June 1709, Preston CT, **Deborah GATES** <Preston CT VR 1:74>, (dau of
    Thomas GATES & Elizabeth FREEMAN), b. 22 Feb. 1683, Stow <Stow VR>, d. pre 15 Jan. 1745 (hus.
    2nd marr.). **Samuel** m.2nd, 15 Jan. 1745, Preston CT, **Hannah (WITTER) Parks** <Preston CT VR 1:
    74>, (dau of Josiah WITTER & Elizabeth WHEELER), b. 17 Mar. 1681, Stonington CT <MFIP #18>,
    d. 25 Nov. 1757, Preston CT <Preston CT VR 1:74>. (Hannah m.1st, 15 Nov. 1703, Preston CT,
    Thomas PARKS <Preston CT VR 1:71> & had 4 chil.) <See Preston CT VR 1:74 for bth. 7 chil. by
    1st wife.>

8. **Mercy STANDISH[3]**, b. (   ), prob. Duxbury, d. 4 Nov. 1748, prob. Salisbury CT <MFIP #21>; m.
    30 Sept. 1726, Windham CT, **Ralph WHEELOCK** <Windham CT VR 1:27>, (son of Eleazer WHEELOCK &
    Elizabeth FULLER), b. 12 Feb. 1682, Mendon <Mendon VR>, d. 13 Oct. 1748, Windham CT <MFIP
    #21>. (Ralph m.1st, 8 Jan. 1707/8, Windham CT, Ruth HUNTINGTON <Windham CT VR 1:27> & had 6
    chil.) <See Windham CT VR 1:100 for one dau.> (See STANDISH Probate Appendix for will of
    Ralph WHEELOCK.)

STANDISH PROBATE APPENDIX

Will of James CARY: <Plymouth Co.PR 2:96>
...18 Oct. 1706, ment. wf Mary; son James CARY; daus Marcy CARY, Mary CARY, Hannah CARY & Elizabeth CARY. Pr. 4 Mar. 1706.
==
Estate of Samuel DELANO: <MDP:439; MD 35:15-6; Plymouth Co.PR 5:424-5>
...28 Sept. 1728, Division, to following chil., viz: Hazadiah DELANOE, Jessee DELANOE, Samuel
DELANOE Jr., Priscilla SIMMONS & hus. Benjamin, Rebeckah SOUTHWORTH & hus. Benjamin, Sarah SIMONS
& hus. Joshua, Jane DELANOE, Mary DELANOE and Joseph CHANDLER.
==
Will of Abraham SAMSON: (husbandman) <Plymouth Co.PR 5:477-80>
...2 Aug. 1725, ment. wf Lorah; sons Nathaniel SAMSON, Abraham SAMSON, Miles SAMSON, Ebenezer
SAMSON; daus Rebecca SAMSON, Sarah SAMSON, Grace SAMSON. Pr. 4 Sept. 1727.
==
Will of Alexander STANDISH[2]: <MD 12:100-8, 176-85; Plymouth Co.PR 1:362>
...21 Feb. 1701/2, ment. unnamed wf and follow. chil., viz: Miles STANDISH (eldest son), Thomas
STANDISH, Ichabod STANDISH, Desire STANDISH, Ebenezer STANDISH, Lorah SAMSON wf of Abraham, Lidia
SAMSON wf of Isaac, Mercy SAMSON wf of Caleb, Elizabeth DELANO wf of Samuel, Sarah SOUL wf of
Benjamin; brother David ALDEN;..."Whatsoever Estate Either in New England or in old which I have
committed into ye hands of Robert orchard to Recover in England by letters of Attorney...Thus
taking my leave of all my near & dear Relations my christian ffriends in church Covenant & all my
loving neighbours I bid you all farewell till we meet in Heaven..." sworn 29 July 1702. (On 10 Aug.
1702 the will was contested by Abraham SAMSON, Isaac SAMSON, Caleb SAMSON & Benjamin SOULE (&
later by Samuel DELANO), the husbands of the daughters. The caveat contains a goldmine of information. "He had by his first wife who was daughter to ye Whorshipfull Mr. John ALDEN a good and a
prudent woman two sons and 5 daughters and after her decease he lived a widdower many years untill all his sd 5 daughters or 4 of them were married...about 16 years before he dyed he married
a second wife...by her he had two sons and one daughter." It also states Alexander was about 76
when he made his will, his eldest son married the daughter of the 2nd wife, son Myles was by the
1st wife, son Ebenezer was the 2nd son by the 1st wife and his 5 daughters by his 1st wife were
all married with children.)
==
Will of Ichabod STANDISH[3] (Alexander[2]): (cooper) <MD 15:190-1; Plymouth Co.PR 21:136>
...8 Mar. 1763, ment. daus Desire HATCH wf of David & her son Ichabod HATCH, Mary STANDISH and
Phebe STANDISH. Pr. 4 May 1772.
==
Will of Capt. Myles STANDISH[1]: <MSR:522-3; MD 3:153-6; Plymouth Col.Wills 3:1:37-40>
...7 Mar. 1655/6, "my body to bee layed as neare as conveniently may bee to my two dear daughters

Lora STANDISH by daughter and Mary STANDISH my daughter-in-law"; ment. wf Barbara; sons Allexander STANDISH, Myles STANDISH, Josias STANDISH and Charles STANDISH (all single); Marcye ROBENSON
"whome I tenderly love for her Grandfathers sake"; ment. all his lands "by lawful decent in Orm-
istick, Bousconge/Borsconge, Wrightington, Maudsley, Newburrow, Cranston/Crawston and the Ile of
man and given to mee as right heire by lawful decent, but surreptitiously/surruptuously detained
from mee my great Grandfather being a 2nd or younger brother from the house of Standish of Standish". Pr. 4 May 1657.

==

Will of **Myles STANDISH**[3] (**Alexander**[2]): (husbandman) <MD 15:123-5; Plymouth Co.PR 8:107>
...31 Aug. 1739, ment. wf Experience; son Miles STANDISH; daus Sarah WESTON wf of Abner, Patience
JENNY wf of Caleb, Priscilla STANDISH & Penelope STANDISH. Pr. 20 Sept. 1739.

==

Will of **Ralph WHEELOCK**: (yeoman) <Windham CT PR #4103, 3:546>
...10 Oct. 1748, ment. wf Mercy; son Eleazer WHEELOCK; daus Elizabeth HENRY, Abigail POMEROY,
Sarah BINGHAM & Mary BINGHAM. Pr. 21 Feb. 1749/50.

NOTES:

JOHN TILLEY

John TILLEY was baptized 19 Dec. 1571, Henlow, Bedfordshire, Eng., the son of Robert TILLEY & Elizabeth (?ELLBORNE) <TAG 52:199,203>. He died between 11 Jan. - 10 Apr. 1621 (N.S.), Plymouth <MD 2:119>. John married 20 Sept. 1596, Henlow, England, Joan (HURST) Rogers <TAG 52:199,203>. Joan was baptized 13 Mar. 1567/8, Henlow, the daughter of William & Rose <TAG 52:204> and died between 11 Jan. - 10 Apr. 1621, Plymouth (N.S.) <MD 2:119>. Joan m.1st, 18 June 1593, Henlow, Thomas ROGERS <TAG 52:204> who died c1594-95 <TAG 52:204 (they had a daughter, Joan, bpt. 26 May 1594, Henlow)>. No connection has been found between Thomas Rogers of the Mayflower and this Thomas.

(See also: TAG 52:198-208, English Ancestry of Seven Mayflower Passengers; TAG 60:171- , Further Traces of John Tilley of the Mayflower.)

John & Joan had 5 children: <TAG 52:203>

I.   Rose, bpt. 23 Oct. 1597, Henlow, d.y.
II.   John, bpt. 26 Aug. 1599, Henlow
III. Rose, bpt. 28 Feb. 1601/2, Henlow
IV.   Robert, bpt. 25 Nov. 1604, Henlow
V.   Elizabeth, bpt. 30 Aug. 1607, St. Mary the Virgin Church, Henlow; see HOWLAND family.

* * * * * * * * * * * * * * * *

II. JOHN TILLEY[2], bpt. 26 Aug. 1599, Henlow, Bedfordshire, England <TAG 52:203; MQ 56:118>. Research has been ongoing to determine if he is the John TILLEY who came to New England. In his articles, "John Tilley, 1599-1636" <MQ 49:16-17, 56:118-21>, Robert L. French suggests he came in the Anne in 1623 and was a member of John Oldham's group, moving on to Cape Anne in 1624, Naumkeag in 1626, Dorchester in 1630 and finally to Windsor CT. Although French presents excellent circumstantial evidence, the final collaborating piece of the puzzle is still missing. The following pertains to the John Tilley of New England who may or may not be John TILLEY[2].

John d. Oct. 1636, Saybrook CT <MQ 49:17 (tortured for 3 days by the Indians)>. He m. (   ) Edith (   ), who d. betw. 1649-1650, Milford or New Haven. Edith m.2nd, c1646, Nicholas CAMP. John & Edith may have been the parents of Elizabeth TILLEY, b. c1632, who married 21 Oct. 1653, Springfield MA, Thomas MERRICK who was b. c1620 and d. 1704; they had 8 chil.

If it can be proven that these two John TILLEYS were the same men, new Mayflower lines will be opened up.

NOTES:

RICHARD WARREN

Richard WARREN was born pre 1590, poss. London, Eng. <MQ 45:125,51:109-12; MD 3:45-6; Stratton: 367>; his origins have not been found. He died in 1628, "This year died Mr. Richard Warren who ...was an useful Instrument and during his life bare a deep share in the Difficulties and Troubles of the first settlement in the Plantation of New-Plimouth" <New England Memorial:68; MD 3:46> Richard married, pre 1610, poss. London, Elizabeth (   ). Despite what has previously appeared in print (e.g. Marsh, Jowett) her maiden name is unknown. Elizabeth was born c1580, England; her obituary states, "Mistris Elizabeth Warren an aged widdow aged above 90 yeares Deceased on the second of October 1673 whoe haveing lived a Godly life Cam to her Grave as a shok of Corn fully Ripe shee was honoralbey buried on the 24th of October aforesaid". (One of the dates is obviously wrong, she could not have died on the 2nd and buried on the 24th; it seems probable that the "twenty" was left off the "second" and that she died on the 22nd.) <PCR 8:35; MD 3:50; MBD 2:455 #1; Plymouth ChR>.

(See also: Mayflower Families In Progress, Richard Warren Of The Mayflower and His Descendants for Four Generations, by Robert S. Wakefield, FASG, Janice A. Beebe, et al, 4th Ed., 1991.)

Richard & Elizabeth had 7 children:

I.   Mary, b. c1610, prob. England
II.   Anna, b. c1612, prob. England
III.   Sarah, b. c1614, prob. England
IV.   Elizabeth, b. c1616, prob. England
V.   Abigail, b. c1618, prob. England
VI.   Nathaniel, b. c1624/5, Plymouth
VII.   Joseph, b. c1626/27, Plymouth

* * * * * * * * * * * * * * *

I. **MARY WARREN**[2], b. c1610, England <MD 2:178,3:105>, d. 27 Mar. 1683, 73rd yr, Plymouth <Plymouth ChR 1:250>; m. c1628/9, Plymouth, **Robert BARTLETT** <MD 3:106>, b. c1603, prob. England <TAG 55:164-8 (poss. the son of Robert BARTLETT & Alice BARKER who was bpt. 27 May 1603, Puddletown, co. Dorset, England)>, d. betw. 19 Sept. - 29 Oct. 1676 <MD 3:114 (will & pr.)>. (Robert's nuncupative will ment. only unnamed wf & unnamed chil.)

8 BARTLETT Children: <MBD 2:395; MD 3:116-7>

1. **Benjamin BARTLETT**[3], b. pre 6 June 1633, Plymouth <MD 3:106, PCR 3:48 (at least 21 when made a freeman 6 June 1654)>, d. betw. 21-28 Aug. 1691, Duxbury <MD 6:44 (will & inv.)>; m.1st, pre 4 Apr. 1654, Plymouth, **Susanna JENNEY** <MD 8:171 (her mother's will of this date ment. "son" Benjamin BARTLETT)>, (dau of John JENNEY & Sarah CAREY), b. aft. 22 May 1627, prob. Plymouth <MD 1:149 (not in the Cattle Division)>, d. prob. pre 4 Apr. 1654, Plymouth <MD 8:171-2 (her mother's will gives to Elder Thomas CUSHMAN "the bible which was my Daughter Susannas"; definitely dec'd by 18 Aug. 1655, her mother's codicil)>. **Benjamin** m.2nd, aft. 4 Apr. 1654, Duxbury, **Sarah BREWSTER**[3], (dau of Love BREWSTER[2] & Sarah COLLIER) - see BREWSTER family. **Benjamin** m.3rd, pre 21 Jan. 1678/9, **Sissillia (   )** <MDP:490; Plymouth Col.Deeds 4:2:281 (wf Sissillia consents to deed)>, b. (   ), d. aft. 1 Sept. 1691 <MD 6: 48-9 (receipts to hus.est.)>. <See MBD 2:395 & MQ 51:133 for 3 chil. by 2nd wf and 3 chil. by 3rd wf.> (See WARREN Probate Appendix for will of Benjamin BARTLETT.)

2. **Rebecca BARTLETT**[3], b. pre 1633, Plymouth <MD 3:106>, d. betw. 2 June 1657 (bth.last ch.) - 15 July 1658 (hus.remarr.) <MD 12:195>; m. 20 Dec. 1649, Plymouth, **William HARLOW** <PCR 8:8; MD 3:109,12:195; MSR:544>, b. c1624, prob. England <MD 12:193 (aft. 25 Aug. 1624)>, d. 25 Aug. 1691, 67th yr, Plymouth <Plymouth VR 1:202; Plymouth ChR 1:271 ("67th yeare neer finished"); MD 12:193,16:62>. <See MBD 2:432, MD 12:195 for bth. 4 chil.; PCR 8:10 (1), 14 (1), 17 (2); MD 16:235 (1), 235 (1), 238 (1), 17:72 (2).> (William m.2nd, 15 July 1658, Mary FAUNCE <PCR 8:21; MD 12:195>, (dau of John FAUNCE & Patience MORTON), b. (   ), Plymouth, d. 4 Oct. 1664, Plymouth <PCR 8:25; MD 12:195>; they had 4 chil. <MD 12:195; PCR 8:22 (2), 23 (1), 25 (1)>. William m.3rd, 25 Jan. 1665, Plymouth, Mary SHELLEY <PCR 8:26; MD 12:195>, (dau of Robert SHELLEY & Judith GARNETT), bpt. 2 Nov. 1639, Barnstable <NEHGR 9:281>, d. aft. 30 Jan. 1693/4 (her 3rd marr.); they had 6 chil. <MD 12:195; PCR 8:31-35 (5)>. Mary SHELLEY m.2nd, 18 Oct. 1692, Plymouth, Ephraim MORTON <MD 13:205>, (son of George MORTON & Julianna CARPENTER), b. c1624, Plymouth, d. 5 Oct. 1693 <MD 16:63,17:45>. Mary SHELLEY m.3rd, 30 Jan. 1693/4, Plymouth, Hugh COLE <PN&Q 3:121>. Ephraim MORTON m.1st, 18 Nov. 1644, Plymouth, Ann COOPER <Plymouth Col.Court Orders 2:107> & had chil. <PCR 8:5,11,15>.) <See WARREN Probate Appendix for will of Sergt. William HARLOW.)

3. **Mary BARTLETT**[3], b. c1634, Plymouth, d. 26 Sept. 1692, Plymouth <MD 16:63; Plymouth VR 1:202>; m.1st, 10 Sept. 1651, Plymouth, **Richard FOSTER** <PCR 8:13; MD 3:109,16:237; MSR:545>, b. (   ) prob. England, d. betw. 2 Feb. 1657/8 <PCR 3:127 (when Jonathan Morey was warned not to fre-

quent the house of Richard FOSTER in his absence)> - 27 June 1659, Plymouth <MD 3:110,14:15, 16 (called dec'd in deed & marr. agreement betw. Mary & Jonathan)>. **Mary** m.2nd, 8 July 1659, Plymouth, **Jonathan MOREY** <MD 3:111,17:182; PCR 8:22; MSR:545>, (son of Roger MOWREY & Mary JOHNSON), bpt. 2 Apr. 1637, Salem <Salem VR>, d. 19 May 1708, 75th yr, Plymouth <MD 16:64>. (Jonathan m.2nd, c1693/4, Hannah (PINCHEN)(Young) Witherell who d. aft. 12 May 1720 <MDP:507; Plymouth Co.PR 4:219 (receipted to hus. est.)>.) <See MBD 2:429 for 2 chil. by 1st hus.; MD 16:238 (1). See MBD 2:430 for 3 chil. by 2nd hus.> (See WARREN Probate Appendix for will of Jonathan MOREY.)

4. **Sarah BARTLETT[3]**, b. (   ), d. pre 14 June 1680, Plymouth <MSR:547 (hus.remarr.)>; m. 23 Dec 1656, Plymouth, **Samuel RIDER/RYDER** <PCR 8:17; MD 3:110,11:182; MSR:545>, (son of Samuel RIDER & Anne GAMLETT), bpt. 25 Nov. 1632, All Saints Parish, co. Northampton, Eng. <TAG 43:117-24>, d. 18 July 1715, 85th yr <MD 16:85; Plymouth TR 1:205; Plymouth ChR 1:214; Drew:147 (no day)> (Samuel m.2nd, 14 June 1680, Taunton, Lydia TILDEN <PCR 8:82; MD 11:182; MSR:547>, (dau of Thomas TILDEN & Elizabeth (BOURNE) Waterman, b. 26 Apr. 1658, Marshfield <MD 2:7; Marshfield VR:5>, d. 17 Sept. 1740, 83rd yr, Plymouth, Manomet cem. <MD 11:182>; they had 12 chil. <MD 1:210 (11), 211 (2).) <See MBD 2:440 & MD 11:183-4 for bth. 3 chil.; PCR 8:17 (1).> (See WARREN Probate Appendix for will of Samuel RIDER.)

5. **Joseph BARTLETT[3]**, b. c1639, Plymouth <PN&Q 3:68 (ae 41 or thereabouts in 17 July 1680 deposition)>, d. 18 Feb. 1711/2, 73rd yr, Plymouth g.s. <Plymouth VR 1:204; MD 12:14,16:64; Drew: 147 (says 13th; "lo here their bodys near togather lay/till ye bright morn of ye Resurrection day")>; m. c1662, Plymouth, **Hannah POPE** <NEHGR 148:317; MD 12:14 (name)>, (dau of Thomas POPE & Ann FALLOWELL), b. c1638, Plymouth <NEHGR 148:317>, d. 12 Mar. 1709/10, 72nd yr, Plymouth <MD 12:14,16:64 (yr, 170-)>. <See MBD 2:407 for 7 chil.>

6. **Elizabeth BARTLETT[3]**, b. c1643, Plymouth, d. 17 Feb. 1712/3, Hingham <Hingham VR 1:157; Lincoln 3:164>; m. 26 Dec. 1661, Plymouth, **Anthony SPRAGUE** <PCR 8:23; MD 3:111,18:220>, (son of William SPRAGUE & Milicent EAMES), bpt. 23 May 1636, Charlestown <MBD 2:402>, d. 3 Sept. 1719, 84th yr, Hingham <Lincoln 3:164>. <For bth. 11 chil. see MBD 2:402 & Hingham VR 1:5,13,18,25,32,43,52,56.> (See WARREN Probate Appendix for will of Anthony SPRAGUE.)

7. **Lydia BARTLETT[3]**, b. 8 June 1648, Plymouth <PCR 8:4; MD 15:27>, d. 11 Sept. 1691, 44th yr, Plymouth <Plymouth ChR 1:271; Plymouth VR 1:202; MD 16:62>; m.1st, pre 14 June 1670, prob. Plymouth, **James BARNABY** <MD 3:112; MDP:488, Plymouth Col.Deeds 3:297 (deed from father-in-law, Robert BARTLETT)>, b. (   ), prob. England, d. pre 30 Oct. 1677 <Plymouth Col.PR 3:2: 98 (inv.)>. **Lydia** m.2nd, soon after 30 Oct. 1677, prob. Plymouth, **John NELSON** <PCR 5:247 (sett. 1st hus. est. says she is about to marry John NELSON)>, (son of William NELSON & Martha FORD), b. c1643/4, Plymouth, d. 29 Apr. 1697, "entered into" 54th yr, Plymouth <MD 16:63, 19:190>. (John m.1st, 28 Nov. 1667, Plymouth, Sarah WOOD <PCR 8:31>, (dau of Henry WOOD & Abigail JENNEY), b. (   ), d. 4 Mar. 1675, Plymouth <PCR 8:64>; they had 3 chil. <MD 1:220> John m.3rd, 4 May 1693, Plymouth, Patience MORTON <MD 13:206; PN&Q 3:121>, (dau of Ephraim MORTON[2] (George[1]) & Ann COOPER), b. (   ), d. 3 May 1715, Plymouth <MD 16:85>; they had 2 chil. <MD 1:210,19:190>.) <See MBD 2:426 for 2 chil. by 1st and 2 by 2nd hus.; MD 1:210, 2 chil. by 2nd.> (See WARREN Probate Appendix for will of John NELSON.)

8. **Mercy BARTLETT[3]**, b. 10 Mar. 1650/1, Plymouth <PCR 8:11>, d. (   ); m. 25 Dec. 1668, Plymouth, **John JOY** <PCR 8:32; MD 3:111,18:57; although the sources state his name was John IVEY, MFIP #16 states a close examination of the original rec. shows the surname is JOY and he was poss. the son of Thomas JOY & Joan GALLOP, bpt. 10 8mth 1641, d. pre 8 July 1677 (fath.will)> <See Boston Rcd.Com.9:11 for bth. 1 child.>

II. **ANNA WARREN[2]**, b. c1612, prob. England <MSR:543; MD 2:178,19:134 (ae 60 or thereabouts in 6 June 1672 deposition)>, d. aft. 19 Feb. 1675/6, Marshfield <MD 4:161 (son's will).>; m. 19 Apr. 1633, Plymouth, **Thomas LITTLE** <Plymouth Col.Court Orders 1:15; MD 13:83>, b. (   ), bur. 12 Mar. 1671/2, Marshfield <Marshfield VR:427; MD 4:161; MSR:248>. (See WARREN Probate Appendix for will of Thomas LITTLE.) <Note: MBD 2:341 & 457, delete footnote #39.>

9 LITTLE Children: <MBD 2:336>

1. **Abigail LITTLE[3]**, b. c1635, Plymouth, d. pre c1660, prob. Marshfield (hus.2nd marr.); m. c1654 -1656, Marshfield, **Josiah KEEN/KEENE** <MD 19:128,28:1,5>, (son of John & Martha), b. (   ), prob. London <TAG 63:122; MD 28:5 ("on London Bredg/Bridge")>, d. betw. 28 May 1695 - 15 Sept 1710, prob. Duxbury <MD 19:128 (will & pr.)>. (Josiah m.2nd, c1660, Hannah DINGLEY (dau of John), b. (   ), d. aft. 15 Sept. 1710 <MD 19:130 (hus.pr)>; they had 7 chil. <MD 19:128>.) <See MBD 2:336 & MD 19:128 for bth. 2 chil. See also MD 28:1-6 for "Hezekiah Keen's Account Book with Family Records.> (See WARREN Probate Appendix for will of Josiah KEEN/KEENE Sr.)

2. **Ruth LITTLE[3]**, b. (   ), Plymouth, d. aft. 19 Feb. 1675/6 <MD 4:164 (will of bro. Thomas)>.

3. **Hannah LITTLE[3]**, b. c1636/7, Plymouth, d. 13 May 1710, Scituate <Scituate VR 4:4:5>; m. 15 Jan 1661/2, Scituate, **Stephen TILDEN** <PCR 8:29; MD 2:34 (says 25th), 17:202; MSR:623>, (son of Nathaniel TILDEN & Lydia HUCKSTEP), bpt. 11 Oct. 1629, Tenterden, co. Kent, Eng. <NEHGR 65: 314-33>. <See MBD 2:349 & Scituate VR for bth. 12 chil.; MD 17:202 (1), 19:23 (1).>

4. **Patience LITTLE**[3], b. c1639, Plymouth, d. 25 Oct. 1723, ae 84, Hingham <Lincoln 2:357>; m. 11 Nov. 1657, Weymouth, **Joseph JONES** <Weymouth VR>, (son of Robert), b. (   ), prob. England, d. 18 July 1714, Hingham <Hingham TR 1:161>. <See MBD 2:360 for 10 chil.; for 7 chil. see Hingham TR 1:7,14,19,24,29,38,50.> (See WARREN Probate Appendix for will of Joseph JONES.)

5. **Mercy LITTLE**[3], b. c1645, Plymouth, bur. 10 Feb. 1693, Marshfield <Marshfield VR:19; MD 5:233; MSR:250>; m. 30 Nov. 1666, Marshfield, **John SAWYER** <Marshfield VR:5; MD 2:111; MSR:242>, b. (   ), d. aft. 8 Mar. 1704/5 <MDP:466 (deed); prob. aft. 28 Apr. 1711 when 2nd wf is called his wife, not widow, at her death>. (John m.2nd, 23 Nov. 1694, Marshfield, Rebecca (BARKER) Snow <Marshfield VR:19; MD 4:126> - see under Josiah SNOW[3] (Abigail Warren[2]). <See MBD 2:358 for 7 chil.; Marshfield VR:13 (dth), 15 (6); MD 2:250 (1), 3:41 (4), 42 (2).>

6. **Isaac LITTLE**[3], b. c1646, Plymouth, d. 24 Nov. 1699, ae about 53 yr, Marshfield, Winslow cem. <Marshfield VR:23,388; MD 10:49,24:1>; m. c1673, prob. Marshfield, **Bethiah THOMAS** <MD 24:1>, (dau of Nathaniel & Mary), b. (   ), prob. Marshfield <MD 24:1>, d. 23 Sept. 1718, bur. Winslow cem., Marshfield <Marshfield VR:388; MD 10:49,24:1; MFIP #21 says she prob. d. at Pembroke; she was called "of Pembroke" in a deed dated 8 Sept. 1718 <MD 24:1>.> <See MBD 2: 354 for bth. 11 chil. (MFIP #21 gives 12 chil., which incl. 3 daus named Bethiah, with 2 of them dying in the same year which is clearly in error.); Marshfield VR:10 (1), 14 (1), 15 (1) 16 (1), 17 (1), 18 (2); MD 2:182 (1), 251 (1), 3:42 (1), 187 (2), 189 (2).> (See WARREN Probate Appendix for will of Lieut. Isaac LITTLE.)

7. **Ephraim LITTLE**[3], b. 17 May 1650, Plymouth <PCR 8:10; MD 16:235,34:146 (says 10th); MD 19:134 (ae 22 or thereabouts in 6 June 1672 deposition)>, d. 24 Nov. 1717, 68th yr, Scituate g.s. <MD 8:116,34:146-8>; m. 22 Nov. 1672, Scituate, **Mary STURTEVANT** <MD 2:195,34:146; Torrey:467> (dau of Samuel STURTEVANT & Ann (?LEE)), b. 7 Dec. 1651, Plymouth <PCR 8:13; MD 16:237>, d. 10 Feb. 1717/8, 66th yr, Scituate g.s. <MD 8:116,34:146,148>. <See MBD 2:341 & MD 34:146; MD 2:181 (1); Marshfield VR:9 (1), 11 (1), 14 (1); see also MD 34:145-49, "A Little Family Record"> (See WARREN Probate Appendix for will of Ephraim LITTLE.)

8. **Thomas LITTLE**[3], b. pre 19 Feb. 1654/5, Marshfield (if at least 21 when he wrote will), d. 26 Mar. 1676, King Phillip's War, Rehoboth, unm. <MD 4:161>. (See WARREN Probate Appendix for will of Thomas LITTLE Sr.)

9. **Samuel LITTLE**[3], b. c1655, Marshfield <MD 2:248 (ae 33 or thereabouts in 31 July 1688 deposition)>, d. 16 Jan. 1707, Bristol MA (now RI) <VR RI (Bristol):145 (or Bristol VR:145)>; m. 18 May 1682, Marshfield, **Sarah GRAY**[4] <Marshfield VR:19; MD 4:126; MSR:243>, (dau of Edward GRAY & Mary WINSLOW[3] (Mary Chilton[2] - see CHILTON family)), b. 12 Aug. 1659, Plymouth <PCR 8:22; MD 17:183>, d. 14 Feb. 1736/7, Bristol MA (now RI) <VR RI (Bristol):145 (or Bristol VR:145)>. <See MBD 2:363 for 3 chil.; Marshfield VR:20 (3); MD 5:234 (3), 11:38 (3 bpt.).> (See WARREN Probate Appendix for will of Samuel LITTLE.)

III **SARAH WARREN**[2], b. c1614, prob. England, d. aft. 15 July 1696 <MD 3:33 (hus.adm.)>; m. 28 Mar. 1634, Plymouth, **John COOKE**[2] <MD 13:83>. See COOKE family.

IV **ELIZABETH WARREN**[2], b. c1616, prob. England, d. 9 Mar. 1669/70, Hingham <Hingham TR 1:20; MD 5:118; NEHGR 121:124>; m. pre 14 Mar. 1635/6, Plymouth, **Richard CHURCH** <TAG 60:129; MD 3:47; Plymouth Col.Court Orders 1:89>, b. c1608, England <MD 4:152,5:118; Plymouth Col.Court Orders 4:92 (ae about 56 in 25 Aug. 1664 deposition)>, d. 27 Dec. 1668, Dedham (bur. Hingham) <MD 5: 118; Hingham TR 1:17>.

11 CHURCH Children: <MBD 2:365>

1. **Elizabeth CHURCH**[3], b. c1636, Plymouth, d. 3 Feb. 1658/9, Hingham <NEHGR 121:109>; m. 8 Jan. 1657/8, Hingham, **Caleb HOBART** <NEHGR 121:109>, (son of Thomas), b. c1622/3, d. 4 Sept. 1711, ae about 87, Braintree g.s. <Braintree VR:722; NEHGR 11:299>. (Caleb m.2nd, 13 Apr. 1662, Braintree, **Mary ELIOT** <NEHGR 121:113> & had 5 chil.; he m.3rd, 15 Jan. 1675/6, Braintree, **Sarah GRAY**[4] <Braintree VR:718>, b. c1633, d. 9 Aug. 1704, ae 71, Braintree g.s. <NEHGR 11:299> and had 1 son.) <See MBD 2:365 for bth. 1 son.>

2. **Joseph CHURCH**[3], b. c1638, Plymouth, d. 5 Mar. 1710/1, ae 73, Little Compton RI g.s. <MD 24: 130 (from The Boston News-Letter of Monday Mar. 12th 1710, "Little Compton, March 8. On Monday the 5th Currant Dyed here the Honourable Joseph Church Esq. lately of Her Majestys Council for this Province in the 73 year of his Age"); NEHGR 115:265>; m. 13 Dec. 1660, Hingham, **Mary TUCKER** <MD 22:22 (no date); NEHGR 121:111>, (dau of John), bpt. 8 Oct. 1640, Hingham <NEHGR 121:13>, d. 21 Mar. 1709/10, ae 69, Little Compton g.s. <VR RI 4:6:101; NEHGR 115:265> <For 10 chil. see MBD 2:383 & NEHGR 121:114,115,118,121,125,191,192,197,199; Hingham VR 1:8 (5).> (See WARREN Probate Appendix for will of Joseph CHURCH.)

3. **Benjamin CHURCH**[3], b. c1639/40, Plymuth, d. 17 Jan. 1717/8, 78th yr, Little Compton <MD 7:100, 24:130; NEHGR 115:267>; m. 26 Dec. 1667, poss. Duxbury, **Alice SOUTHWORTH** <NEHGR 121:121>, (dau of Constant SOUTHWORTH & Elizabeth COLLIER), b. c1646, Duxbury, d. 5 Mar. 1718/9, 73rd

yr, Little Compton <NEHGR 115:267>. <See MBD 2:369 for 7 chil. (Bowman errs in giving 8th
ch., Martha; see Probate Appendix)> (See WARREN Probate Appendix for estate and obit of
Benjamin CHURCH.)

4. **Nathaniel CHURCH**[3], b. c1642, Plymouth, d. pre 29 Oct. 1689, Scituate <PN&Q 5:91 (inv.)>; m.
pre 8 June 1666, (   ), **Sarah BARSTOW** <PCR 8:116,117 (they each owed 5 pounds in fines on
this date which indicates fornication charges); see SOULE family p.102 for Nathaniel's fornication charges with Elizabeth SOULE in 1663>, (prob. dau of William BARSTOW & Ann HUBBARD),
<MFIP #27>, b. (   ), d. aft. 4 Nov. 1717 (deed) <MDP:480; Plymouth Co.Deeds 13:113>. <See
MBD 2:385 & Scituate VR 1:71 for bth. 7 chil.> (See WARREN Probate Appendix for estate of
Nathaniel CHURCH.)

5. **Richard CHURCH**[3], b. (   ), d. aft. 9 Apr. 1649 <PCR 12:165>. (Bowman <MBD 2:365> includes
him, MFIP #5 questions him.)

6. **Charles CHURCH**[3], b. c1644, Plymouth, d. 30 Oct. 1659, Hingham <NEHGR 121:110>.

7. **Caleb CHURCH**[3], b. c1647, Plymouth <PN&Q 2:47, Middlesex Deeds 10:602 (ae about 39 in 1 Apr.
1686 deposition)>, d. pre 26 June 1722, Watertown (inv.) <MDP:475; Middlesex Co.PR #4449, 16:
459>; m.1st, 16 Dec. 1667, Hingham, **Joanna SPRAGUE** <Hingham VR 1:14; NEHGR 121:121>, (dau of
William SPRAGUE & Milicent EAMES), bpt. Dec. 1645, Hingham <NEHGR 121:118; Lincoln 2:126>, d.
11 July 1678, Watertown <Watertown VR 1:444>. **Caleb** m.2nd, pre 8 June 1680, (   ), **Deborah
(   )** <Middlesex Co.Deeds 7:283-4 (wf Deborah ack.deed)>, b. (   ), d. 17 Jan. 1690,
Watertown <Watertown VR 1:62>. (Bowman <MM:298> gives only 2 marriages for Caleb and states
<MBD 2:374> the Deborah Church who d. in 1690 was a dau.) **Caleb** m.3rd, 6 Nov. 1691, Water-
town, **Rebecca (   ) SCOTTOW** <Watertown VR 1:64>, b. (   ), d. aft. 1 Apr. 1715 (ack.deed)
<MDP:476>. (Rebecca m.1st, John SCOTTOW.) <See MBD 2:374 for 8 chil. incl. twins (9th ch.,
Deborah, is an error); Watertown VR 1:43 (1), 44 (2), Dedham VR:12,13 (3).> (See WARREN Probate Appendix for estate of Caleb CHURCH.)

8. **Abigail CHURCH**[3], b. 22 June 1648, Plymouth <PCR 8:4; MD 15:27>, d. 25 Dec. 1677, ae 30, Hingham <MD 23:145>; m. 19 Dec. 1666, Hingham, **Samuel THAXTER** <MD 23:145; NEHGR 121:119>, (son of
Thomas & Elizabeth), b. 19 May 1641, Hingham <Hingham VR 3:230; NEHGR 121:13>, d. 27 May 1725
ae 84, Hingham <Hingham VR 3:231>. (Samuel m.2nd, 13 June 1678, Hingham, Deborah LINCOLN <MD
23:145; NEHGR 121:201>, b. (   ), d. 7 Dec. 1694, Hingham <MD 23:145>; they had 3 chil.
<Hingham TR 1:49,55,64.) <See MBD 2:365 & MD 23:145-6 for 7 chil.> (See WARREN Probate App-
endix for will of Samuel THAXTER.)

9. **Sarah CHURCH**[3], b. 1650's, d. betw. 29 Sept. 1688 (deed) <MDP:483; Bristol Co.Deeds 1:97> -
c1693 (hus.remarr.), Bristol; m. 8 Dec. 1674, Hingham, **James BURROUGHS/BURROWES** <Hingham TR
1:33; NEHGR 121:113>, b. c1650, d. aft. 10 Oct. 1699 <MFIP #30, Bristol Co.Court of General
Sessions (1697-1701):41 (He is ment. on this date in connection with his dau. Elizabeth BURR-
OUGHS who d. pre 7 Aug. 1699 after giving birth to an illegitimate child by a negro servant)>
(James m.2nd, c1693, Anne (   ) <MDP:483; Bristol Co.Deeds 51:251 (pre 30 July 1694 deed)>;
they had one son <Bristol VR 1:141>.) <For 4 chil. see MBD 2:389,462 #162; Boston Rcd.Com.9:
141 (1), 148 (1), Bristol VR 1:141 (1).>

10. **Mary CHURCH**[3], b. (   ), d. 30 Apr. 1662, Duxbury <NEHGR 121:113>.

11. **Deborah CHURCH**[3], b. 27 Jan. 1656/7, Hingham <TAG 40:101>. (She poss. m. **Sylvanus WHITE**[3]
(son of Peregrine WHITE[2] & Sarah BASSETT) -see WHITE family.)

V. **ABIGAIL WARREN**[2], b. c1618, prob. England, d. aft. 3 Jan. 1692/3, Marshfield <MD 5:5 (swore to
hus.inv.)>; m. 8 Nov. 1639, Plymouth, **Anthony SNOW** <Plymouth Col.Court Orders 1:216; MD 13:
85>, b. (   ), Eng., d. betw. 8 Aug. (codicil) - 31 Aug. 1692 (d. _in_ Aug.), Marshfield
<Marshfield VR:17; MD 3:187,5:1; MSR:249>. (See WARREN Probate Appendix for will of Anthony
SNOW.)

6 SNOW Children: <MBD 2:329>

1. **Lydia SNOW**[3], b. c1640-45, Plymouth, d. 17 Mar. 1711, Sandwich g.s. <Sandwich VR; MD 29:23
(g.s. says 1713 ae 74)>; m. c1665, (   ), **Stephen SKIFF/SKEEFE** <MM:283>, (son of James &
Mary), b. 14 Apr. 1641, Sandwich <MD 14:167,29:69>, d. 8 June 1710, Sandwich g.s. <MD 29:22;
(g.s. says 19 June)>. <See MBD 2:332 for 5 chil.; MD 29:21 (2), 22 (1), 70 (1).> (See WAR-
REN Probate Appendix for will of Stephen SKIFF/SKEEFE.)

2. **Josiah SNOW**[3], b. c1645, Plymouth, d. Aug. 1692, Marshfield <Marshfield VR:17; MSR:250; MD 3:
187, 5:2 (aft. 8 Aug. as his father's codicil would have ment. his decease); see MDP:450 for
estate and deeds of heirs>; m. c1669, prob. Marshfield, **Rebecca BARKER** <Marshfield VR:427,
MSR:243 (date not entered)>, (dau of Robert), b. (   ), d. 28 Apr. 1711, Marshfield <Marsh-
field VR:33; MD 7:120; MSR:250>. (Rebecca m.2nd, 23 Nov. 1694, Marshfield, John SAWYER <Mar-
shfield VR:19> who m.1st Mercy LITTLE[3] (Anna Warren[2]) - see under Mercy.) <See MBD 2:331 for
10 chil.; Marshfield VR:9 (1, dth), 12 (2), 13 (1), 15 (4), 18 (1); MD 2:181 (1), 250 (1),
251 (1), 3:42 (4).>

3. **Abigail SNOW**[3], b. c1647-49, Plymouth, bur. 26 June 1682, Marshfield <Marshfield VR:13; MD 2: 280; MSR:249>; m. 12 Dec. 1667, Marshfield, **Michael FORD** <Marshfield VR:10; MD 2:182>, (son of William FORD & Anna/Hannah (   ) - NEHGR 119:23 suggests she is Hannah EAMES), b. (   ), d. 27 Mar. 1729, Marshfield <Marshfield VR:85; MD 30:153>. (Michael m.2nd, 29 Mar. 1683, Marshfield, Bethia HATCH <Marshfield VR:16; MD 3:43; MSR:243>, (dau of Walter HATCH & Elizabeth HOLBROOKE), b. 31 Mar. 1661, Scituate <PCR 8:29; MSR:317>, d. 22 Nov. 1728, ae 67, Marshfield <Marshfield VR:401> & had 13 chil. <MBD 2:329; Marshfield VR:14 (2), 15 (1), 18 (2), 20 (4), 21 (2)>.) <See MBD 2:329 for bth. 6 chil.; MD 2:180 (1), 249 (1), 3:42 (1); Marshfield VR:8 (1), 12 (1); MFIP #33 gives a 7th ch., dau Bathsheba who was bur. 12 Mar. 1680/1 however this is an error; she was b. 3 Feb. 1680, dau of William Ford <Marshfield VR:11; MD 2:249> and was bur. 12 Mar. 1680/1, dau of William <Marshfield VR:12; MD 2:250>.> (See WARREN Probate Appendix for will of Michael FORD.)

4. **Sarah SNOW**[3], b. cJune 1651, (   ), d. 11 Sept. 1741, ae 90y3m, Marshfield, Winslow cem. <Marshfield VR:389; MD 10:50,24:146>; m. c1673, prob. Marshfield, **Joseph WATERMAN** <MD 24:145> (son of Robert WATERMAN & Elizabeth BOURNE), b. c1649, Marshfield <MFIP #34>, d. 3 Jan. 1710/ 11, ae 62, Marshfield, Winslow cem. <Marshfield VR:389 (no day); MD 8:177 (yr worn), 10:50 (no day), 24:146>. <For 7 chil. see MBD 2:333, Marshfield VR:11 & MD 2:183, 24:145-6.> (See WARREN Probate Appendix for will of Joseph WATERMAN.)

5. **son,** b. 25 Mar. 1655, Marshfield, d.y. <Marshfield VR:3; MD 2:6>.

6. **Alice SNOW**[3], b. 18 Jan. 1657, Marshfield <Marshfield VR:4; MD 2:7>, d. aft. 5 Sept. 1697 (bth last ch.), prob. Duxbury; m. c1681, (   ), **Robert BARKER** <MFIP #35>, (son of Robert), b. c1651, d. 25 Sept. 1729, ae 78, Duxbury <Duxbury VR>. (Robert m.2nd, soon aft. 9 Oct. 1705, Phebe (COOK)(Arnold) Marsh <MFIP #35 (no reason for date)>.) <See Duxbury VR & MFIP #35 for bth. 8 chil.> (See WARREN Probate Appendix for will of Robert BARKER.)

VI **NATHANIEL WARREN**[2], b. c1624/5, Plymouth <MD 2:178-9,3:46 (ae 37 or thereabouts in 15 Oct. 1661 deposition)>, d. betw. 16 July - 21 Oct. 1667, Plymouth <MD 2:36-40 (codicil & inv.)>; m. 19 Nov. 1645, Plymouth, **Sarah WALKER** <Plymouth Col.Court Orders 2:125>, (dau of William), poss. bpt. 10 Nov. 1622, St. Olave's, Southwark, co. Surrey, Eng. <TAG 51:92>, d. 24 Nov. 1700, Plymouth <MD 16:63>. (See WARREN Probate Appendix for will of Nathaniel WARREN.)

   12 WARREN Children: <MBD 2:441; PCR 8:24 (MD 17:284) gives chil. 3-11 & states 2 older chil. are also rec.; Sarah is found but Richard is not.>

1. **Richard WARREN**[3], b. c1646, Plymouth, d. 23 Jan. 1696/7, Plymouth <MD 16:63>; m. c1678, (   ) **Sarah TORREY** <MFIP #24; MM:327,331>, (dau of James TORREY & Ann HATCH), b. 9 Feb. 1660/1, Scituate <Scituate VR; PCR 8:29>, d. aft. 6 Nov. 1722 <MFIP #24 (no reason given)>. (Sarah m.2nd, 18 Sept. 1712, Barnstable, Thomas EWER <MD 14:226>, (prob. son of Thomas & Hannah), b. (   ), d. Sept. 1722, Barnstable <MD 14:226>; Otis 1:362 cites the will of Thomas EWER (no date) which ment. wf Sarah & sons Thomas, John & Nathaniel.) <See MBD 2:449 for 6 chil.; PCR 8:72 (1), 75 (2).>

2. **Sarah WARREN**[3], b. 29 Aug. 1649, Plymouth <PCR 8:7; MD 16:120>, d. aft. 4 Mar. 1692/3 (consented to deed) <MD 7:146>; m. c1673, (   ), **John BLACKWELL** <MM:329>, (son of Michael), b. c1646, prob. Sandwich, d. pe 28 Nov. 1688 (inv.) <MD 10:7>. <See MBD 2:453 for 7 chil.; PCR 8:64 (1), 108 (1), 109 (3); MD 14:166 (1), 169 (1).>

3. **Hope WARREN**[3], b. 6 or 7 Mar. 1650/1, Plymouth <PCR 8:11 & MD 16:236 (6th); PCR 8:24 & MD 17: 184 (7th)>, d. pe 9 Jan. 1689/90 (fath.est.) <MD 7:143-46>.

4. **Jane WARREN**[3], b. 31 Dec. 1652, Plymouth <PCR 8:14; MD 16:238; PCR 8:24 & MD 17:184 say 10 Jan. 1652/3>, d. 27 Feb. 1682/3, Barnstable <MD 11:98>; m. 19 Sept. 1672, Barnstable, **Benjamin LOMBARD** <MD 11:98>, (son of Thomas & Joyce), b. 26 Aug. 1642, Barnstable <MD 11:97>, d. aft. 11 Feb. 1704/5 (last ch.bpt.) <MFIP #38 (poss. d. 2 Aug. 1725)>. (Benjamin m.2nd, 19 Nov. 1685, Barnstable, Sarah WALKER <MD 11:98>, (poss. the dau of William WALKER & Sarah SNOW[3] (Constance Hopkins[2])), b. 30 July 1662, Eastham <MD 6:206>), d. 6 Nov. 1693, Barnstable <MD 11:98; Note: MBD 2:468 #345 should be "b." not "d.">; they had 4 chil. <MD 11:98>. Benjamin m.3rd, 24 May 1694, Barnstable, Hannah (   ) WHETSTONE <MD 11:98>; they had 2 chil. <MD 11:98>.)

5. **Elizabeth WARREN**[3], b. 15 Sept. 1654, Plymouth <PCR 8:24; MD 17:184>, d. aft. 10 Jan. 1689/90 (consented to deed) <MD 7:146>. (On 27 Oct. 1674 she accused Joseph DOTEN[2] of fathering her unborn child <PCR 5:156> - see DOTY family.) **Elizabeth** m. c1683, (   ), **William GREEN** <MD 7:144>, b. (   ), d. 7 Oct. 1685, Plymouth <MD 15:213>. <See MBD 2:444 & MD 1:146 for bth. 1 son.>

6. **Alice WARREN**[3], b. 2 Aug. 1656, Plymouth <PCR 8:24; MD 17:184>, d. betw 4 Mar. 1692 (consented to deed) - 23 June 1725 (hus.will) <MD 7:146,23:123-5>; m. 23 Dec. 1674, Sandwich, **Thomas GIBBS** <MD 14:111,23:123>, (son of Thomas), b. 23 Mar. 1636/7, Sandwich <MD 14:170; MFIP #43 has changed this date to 1646/7>, d. 7 Jan. 1732/3, Sandwich <MD 23:124,29:22; Gen.Adv.4:14>. <See MBD 2:442 & MD 23:123 for bth. 8 chil.; MD 14:107 (1), 111 (1). Note: MBD 2:442 as all

the children are listed, delete "(3 of 8)".> (See WARREN Probate Appendix for will of Thomas GIBBS Sr.)

7. **Mercy WARREN**[3], b. 20 Feb. 1657, Plymouth <PCR 8:24; MD 17:184>, d. aft. 6 Nov. 1727 <NEHGR 7: 136 (letter of son Jabez)>; m. 28 Feb. 1677/8, Dartmouth, **Jonathan DELANO** <MD 3:218,23:148>, (son of Philip DELANO & Hester DEWSBERY) <MFIP #41>, b. c1647, Plymouth, d. 28 Dec. 1720, 73rd yr, Dartmouth <Dartmouth VR, MFIP #41>. <See MBD 2:448, Dartmouth VR & MD 3:218 for bth of 13 chil.> (See WARREN Probate Appendix for will of Jonathan DELANO.)

8. **Mary WARREN**[3], b. 9 Mar. 1660, Plymouth <PCR 8:24; MD 17:184>, d. pre 9 Jan. 1689/90 (fath. est.) <MD 7:143-6>.

9. **Nathaniel WARREN**[3], b. 10 Mar. 1661, Plymouth <PCR 8:24; MD 17:184>, d. 29 Oct. 1707, 48th yr, Plymouth g.s. <MD 16:64,22:43; Drew:293 (first name worn)>; m. pre 24 Feb. 1693/4, (   ), **Phebe MURDOCH/MURDOCK** (deed) <Bristol Co.Deeds 3:115>, b. (   ), d. betw. 16 May 1746 - 15 Dec. 1746 (will & pr.) <RI Gen.Reg.4:340>. No known issue. (Phebe m.2nd, betw. 21 Dec. 1708 (ack.deed) <MD 21:84> - 24 June 1709 (swore to 1st hus. inv. as Phebe Gray) <MDP:519>, Capt. Thomas GRAY <MD 22:43>, (son of Edward GRAY & Dorothy LETTICE) <MFIP #118>, b. c1670, Plymouth, d. 5 Nov. 1721, 52nd yr, Little Compton <MFIP #118; VR RI (Little Compton)>. Thomas m.1st, 3 July 1694, Boston, Anna LITTLE[4] <Boston Rcd.Com.9:217; Marshfield VR:352; MD 34:148> (dau of Ephraim LITTLE[3] (Anna Warren[2]) & Mary STURTEVANT - see Ephraim), b. 23 Aug. 1673, Marshfield <MD 34:146>, d. 16 Oct. 1706, 34th yr, Little Compton <MD 34:146>; they had 7 chil <VR RI (Little Compton)>.) (See WARREN Probate Appendix for will of Capt. Thomas GRAY.)

10. **John WARREN**[3], b. 23 Oct. 1663, Plymouth <PCR 8:24; MD 17:184>, d. pre 9 Jan. 1689/90 (fath. est.) <MD 7:143-6>.

11. **James WARREN**[3], b. 7 Nov. 1665, Plymouth <PCR 8:24,25; MD 17:184,25:3>, d. 29 or 30 May 1715, 50th yr, Plymouth g.s. <MD 16:85; Plymouth TR; Drew:293 (g.s. says 29 June); Plymouth ChR 2:214 ("In June 1715 An Exceeding loss to ye church Town & Country"); MD 25:4-5 (Bowman shows he d. betw. 25 May - 7 June 1715, therefore the date of 29 June is in error)>; MD 25:4, MBD 2:467 #330 (The Boston News-Letter of 13 June 1715, "On the 29th of May last Dyed James Warren Esq. of this Town, who was taken suddenly Ill as he was going to the General Assembly, he was a Gentleman of great Integrity and Capacity and his loss is Universally Lamented".)>; m. 21 June 1687, Plymouth, **Sarah DOTY**[3] <MD 13:204,25:3>, (dau of Edward DOTY[2] - see DOTY family) <For bth. 10 chil. see MBD 2:446; MD 1:208, 25:3-4; Plymouth VR.> (See WARREN Probate Appendix for will of Capt. James WARREN.)

12. **Jabez WARREN**[3], b. c1667, Plymouth, d. 19 Apr. 1701, drowned at sea <MD 16:63>.

VII **JOSEPH WARREN**[2], b. c1626/7, Plymouth <MD 3:46,51; 1:152 (pre 22 May 1627)>, d. 4 May 1689, Plymouth <Plymouth TR 1:201; MD 4:14,16:62>; m. c1652, Plymouth, **Priscilla FAUNCE** <MM:303>, (dau of John FAUNCE & Patience MORTON), b. c1633/4, Plymouth, d. 15 May 1707, near 74 yrs, Plymouth <Plymouth TR 1:204; Plymouth ChR 1:205 (ae about 74); MD 4:14,16:64>. (See WARREN Probate Appendix for will of Joseph WARREN.)

6 WARREN Children: <MBD 2:389>

1. **Mercy/Marcy WARREN**[3], b. 23 Sept. 1653, Plymouth <PCR 8:33; MD 18:69>, d. Mar. 1747, ae 93y6m, Kingston <MD 7:23>; m. 6 Jan. 1674, Plymouth, **John BRADFORD**[3] <MD 13:205>, (son of William BRADFORD[2] & Alice RICHARDS) - see BRADFORD family.

2. **Abigail WARREN**[3], b. 15 Mar. 1655, Plymouth <PCR 8:34; MD 18:69>, d. pe 4 May 1689 (fath. will) <MD 4:14-17>.

3. **Joseph WARREN**[3], b. 8 Jan. 1657, Plymouth <PCR 8:34; MD 18:69>, d. 28 Dec. 1696, Plymouth <Plymouth TR 1:203; MD 16:63>; m. 20 Dec. 1692, Plymouth, **Mehitabel WILDER** <MD 13:206; also rec. at Hingham as 25 Dec.>, (dau of Edward WILDER & Elizabeth EAMES), b. c1661, Hingham <MFIP #45>, d. aft. 21 June 1716, of Hingham <Plymouth Co.PR 3:404 (sett.hus.est.)>. In 1709 Mehitabel was acquitted on witchcraft charges <MFIP #45; MBD 2:462 #176>. <See MBD 2:392 for bth. 3 chil.; MD 2:224 (2); Hingham VR 1:91 (1); see MD 40:34 for his est.>

4. **Patience WARREN**[3], b. 15 Mar. 1660, Plymouth <PCR 8:34; MD 18:69,27:21>, d. aft. 9 Mar. 1719 (deed) <MD 27:22-3; Plymouth Co.Deeds 14:244>; m. 16 Dec. 1686, Plymouth, **Samuel LUCAS** <MD 13:205,27:21>, (son of Thomas), b. 15 Sept. 1661, Plymouth <PCR 8:23; MD 17:184,27:21>, d. 17 Jan. 1715/6, ae 54, Plymouth <MD 16:85,27:21>. <For bth. 4 chil. see MBD 2:393; MD 1:206, 27:22; Plymouth VR.> (See WARREN Probate Appendix for will of Samuel LUCAS Sr.)

5. **Elizabeth WARREN**[3], b. 15 Aug. 1662, Plymouth <PCR 8:34; MD 18:69,20:97>, d. betw. 9 Mar. 1719 (deed) <MD 27:23-4; Plymouth Co.Deeds 14:244> - 2 Jan. 1723 (hus.will) <MD 20:97>; m. 19 Jan. 1687/8, Plymouth, **Josiah PHINNEY** <MD 13:205,20:97>, (son of John PHINNEY & Elizabeth BAILEY), b. 11 Jan. 1660/1, Barnstable <PCR 8:47; MD 11:130,20:97>, d. betw. 2 Jan. 1723 (will) - 2 Jan. 1726/7 (pr.) <MD 20:97; Plymouth Co.PR 5:219-22>. (Josiah m.2nd, 14 Sept. 1726, Marshfield, Mercy (FORD) Thomas <Marshfield VR:145,428>, (dau of William FORD & (   ) DINGLEY),

<NEHGR 148:326>, b. 29 Apr. 1662, Marshfield <Marshfield VR:8>, d. (   ). Mercy m.1st, 27
May 168(-), Marshfield, Samuel THOMAS <Marshfield VR:16>, (son of John THOMAS & ?Sarah PIT-
NEY), b. 6 Nov. 1655, Marshfield <Marshfield VR:7>, d. 2 Sept. 1720, ae 65, Marshfield <Mar-
shfield VR:38,389>; for 4 chil. see Marshfield VR:13,14,16,18.) <For bth. 8 chil. see MBD
2:391, MD 1:208 & Plymouth VR. See also NEHGR 148:315-317, The Finney Family of Lenton, Nottinghamshire And Plymouth Mass.> (See WARREN Probate Appendix for will of Lieut. Josiah
FINNEY/PHINNEY.)

6. **Benjamin WARREN³**, b. 8 Jan. 1670, Plymouth <PCR 8:34; MD 18:69>, d. 30 May 1746, 76th yr,
    Plymouth g.s. <MD 16:86 (no yr), 23:152; Drew:14>; m.1st, 22 Apr. 1697, Plymouth, **Hannah**
    MORTON <MD 13:206,23:152>, (dau of Ephraim MORTON³⁻² (George¹) & Hannah FINNEY), b. 7 Nov.
    1677, Plymouth <MD 1:147>, d. 3 Nov. 1715, Plymouth <MD 16:85>. **Benjamin** m.2nd, 25 Oct. 1716
    Plymouth, **Esther/Hester (BARNES) Cushman** <MD 14:38,23:152>, (dau of Jonathan BARNES & Eliza-
    beth HEDGE), b. 18 Feb. 1682, Plymouth <Savage 1:121>, d. 1 Nov. 1770, ae 88, Plymouth g.s.
    <Drew:14> (Esther/Hester m.1st, 23 Feb. 1702/3, Plymouth, Elkanah CUSHMAN⁴ <MD 14:35>, (son
    of Elkanah CUSHMAN³ (Mary Allerton²) & Elizabeth COLE - see ALLERTON family), b. 15 Sept.
    1678, Plymouth <MD 1:142> d. 9 Jan. 1714/15, Plymouth, ae 37 <Kingman:10>; they had 4 chil.
    <MBD 2:73; MD 2:226 (3)>.) (See WARREN Probate Appendix for est. of Elkanah CUSHMAN.)

WARREN PROBATE APPENDIX

Will of Robert BARKER Sr.: <MD 31:102=104; Plymouth Co.PR 1:123>
...18 Feb. 1689, asks to be "Buried as near unto my welbeloved wife and my Eldest Son as Conveniently may be"; ment. sons Francis BARKER, Robert BARKER; daus Rebeckah SNOW, Abigail ROGERS;
grandsons Samuel BARKER (under 21), Francis BARKER, Robert BARKER, Jabiz BARKER (under 21), Isaac
BARKER (under 21), six daus of son Isaac BARKER, viz: Rebeckah, Mary, Lidia, Judeth, Martha "and
the youngest of all" (no name), when they reach 21 or marry. Inv. taken 15 Mar. 1691/2. (The
division of lands states the 5 Barker grandsons were sons of son Isaac.)
==
Will of Benjamin BARTLETT³ (Mary Warren²): <MD 6:44-9; Plymouth Co.PR 1:113-115,135>
...21 Aug. 1691, ment. pre-marital agreement with present wf Sissilla; sons Benjamin BARTLETT,
Samuel BARTLETT (land that belonged to his father in law PABODY), Ebenezer BARTLETT, Ichabod BAR-
TLETT; dau Rebecka BRADFORD & her two daus (Alice & Sarah) that she had by William BRADFORD; bro-
ther Joseph BARTLETT; Sarah COVEL "my wife her Aunt"; Indian servant Roben. Inv. 28 Aug. 1691.
==
Estate of Benjamin CHURCH³ (Elizabeth Warren²): <MD 7:100-7; Bristol Co.PR 3:563>
...27 Mar. 1719, Division between follow. chil., viz: Thomas CHURCH, Capt. Constant CHURCH, Charles CHURCH, Martha CHURCH widow of Edward, Elizabeth SAMPSON & hus. John SAMPSON. Ack. by all 16
Apr. 1719. (Bowman states "It is a curious fact that, although Martha CHURCH did not sign the
original document consenting to the sale of land, her name appears in the record". He believed
she was a daughter <MBD 2:369> but as is shown, she was a daughter-in-law; her name should be
deleted as a daughter in MBD.)

(Obit, MD 24:130: The Boston News-Letter of Monday, Feb. 3rd 1718, "Little Compton, January 18.
Yesterday the 17th Currant, The Honourable Col. Benjamin CHURCH Esq., Riding out to his Farm, his
Horse stumbled and he fell, pitched upon his Head and Shoulders, was immediately taken up and
carried to the next House, but never spoke a word after, but it's thought by the motions and
signs he made, that he had his Senses and Died about six hours after in the 78th Year of his Age.
He was a true lover of his Country and approved himself so, by venturing his Life so often in its
Defence in the several wars & many Services he has done for it, as also in his Stedfast adherence
to its Interest in times of Temptations to the contrary: a Gentleman also that has been a great
Friend and Incourager of Virtue and Religion, especially in this corner of the Province, where
Providence disposed the bounds of his Habitation".)
==
Estate of Caleb CHURCH³ (Elizabeth Warren²): <MDP:476; Middlesex Co.PR #4449, 17:439>
...18 Apr. 1726, Settlement among follow. chil., viz: Isaac CHURCH, Hannah BOOMER wf of Matthew,
Ruth INGERSOLE wf of Thomas, Rebecca WARREN wf of Joshua. (See MDP:476 for letter dated 1722
from Ruth INGERSOLE to son John MADDOCKS.)
==
Will of Joseph CHURCH³ (Elizabeth Warren²): <MD 22:22-5; Bristol Co.PR 3:21>
...15 Feb. 1710/11, ment. sons Joseph CHURCH (eldest son), John CHURCH; daus Elizabeth BLACKMAN
wf of Joseph, Mary WOOD wf of Lieut. John, Deborah GRAY wf of Samuel, Abigail SIMONS wf of William; Mary TOCOCKONOE "for her former kindnesses to my wife & since to my self"; Indian boy Amos
(to receive half a 15 acre lot when he serves out his time. Wit. made oath 12 Mar. 1710/11.
==
Estate of Nathaniel CHURCH³ (Elizabeth Warren²): <PN&Q 5:91-3; Plymouth Co.PR 3:20>
...5 Mar. 1707/8, Settlement, states he left a widow Sarah and 7 chil., viz: Richard CHURCH (the
eldest son since dec'd leaving 3 chil.), Nathaniel CHURCH, Joseph CHURCH (3rd son, since dec'd
leaving one dau.), Charles CHURCH, Abigaill, Alce/Alice & Sarah. Signed by the widow Sarah
CHURCH; William BEARSTOW as gdn. to chil. of Richard CHURCH; Nathaniel CHURCH; Judith CHURCH the
widow of Joseph; Charles CHURCH; Nathaniel HARLOW, Abigail HARLOW; Sarah CHURCH. <4:31>...4 Nov.
1717, dau Sarah HOLMES & hus. John HOLMES signed.
==

Will of **Richard CHURCH**: <MD 5:118-20; Suffolk Co.PR 6:21>
...25 Dec. 1668, ment. wf Elizabeth; son Joseph CHURCH to have a double portion "by reason of the lamnes of his hand, whereby hee is disinabled above the rest of my children, for the getting of a livlihood"; unnamed chil. Inv. taken 1 Jan. 1668/9.
===

Estate of **Elkanah CUSHMAN**: <Plymouth Co.PR 4:20>
...22 June 1717, Division among the widow, Hester WARREN now the wife of Benjamin WARREN and follow. chil., viz: Elkanah CUSHMAN, James CUSHMAN, Elizabeth and Hannah.
===

Will of **Jonathan DELANO**: (yeoman) <MD 23:148-51; Bristol Co.PR 3:707>
...17 Dec. 1720, ment. wf Mercy; sons Nathaniel DELANO, Jethro DELANO (under 21), Thomas DELANO
(under 21), Jonathan DELANO, Jabez DELANO; daus Esther DELANO, Mercy HATCH; granddaus. Meribah
DELANO, Susanna NYE. Codicil, 22 Dec. 1720, ment. sons Nathaniel, Jethro & Thomas. Pr. 6 Mar.
1720/1.
===

Will of **Josiah FINNEY/PHINNEY**: (Lieut.) <MDP:485; MD 20:97-100; Plymouth Co.PR 5:219>
...2 Jan. 1723, ment. sons Robert FINNEY, Josiah FINNEY, John FINNEY, Joshua FINNEY; daus Elizabeth BRADFORD, Precilah MARSHALL, Pheby FINNEY; my negro man. Pr. 2 Jan. 1726.
===

Will of **Michael FORD**: <MDP:449; Plymouth Co.PR 5:498>
...12 June 1719, ment. wf Bethiah; sons William FORD, James FORD, Thomas FORD, Ephraim FORD, Elisha FORD; daus Bathsheba, Mehitable & Mercy. Pr. 16 May 1729.
===

Will of **Thomas GIBBS Sr.**: (husbandman) <MDP:518; MD 23:123-5; Barnstable Co.PR 5:24>
...23 June 1725, ment. sons Thomas GIBS, Cornelius GIBBS, Warren GIBBS; sons Ebenezer GIBBS &
Jabez GIBBS "beyond the sea if they return"; dau Abigail; chil. of daus Bethiah & Sarah. Wit.
sworn 12 Jan. 1732/3.
===

Will of **Capt. Thomas GRAY**: (yeoman) <MDP:456; MD 21:84-8; Bristol Co.PR 4:19>
...21 Sept. 1721, ment. wf Phebe; sons Thomas GRAY, Edward GRAY; dau Anna RICHMOND, Rebeccah GRAY
(under 24); 3 grandchil., viz: Barzeller RICHMOND, Mary GRAY, Anstes GRAY; kinsman Nathaneil/
Nathaniel GIBES/GIBS son of Warren GIBS; negro woman Sarah; melattow/mulatto boy Sollomon. Codicil, 21 Oct. 1721, ment. wf Phebe and sons Thomas & Edward. Inv. 7 Nov. 1721.
===

Estate of **Sergt. William HARLOW**: <MDP:509; MD 12:193-7; Plymouth Co.PR 1:104-5>
...18 Sept. 1691, Settlement, ment. the widow Mary; 7 unnamed daus.; sons Samuel HARLOW, William
HARLOW, Nathaniel HARLOW, Benjamin HARLOW.
===

Will of **Josiah KEEN/KEENE Sr.**: <MD 19:128-30; Plymouth Co.PR 2:160>
...28 May 1695, ment. son Josiah KEEN; unnamed wf; sons Mathew KEEN, John KEEN, Ephraim KEEN; 4
unmarried & unnamed daus.; unnamed grandch. Pr. 15 Sept. 1710.
===

Will of **Ephraim LITTLE[3] (Anna Warren[2])**: (yeoman) <MD 19:159-61; Plymouth Co.PR 4:113>
...7 Mar. 1715, ment. wf Mary; sons Ephraim LITTLE (eldest son), David LITTLE, John LITTLE; daus
Mercy OTIS, Ruth AVERY & chil. of dec'd dau Anna GRAY; "my Negro Man Named Stuard be kindly and
Favourable dealt with in his Old Age And that he be allowed during his Naturall life, for Rest
and Recreation, One day in Every Month, Over and Above what the Law Allows." Pr. 24 Dec. 1717.
===

Will of **Lieut. Isaac LITTLE[3] (Anna Warren[2])**: <MD 24:17; Plymouth Co.PR (original)>
...18 Nov. 1699, nuncupative will, "on his Death bed", ment. sons Thomas LITTLE (eldest son),
Isaac LITTLE, Charles LITTLE, Nathaniel LITTLE, William LITTLE, Lemuel LITTLE (youngest son); 2
unnamed daus; unnamed wf; brothers Maj. Nathaniel THOMAS, Ephraim LITTLE; "Most of his children
being present he charged them to take notice as they would Answer it at that great day that this
was his Will: he also told his Son Thomas that he had done Considerably for him already: And So
Charged them all to fear God & obey their Mother and to live in Love one with Another." Wit.
made oath 6 Mar. 1699/1700. <3:283>...29 Mar. 1712, Division among widow Bethiah and follow.
chil., viz: Thomas LITTLE, Isaac LITTLE, Charles LITTLE, Nathaniel LITTLE, William LITTLE, Lemuel
LITTLE, Abigail LITTLE, Bethiah LITTLE. (William, Lemuel & Bethiah appear to be the youngest and
were not of full age.) On 7 Mar. 1712/3, William LITTLE "being then of full age" ack. On 3 Apr.
1714, Thomas BARKER & wf Bethiah BARKER ack. On 3 May 1718, Lemuel LITTLE ack.
===

Will of **Samuel LITTLE[3] (Anna Warren[2])**: (joyner) <MD 17:83-5; Bristol Co.PR 2:196>
...13 Jan. 1707/8, "being in much Paine & other Illness of body", ment. wf Sarah; eldest son
Samuel LITTLE; granddau. Sarah BILLINGS Jr.; youngest son Edward LITTLE; grandson Richard BILLIN-
GS Jr.; dau Sarah BILLINGS wf of Richard. Inv. 4 Feb. 1707/8.
===

Estate of **Sarah (GRAY) Little**: (widow) <MD 17:85-7; Bristol Co.PR>
...7 Mar. 1736/7, Petition of son Edward LITTLE for probate and asks that "those persons whom
there is grounds to Think may Conceale or Embezzled my mother's goods & Estate may be cited". A
cittion dated 3 May 1737 states son Samuel LITTLE has filed a complaint, "that he harth Great
Reason to Suspect that Edward LITTLE of Bristol aforsaid her other Son in the Life Time of the
Said Sarah LITTLE While she Lived by her self Alone Did Conceal Imbezel or Convey Away Considerable of her money Goods or Chattles."
===

Will of **Thomas LITTLE**: <MD 4:162-3; Plymouth Col.Wills 3:1:46>
...17 May 1671, ment. unnamed wf; sons Isacke LITTLE (eldest son), Ephraim LITTLE (unm.); young-

est sons Thomas LITTLE & Samuel LITTLE; grandchild John JONES. Pr. 1 July 1672.

Will of **Thomas LITTLE Sr.**[3] **(Anna Warren**[2]**)**: <MD 4:164; Plymouth Col.Wills 3:1:165>
...19 Feb. 1675/6, ment. brother Samuel LITTLE; "all my wages which is Due to mee for being a souldier"; sisters Ruth, Hannah, Patience, Mercye; unnamed mother; brothers Isack LITTLE, Ephraim LITTLE. Wit. made oath 31 May 1676.

Will of **Samuel LUCAS Sr.**: <MD 27:22-3; Plymouth Co.PR>
...4 July 1715, ment. son Joseph LUCAS; unnamed wf; son William LUCAS; dau Patiance. Wit. sworn 8 Mar. 1715/6.

Will of **Jonathan MOREY/MORY**: <MDP:507; Plymouth Co.PR 2:133>
...24 Feb. 1699/1700, ment. wf Hannah; son John MOREY; dau Hannah BUMPAS; son Jonathan MOREY. Pr. 16 June 1708.

Will of **John NELSON**: <MD 19:190-92; Plymouth Co.PR 1:270>
...29 Apr. 1697, ment. minor son Samuel NELSON; daus Mehetabel DOTY, Joanna (under 18); wf Patience; son-in-law John DOTEY Jr. Pr. 16 June 1697.

Will of **Samuel RIDER**: (yeoman) <MD 11:185-6; Plymouth Co.PR 3:377-8>
...7 Apr. 1714, ment. son William RIDER; wf Lydia; daus Hannah, Sarah, Lydia, Mary, Elizabeth & Abigail; sons John RIDER, Samuel RIDER, Benjamin RIDER; dau Mercy; sons Joseph RIDER, Josiah RIDER. Pr. 23 Sept. 1715.

Will of **Stephen SKEFFE/SKIFF**: <Barnstable Co.PR 3:137-9>
...7 May 1701, ment. wf Lydia; granddau. Keziah; son Stephen SKEFFE; daus Abigail SMITH, Deborah PRESBURY, Mary CHIPMAN, Lydia BLACKWELL. Codicil, 20 Aug. 1708, ment. marriage of granddau. Keziah. Pr. 28 June 1710.

Will of **Anthony SNOW**: <MD 5:1-5; Plymouth Co.PR 1:156-8>
...28 Dec. 1685, ment wf Abigall; grandson Jams/James FORD; son Josias SNOW & his wf; daus Lidia, Sarah & Alis/Alice; chil. of dau Abigall; grandchildren Hannah FORD & Abigail FORD; brother Joseph WARREN. Codicil, 8 Aug. 1692, ment. wf; unnamed chil. & grandch.; three of dau Abigall's chil.; dau Sarah and "other daus". Pr. 3 Jan. 1692/3.

Will of **Anthony SPRAGUE**: (yeoman) <MD 18:220-24; Suffolk Co.PR 21:493,496>
...21 July 1716, ment. son Anthony SPRAGUE & his son Anthony; sons Richard SPRAGUE, James SPRAGUE Samuel SPRAGUE, Mathew SPRAGUE, Josiah SPRAGUE, Jeremiah SPRAGUE; dau Sarah BATE. Inv. 24 Sept. 1719.

Will of **Samuel THAXTER**: (wheelwright) <MD 23:145-7; Suffolk Co.PR 24:212>
...12 July 1723, ment. daus Sarah DUNBAR, Deborah BEAL, Abagail THAXTER; son David THAXTER. Pr. 6 Oct. 1725.

Will of **Capt. Benjamin WARREN**[3] **(Joseph**[2]**)**: (yeoman) <MDP:483; MD 23:152-54; Plymouth Co.PR #21858, 10:301,303>...8 May 1745, "aged", ment. wf Esther and follow. chil., viz: Nathaniel WARREN, dec'd son Benjamin WARREN, Abigail RIDER widow of Joseph, Hannah FAUNCE wf of Eleazer, Priscilla, Patience & Mercy; Benjamin WARREN, only son of son Benjamin. Pr. 8 July 1746.

Will of **Capt. James WARREN**[3] **(Nathaniel**[2]**)**: <MD 25:6-12; Plymouth Co.PR #21874, 3:360>
...28 Jan. 1711/12, ment. wf Sarah; only son James WARREN (under 21); dau Sarah; dec'd brother Nathaniel WARREN; unnamed daus (some under 16). Pr. 23 June 1715.

Will of **Joseph WARREN**[2]: <MD 4:14-17; Plymouth Co.PR 1:38-9>
...4 May 1689, ment. wf Pricilla; sons Joseph WARREN, Benjamin WARREN; daus Mercy BRADFORD, Patience & Elizabeth; brother Thomas FAUNCE. Inv. 14 May 1689.

Will of **Nathaniel WARREN**[2]: <MD 2:36-40; Plymouth Col. Wills 2:2:46-7>
...29 June 1667, ment. wf Sarah; unnamed chil.; unnamed eldest son; "incase my Deare Child my Daughter Hope shall Continew lame and Impotent"; brother Joseph WARREN; regarding the marriages of his children he asks, "That they bee matched with such as may be fitt for them both in reference to their sperituall and outward estate". Codicil, 16 July 1667, ment. mother Elizabeth WARREN; brother Joseph WARREN, sisters Mary BARTLETT Sr., Ann LITTLE, Sarah COOKE, Elizabeth CHURCH & Abigaill SNOW. Inv. 21 Oct. 1667.

Will of **Nathaniel WARREN**[3] **(Nathaniel**[2]**)**: <MDP:518; MD 22:43-7; Plymouth Co.PR #21896, 2:140>
...28 Oct. 1707, "God in his holy providence having denyed me the blessing of a natural ofspring" ment. wf Phebe and following "kindred & relations", viz: Warren GIBBS; James WARREN & Sarah WARREN the chil. of brother James WARREN; Sarah GIBBS alias CUSHMAN wf of Isaac Jr.; Alice BLACKWELL alias SPOONER wf of William; Mercy LUMBARD alias BURGES wf of Ebenezer; James WARREN son of dec'd brother Richard WARREN; Desire BLACKWELL alias GENNINGS/JENNINGS wf of Lettice; negro girl Pegg. Inv. 14 Dec. 1707.

Will of **Joseph WATERMAN**: <MDP:451; MD 24:145-9; Plymouth Co.PR #22163, 3:33,34>
...6 Aug. 1709, ment. wf Sarah and following chil., viz: Joseph WATERMAN, Anthony WATERMAN,

Sarah HEWETT, unnamed chil. of dec'd dau Elizabeth BARTLETT, Abigall WINSLOW, Bethiah & Lidia; Joseph RYDER "my sister's son"; ment. lands exchanged with sons Joseph WATERMAN & Kenelm WINSLOW; Mary OKESMAN, whom he had "brought up". Inv. taken 16 Feb. 1710/11.

NOTES:

WILLIAM WHITE

William WHITE was probably born in England, although his origins are unknown. He was possibly connected with the Whites of Sturton-le-Steeple, Nottinghamshire <MQ 54:284>. William died 21 Feb. 1620/1, Plymouth, during the General Sickness of the first winter <MD 30:3>. His wife was Susanna (   ), origins and maiden name unknown. Despite the oft repeated claim that she was the Anna, sister of Dr. Samuel & Edward Fuller, the known facts do not support this assumption. Sister Anna was born in 1577; Susanna's first child was born c1615, her last child was born c1630's and her 2nd husband was born in 1595. Using Anna's birth date, this would make Susanna 38 when her first child was born, over 53 when her last child was born and she would have been 18 years older than her 2nd husband! <See MBD 2:486 #1 which discusses these and other facts.> Susanna married as her 2nd husband, Edward WINSLOW (See WINSLOW family). She died after 18 Dec. 1654 (will of 2nd hus.) and possibly pre 2 July 1675 (will of son Josiah who makes no provision for her).

(See also: Mayflower Families Through Five Generations (MF5G), William White of the Mayflower, by Ruth W. Sherman, F.A.S.G. and Robert M. Sherman, C.G., F.A.S.G., vol. 1, (1975), 4th printing 1988 with addendum.)

William & Susanna had 2 children:

I.   Resolved, b. c1615/6, England or Holland
II. Peregrine, b. betw. 27 Nov. - 30 Nov. 1620 (O.S.), Cape Cod Harbour.

* * * * * * * * * * * * * * *

I.   **RESOLVED WHITE[2]**, b. c1615/6, England or Holland <MD 33:99 (ae about 59 when he wit. receipt on 4 July 1674)>, d. prob. aft. 19 Sept. 1687 <Plymouth Co.Deeds 1:38 (son is called son of Resolved - he is not called dec'd); MBD 2:471 (Bowman states he d. betw. 1690-94 with no source or reason)>; m.1st, 5 Nov. 1640, Scituate, **Judith VASSALL** <MD 2:32; MD 17:74 (says 8 Apr.)>, (dau of William VASSALL & Ann KING), b. c1605/6, England <MF5G 1:100 (ae 74 in deposition dated 2 Mar. 1679/80; however in saying this, MF5G gives her a birth of 1619!)>, bur. 3 Apr. 1670, Marshfield <Marshfield VR:10, MSR:248, MD 2:182 (name worn)>. **Resolved** m.2nd, 5 Oct. 1674, Salem, **Abigail (   ) LORD** <MM:336; MD 2:120 (N.S.)>, b. ?c1606, prob. England, d. betw. 26 Apr. 1682 - 27 June 1682 (will & pr), Salem <Essex Inst.Hist.Coll.3:189; MF5G 1:99 & MBD 2:481 state she d. aft. 15 June with no reason given>. (Abigail m.1st, William LORD <MF5G 1:99> who d. betw. 2 Mar. 1668 - 24 June 1673 (will & pr.) <Essex Co.PR 2:352-3>.)

8 WHITE Children: (by 1st wf) <MBD 2:480; MSR:312-15 (Norwell ChR, bpt. 3-8)>

1.   **William WHITE[3]**, b. 10 Apr. 1642, Scituate <PCR 8:19; MD 17:74>, d. 24 Jan. 1695, Marshfield, unm. <Marshfield VR:19; MD 5:233; MSR:250>.

2.   **John WHITE[3]**, b. 11 Mar. 1644, Scituate <PCR 8:19; MD 17:74>, d. prob. pre 13 Mar. 1684/5 <PN&Q 5:87 (deed of father & brothers, he is not ment.)>.

3.   **Samuel WHITE[3]**, b. 13 Mar. 1646, Scituate <PCR 8:19; MD 12:97,17:74>, d. betw. 20 Sept. 1720 <MBD 2:480, MF5G 1:104 (apparently a deed - where is it?)> - 11 Aug. 1731 <MD 9:219 (dec'd in son John's deposition); MD 9:220 (poss. pre 21 Apr. 1731 when son is called "Samuel Sr.")>; m. c1668, prob. Sandwich or Scituate, **Rebecca (   )**, b. c13 Mar. 1646 <MD 12:97>, (she is prob. **Rebecca LAPHAM**, dau of Thomas, bpt. 15 Mar. 1645/6, Scituate <MSR:312 (Samuel was bpt. same day)> d. 25 June 1711, 65th yr, Rochester <MD 12:97>. <For bth. 9 chil. (incl. twins) see MBD 2:481-2, MD 12:97 & Rochester VR.>

4.   **Resolved WHITE[3]**, b. 12 Nov. 1647, Scituate <PCR 8:19; MD 17:75>, bur. 27 Mar. 1670, Marshfield <Marshfield VR:10 & MD 2:182 (1st name worn)>.

5.   **Anna WHITE[3]**, b. 4 June 1649, Scituate <PCR 8:19; MD 17:75>, d. 25 May 1714, ae 64, Concord <Concord VR>; m. 2 June 1671, Concord, **John HAYWARD** <Concord VR>, (son of George & Mary), b. 20 Dec. 1640, Concord <Concord VR; MBD 2:481>, d. 22 Nov. 1718, ae 78, Concord <Concord VR; MBD 2:481>. <See MBD 2:481,488 #36 for bth. 7 chil.>

6.   **Elizabeth WHITE[3]**, b. 4 June 1652, Scituate <PCR 8:19; MD 17:75>, d. aft. 10 Mar. 1712/3 (ack.deed) <Middlesex Co.Deeds 17:467>; m. 17 July 1672, Concord, **Obadiah WHEELER** <Concord VR:16>, (son of Obadiah), b. c1650, Concord, d. aft. 10 Mar. 1712/3 (ack.deed) <Middlesex Co. Deeds 17:467>. <For bth. 9 chil. see MBD 2:481, MF5G 1:105, Concord VR:17,19,21,24,26,28,34, 38,41.>

7.   **Josiah WHITE[3]**, b. 29 Sept. 1654, Scituate <PCR 8:19; MD 8:165,17:175>, d. betw. 3 Mar. - 5 June 1710, Boxford <MDP:538 (will & pr.)>; m. pre 30 Dec. 1680, **Remember READ** <MDP:537; Essex Co.Deeds 5:101>, (dau of Thomas), bpt. 26 Apr. 1657, Salem <MD 8:165>, d. aft. 20 May 1721,

Salem (ack.deed) <MDP:539; Essex Co.Deeds 38:79>. <See MF5G 1:106 for 6 chil.; see also MD
8:165-170 for descendants of Josiah WHITE.> (See WHITE Probate Appendix for will of Josiah.)

8. **Susanna WHITE**[3], b. Aug. 1656 <MF5G 1:101>, bpt. 8 Nov. 1656, Scituate <MSR:315>.

II. **PEREGRINE WHITE**[2], b. betw. 27 Nov.-30 Nov. 1620 (O.S.), Cape Cod Harbour <MD 30:3,145-6,31:
145-7; PN&Q 5:83-4 & Plymouth Col.Court Orders 4:112 (On 11 Oct. 1665, he was granted 200
acres "in Respect that hee was the first of the English that was borne in these ptes" - MF5G
1:102 gives the year as 1655 (as does Stratton:370), citing PN&Q (which says 1665) but not
citing the original records so I assume 1655 is a typo error); MD 11:38 ("Capt. Peregrine
White the first born Child of New England born November 1620 was admitted into this Church
May 22 1698 in the 78th Year of his age. Mat.20.6.7.")>, d. 20 July 1704, ae 83y8m, Marshfield <Marshfield VR:43; MSR:250; MD 24:128,30:145,31:145; note that in his daughter's obit
his dth. date is given as 22 July>; m. pre 6 Mar 1648/9, prob. Marshfield, **Sarah BASSETT** <MBD
2:486 #4, Plymouth Col.Court Orders 2:183 (they were fined for fornication before marriage or
contract)>, (dau of William & Elizabeth), b. (   ), d. 22 Jan. 1711, Marshfield <Marshfield
VR:33; MD 7:120; MSR:250>. (See WHITE Probate Appendix for will & obit of Peregrine WHITE.)

7 WHITE Children: <MBD 2:471>

1. **Daniel WHITE**[3], b. c1649 or c1654, Marshfield, d. 6 May 1724, ae 70 or 75, Marshfield g.s.
<MD 20:61; 70th yr -MSR:251 & MD 30:154; ae 75, g.s. - Marshfield VR:413 & MD 13:133>; m.
19 Aug. 1674, Marshfield, **Hannah HUNT** <Marshfield VR:8; MD 20:61>, b. (   ), d. aft. 25
May 1721 (hus.will) <MD 20:62>. <For bth. 7 chil. see MBD 2:471, MD 7:119 & Marshfield VR:
31 (2), 32 (5).> (See WHITE Probate Appendix for will of Daniel WHITE.)

2. **child**, b. c1650/51, d.y. <Bradford stated Peregrine had 2 chil.>

3. **Jonathan WHITE**[3], b. 4 June 1658, Marshfield <MD 2:207>, d. betw. 14 July 1736 - 22 Feb. 1737,
Yarmouth <MD 9:122-3 (will & pr.)>; m.1st, 2 Feb. 1682/3, Yarmouth, **Hester NICKERSON** <MD 2:
209>, (dau of Nicholas & Mary), b. last week Oct. 1656, Yarmouth <MD 2:208>, d. 8 Feb. 1702/
03, Yarmouth <Yarmouth VR 3:5>. **Jonathan** m.2nd, (   ), **Elizabeth** (   ), b. (   ), d.
12 Apr. 1718, Yarmouth <Yarmouth VR 3:29>. <See MBD 2:477 for 7 chil. by 1st wf.> (See
WHITE Probate Appendix for will of Jonathan WHITE.)

4. **Peregrine WHITE**[3], b. c1661/2, Marshfield <MF5G 1:108 (bpt. 16 Feb. 1723/4, ae 62, Boston)>,
d. 20 Nov. 1727, ae 66, Boston g.s. <MF5G 1:108>; m.1st c1684, (   ), **Susanna** (   ), b.
(   ), d. (   ). **Peregrine** m.2nd, pre 9 June 1696 <MF5G 1:108 (reason?)>, **Mary** (   ),
b. (   ), d. aft. 13 Mar. 1755 <MF5G 1:108 (reason?)>. (Mary m.2nd, 1728, Cornelius JUDE-
VINE <MF5G 1:108>.) <See MBD 2:478 & Weymouth VR for bth. 1 son.>

5. **Sarah WHITE**[3], b. c1663, Marshfield, d. 9 Aug. 1755, 92nd yr, Scituate <MD 24:129>; m. Jan.
1688/9, Scituate, **Thomas YOUNG** <MD 2:87; MSR:618>, (son of George YOUNG & Hannah PINSON), b.
5 Nov. 1663, Scituate, d. 25 Dec. 1732, ae 69y1m20d, Scituate g.s. <MD 8:118; MSR:618>.
<See MBD 2:480 & Scituate VR 4:66 for bth. 9 chil.> (See WHITE Probate Appendix for obit of
Sarah (WHITE) Young.)

6. **Sylvanus WHITE**[3], b. prob. pre 1667, Marshfield (if at least 21 when his est. was adm.),
d. pre "last of" June 1688 (adm.) <PN&Q 4:123-4 (30th June was written but crossed off)>.

7. **Mercy WHITE**[3], b. c1670, Marshfield, d. 12 June 1739, ae 69, Marshfield <MD 13:110>; m. 3 Feb.
1697, Marshfield, **William SHERMAN**[3] <MD 5:237,25:133>, (son of William SHERMAN & Desire
DOTY[2]). See DOTY family.

WHITE PROBATE APPENDIX

<u>Will of **Daniel WHITE**[3] (Peregrine[2]):</u> <MDP:530; MD 20:62-3; Plymouth Co.PR #22533, 4:446-8>
...25 May 1721, "being aged & Infirm", ment. wf Hannah and follow. chil., viz: John WHITE, Joseph
WHITE, Thomas WHITE, Cornelius WHITE, Benjamin WHITE, Eleazer WHITE, Ebenezer WHITE. Pr. 8 May
1724.

==

<u>Will of **Jonathan WHITE**[3] (Peregrine[2]):</u> (yeoman) <MD 9:122-3; Barnstable Co.PR 5:304>
...14 July 1736, ment. sons Jonathan WHITE (eldest son), Joseph WHITE (3rd son), Ebenezer WHITE;
daus Elizabeth WHITE, Esther DRAKE, Sarah WHITE, Mary RUSSELL; minor grandson Jonathan DELL. Pr.
22 Feb. 1737.

==

<u>Will of **Josiah WHITE**[3] (Resolved[2]):</u> (yeoman) <MDP:538; MD 8:166; Essex Co.PR 310:244>
...3 Mar. 1710, ment. wf Remember; sons Josiah WHITE, Joseph WHITE, Samuel WHITE (under 21); daus
Sarah WHITE, Hannah WHITE (under 18). Wit. made oath, 28 May 1724.

==

Will of **Peregrine WHITE**[2]: <MD 1:129-31; Plymouth Co.PR 2:48>
...14 July 1704, "being aged and under many Weaknesses and Bodily Infirmities", ment. wf Sarah;
eldest son Daniel WHITE; daus Sarah & Mercy; son Jonathan WHITE and his eldest unnamed son; son
Peregrine WHITE. Pr. 14 Aug. 1704.

Obit: <MD 24:128,30:145; MBD 2:486 #2>
The Boston News-Letter of Monday, 31 July 1704, "Marshfield, July 22, Capt. Peregrine White of
this Town, Aged Eighty three years and Eight Months died the 20th Instant. He was vigorous and
of a comly Aspect to the last: Was the Son of Mr. William White and Susanna his Wife: born on
board the Mayflower, Capt. Jones Commander in Cape Cod Harbour, November, 1620, was the First En-
glishman born in New England. Altho' he was in the former part of his Life extravagent yet was
much Reform'd in his last years and died hopefully." (See daughter's obit below.)
===
Obit of **Sarah (WHITE**[3]**) Young**: <MD 24:129; MBD 2:486 #4a>
The Boston News-Letter of Friday, 29 Aug. 1755, "Saturday August 9th died at Scituate in the 92nd
Year of her Age, Mrs. Sarah Young, the virtuous widow of Mr. Thomas Young and eldest Daughter of
That Mr. Peregrine White of Marshfield, who was the First Born English Child in New-England: Be-
ing Son of William and Susannah White, born on board the ship in Cape Cod Harbour in the latter
Part of November 1620, in which Governor Carver and the Rest of our Plimouth Planters came to New
England, before the Ship left said Harbour and set sail for said Plimouth. Said Peregrine White
liv'd in great Health and Vigour to the 84th Year of his Age, when a Fever carried Him off on
July 22, 1704 as our News-Letter soon after inform'd the Publick. And this his Eldest Daughter
was Born at Marshfield in Oct. 1663, enjoy'd her Senses and Health in good measure, till towards
her End, and left four Sons surviving. Two observable Instances of the Long Lives of the very
first and second Race of Children born in this happy Country."

NOTES:

EDWARD WINSLOW

Edward WINSLOW was born 18 Oct. 1595, Droitwich, Worcestershire, England, the son of Edward WIN-SLOW & Magdalene OLIVER <NEHGR 4:297-303>. He "fell sick at sea betwixt Domingo & Jamaica" and died 8 May 1655 in his 61st year <MD 4:1-3; see MD 5:224-33 for account of his life>. Edward married 1st, c12 May 1618, Leyden, Elizabeth BARKER <MD 8:100,22:66-7 (3rd bans were published 12 May so the marriage took place on or soon after this date)>. Elizabeth's origins are unknown, however the marriage record states she was from Chatsum, co. Suffolk, England. She died 24 Mar. 1621, Plymouth <MD 30:3>. Edward married 2nd, 12 May 1621, Plymouth, Susanna (   ) WHITE <MD 30:4>, the widow of William WHITE (see WHITE family). (See WINSLOW Probate Appendix for will of Edward WINSLOW.)

(See also: Mayflower Families Through Five Generations (MF5G), Edward Winslow of the Mayflower, by Ruth C. McGuyre and Robert S. Wakefield, F.A.S.G., vol. 5, 1991; NEHGR 4:297, Genealogical Memoir of the Descendants of Edward Winslow, Governor of Plymouth Colony; NEHGR 17:159, Genealogy of the Winslow Family; NEHGR 121:25,122:175,124:182, The Mayflower Winslows - Yeomen or Gentlemen?; TAG 41:168, Clues to the Ancestry of Winslow of Droitwich; TAG 42:52, Governor Edward Winslow's Mother's Family, the Olivers; TAG 42:52, A Note on the Winslow Births in England; TAG 43:239, A Winslow Pilgrim Note - Addendum.)

Edward and Susanna had 5 children: <In a letter to Gov. Winthrop, 28 Nov. 1640, Edward states one child has died; Bradford states in 1650/1 that he has two children.>

I.   child, b. & d. 1623 <NEHGR 109:242-3 (in a letter to Uncle Robert Jackson in England, dated 30 Oct. 1623, Edward states "My wife hath had one child by me, but it pleased him that gave it to take it again unto himselfe")>.
II. Edward, b. c1624 (above letter of 1623, Edward states "I left her with child at my departure (whom God Preserve) but hope to be with her before her delivery.), d. betw. 22 May 1627 <MD 1:150 (Cattle Division)> - 1640 or 1650/1.
III. John, b. c1626, d. betw. 22 May 1627 <MD 1:150 (Cattle Division)> - 1640 or 1650/1.
IV. Josiah, b. c1628, Plymouth.
V.   Elizabeth, b. c1630's, Plymouth.

                    * * * * * * * * * * * * * * *

IV JOSIAH WINSLOW[2], b. c1628, Plymouth, d. 18 Dec. 1680, ae 52, Marshfield g.s. <Marshfield VR:390; MD 5:82,10:51; MSR:241>; m. 1651 or 1657, London or Boston, Penelope PELHAM <MF5G 5:7>, (dau of Herbert PELHAM & Jemima WALDEGRAVE), bpt. 1633, Bures, co. Essex, England <NEHGR 33:285-91>, d. 7 Dec. 1703, ae 73, Marshfield g.s. <Marshfield VR:43,390; MD 10:51; MSR:241,250> (See WINSLOW Probate Appendix for will of Josiah WINSLOW.)

4 WINSLOW Children: <MBD 2:490>

1. dau., b. 13 Mar. 1658, Marshfield <Marshfield VR:5; MD 2:7>, bur. 15 Mar. 1658, Marshfield <Marshfield VR:3; MD 2:5>.

2. Elizabeth WINSLOW[3], b. 8 Apr. 1664, Marshfield <Marshfield VR:6; MD 2:111>, d. 11 July 1735, ae 72, Pembroke, Centre cem. <Pembroke VR:394; MD 9:112>; m. 4 Sept. 1684, Marshfield, Stephen BURTON <Marshfield VR:11; MD 2:183,10:56; MSR:243>, (son of Stephen), b. (   ), prob. England, d. 22 July 1693, Bristol <VR RI (Bristol) 6:121; Gen.Adv. 4:125 "Whereas Mr. Stephen Burton somtime Clerk of the peace for the County of Bristol Dec'd: by Reason of some Distempter in his head A Considerable time before his Death: was very remiss in Recording & Keeping the Records of the Court...8 Aug. 1694">. (Stephen m.1st, aft. 9 Feb. 1673, Abigail BRENTON <MF5G 5:9>, (dau of William), b. (   ), bur. 30 Mar. 1684, Bristol <VR RI (Bristol) 6:121>; see MD 10:56-9 for 1 ch. <See MF5G 1:10 for 4 chil.; MBD 2:490 (3), omits child who d.y.>

3. Edward WINSLOW[3], b. 14 May 1667, Marshfield <Marshfield VR:6; MD 2:111>, bur. 11 Dec. 1667, Marshfield <Marshfield VR:427; MSR:248>.

4. Isaac WINSLOW[3], b. c1671, Marshfield, d. 14 Dec. 1738, ae 67, Marshfield g.s. <Marshfield VR:47,390; MD 9:184,24:132; MSR:241>; m. 11 July 1700, Boston, Sarah WENSLEY <Marshfield VR:22; Boston Rcd.Com.28:2; MD 5:236,24:30>, (dau of John WENSLEY & Elizabeth PADDY), b. 11 Aug. 1673, Boston <Boston Rcd.Com.9:130>, d. 16 Dec. 1753, ae 80, Marshfield g.s. <Marshfield VR:47; MD 9:185,24:31>. <For bth. 6 chil. see MBD 2:490, MD 7:118 & Marshfield VR:31. (See WINSLOW Probate Appendix for wills of Hon. Isaac WINSLOW & wife)

V. ELIZABETH WINSLOW[2], b. c1630's, Plymouth, d. betw. 25 Dec. 1696 <Essex Co.Court Rec.15:102> - 23 Apr. 1698, Boston (adm.) <MDP:548; MD 1:240; Suffolk Co.PR #2447, 8:140; Boston Rcd.Com.9:237 (prob. the Mis. Curwin who d. 23 Sept. 1697)>; m.1st, pre 1656, poss. England, Robert

BROOKS <MD 1:239>, (poss. son of Robert & Anne), b. (   ), prob. England <MF5G 5:8>, d. pre 22 Sept. 1669 (wf remarr.). **Elizabeth** m.2nd, 22 Sept. 1669, Salem, **George CURWEN/CORWIN** <MD 1:239; Salem VR>, b. 10 Dec. 1610, Workington, co. Cumberland, Eng. <MF5G 5:8>, d. 3 Jan. 1684/5, Salem <MD 1:239>. (George m.1st, Elizabeth (HERBERT) White & had 7 chil. <MF5G 5:8>) (See WINSLOW Probate Appendix for estate of Capt. George CORWIN.)

1 BROOKS child, 2 CORWIN children: <MBD 2:490>

1. **John BROOKS/BROOK**[3], b. c1656, poss. Eng., d. 25 Dec. 1687, ae 31, unm., Charlestown g.s. <Charlestown VR 1:118; MD 1:239>.

2. **Penelope CORWIN**[3], b. 7 Aug. 1670, Salem <Salem VR 1:210>, d. 28 Dec. 1690, Salem <Salem VR 6: 341>; m. 19 Feb. 1684/5, Salem, **Josiah WALCOTT** <Salem VR 3:246>, b. c1657, poss. Eng., d. 9 Feb. 1728/9, ae 71, Salem <Boston News Obits 3:586>. (Josiah m.2nd, 1 May 1694, Boston, Mary FREKE <Boston Rcd.Com.9:218> & had 8 chil. <Salem VR 2:439>.) <See MBD 2:490 & Salem VR 2: 439 for bth. 2 chil.

3. **Susanna CORWIN**[3], b. 10 Dec. 1672, Salem <Salem VR 1:210>, d. pre 22 Oct. 1696, Salem (hus.re-marr.); m. 29 Nov. 1694, Salem, **Edward LYDE** <Salem VR 3:246>, (son of Edward LYDE & Mary WHEELWRIGHT), b. c1662, Boston, d. betw. 18 Jan. 1722 – 25 May 1724 (will & pr.). (Edward m.2nd, 22 Oct. 1696, Boston, Deborah BYFIELD <Savage 3:133> & had 4 chil. <Boston Rcd.Com.9: 241,24:8,29,49>; he m.3rd, 6 June 1709, Boston, Katherine (   ) BRINLEY <Boston Rcd.Com.28: 24>.) No known issue.

WINSLOW PROBATE APPENDIX

Estate of Capt. George CORWIN: <MDP:548; Essex Co.Court Papers 44:96>
...(not dated but is among those dated June–Sept. 1685) This is a very interesting list of items inventoried by his widow Elizabeth as items which belong to her and is reflective of a wealthy family. Among the items listed are "a turkie carpet...pomander basket in ye glas Chamber...small Japan Trunke...soe much gold ye Capt. received of Mr. Pope pr the produce of an Indian boy sent me from Plimouth pr ye Governor & Councill...large tankerd, plate, that was my former Husband's Mr. Robert BROOKES with our Armes...a plate sugar box given me by Gov. Winslow...a porringr sent John BROOK by Gov. Winslow...a smale hand silver candestick given John BROOK by Herbert PELHAM... one silver spoone given pr ye Lord Mayor...chaires & Screetore of Gilded Leather in the Red Cham-ber which I bought with the produce of som Adventures the Capt. had given me..." MF5G 5:8 states Capt. Corwin's estate was appraised at nearly 6,000 pounds when it was administered in Apr. 1685. Distribution was made to the widow, son Jonathan CORWIN, chil. of dec'd son John CORWIN, dau Sus-anna, Josiah WALCOTT & James RUSSELL for their wives, and other unnamed chil. Samuel GARDNER filed a claim on behalf of his wife.
==
Will of Edward LYDE: <Suffolk Co.PR #4909, 5:186>
...18 Jan. 1722, ment. wf Katherine and follow. chil., viz: Byfield LYDE, Deborah BRINDLE, Mary CRADDOCK. Pr. 25 May 1724.
==
Will of Edward WINSLOW[1]**:** <MD 4:1-3>
...18 Dec. 1654, of London, "being now bound on a voyage to sea in the service of the comon welth"; ment. only son Josias WINSLOW; unnamed wf; dau "Elizabet"; unnamed brothers; ment. per-sonal estate in England.
==
Will of Hon. Isaac WINSLOW[3] **(Josiah**[2]**):** <MDP:549; MD 24:30-3; Plymouth Co.PR #23184, 8:27>
...24 May 1736, ment. wf Sarah; sons John WINSLOW, Edward WINSLOW; daus Penelope WARREN wf of James, Elizabeth MARSTON wf of Benjamin. Pr. 6 Apr. 1739. <MDP:549, Bowman's files give the date as the 4th, however MD says 24th so the date should be changed in MDP.>
==
Will of Sarah (WENSLEY) Winslow: (widow) <MDP:549; MD 24:33-5; Plymouth Co.PR 23233, 13:201>
...5 Sept. 1753, ment. sons John WINSLOW, Edward WINSLOW; sister Hopestill OLIVER; dau Elizabeth MARSTON; grandchildren James WARREN Jr., Anna WARREN & Sarah WARREN the chil. of dec'd dau Pene-lope WARREN. Pr. 4 Feb. 1754.
==
Will of Josiah WINSLOW[2]**:** <MD 5:82-6; Plymouth Col.Wills 4:2:115-17>
...2 July 1675, ment. sister Elyzabeth CORWIN & her hus. Capt. George CORWIN & her son John BROOK brothers Resolved WHITE & Peregrine WHITE; kinsman William WHITE; Aunt Mrs. Elyzabeth PELHAM; brother Edward PELHAM "if he returne againe to New England"; dau Elyzabeth WINSLOW (under 18); son Isack WINSLOW (under 21); cuzens Peter SERGIANT, Nathaniel WINSLOW; wf Penelope. Pr. 2 Mar. 1680/1.

APPENDIX A

GOVERNOR BRADFORD'S

LIST OF THE MAYFLOWER PASSENGERS

AND THE INCREASINGS & DECREASINGS

The names of those which came over first, in ye year .1620 and were (by the blesing of God) the first beginers, and (in a sort) the foundation, of all the plantations, and Colonies, in New England. (And their families.)

m^r John Carver. Kathrine his wife. Desire Minter; & .2. man-servants
.8. John Howland Roger Wilder. William Latham, a boy & a maid servant & a child y^t was put to him called, Jasper More

m^r William Brewster. Mary his wife, with .2. sons, whose names were Love, 7 Wrasling. and a boy was put to him called Richard More; and
.6. another of his brothers the rest of his children were left behind & came over afterwards

m^r Edward Winslow Elizabeth his wife, & 2. men servants, caled Georg
.5. Sowle, and Elias Story; also a litle girle was put to him caled Ellen, the sister of Richard More.

.2. William Bradford, and Dorathy his wife, having but one child, a sone left behind, who came afterward.

m^r Isaack Allerton, and Mary. his wife; with .3. children Bartholomew
.6. Remember, & Mary. and a servant boy, John Hooke.

.2. m^r Samuell Fuller; and a servant, caled William Butten. His wife was behind & a child, which came afterwards.

.2. John Crakston and his sone John Crakston

.2. Captin Myles Standish and Rose, his wife

.4. m^r Christpher Martin, and his wife; and .2. servants, Salamon prower, and John Langemore

.5. m^r William Mullines, and his wife; and .2. children Joseph, & priscila; and a servant Robart Carter.

m^r William White, and Susana his wife; and one sone caled resolved, and
.6. one borne a ship-bord caled perigriene; & .2. servants, named William Holbeck, & Edward Thomson

m^r Steven Hopkins, & Elizabeth his wife; and .2. children, caled Giles, Constanta a doughter, both by a former wife. And .2. more by this wife,
.8. caled Damaris, & Oceanus, the last was borne at sea. And .2. servants, called Edward Doty, and Edward Litster.

.1. m^r Richard Warren, but his wife and children were lefte behind and came afterwards

4   John Billinton, and Elen his wife: and .2. sones John, & Francis.

.4. Edward Tillie, and Ann his wife: and .2. childeren that were their cossens; Henery Samson, and Humility Coper

.3. John Tillie, and his wife; and Eelizabeth their doughter

.2. Francis Cooke, and his sone John; But his wife & other children came afterwards.

.2. Thomas Tinker, and his wife and a Sone.

2. John Rigdale; and Alice his wife.

3. James Chilton, and his wife, and Mary their doughter; they had another doughter y^t was maried came afterward.

.3. Edward fuller, and his wife; and Samuell their sonne

.3. John Turner, and .2. sones; he had a doughter came some years after to
Salem, wher she is now living.

.3. Francis Eaton. and Sarah his wife, and Samuell their sone, a yong child

Moyses fletcher, John Goodman, Thomas Williams, Digerie Preist, Edmond
.10. Margeson, Peter Browne, Richard Britterige, Richard Clarke, Richard
Gardenar, Gilbart Winslow

John Alden was hired for a cooper, at South-Hampton wher the ship was
.1. victuled; and being a hopefull yong man was much desired, but left to
his owne liking to go, or stay when he came here, but he stayed, and
maryed here.

John Allerton, and Thomas Enlish were both hired, the later to goe m^r
of a shalop here, and ye other was reputed as one of ye company, but
.2. was to go back (being a seaman) for the help of others behind. But
they both dyed here, before the shipe returned.

Ther were allso other .2. seamen hired to stay a year here in the
.2. country, William Trevore; and one Ely. But when their time was out
they both returned.

These bening aboute a hundred sowls came over in this first ship; and began
this worke, which god of his goodnes hath hithertoo blesed; let his holy name
have ye praise.

* * * * * *

And seeing it hath pleased him to give me to see .30. years compleated,
since these beginings. And that the great works of his providence are to be
observed. I have thought it not unworthy my paines, to take a view of the
decreasings, & Increasings of these persons, and such changs as hath pased
over them, & theirs, in this thirty years. It may be of some use to such as
come after; but however I shall rest in my owne benefite.

I will therefore take them in order as they lye.

m^r Carver and his wife, dyed the first year, he in ye spring, she
in ye somer; also his man Roger, and ye litle boy Jasper, dyed before either of them, of ye commone Infection. Desire Minter, returned to her freind & proved not very well, and dyed in England.
His servant boy Latham after more then .20. years stay in the country went into England; and from thence to the Bahamy Ilands in y^e
west Indees; and ther with some others was stavred for want of food.
15   His maid servant maried, & dyed a year or tow after here in this
place. His servant John Howland maried the daughter of John Tillie,
Elizabeth, and they are both now living; and have .10. children now
all living and their eldest doughter hath .4. children And ther .2.
doughter, one, all living and other of their Children mariagable,
so .15. are come of them.

m^r Brewster lived to a very old age; about .80. years he was when
he dyed, having lived some .23. or .24. years here in ye countrie.
& though his wife dyed long before, yet she dyed aged. His sone
4.   Wrastle dyed a yonge man unmaried; his sone Love, lived till this
year .1650. and dyed, & left .4. children, now living. His doughters which came over after him, are dead but have left sundry child-
2.   ren alive; his eldst sone is still liveing, and hath .9. or .10.
children, one maried, who hath a child, or .2.

Richard More, his brother dyed the first winter; but he is maried,
4.   and hath .4. or .5. children, all living.

m^r Ed: Winslow, his wife dyed the first winter; and he maried with
2.   the widow of m^r White and hath .2. children living by her marigable,
besids sundry that are dead. one of his servants dyed, as also the
litle girle soone after the ships arivall. But his man Georg Sowle,
is still living, and hath .8. children.

William Bradford, his wife dyed soone after their arivall; and he
4   maried againe; and hath .4. children, .3: wherof are maried.

(who dyed 9 of May, 1658**)

m^r Allerton his wife dyed with the first, and his servant John Hooke.
his sone Bartle is maried in England but I know not how many children
he hath. His doughter remember is maried at Salem & hath .3. or .4.

.8. children living. And his doughter mary is maried here, & hath .4.
children. Him selfe maried againe with ye dougter of m^r Brewster, &
hath one sone living by here but she is long since dead. And he is
maried againe, and hath left this place long agoe. So I account his
Increase to be :8: besids his sons in England.

m^r ffuller, his servnt dyed at sea; and after his wife came over,
.2. he had tow children by her; which are living and growne up to years.
but he dyed some .15. years agoe.

John Crakston dyed in the first mortality; and about some .5. or .6.
years after his sone dyed, having lost him selfe in ye wodes, his
feet became frosen, which put him into a feavor, of which he dyed.

Captain Standish his wife dyed in the first sicknes; and he maried
.4. againe, and hath .4. sones liveing, and some are dead.

(who dyed .3. of Octob. 1655.**)

m^r Martin, he, and all his, dyed in the first Infection; not long
after the arivall.

m^r Molines, and his wie, his sone, & his servant dyed the first
winter. Only his dougter priscila survied, and maried with John
.15. Alden, who are both living, and have .11. children. And their
eldest daughter is maried & hath five children.

(See N.E. Memorial, p.22**)

m^r White, and his .2. servants dyed soone after ther landing. His
wife maried with m^r Winslow (as is before noted) His .2. sons are
.7. maried, and resolved hath .5. children; perigrine tow, all living.
So their Increase are :7.

m^r Hopkins, and his wife are now both dead; but they lived above
.20. years in this place, and had one sone, and .4. daoughters
.5. borne here. Ther sone became a seaman, & dyed at Barbadoes, one
doughter dyed here. and .2. are maried. one of them hath .2. children, and one is yet to mary. So their Increase, which still
survive, are .5.
4. But his sone Giles is maried, and hath .4. children.
.12. his doughter Constanta, is also maried, and hath .12. children all
of them living, and one of them maried.

m^r Richard Warren lived some .4. or .5. years, and had his wife come
over to him, by whom he had .2. sons before dyed; and one of them is
4 maryed, and hath .2. children So his Increase is .4. but he had .5.
doughters more came over with his wife, who are all maried, & living & have many children.

John Billinton after he had bene here .10. yers, was executed, for
.8. killing a man; and his eldest sone dyed before him; but his .2.
sone is alive, and maried, & hath .8. children

Edward Tillie, and his wife both dyed soon after their arivall; and
.7. the girle Humility their cousen, was sent for into Ento England,
and dyed ther. But the youth Henery Samson, is still liveing, and
is maried, & hath .7. children.

John Tillie, and his wife both dyed, a litle after they came a-
shore; and their daughter Elizabeth maried with John Howland and
hath Isue as is before noted.

Francis Cooke^+ is still living, a very olde man, and hath seene
his childrens, children, have children: after his wife came over.
.8. (with other of his children) he hath .3. still living by her, all
maried, and have .5. children so their encrease is .8. And his
.4. sone John which came over with him, is maried, and hath .4. children living.

Thomas Rogers dyed in the first sicknes, but his sone Joseph is
.6. still living, and is maried, and hath .6. children. The rest of
Thomas Rogers came over, & are maried, & have many children.

Thomas Tinker, and his wife, and sone, all dyed in the first sicknes.

And so did John Rigdale, and his wife.

James Chilton, and his wife also dyed in the first Infection. but
.10. their daughter mary, is still living and hath .9. children; and
one daughter is maried, & hath a child; so their Increase is .10.

Edward ffuller, and his wife dyed soon after they came ashore; but
4 their sone Samuell is living, & maried, and hath .4. children or
more.

John Turner, and his .2. sones all dyed in the first siknes. But
he hath a daugter still living, at Salem, well maried, and approved
of.

Francis Eeaton, his first wife dyed in the generall sicknes; and he
maried againe, & his .2. wife dyed, & he maried the .3. and had by
4 her .3. children. one of them is maried, & hath a child; the other are living, but one of them is an Ideote. He dyed about .16.
years agoe.

.1. his sone Samuell, who came over a sucking child is allso maried, &
hath a child.

Moyses fletcher Thomas Williams Digerie preist John Goodman Edmond
Margeson Richard Britterige Richard Clarke All these dyed sone after their arivall. in the Generall sicknes that befell. But Digerie preist had his wife & children sent hither afterwards she being
m^r Allertons sister. But the rest left no posteritie here.

Richard Gardinar, became a seaman, and dyed in England, or at sea.

Gilbert Winslow after diverse years aboad here, returned into England and dyed ther.

Peter Browne maried twise, by his first wife he had .2. children,
who are living, & both of them maried, and the one of them hath
6 .2. children. by his second wife, he had .2. more; he dyed about
16 years since

Thomas English; and John Allerton, dyed in the generall siknes.

John Alden maried with priscila, m^r Mollines his doughter, and had
Isue by her as is before related.

Edward Doty, & Edward Litster the servants of m^r Hopkins. Litster
After he was at liberty, went to Virginia, & ther dyed. But Edward
Doty by a second wife hath .7. children and both he and they are
living

Of these 100 persons which came first over, in this first ship together;
the greater halfe dyed in the generall mortality; and most of them in .2. or
three monthes time. And for those which survied though some were ancient &
past procreation; & others left ye place and cuntrie. yet of those few remaining are sprunge up above .160. persons; in this .30. years. And are now
living in this presente year .1650. besids many of their children which are
dead and come not within this account.

And of the old stock, (of one & other) ther are yet living this present
year .1650. nere .30. persons. Let the Lord have ye praise; who is the High
preserver of men.

(The following entries were added later, in two different hands.)

Twelfe persons liveing of the old Stock this present yeare 1679.

Two persons liveing tht come over in the first Shipe 1620 this present
yeare 1690. Resolved White and Mary Cushman the Daughter of m^r Alderton.

and John Cooke the Son of frances Cooke that Came in the first ship is
still liveing this present yeare 1694

& Mary Cushman. is still liveing this present yeare 1698

**these three entries are in the same hand and the year is incorrect in both
†in the margin is "dyed 7 of April 1663 above 80." in a different hand

APPENDIX B

1627 CATTLE DIVISION

At a publique court held the 22th of May it was concluded by the whole Companie, that the cattell wch were the Companies, to wit, the Cowes & the Goates should be equall devided to all the psonts of the same company & soe kept untill the expiration of ten yeares after the date above written. & that every one should well and sufficiently pvid for there owne pt under penalty of forfeiting the same.

That the old stock with halfe th increase should remaine for comon use to be devided at thend of the said terme for otherwise as ocation falleth out, & the other halfe to be their owne for ever.

Uppon wch agreement they were equally devided by lotts soe as the burthen of keeping the males then beeing should be borne for common use by those to whose lot the best Cowes should fall & so the lotts fell as followeth. thirteene psonts being pportioned to one lot.

1 The first lot fell to ffrancis Cooke & his Companie Joyned to him his
    wife Hester Cooke
   3 John Cooke
   4 Jacob Cooke
   5 Jane Cooke   To this lot fell the least of
   6 Hester Cooke   the 4 black Heyfers Came in the
   7 Mary Cooke   Jacob, and two shee goats.
   8 Moses Simonson
   9 Phillip Delanoy
  10 Experience Michaell
  11 John ffance
  12 Joshua Pratt
  13 Phinihas Pratt

2 The second lot fel to Mr Isaac Allerton & his Companie joyned to him his
    wife ffeare Allerton.
   3 Bartholomew Allerton
   4 Remember Allerton
   5 Mary Allerton   To this lot fell the Greate Black
   6 Sarah Allerton   cow came in the Ann to which they
   7 Godber Godberson   must keepe the lesser of the two
   8 Sarah Godberson   steers, and two shee goats.
   9 Samuell Godberson
  10 Marra Priest
  11 Sarah Priest
  12 Edward Bumpasse
  13 John Crakstone

3 The third lot fell to Capt Standish & his companie Joyned to him his wife
   2 Barbara Standish
   3 Charles Standish
   4 Allexander Standish   To this lot fell the Red Cow w^{ch}
   5 John Standish   belongeth to the poore of the Col-
   6 Edward Winslow   onye to wch they must keepe her Calfe
   7 Susanna Winslow   of this yeare being a Bull for the
   8 Edward Winslow   Companie. Also to this lott Came too
   9 John Winlsow   she goats.
  10 Resolved White
  11 Perigrine White
  12 Abraham Peirce
  13 Thomas Clarke

4 The fourth lot fell to John Howland & his company Joyned to him his wife
   2 Elizabeth Howland
   3 John Howland Juno^r
   4 Desire Howland   To this lot fell one of the 4 hey-
   5 William Wright   fers Came in the Jacob Called Rag-
   6 Thomas Morton Juno^r horne.
   7 John Alden
   8 Prissilla Alden
   9 Elizabeth Alden
  10 Clemont Briggs
  11 Edward Dolton
  12 Edward Holdman
  13 Joh. Alden

5 The fift lot fell to M[r] Willm Brewster & his companie Joyned to him
  2 Love Brewster
  3 Wrestling Brewster
  4 Richard More
  5 Henri Samson
  6 Johnathan Brewster
  7 Lucrecia Brewster
  8 Willm Brewster
  9 Mary Brewster
10 Thomas Prince
11 Pacience Prince
12 Rebecka Prince
13 Humillyty Cooper

> To this lot ffell one of the fower Heyfers Came in the Jacob Caled the Blind Heyfer & 2 shee goats.

6 The sixt lott fell to John Shaw & his companie Joyned
  1 to him
  2 John Adams
  3 Eliner Adams
  4 James Adams
  5 John Winslow
  6 Mary Winslow
  7 Willm Basset
  8 Elizabeth Bassett
  9 Willyam Basset Juno[r]
10 Elyzabeth Basset Juno[r]
11 ffrancis Sprage
12 Anna Sprage
13 Mercye Sprage

> To this lot fell the lesser of the black Cowes Came at first in the Ann wth which they must keepe the bigest of the 2 steers. Also to this lott was two shee goats.

7 The seaventh lott fell to Stephen Hopkins & his companie Joyned to him his wife
  2 Elizabeth Hopkins
  3 Gyles Hopkins
  4 Caleb Hopkins
  5 Debora Hopkins
  6 Nickolas Snow
  7 Constance Snow
  8 Willam Pallmer
  9 ffrances Pallmer
10 Willm Pallmer Jno[r]
11 John Billington Seno[r]
12 Hellen Billington
13 ffrancis Billington

> To this lott fell A Black weining Calfe to w[ch] was aded the Calfe of this yeare to come of the black Cow, w[ch] fell to John Shaw & his Companie, w[ch] pveing a bull they were to keepe it ungelt 5 yeares for common use & after to make there best of it. Nothing belongeth of thes too, for y[e] companye of y[e] first stock: but only halfe y[e] Increase. To this lott ther fell two shee goats: which goats they posses on the like terms which others doe their cattell.

8 The eaight lott fell to Samuell ffuller & his company Joyned to him his wife
  2 Bridgett ffuller
  3 Samuell ffuller Junior
  4 Peeter Browne
  5 Martha Browne
  6 Mary Browne
  7 John fford
  8 Martha fford
  9 Anthony Anable
10 Jane Anable
11 Sara Anable
12 Hanah Anable
13 Damaris Hopkins

> To this lott fell A Red Heyfer Came of the Cow w[ch] belongeth to the poore of the Colony & so is of that Consideration.(viz[t]) thes psonts nominated, to have halfe the Increace, the other halfe, with the ould stock, to remain for the use of the poore. To this lott also two shee goats.

9 The ninth lot fell to Richard Warren & his companie Joyned wth him his wife
  2 Elizabeth Warren
  3 Nathaniell Warren
  4 Joseph Warren
  5 Mary Warren
  6 Anna Warren
  7 Sara Warren
  8 Elizabeth Warren
  9 Abigall Warren
10 John Billington
11 George Sowle
12 Mary Sowle
13 Zakariah Sowle

> To this lott fell one of the 4 black Heyfers that came in the Jacob caled the smooth horned Heyfer and two shee goats.

10 The tenth lot fell to ffrancis Eaton & thos Joyned wth him his wife
  2 Christian Eaton
  3 Samuell Eaton
  4 Rahell Eaton
  5 Stephen Tracie
  6 Triphosa Tracie
  7 Sarah Tracie
  8 Rebecka Tracie
  9 Ralph Wallen
10 Joyce Wallen
11 Sarah Morton
12 Robert Bartlet
13 Tho: Prence

> To this lott ffell an heyfer of the last yeare called the white belyd heyfer & two shee goats.

11 The Eleventh lott ffell to the Governo^r Mr William Bradford and those with him, to wit, his wife
  2 Alles Bradford and
  3 William Bradford, Junior
  4 Mercy Bradford
  5 Joseph Rogers
  6 Thomas Cushman
  7 William Latham
  8 Manases Kempton
  9 Julian Kempton
10 Nathaniel Morton
11 John Morton
12 Ephraim Morton
13 Patience Morton

> To this lott fell An heyfer of the last yeare wch was of the Greate white back cow that was brought over in the Ann, & two shee goats.

12 The twelveth lott fell to John Jene & his companie joyned to him, his wife
  2 Sarah Jene
  3 Samuell Jenne
  4 Abigall Jene
  5 Sarah Jene
  6 Robert Hickes
  7 Margret Hickes
  8 Samuell Hickes
  9 Ephraim Hickes
10 Lidya Hickes
11 Phebe Hickes
12 Stephen Deane
13 Edward Banges

> To this lott fell the greate white backt cow wch was brought over with the first in the Ann, to wch cow the keepeing of the bull was joyned for thes psonts to pvide for. heere also two shee goats.

1627, May the 22. It was farther agreed at the same Court: That if anie of the cattell should by acsident miscarie or be lost or Hurt: that the same should be taken knowledg of by Indifferent men: and Judged whether the losse came by the neglegence or default of those betrusted and if they were found faulty, that then such should be forced to make satisfaction for the companies, as also their partners dammage:

APPENDIX C

REFERENCE LIST

Adventurers of Purse & Person
Meyer, Virginia M. and Dorman, John F. Adventurers of Purse and Person, Virginia, 1606-1625. Richmond, 1987.

Banks
Banks, Charles E. English Ancestry and Homes of the Pilgrim Fathers. N.Y., 1921; repr. Baltimore, 1976.

Banks' Martha's Vineyard
Banks, Charles E. History of Martha's Vineyard, with Genealogy. 3 vols. Boston, 1911-25; repr. Edgartown, 1966

Banks' Planters
Banks, Charles E. The Planters of the Commonwealth. Boston, 1930; repr. Baltimore, 1979.

Boston News Obits
Index of Obituaries in Boston Newspapers 1704-1800. 3 vols. Boston, 1968.

Boston Rcd.Com.
Reports of the Record Commissioners of the City of Boston; Vol. 9, Births, Baptisms, Marriages & Deaths, 1630-99; Vol. 24, Births, 1700-1800; Vol. 28, Marriages, 1700-1751; Vol. 30, Marriages, 1752-1809. Boston, 1898, 1902; repr. Baltimore, 4 vols in 2, 1977, 1978.

Bradford
Bradford, William. Of Plymouth Plantation, 1620-1647. Morison, Samuel E., ed. NY, 1952; repr. N.Y., 1970.

Bradford Desc.
Hall, Ruth G. Descendants of Governor William Bradford Through the First Seven Generations. Ann Arbor MI, 1951.

Brewster Gen.
Jones, Emma C. The Brewster Genealogy, 1566-1907, A Record of the Descendants of William Brewster of the Mayflower, Ruling Elder of the Pilgrim Church Which Founded Plymouth Colony in 1620. 2 vols, 1908.

Cambridge Epitaphs
Harris, William T. Epitaphs from the Old Burying Ground in Cambridge, with Notes. 1845.

Caulkins
Caulkins, Francis M. History of New London, Connecticut from the first survey of the coast in 1612 to 1860. New London, 1895.

Columbia Co.NY Hist.
Franklin, Ellis. History of Columbia County NY. Philadelphia, 1878.

Dexter
Dexter, Henry M. & Morton. The England and Holland of the Pilgrims. Boston, 1905; repr. Baltimore, 1978.

Doty Gen.
Doty, Ethan A. The Doty-Doten Family in America. 2 vols. Brooklyn NY, 1897; repr. 1 vol., 1985

Drake
Drake, Samuel G. The Founders of New England. Boston, 1860; repr. Baltimore, 1969.

Drew
Drew, Benjamin. Burial Hill: Monuments & Gravestones. 1894.

Early CT PR
Manwaring, Charles W. A Digest of the Early Connecticut Probate Records, 1635-1750. 3 vols. Hartford, 1902-6.

Gen.Adv.
Greenlaw, Lucy H., ed. The Genealogical Advertiser, A Quarterly Magazine of Family History. 4 vols. Cambridge, 1898-1901; repr. 4 vols in 1, Baltimore, 1994.

Giles Mem.
Vinton, John A. The Giles Memorial, Genealogical Memoirs of the Families Bearing the Names of Giles, Gould, Holmes (and others). Boston, 1864.

Hawkes Gen.
Smith, Ethel F. Adam Hawkes of Saugus, Mass, 1605-1672. 1980

Hist. of Gorham
McLellan, Hugh D. and Lewis K. History of Gorham ME. Portland, 1903.

Hist. Hingham (see Lincoln)

Hist. New London (see Caulkins)

Hist. Montville
Baker, Henry A. History of Montville, formerly the north parish of New London, from 1640-1896.
Hartford, 1895.

Kingman
Kingman, Bradford. Epitaphs from Burial Hill, Plymouth, Mass. from 1657-1892; With biographical
and historical notes. Brookline, 1892; repr. Baltimore, 1977.

Lincoln
Lincoln, George. History of the Town of Hingham, Mass. 3 vols. Hingham, 1893; repr. Somersworth
NH, 1982.

Little Compton Fam.
Wilbour, Benjamin F. Little Compton Families, pub. by the Little Compton Historical Society from
the records compiled by Benjamin F. Wilbour. Providence RI, 1967.

MA Hist.Coll.
Collections of the Massachusetts Historical Society. Boston, vol.1- , 1879- .

Marshfield VR
Sherman, Robert M. and Ruth W. Vital Records of Marshfield Massachusetts to the year 1850. Camden ME, 1969, 1980, 1993.

MBD
Roser, Susan E. Mayflower Births & Deaths: From The Files Of George Ernest Bowman At the Massachusetts Society of Mayflower Descendants. 2 vols. Baltimore, 1992.

MD
The Mayflower Descendant: A Quarterly Magazine of Pilgrim History and Genealogy. Vol.1-34, Boston, 1899-1940, Bowman, George E., ed.; Vol.35- , Boston, 1985- , Williams, Alicia C., ed.
Pub. by the Massachusetts Society of Mayflower Descendants.

MDP
Roser, Susan E. Mayflower Deeds & Probates: From The Files Of George Ernest Bowman At the Massachusetts Society of Mayflower Descendants. Baltimore, 1994.

ME NH Gen.Dict.
Noyes, Sybil, Libby, Charles T. and Davis, Walter G. Genealogical Dictionary of Maine and New
Hampshire. 5 vols. 1928-35; repr. Baltimore, 5 vols. in 1, 1972.

MFIP
Mayflower Families In Progress, pub. by the General Society of Mayflower Descendants (volumes are
cited under pertinent family).

MF5G
Mayflower Families Through Five Generations, pub. by the General Society of Mayflower Descendants
(volumes are cited under pertinent family).

MM
Roser, Susan E. Mayflower Marriages: From The Files Of George Ernest Bowman At the Massachusetts
Society of Mayflower Descendants. Baltimore, 1990.

MQ
The Mayflower Quarterly, pub. by the General Society of Mayflower Descendants. Vol.1- , 1935- .

MSR
Roberts, Gary B., ed. Mayflower Source Records, from the New England Historical & Genealogical
Register. Baltimore, 1986.

NEHGR
The New England Historical & Genealogical Register, pub. by the New England Historic Genealogical
Society. Boston, 1847- , Vol. 1- .

NJ Archives
New Jersey Archives, 1st series, 1880-1949; 2nd series, 1901- .

NJ Gen.Mag.
Genealogical Magazine of New Jersey, pub. by the Genealogical Society of New Jersey. Newark, vol. 1- , 1925- .

NJHS
Proceedings of the New Jersey Historical Society; vol. 1- . Princeton, 1845- .

NYGBR
The New York Genealogical and Biographical Record, pub. by the Society. Vol.1- , 1870- .

Otis
Swift, Charles F., ed. Genealogical Notes of Barnstable Families, Being a Reprint of the Amos Otis Papers, Barnstable MA 1888-90; repr. Baltimore, 1979.

PCR
Shurtleff, Nathaniel B. and Pulsifer, David, eds. Records of the Colony of New Plymouth in New England. 12 vols. Boston, 1855-61; repr. 6 vols, NY, 1968.

PCR
Shurtleff, Nathaniel B., ed. Records of Plymouth Colony: Births, Marriages, Deaths, Burials and Other Records, 1633-1689; repr. of vol.8 of above, Baltimore, 1976.

Plymouth ChR
Plymouth Church Records, 1620-1859. 2 vols. NY, 1920,1923; repr. Baltimore, 1975.

PN&Q
Bowman, George E., ed. Pilgrim Notes and Queries; supplement to The Mayflower Descendant; pub. by the Massachusetts Society of Mayflower Descendants. 5 vols. Boston, 1913-17.

RI Gen.Dict.
Austin, John O. The Genealogical Dictionary of Rhode Island, Comprising Three Generations of Settlers Who Came Before 1690. Albany NY, 1887; repr. Baltimore, 1982.

Royal Descent
Roberts, Gary B. The Royal Descent of 500 Immigrants to the American Colonies or the United States. Baltimore, 1993.

Salem Witchcraft
Upham, Charles W. Salem Witchcraft, With an Account of Salem Village and A History of Opinions on Witchcraft and Kindred Subjects. Vol. 2. NY.

Savage
Savage, James. Genealogical Dictionary of the First Settlers of New England, showing three generations of those who came before May 1692. 4 vols. Boston, 1860-62; repr. Baltimore, 1986.

Sherman Fam.
Holman, Mary L. Descendants of William Sherman of Marshfield, Mass. Concord NH, 1936.

Stratton
Stratton, Eugene A. Plymouth Colony, Its History & People, 1620-1691. Ancestry, 1986.

TAG
Green, David L., ed. The American Genealogist. Vol.1- , 1922- , Demorest GA.

TG
Thompson, Neil D., ed. The Genealogist. Vol.1- , NY, 1980- .

Thayer Mem./Gen.

Thayer, Bezaleel. Memorial of the Thayer Name from the Massachusetts Colony of Weymouth and Braintree, Embracing Genealogical and Biographical Sketches of Richard and Thomas Thayer and Their Descendants from 1636 to 1874. 1874.

Thayer, Elisha. Family Memorial. Part 1: Genealogy of Fourteen Families of the Early Settlers of New England of the Names of Alden, Adams, Arnold, Bass, Billings, Capen, Copeland, French, Hobart, Jackson, Paine, Thayer, Wales and White. Collected from Ancient Records, Manuscripts and Printed Works. Part 2: Genealogy of Ephraim and Sarah Thayer, with Their Fourteen Children, From the Time of Their Marriage to 1835, with Notes of References as in Part 1. Hingham MA, 1835.

Torrey
Torrey, Clarence A. New England Marriages Prior to 1700. Baltimore, 1985.

Underhill
Underhill, Lora A. Descendants of Edward Small of New England and the Allied Families, with Tracings of English Ancestry. 3 vols. 1910; repr. Boston & NY, 1934.

VG
The Virginia Genealogist. Vol.1-   , Washington, 1952-   .

Virg.Mag.
The Virginia Magazine of History and Biography; pub. by the Virginia Historical Society.   Vol.1-
Richmond, 1893-   .

VR RI
Arnold, James N.   Vital Records of Rhode Island, 1636-1850.   21 vols. Providence, 1891-1912.

Waterman Gen.
Jacobus, Donald L.   Descendants of Robert Waterman of Marshfield, Mass.   Vol.1 & 2, New Haven,
1939-42.   Descendants of Richard Waterman of Providence RI.   Vol.3, New Haven, 1954.

Winsor
Winsor, Justin.   History of the town of Duxbury, Mass. with Genealogical Registers.   Boston,
1848; repr. Boston, 1985.

Wood
Wood, Alfred.   Record of Deaths, Middleboro, Mass.   Boston, 1947.

INDEX